Date Due

AUG 3 0 00

LAND TITLE ORIGINS

A Tale of Force and Fraud

ALFRED N. CHANDLER

LAND
TITLE ORIGINS

A TALE OF FORCE AND FRAUD

1945

———◆———

Robert Schalkenbach Foundation

New York

To my first American paternal ancestors,

GEORGE and JANE CHANDLER

who, with their seven children, in 1687, left their home in Wilt-shire, England (where their forebears had lived for more than five centuries), venturing on a tempestuous two months' voyage in an insanitary ship of the time, to obtain land in Pennsylvania for the economic betterment of themselves and their descendants, this volume is gratefully dedicated.

Encomium

Land Title Origins makes fascinating reading. I may add that I am greatly impressed—amazed would hardly be too strong a word—at the amount of historic investigation that is represented.

The research is the more impressive and creditable because, as far as I know, it brings together for the first time materials that are widely scattered.

In addition to deserving publication as a piece of historical inquiry into a very important aspect of the development of the United States, it merits it as a contribution to present economic issues.

Either count alone more than justifies publication of the book.

JOHN DEWEY

Preface

A LARGE PART OF THE HISTORY OF MANKIND is the story of increase in population compelling the migration of people to acquire land on which to live and maintain themselves, and of wars to govern and exact tribute of others.

Mass migration of Europeans to America was caused, not by widespread desire for religious freedom as often declared but, as here shown, by craving for land, and to escape the poverty in Europe emanating from feudalism.

This, it has been justly said, affords a study which is one of the most interesting in American history.

Without some knowledge of the claims of ownership of land, the location of settlements on the North American Continent by five European nations and the many naval and military fights between them during a long period of time to uphold such claims, the study of the history of the United States would be superficial, for a large part of that history must be written in terms of land.

The facts are historic. New and timely interpretations of many neglected facts are here presented.

Here are related the unscrupulous aims, objects and methods of European potentates and their favored grantees to possess all the land on a continent they had never seen.

After the English conquest of other nationals, all the land in the English colonies in America was, by royal edict, claimed as the personal property of successive British monarchs, to do with as they pleased.

ix

The mere scratch of a goose-quill in the hand of a European monarch, giving to his court favorites, their heirs and assigns, title to land and, supported by armed force, the right to exact tribute of all who settled or were afterwards born in America, was without justification of any kind.

Here for the first time in integral parts, disassociated from extraneous matter, are shown the methods of favor, fraud and force by greedy and unscrupulous men of great political power and influence in the United States government during the first century of its existence. Here also is told how they grabbed the vast expanses of fertile prairies and valleys, forests, mineral wealth and potential water-powers of the public domain, and proceeded to exploit and despoil succeeding generations of their rightful share of the common heritage.

The reader may be astonished to find amongst these despoilers the names of some of the most illustrious political leaders of the past.

Tangible facts can be more easily comprehended than can communicated impressions. For that reason I have simply presented facts, letting them show for themselves, rather than pressing upon the reader my own conclusions, other than to give the facts what I consider to be their real significance.

Some of the best work when presented, has seemed to be in opposition to some existing policy, but when it has had time to prove its wisdom has been accepted and acclaimed as an enlightened contribution.

With but relatively few individual exceptions in each generation, people seem to hold to beliefs with which they have grown up, until it is demonstrated that such beliefs are not justified by facts—and any attempt at such demonstration is usually resented.

It long has been a popular belief that the existing universal land policy is sacrosanct and must not be questioned, but now many outstanding thinkers, men and women, in different parts of the world are expressing their misgivings respecting the wisdom of it.

What effect the land policy, whether in America or elsewhere, has upon the cause of economic conflicts and international wars, and upon social welfare—upon unemployment and its many concomitants, and upon agriculture, industry, and public buying-power—is here indicated.

American civilization is still in the embryonic state, with inestimable possibilities of growth. The success or failure may well be determined by what the future land policy may be. The first step to arrive towards understanding is a critical examination of the subject and of ourselves. To that understanding this book is devoted.

The chapters have been entered chronologically as nearly as may be, and each chapter is likewise so treated.

The first seven chapters are preliminary but essential to a full understanding of the subject.

A chapter on any specific colony, state or region does not necessarily present all that the volume contains relating to that area. There were some conditions and actions which were alike in different parts of the country. To avoid repetition, such are generally noted in but one chapter, although there is occasional reference to kindred chapters.

To elucidate what may appear confusing: several different governmental agencies in London named in the text as dealing with land and government in the colonies were committees of the Privy Council, but in some instances have been inexactly designated.

Numerals in brackets in the text refer to the authors whose names are given in the bibliography.

ALFRED N. CHANDLER

Maplewood, New Jersey

Acknowledgments

To the authors named in the bibliography I extend my appreciation for the help I have received from their writings.

For the courtesies extended by members of the staffs of the Library of Congress, New York Public Library, Newark Public Library and many State libraries, and for information given me by many persons, including officials of Historical Societies, I herewith extend my thanks.

Also to Mr. Andrew Markhus of the United States General Land Office for his patience in elucidating some perplexing problems.

And to Mr. William Mill Butler of the Rochester, New York, Historical Society, Mr. James LeBaron and Miss V. G. Peterson, of the publishers, each for reading the manuscript, correcting errors and making valued suggestions.

Contents

LAND TITLE ORIGINS

A Tale of Force and Fraud

1

Dawn of the American Conquest

IMMEDIATELY upon the return of Columbus to Barcelona, in 1492, Ferdinand and Isabella sent an ambassador to Rome to obtain a grant to them by the Pope of the newly discovered land in the West.

The Pope, Alexander VI, a Spaniard, on May 3, 1493 issued a bull granting to Ferdinand and Isabella all lands discovered or to be discovered on the western ocean and threatened excommunication of any person who should disregard this declaration.

This grant, the Pope announced, was made "out of our pure liberality, infallible knowledge, and plenitude of apostolic power, and by virtue of the authority of omnipotent God granted to us in St. Peter, and of the Vicarship of Jesus Christ which we administer upon the Earth."

To avoid a quarrel between the monarchs of Spain and Portugal, the Pope, on the following day issued a second bull, which decreed that all lands discovered or to be discovered to the west of a meridian a hundred leagues west of the Azores and Cape Verde Islands should belong to the Spanish monarchs.

This was not satisfactory to King John of Portugal, and in June, 1494, the treaty of Tordesillas was concluded between Spain and Portugal, stipulating that the Spanish monarchs should have all land discovered west of a straight line drawn from the Arctic pole to the Antarctic pole at a distance of 370 leagues (1,110 miles) west of the Cape Verde Islands, while all land east thereof should belong to the King of Portugal. Owing to the treaty makers' lack of geographical knowledge, this line ran through the eastern part of Brazil, giving a small part of that country to King John, while Ferdinand and Isabella were assigned the main part on the west; thus arose the expression, "the Brazils."

A proclamation by the Spanish sovereigns in April, 1495, gave to all Spaniards the privilege of voyaging to, and trafficking with, the natives in the newly discovered "Indies," and those who settled there were to be granted land. Columbus protested the proclamation, claiming a monopoly of the land and trade in that region.

Columbus' claim was not justified by the terms of the royal authority granted him. The license to Columbus by Ferdinand and Isabella, dated April 30, 1492, was to sail to the westward on a voyage of discovery. He was granted the title of Admiral and Don; to be perpetual governor and to have all salaries, perquisites and honors. Nothing was contained therein respecting land.

Shortly thereafter, John Cabot, a native of Venice who had lived in Bristol, England, for many years, applied to King Henry VII of England for authority and aid for an expedition to discover, by sailing to the West, a route to the source of the spices and rich silks of the East.

The king offered no financial help, but in March, 1496, issued to Cabot and his three sons a patent for the discovery of new and unknown lands, of which the following is an excerpt:

"Be it known that we give and grant for us and our heirs to our well beloved John Cabot citizen of Venice, to Lewis, Sebastian and Sancius, his sons and to their heirs full leave to sail to all parts with five ships at their own cost and charge to discover islands and continents, and give them license to set up our banners therein, getting to us the rule, title and jurisdiction of the same; yet so that the aforesaid John, his sons and heirs, be holden of all the fruits and profits growing out of such voyage, paying to us in wares or money the one-fifth part of the capital gain so gotten. . . . We give to them and their heirs all the land they shall find."

Financed by Bristol merchants as participants in the prospective profits, Cabot sailed from Bristol in May, 1497, in the ship

"Matthew," with a crew of eighteen. He sighted Newfoundland and adjacent islands, for which, upon return of the voyagers to England, Henry gave Cabot £10, and an annual pension of £20.

Another voyage was made the following year with perhaps as many as six ships. To avoid the Spaniards, whose claim to the Western Hemisphere by the bull of Pope Alexander was recognized by the British monarch, Cabot's explorations were limited to the northeast and west of England. He is variously reported to have sailed as far south as 38° 67′ (Delaware Capes), or 38° (Cape Hatteras), and occasionally to have seen land at a distance, the sovereignty of which he claimed for the English king.

These voyages of Cabot are the basis on which British monarchs subsequently, with force of arms, claimed sovereignty and exclusive ownership of all the land between Florida and the eastern boundary of Maine.

Francis I of France had slight reverence for the bulls of the Pope parceling out the Earth between the Spanish and Portuguese monarchs. Twenty-three years after the discovery he sent to Charles V, King of Spain, asking by what right he and the King of Portugal undertook to monopolize all the land on Earth? Had our first father, Adam, made them his sole heirs? If so, it would be more than proper for them to produce a copy of the will. Meanwhile he should feel at liberty to seize upon all the land he could get.[a]

During the sixteenth century numerous voyages of exploration were made to North America from England, France, Portugal and Spain, and during the seventeenth century, from Holland and Sweden. Some of these voyages were under the patronage of monarchs with a view to extending their dominions, while others were made by individual adventurers, or by companies of merchants. All sailed in hope of gaining sudden wealth and fame by obtaining land and a share of the rich commerce which promised soon to be opened to the world, or by finding a northwestern passage to the East Indies. Many of those voyagers from the four countries first named captured Indians to sell as slaves or for proof of their voyage to America.

Of the voyagers: In 1501, Cortereal, under the patronage of the

[a]Bernal Diaz

King of Portugal, made, with two ships, a second voyage to Labrador, where he enticed aboard fifty Indians whom he sold as slaves in Portugal. [5]

In 1502 Columbus made his fourth and last voyage to the West Indies, and died four years later.

In 1504 French fishermen discovered the Grand Banks and Cape Breton Island.

In 1506 Jean Denys of Normandy, sailed to and charted the St. Lawrence River, prompting venturesome Frenchmen to engage in the fisheries and fur trades. With the later-arriving English, they introduced to the natives the corruptions of European civilization. [58]

In 1508 Thomas Aubert, a Frenchman, sailed with two vessels 240 miles up the St. Lawrence, and took back to France seven Indians. [49]

In 1513 Ponce de Leon discovered Florida; and from the Isthmus, Balboa sighted the Pacific Ocean.

In 1519 Pineda, a Spaniard, is said to have been the first European to explore the mouth of the Mississippi River; the same year Magellan discovered the strait which bears his name.

In 1520, Alvarez Fagundes, a Portuguese, explored the Gulf of St. Lawrence and was granted land there by the King of Portugal.

In 1520 d'Ayllon, of Spain, obtained from King Charles V a grant of land in the Chesapeake Bay region, and two years afterward made a settlement on the James River eighty-one years before the English settled there. His colony included six hundred men and women and one hundred horses, but upon his death shortly after founding the settlement, it was abandoned.

In 1524, eighty-five years before Henry Hudson, Verrazzano, a Florentine in the service of King Francis I of France, seeking a northwestern passage, sailed into the Hudson River and thence to the Gulf of St. Lawrence.

Ten years later Jacques Cartier voyaged from France and erected crosses on Prince Edward and Anticosti Islands. On the basis of these voyages, France claimed all the country between the latitude of Philadelphia and a line north of Montreal.

In 1539, with 9 vessels, 570 men, 223 horses, 300 hogs, and cattle and bloodhounds, DeSoto, a Spaniard, landed presumably at Tampa Bay. During the following three years he traveled over parts of Georgia, Alabama, Tennessee and Mississippi, and crossed the Mississippi River into Arkansas.

But, as with Pineda twenty years earlier, the sighting of that river added nothing to geographical knowledge. The Mississippi remained unknown to the world until LaSalle, 143 years later, explored and made it known. Coronado, another Spaniard, was exploring the country between Mexico and Kansas at that time and reported seeing cows, which no doubt were buffalo.

On a globe made in Spain in 1540, was traced Chesapeake Bay. That year French fur traders had a fort on the Hudson River below Albany and two years later, a fort on Manhattan Island.

The name North America appeared on a map published in 1522, but not until forty-nine years after the discovery of the West Indies were the names North and South America shown, and the theory that these were a part of the east coast of Asia finally exploded. [37]

The Pope's authority in granting land lost its efficacy after a while; both because he had made, from what did not belong to him, a donation of infinite extent, and because such gifts became injurious restrictions on international commerce and enterprise. Also, with justice, it began to be denied that any nation had the right to exclude all others from vast and undefined regions which it could not itself people nor cultivate. No longer was territory to be claimed merely by gift, or priority of discovery, without such possession being taken of the land as implied a permanent occupancy. The rights or desires of the natives of the newly discovered lands were, of course, not considered by the rival European monarchs. [126]

Henry VIII of England, about 1533 changed his policy, divorcing Catherine, his Spanish wife, and thus divorcing himself from the King of Spain and the Pope of Rome.

For fear of the mighty power of the Spanish and Portuguese navies guarding the South Atlantic routes, British commerce could not be extended to the Far East by way of the Cape of Good Hope. A company was formed in England in 1553 with the corporate name, "The Mysterie and Companie of the Merchant Adventurers for Discoverie of Regions and Dominions,

Islands and Places Unknown," which became known as the Russian or Muscovy Company. Sebastian Cabot was recalled from Spain by Edward VI and made governor of the company for life. It was given a charter similar to the Cabot charter of fifty-seven years previous, but this later charter omitted restrictions on explorations beyond the limit fixed by Pope Alexander.

King Philip II of Spain seemed determined, in 1558, to claim as widespread an area as possible in America, to forestall the monarchs of other European nations. Because of extensive explorations along the North Atlantic coast, all America south of 44° (Kennebec River, Maine) was then generally recognized as Spanish. [17]

In 1570 a Jesuit mission was located at Occoquan, on the Potomac River, about twenty miles below Washington; this was fourteen years before the Raleigh colony located at Roanoke, and thirty-seven years before the English settled at Jamestown. The mission was destroyed by Indians. An exact description of Chesapeake Bay, with Spanish place-names, was written soon after, presumably by one of this expedition. [153]

From these voyages arose the conflicting claims of the sponsoring monarchs to various portions of North America. Repeated fights took place between the British, French, Spaniards, Dutch and Swedes. The land was not claimed for the people of those nations, but for the reigning monarchs personally, or for some incorporated company. More than a hundred years passed between the time of the first discovery and the establishment by Europeans of any permanent settlement north of Florida.

All grants for overseas adventures issued by European monarchs to their subjects, prior to Queen Elizabeth, had been to establish royal sovereignty, or for the avowed purpose of seeking wealth through finding gold, or of extending trade by discovery of a route to the source of the spices. But with the grant by Elizabeth to Sir Humphrey Gilbert in 1578, desire for profiteering by land ownership made its appearance and a quarter of a century later, English settlement in America began. An excerpt from the grant read:

"Elizabeth by Grace of God, Queen of England; to all people to whom these presents shall come, greeting:

"Know ye that we give and grant to our trustie and well-beloved servant Sir Humphrey Gilbert of Compton, Devonshire, and to his heirs and assigns for ever, free license to discover remote lands not possessed by any Christian prince or people and the same to have and enjoy for ever, paying unto us, our heirs and successors one-fifth of all gold and silver discovered."

He was, furthermore, authorized to expel from the countries discovered all persons there without his permission, and to seize any ship trading there without his license, and to appropriate its cargo.

In a will made prior to embarking on a voyage, Gilbert directed his executor to grant to his widow and sons fifty square miles of the land so discovered, and twenty square miles to each of his daughters, which they might sell or rent to others.

Anyone who took, or promoted the sending of, five settlers to a colony in such discovered territory was to receive two thousand acres, on which they were to pay to Gilbert, or his heirs and assigns, an annual land rent of 20s on each thousand acres. Each of the five settlers was to receive 120 acres on rent. This seems like "counting chickens before they are hatched," and it was the first recorded instance of an annual land rent, or price of any kind, being exacted for the right to hold land across the seas.

Gilbert thus was the forerunner of Sir William Alexander on Long Island; Ferdinando Gorges in Maine; Cecilius Calvert in Maryland; George Carteret in New Jersey and Carolina; and William Penn in New Jersey and Pennsylvania.

Gilbert, planning a voyage of discovery, solicited expense funds. For every £5 subscribed he would grant land at a perpetual annual land rent of 10s per thousand acres.

He encouraged some of his friends to establish, upon that basis of rent to him, subsidiary proprietories within his prospective domain; among them were Sir Thomas Gerrard and Sir George Peckham—to each of whom he granted 1,500,000 acres to be located between Florida and Cape Breton; and Sir Philip Sidney, who was granted 3,000,000 acres. [112]

Gilbert, with four or five ships and 260 men set sail, and reached Newfoundland in June, 1583. Upon arrival there he proclaimed to the assembled fishermen of several nationalities his ownership, by royal grant, of all land within six hundred miles. He granted various tracts of land in and about St. John's to the astonished fishermen, to be held by them so long as they paid him rent for the land, the use of which hitherto had been "free to all the children of men." On his homeward voyage his ship, the "Squirrel," foundered, and Gilbert, with all on board, was lost. [112]

With Gilbert dead and his grant expired, Queen Elizabeth in 1584 reissued it to Gilbert's half-brother, Walter Raleigh. It gave him, his heirs and assigns, land which he might discover, the same to have, hold and enjoy for ever thereafter, reserving to Elizabeth, her heirs and successors, one-fifth part of all gold and silver discovered.

Although Raleigh, now a knight, was aware that Spain claimed all America by virtue of the bull of Pope Alexander ninety-two years previously, he sent a fleet of seven vessels with 120 men across the Atlantic, in command of Sir Richard Grenville and Captain Ralph Lane. Raleigh never was in North America.

Grenville and Lane, arriving on the American coast, unfortunately entered an inlet of Pamlico Sound, North Carolina. This was the least desirable spot for harboring on the entire coast, difficult and generally impossible of ingress or egress by ocean-going vessels. They left settlers on Roanoke Island, who remained one year, and were then returned to England.

Another Raleigh colony of 118 men and women was left at Roanoke in July, 1587, and Virginia Dare was born there. When, a few years afterward, the settlers were sought, they could not be found. Many stone tablets found in North Carolina, South Carolina and Georgia during recent years and now in possession of Brenau College, Gainesville, Georgia, tell of the wanderings for sixteen years and final death of many of the colonists. The authenticity of these stones is doubted by some persons.

Although the naval power of Spain had long restricted the commerce and maritime adventures of other nations, Spanish ships were often taken by the British and, in later years, by the Dutch. In fact, the popular sport of naval and maritime captains seems, during the 1500's and early 1600's, to have been capturing or sinking the ships of one another.

To clear the ocean of British ships and prevent further capture by them of Spanish commerce and treasure ships from Panama, Spain sent to the English Channel in July, 1588, the mighty Spanish Armada, composed of 132 ships, with 30,000 men, 3,000 cannon and 90 executioners with implements of torture.

To meet them, the British had almost as many ships and, though smaller, these were speedier, with fewer but longer range guns. From the fight and the terrific gale, which the remnant of the fleet encountered in returning home north of Scotland, the Spaniards lost seventy-seven ships and twenty thousand men, while the British, with sixty-eight men killed or wounded, did not lose a vessel.

The final blow to the Spanish navy occurred eight years after the defeat of the Armada, when the British destroyed at Cadiz what remained of the fleet. This victory cleared the North Atlantic of the Spanish navy and, for the first time, made possible uninterrupted European settlement in America.

Numerous other British and French expeditions sailed to the Western Hemisphere during the sixteenth century, but The Netherlands, which had thrown off the yoke of Spain, were soon to be reckoned with.

The Portuguese had rounded the Cape of Good Hope, and were profitably importing spices and luxuries from the East Indies. The demand for spices and East Indian products was increasing, and the Dutch decided to make an effort to discover a route to the East.

Several important joint stock companies were formed both in England and The Netherlands at the beginning of the seventeenth century; among them, the East India Company of each country. Some vessels of these companies rounded the Cape of Good Hope, while others were sent to America in search of a northwestern passage to the Far East.

Bartholomew Gosnold, one of Raleigh's captains, with thirty-two men, of whom eight seamen and twenty others were to settle in America, sailed from England in 1602, over the usual course via the Azores. In seven weeks he reached the Kennebec River, Maine. There he found a French-built shallop, but Gosnold is believed to have been the first Englishman ever on that coast. From there he sailed to, and named Martha's Vineyard, Buzzard's Bay and Cuttyhunk. At the last named place he made a settlement, but soon abandoned it and returned to England.

In 1603 Martin Pring of England, aged twenty-three years, commanded an expedition to Penobscot Bay, Maine.

While the destruction of the Armada, and these several voyages, stimulated preparations for, and made possible, colonization in America, it is doubtful if at the close of Elizabeth's reign, in 1603, a single Englishman remained in North America. [105]

Some French merchants at Rouen formed a company in 1603 for adventuring in America. Henry IV of France granted to a Huguenot member of his suite, Pierre du Gast, Sieur de Monts, all the land in North America between 40° and 46° N. lat. (Philadelphia–Montreal) and created him Lieutenant-General in New France. To assure him an armed garrison, de Monts was permitted to impress for the expedition vagabonds, idlers and masterless men, and all criminals condemned to banishment. [72]

This was three years before James I granted to the shareholders of the Virginia Company all the land between and including Maine and North Carolina, extending from the Atlantic Ocean to the South Sea.

With the financial aid of the Marchioness de Guerchevilles, a devout Roman Catholic, wife of the governor of Paris and the first equerry of the king, the expedition of two ships sailed from Havre in April, 1604, taking a Protestant minister, a Catholic priest, and a large number of Jesuits. Samuel de Champlain du Brouage, a French naval officer, known to history as Champlain, was of the party.

One ship reached the present location of Liverpool, Nova Scotia, where a French captain, Rossignol, was discovered to be trading in furs and his ship confiscated. The other ship, in command of de Poutrincourt, arriving later made a landing and set up the French standard at the Island of St. Croix, in Passamaquoddy Bay. [80]

De Poutrincourt also built a fifteen ton pinnace, probably the first American built vessel, and the next summer used it to explore the coast between Maine and Long Island Sound, entering the Penobscot, Kennebunk and Saco Rivers, before returning to Acadia. [80]

By the favor of de Monts, Poutrincourt became possessed of the site of Port Royal (now Annapolis), Nova Scotia. In 1606 it was decided to make a permanent settlement at Port Royal, and no further attempt was made under this charter to plant colonies within the present limits of Maine.

Madame de Guerchevilles bought of de Monts all that had been granted to him in New France except the site of Port Royal. Whereupon Louis XIII, after the assassination of Henry IV in 1610, granted to her all the land in New France between the Great River (St. Lawrence) and Florida. She was the only woman ever possessed of sovereignty in America. [72] Further development under this grant appears in the chapter on New England.

Captain Weymouth, failing in his search for a northwestern passage, sailed from England in 1605, with a company of twenty-seven men. After a ten weeks' voyage he arrived at Monhegan Island, Maine, and explored the Maine coast. To prove that he had been to America he kidnapped five Indians and took them to England.

Ferdinando Gorges, commander of the fort at Plymouth, learned from Weymouth of the great expanse of land in Maine uninhabited by any civilized people, and with Lord Chief-Justice Popham, laid plans to get possession of an extensive part of it. They became in 1606, two of the land grantees under the Virginia grant, from which sprang the London (southern) and Plymouth (northern) companies, and the beginning of permanent English colonization in America.

James I, King of England, claimed by royal edict (as did all succeeding British monarchs prior to the American Revolution), all the land in America between the French settlements in the St. Lawrence region and the Spanish settlement in Florida. Each reigning British monarch considered his American territory personal property to do with as he pleased.

2

Who Owned America?

INTERNATIONAL law has never been anything better than a delicate flower surrounded by the weeds of greed, wilfulness, shrewdness and strategy.[a] So it was after discovery of America, when various European monarchs issued edicts which they aimed, by force of arms, to mask as international law.

A search for the owners of the land in Colonial America leads far beyond the race of American Indians, who undoubtedly migrated from Asia; to the moundbuilders; and before them to the basketmakers who lived, at best estimates, as far back as 1,500 B.C.; and to races yet ages before them.

It is known that man lived in Europe at the time of the mammoth, after the last ice age, twenty-five thousand years ago. Recent discoveries in New Mexico seem to indicate that he lived in America during the same period.[b]

But none of these races passed down to succeeding races parchment deeds upon which legal ownership of land can today be based.

Hugo Grotius (1583–1645), an eminent Dutch jurist who was widely recognized as an advocate of international law, declared: "The particular right we have to a thing is either by original or derivative acquisition. It is called original when a thing which before belonged to no man begins to be the property of some particular person. It is derivative when the right of property already established passes from one to another."

[a]Editorial, Newark Ledger
[b]E. B. Howard, Acad. Nat. Sc. Philadelphia

Some authorities have represented a right from discovery as being of so imperfect a nature as to be nearly incapable of distinct existence. [105]

Discovery of an island by Columbus did not give all islands to the Spanish monarchs. Sighting land by Cabot from the deck of his ship did not give British monarchs an entire continent.

It must be allowed that the Right of Discovery of an hitherto unknown land is generally but a slender right unless promptly followed by occupancy. But between the time of the Cabot voyages, the basis of the British claim to land in America, and the first British settlement in the Western Hemisphere, a century and a quarter passed.

Dr. O'Callaghan [111] wrote: "The principle, that mere discovery of a country does not confer title unless followed by actual possession, was laid down and acted upon by Queen Elizabeth as far back as 1580, when resisting the pretensions of Spain to the exclusive ownership of the Western Hemisphere through donation by Pope Alexander VI.

"Elizabeth thus refused to recognize any right to places other than those of which the Spaniards were in actual possession, for their having touched only here and there upon a coast, and given names to a few rivers and capes, were such insignificant things as could in no way entitle them to a propriety farther than in the parts where they actually settled and continued to inhabit.

"But in the next century England realized that what had been good logic for England against Spain, was bad logic for England as against the Dutch in America.

"The assumed right of England which rested on the voyages of Cabot, who had not even 'touched here and there on a coast,' thus fell to the ground. The only claim that England could make to the American continent prior to the settlement of the Dutch on Manhattan Island and on the Connecticut and Delaware Rivers, was based on the precarious English settlement on the James River in Virginia.

"The Dutch had as good right to reclaim the American wilderness as any other European nation, and so long as the Dutch could show all the prerequisites insisted upon by England in 1580 for establishing a title, theirs must be considered unobjectionable."

This view of the case is only strengthened by the wording of the New England grant by James I to the Plymouth Company (Council of New England), November 3, 1620, as herein given. This charter conveyed to the Council all the country between 40° and 48° N. lat. (Philadelphia–Newfoundland), with the express reservation which read: "Provided, always, that the said islands or any of the said premises hereinbefore mentioned . . . be not actually possessed or inhabited by any other Christian Prince or Estate." The Dutch were then in actual possession of Manhattan Island and had been for several years before the date of this grant by King James.

3

Why Europeans Migrated to America

WHEN William the Conqueror established the manorial or feudal land system in England, he allotted land to his barons, who were to render to him and his successors certain services. These feudal services were, in effect, a perpetual land rent to provide the requirements of government.

In addition, areas of land were set aside for free use by the landless serfs as commons on which to grow food, pasture their domestic animals, and cut fire wood.

With increasing population causing increasing demand for wool, the barons steadily encroached upon the commons by enclosing them for sheep pasture, and the area of free land allotted to the serfs was continually reduced.

"In this way it came that these poor wretches," Sir Thomas More wrote, "were driven from their native fields without knowing where to go." Cardinal Wolsey issued a decree that all enclosures be reopened, but it was not effective. Starkey, in a *History of England,* said: "Now they go about in England, from door to door, and ask alms for God's sake, and some of them, because they will not beg, do steal, and then be hanged."

Froude, the historian estimated that, up to his time, the ministers of the crown and their friends had appropriated, and divided among themselves lands worth in modern currency about £5,000,-000.

The Duke of Somerset pitied the poor and demanded that enclosed lands be reopened. The landholders' parliament resented this, and the duke was arrested and executed.

During Elizabeth's reign the punishment for begging was ameliorated, being modified to "whipping on the bare back until his body is bloody," and "rogues, victims of eviction and unemployment were trussed up, and there was not a year wherein three hundred or four hundred were not hanged."

In 1606, during the reign of James I (1603–1625), when the lands of the Gunpowder Plot conspirators were confiscated and distributed to court favorites, the new grantees of this land—the new aristocracy—made fresh enclosures and evictions. This caused eight thousand people, led by "Captain Pouch," to assemble in protest.

British soldiers demurred at attacking their fellow countrymen, with whom they sympathized, whereupon the manor lords with their servants attacked the dispossessed. Captain Pouch was hanged, drawn and quartered, but his fellows were "only hanged." These laborers were neither felons nor traitors; they were simply Englishmen defending their use of the common land against private appropriation. [163]

The first English migration to America was just then leaving for Virginia. The Archbishop of York, in a sermon three years later, said: "The lords hath got most of the tillage in their hands. They convert to a shepherd and his dog townships in which there had been one or two hundred communicants. Look seriously to the land and see whether there be not necessity to seek abroad."

Migration to Virginia was widely advocated to draw from England large numbers of the unemployed, diminish begging, vagabondage and crime, and thus lessen the cost of poor relief. [20]

The population of England was then fifty per square mile, while it is now 748 per square mile. The land, source of all employment, was held as it is today in most countries, by the relatively few, at prices and exactions which prevented the more general use by which laborers could maintain themselves.

So many idle and disabled men were turned loose upon the country by the parishes that they threatened a dangerous pestilence of vagabonds. In 1627 to reduce the cost of poor relief, 1,400 children were collected in different parts of England and sent to Virginia. [20]

At that period ocean passage for adults was £6, and freight £3 per ton.

The Puritan exodus to New England, a territory which was entirely English, really commenced in 1629, when Charles I, ruling without a parliament, levied taxes, imprisoned objectors and collected forced loans. In 1642 when the Long Parliament met and civil war began, the Puritan exodus ceased. For more than a century after, there was no considerable migration to New England. [49]

Meanwhile, however, the sale of land in New York and Maryland, and emigration thereto, continued to be actively promoted by the proprietary landholders who were living in Holland and England. A more likely cause of the cessation of emigration to New England at that period was the revocation of the charter of the Council of New England and the distribution to its members of the lands. This took place seven years prior to the date named and left New England without an organized agency for promoting emigration. The Massachusetts Bay Company does not seem to have maintained a sales and emigration agency in England.

In 1649, during the Commonwealth (1649–1660) there arose another rebellion against enclosures, led by Lieutenant-Colonel Lilburne and Gerrard Winstanley. "They had no quarrel with the rights of property, or desire to steal lands of other people; they only wanted restoration of their own rights to common pasturage and tillage. 'Englishmen,' they said, 'are not a free people while the poor are not allowed to dig and labor on the commons.'" Lilburne was imprisoned in the Tower of London, and the diggers were shot down. [163]

During the period many pamphlets were written on the subject of the unemployed. One, by the Rev. J. Moore, on the *Crying Sin of England,* denounced "the broode of those wretches that by their enclosures do unpeople country, cities and towns by their unsocial, covetous and cruel actions in trebling the price of the land which they enclose, which makes such swarms of beggars that go from door to door."

At the Restoration of Charles II in 1660, the enormous annual revenue from land rents payable by the barons to the king was, by act of Parliament, compounded for a cash payment to the king of £100,000 per annum, to be paid by taxation. The barons, thereby being freed for ever of land rents, a proposal was made to raise an equivalent sum by a tax upon land.

An opponent, speaking in the House of Lords, declared: "You can get this money by an easier method. By indirect taxation you can tax the last rag off a man's back, the last mouthful of food from his mouth, and he will not know what is injuring him; he may grumble about hard times, but he will not know that the hard times have been produced by taxation."

The first excise tax in England was imposed on liquors in 1640, and was afterwards extended to other articles. The Parliament, by a majority vote of two, in a membership of three hundred, ordered payments to the king to be made by a general excise (or sales) tax on commodities. The landholding members of parliament, thus voting to abolish all services and payments for land due from the barons to the king, did not abolish the land rent payments due to the barons from their own tenants. [41]

Indirect taxation was, therefore, the next great cause of poverty in England, much as it is today in all countries.

During the reign of Charles II the tax for support of the poor was the heaviest tax, amounting to little less than one-half the entire public revenue. In 1694 during the reign of William III, a land tax of 4s in the pound (20 per cent) raised £2,000,000 with certainty and dispatch. [97]

In 1698, English woolen manufacturers resenting competition, caused similar manufactures in the north of Ireland to be suppressed. Twenty thousand Ulsterites, descendants of those whom James I, grandfather of the reigning king, had earlier in the century sent there from Scotland and the North of England, were deprived of employment. All who could do so migrated to America.

In that year of 1698 Gabriel Thomas, of Wales, wrote from Philadelphia: "The great number of poor men, women and children in England, half starved, visible in their meagre looks, that are continually wandering up and down looking for employment without finding any, if here, need not lie idle a moment. Wages for labor are nearly three times that of labor in England or Wales. There are no beggars to be seen here; . . ."

Emigration to America was not confined to the English, Scotch and Irish. Thousands of Hollanders, Belgians, and Flemish together with some Swedes went, or were sent, to New Netherland. Revocation of the Edict of Nantes by Louis XIV, in 1685, caused no less than five hundred thousand Protestants (Huguenots) to flee from France. Nearly all were of eminent respectability, their ranks including artisans as well as many persons of the ancient nobility, large numbers of whom migrated to America. Concurrently, Penn, who had had his literature regarding Pennsylvania translated into German, was inducing large numbers of Germans and kindred people to go to Philadelphia.

Of the population of 5,500,000 in England, in 1696, it was estimated that one-fourth of them were beggars and on the public charge. All the people in Gloucestershire (and similarly in other shires) were then either living on alms, or being ruined by paying them, and there were serious riots. [97]

The cost of the poor laws enacted during the reign of Elizabeth was fabulous for that time, just as it was in the United States during the 1930's. Less than a century afterwards the tax levy for the poor in England had increased from £730,000 to £7,000,000.

Up to about 1710, enclosures were not sanctioned by law, but the landholders in that year applied to and easily obtained from a Parliament composed largely of landholders, acts enclosing the common land. Thereafter, instead of being robbed without process of law, the landless were by law robbed further of the right to use the commons. [163]

In the six years following 1728 at least four thousand men were imprisoned every year for petty thefts in England, largely because of poverty due to unemployment. [5]

For refusal to take oath of allegiance to the British Crown, seven thousand French in Acadia (Nova Scotia) were, in 1755, transported to American seacoast towns.

Watt perfected the steam engine at about the time of the outbreak of the American Revolution, and factories were established in England for converting into cloth the wool which hitherto had been exported to the continent. Eleven years later the Watt engine was installed in cotton factories. This somewhat relieved unemployment, but unfortunately became the cause of child labor and slum housing in the mill towns, to the great profit of land-holders in those towns.

In 1782 a poor-law act provided outdoor relief for the able-bodied and the practice became common, as it had been eighty-two years previously; this was similar to the unemployment re-lief in the United States 150 years later, in the 1930's.

Professor Ogilvie, an economist of King's College, Aberdeen, in an essay on the rights of property in land, suggested taxation of land values for poor relief.

Parliament enacted numerous land enclosure acts and in 1801 passed a general enclosure act which caused a rapid increase in enclosures. Prothers cites that during the thirty-two years preced-ing 1809 there were 1,651 acts passed permitting the enclosure of more than 4,500,000 acres of the English commons. Thus addi-tional vast numbers of the landless were shut out from use of the commons for cultivation, pasturage and fuel.

At the conclusion of the Napoleonic Wars, in 1815, the British national debt had risen to £846,000,000. Increased indirect taxa-tion levied to pay the interest charges brought still more suffering to the common people.

In some counties the unemployed marched with banners in-scribed "Bread or Blood." Machinery in textile mills was destroyed by the unemployed, who in their ignorance considered it the cause of their distress. One leader, Brandreth, with some followers, was arrested, and though ably defended, he and two others were hanged and then beheaded—at that late period in a presumably cultured society. Some juries before whom prisoners were tried felt pity for the starving unemployed and declared them not guilty. [163]

Ten years later another insurrection by the unemployed oc-curred, and in one day every power-loom in Blackburn and within a radius of six miles was smashed. There, and in other towns, within one week 1,000 power-looms were destroyed. [163]

The condition of the poor in all parts of Great Britain steadily became worse. Meanwhile, thousands of the earlier American settlers were moving into the country west of the Appalachian Mountains to locate on fertile land.

During that period about two hundred books and pamphlets (some by promoters of land settlement in America) were printed in England depicting the misery of the poor there and urging that they be sent to America.

Very few of these writers, however, noted that poverty was directly being caused by appropriation of the land by the British aristocracy, and by indirect taxation of the people. [163]

It was not realized then that non-landholders were being taxed —and but few seem now to realize it. The constant use in common speech and print of the term "the taxpayers" would indicate a separate class of citizens. But as tax after tax is placed on all sorts of articles, every producer and merchant naturally must add the tax to the price of what he sells, and all consumers become taxpayers. Use of the term "the taxpayers," indicating only those who pay taxes on land, buildings and incomes, is fallacious, misleading and a careless use of words. All citizens pay taxes.

Up to the time of the execution of Charles I in 1649, the greater part of the public revenue in Britian was from land rent. When as cited above, the feudal tenures were abolished during the reign of Charles II and the barons were relieved of paying their stipulated land rent, the percentage of public revenue from land rent dropped to 31 per cent of the total revenue; the average during the thirteen years ending in 1727 was 23 per cent; in 1770 it was 15 per cent; in 1798 (after the war with the American colonies which cost Great Britain £98,000,000) the public revenue from land rent had further dropped to 6 per cent; in 1837 to 4 per cent; and in 1908, to 1 per cent. [41]

In Ireland, during the five years following the potato disease and famine, beginning in 1847, there were 221,845 evictions of the agricultural population from their homes. Their houses were destroyed—whole townlands being depopulated—to make room for the cattle and sheep which were more profitable to the absentee, mostly English, landlords. [156]

In Scotland, between 1710 and 1843, it was estimated that by various enclosure acts about seven million acres of land were enclosed for sheep, deer and grouse. Eviction of people began in 1807, accompanied by the tearing down of their houses. The dispossessed, if given any land at all, were given unproductive plots while others were deported by the hundreds to the United States, Canada, West Indies, and Australia with no pretense of consulting their preference. Many more were driven to live in the cellars and attics of the slums of Glasgow. [156]

These deplorable conditions in Ireland and Scotland, the industrial and economic distress in Europe following the Napoleonic Wars, and failure of the revolution in Germany in 1848 accelerated migration to America which continued until the high speculative prices of land resulted in the panic and depression in America in 1857.

The effect during the past several centuries of shutting people out from the use of land and of levying taxes on commodities are here clearly shown.

Under these social and economic conditions, urging migration to America grew into a systematized business for profit conducted by various lords proprietors of royal grants of vast areas of land on the North American Continent. They were interested only in finding buyers for their lands, and to that end became active propagandists in inducing people either to go, or send others, to America for land. These, and some ship captains transporting indentured servants, were, during the early Colonial Period, the only agencies for peopling America.

Among the grantees of land the Virginia Company, the Council of New England, Calvert of Maryland, Carteret of New Jersey and Carolina, Penn of New Jersey and Pennsylvania, and the Dutch patroons of New York were, in their respective provinces, the most proficient.

4

The Indians and Land

HOW the immigrants were received by the strange race of natives they found upon arrival in America; the attitude of each towards the other, and the methods by which the early settlers obtained access to the land, are of interest.

It has been estimated that at the beginning of the European settlement period there were in the present United States somewhat less than 800,000 Indians, in 330 tribes. There are now 361,-816, in 180 tribes, and the tendency is toward increase.

The first contact of Europeans with American Indians was made when Columbus, on his initial voyage, landed at San Salvador. "They are," he reported, "so ingenuous and free with all they have, that no one would believe it who had not seen it; of anything they possess, if it be asked of them they never say no; on the contrary, they invite you to share it, and they show as much love as if their hearts went with it."

The first European settlement north of the Gulf of Mexico seems to have been that of Jean Ribault, who, in command of two French ships carrying a colony of Huguenots landed in 1562 at St. John's River, Florida. There they planted the arms of France and were welcomed with presents by the Indians. Subsequently they proceeded to Port Royal in South Carolina, where they found the Indians friendly. [126]

Ribault, who spent three years in Florida, reported the Indians as "good, and of gentle, courteous and amiable nature, and willingly they obey, yea be contented to serve those that shall with gentleness and humanity go about to allure them, as it is necessary for those that be sent thither hereafter so to do."

Rene Laudonniere, a French naval officer who succeeded Ribault, arrived at St. John's River three years after Ribault. When he visited the fort he found the stone pillar which Ribault had erected garlanded with wreaths and maize, while fruit lay at its base. [169]

He sent one of his ships to Port Royal, where the Indian chief offered land if they would settle there. [126]

Laudonniere wrote that the savages assured him that so long as their corn fields yielded harvests, he and his friends should not want. "I praise God continually for the great love I have found in these savages." [114]

The first Virginia colony on the first sight of land, went ashore for the day at Cape Henry, and was there attacked by Indians. In view of the previous and subsequent reception of settlers by the natives it is not improbable that this attack was an act of retaliation by Indians of the tribe warred on by the English settlers at Roanoke, eighty miles distant.

John Smith, in his book, *The True Relation,* wrote that the Susquehannock Indians, in Virginia, who made war on other tribes, seemed of an honest but simple disposition towards the first English settlers.

Samoset, chief of the Pemaquid Indians, who had learned some English from migratory fishermen along the Maine coast, greeted the Pilgrims upon their arrival at Cape Cod in 1620, with: "Welcome Englishmen."

The Pilgrims, becoming possessed in the following spring of some land which had been previously cultivated by the Indians, planted twenty acres in corn, and were "instructed by the Indian, 'Squanto,' how to fertilize the land with fish, showing them both ye manner how to set it, and after how to dress and tend it." They were also instructed in the arts of woodcraft and the stream. The first settlers in Maryland reported receiving similar help.

A treaty of alliance made in New England that year between the Pilgrims and the Sachem, Massassoit, was kept for more than half a century. [5]

Soon after arrival of a Dutch ship at Manhattan, in 1623,

Indian tribes of the Five Nations "came and made covenants of friendship, bringing presents of beaver." For several years afterwards the Indians "were all as quiet as lambs" and came and traded with the Dutch.

It would have been easy at that early day for the Indians to have exterminated any of these bands of immigrants but, instead, they usually welcomed them with friendship and hospitality. [7]

A colonist in Maryland, one year after arrival of the first English settlers there, wrote: "Experience has taught us that, by kind and fair usage, the natives are not only become peaceable, but friendly, and have upon all occasions performed as many friendly offices to the English in Maryland and New England as any neighbor or friend does in the more civil parts of Christendom." [60]

Thirteen years after the English settled in New Jersey a settler wrote: "The natives are very loving to us except when one has got in his head liquor, which is supplied by white men." [139] A company of 360 colonists arriving at Rancocas Creek in New Jersey five years afterward, sent ten miles to an Indian settlement for food. The sachem directed his people to take it to them.

The proprietors of East Jersey at that time stated that the Indians so far from being injurious, "are really serviceable to the English in hunting food animals and in fishing, and in killing bears, wolves and foxes, which they sell at less price than the value of the time an Englishman must spend to take them." [139]

Rev. Eric Biork, the Swedish pastor, fifty-eight years after the first Swedish settlement in Delaware wrote: "The Indians and we are as one people; we live in much greater friendship with them than with the English. They are very courteous in their behavior and fond of obliging the Swedes; they take great pains to help them, and prevent any harm happening to them."

The chief of the Hackensack Indians repeatedly complained, in 1656, that whole ankers (ten gallons each) of brandy were peddled among his tribe by white men from the Dutch Settlement, in exchange for furs, and that if it were not stopped many troubles would arise.

The actions of the migratory fishermen along the Maine coast towards the Indians were often disreputable: making the men drunk, taking advantage of them in trade, and outraging their women—all gave the Indians reasons for seeking revenge. [80]

Mohawk chiefs, in 1659, appealed at Fort Orange (Albany) that no more brandy be sold to their people; that their warriors got drunk and could not fight the French. Sale of liquor to the Indians became a crying evil throughout East Jersey in the 1670s.

Indians in Pennsylvania, in 1681, complained to the newly-arrived deputy-governor that their people bought rum at New Castle and became debauched.

A disgusted settler, in 1692, wrote: "Instead of converting the Indians to the Gospel, we have, among other sins, taught them to be drunkards." [62]

The proprietors in England, in 1671, wrote their governor in Carolina: "It is ordered by the grand council that if the Indian tribe wishes to ransom any of our Indian captives they may do so; such ransom to be shared equally among the company of soldiers that took them captive." Some of these captives were sold as slaves to the West India English sugar-planters as the cheapest means of encouraging the soldiers of their infant colony. The council, in accord with the policy of the Carolina proprietors, later freed those held as slaves by the whites in the colony. [126]

But Indian slavery was not eradicated. Years later, a letter to the lords proprietors of Carolina, in London, signed by 150 of the principal inhabitants of Carolina including some members of the assembly, said: "Notwithstanding your lordships' repeated commands to be neighborly with the Indians, the late Governor Moore engaged in the Indian fur trade for his own profit and turned it into Indian catching or slave making. He granted licenses to others to kill, or take captive, as many Indians as they could, the profit and produce of the slaves being turned to his own profit. This will likely draw upon us an Indian war with all the consequences."

Other colonies where, as noted in the chapters on those regions, there occasionally was Indian slavery, were: in New England, by the English; in New Netherland, by the Dutch; and in Louisiana by the French.

The haughty spirit of the Indian made him a poor worker under the lash. [10]

King Louis XIV of France ordered De La Barre, his governor in Canada, to "diminish as much as possible the number of Iroquois; and moreover, as the savages who are very strong and robust will serve usefully in my galleys, I will that you do everything in your power to make a great number of them prisoners of war and have them conveyed to France."

The lords proprietors based their ownership of the land not upon consent of the natives, but upon the grants made them by various kings and rulers in Britain, France, Holland and Sweden. These grants gave to the proprietary grantees a strict monopoly of all the land in America, and this monopoly was maintained by force based upon monarchial edicts which satisfied the public conscience.

In an affidavit in 1664, Edward Sackville, gent, said: "To my certain knowledge Governor Philip Carteret of New Jersey gave to the Indians goods that the lords proprietors might enjoy their land quietly, otherwise they could not have inhabited the same."

The proprietors of East Jersey, four years later ordered in London: "When it is proposed to take over land of the natives the commissioners shall give the natives what present they shall agree upon, for their good will or consent."

Stuyvesant, in 1652, forbade the settlers buying land from the Indians without the consent of the Dutch West India Company. In 1683 an act of the East Jersey council forbade the purchase of land from the Indians without license from the governor, except in the name of the lords proprietors, "upon pain of being prosecuted as seditious persons and as breakers of the king's peace." And twenty years later, "if any one, except in the name of the lords proprietors, should make a purchase of land from the Indians such a one shall forfeit 40s per acre for every acre so purchased." Similar ruling prevailed in all the proprietary colonies.

Queen Anne of England, in 1702, instructed her newly-appointed governor of New York and New Jersey: "You shall not permit any person besides the lords proprietors to purchase any land whatsoever in New Jersey from the natives. Further, you are to take care that all lands purchased from these proprietors shall be cultivated and improved by the possessors thereof." The latter was a wise provision, but the craze for land speculation, even at that early day, was too great to admit of its enforcement.

Ownership of land by the Indians, although they had been in possession of it for immemorial ages, was not recognized by European monarchs.

In some colonies, "making terms" with the Indians was a prerequisite to obtain a grant of land from the English or Dutch overlord. But, by decision of the United States Supreme Court, purchase of land from Indians has never been recognized in any part of the United States as giving a legal title to such purchaser.

Governor Yeardley of Virginia made a grant of land to one Barkham in 1620, on condition that Barkham obtain the consent of the Indian chief. The officers of the company in London, grantees of the crown, repudiated and condemned this as a recognition that the Indians had a title to the land, and declared it to be "dishonorable and prejudicial to the company." As late as 1646, an Indian chief was obliged by the governor of Virginia to acknowledge that he held his land under authority of the King of England. [20]

A reply on the part of Charles I and the Lords Commissioners of England, in 1632, in support of the British claim to those parts of North America then in possession of the Dutch West India Company, said: "It is denied, first, that the savages were possessors *bona fide* of those countries so as to be able to dispose thereof either by sale or gift, their habitations being changeable, uncertain and only in common. Secondly, it cannot be proved, *de facto,* that all the natives of said countries were parties to the said pretended sale . . . ."

The Massachusetts general court, in 1636, declared that the Indians had a natural right to only that land which they could improve, and that other land was open to those who could and would use it. Such men as Cotton Mather deemed it unnecessary to recognize in any way an Indian title to land.

Roger Williams, on the contrary, contended that settlers could have no just land title except it were derived from the Indians. So strong was public opinion against recognizing aboriginal ownership, and in upholding ownership by the crown, that Williams was summoned before the court and condemned to banishment by a council of ministers. [42]

An opinion of eight English lawyers stated: "Though it is the practice of all lords proprietors to give the Indians some recompense for their land it so seems to purchase it of them, it is not done for want of sufficient title from the king, but out of prudence, otherwise the Indians might have destroyed the first settlers (who are usually too few to defend themselves), or refused all commerce or conversation with them." [162]

The proprietors of East Jersey in December, 1700, stated to the Lords Commissioners of Trade in London: "Purchase of the land from the Indians (which is done for a trifle) is not for defect of sufficient title in the crown, or its grantees, but merely to avoid wars with the savage nations. This method of purchasing is not practiced in all the English plantations, and not at all in Virginia and Maryland, the planters there, locating on land by virtue of the governor's warrant only, without leave or consent of the natives." [162]

Much has been said in American history of the righteousness and magnanimity of the royal grantees and colonists in buying the land of the Indians before occupying it. This is pure fiction and ennobling reading for children. Written history often is not history at all. And the pity is that school children learn a great deal of such history which takes them years to unlearn. Later they have no inclination to examine history. [72]

The lands occupied by the Indians were disposed of by European monarchs to their court favorites as if the lands had been found uninhabited.

Agents of the Federal government, as late as 1850, made treaties with Indians as if they had a title to the land, but the United States Senate rejected these, and as Spain and Mexico had done, ignored the Indian claim of land ownership.

In some colonies rum and trinkets and, in few instances, fish hooks, clothing and utensils, all of insignificant pecuniary value, were given the Indians, not for purchase of land—to which the Indians could not give a legal title—but for reasons as will appear.

Fiske [49] said: "To an Indian, the selling of land meant little
more than granting permission to pass over it unhindered. The
Indians had not arrived at the point where the sale of land conveys to the vendee the right to exclude the vendor; but his mind
was open to a suggestion of Father Rale, that no sale of land by
an Indian sachem could be other than void, because the land
was the property of the tribe, and must be kept in trust for the
children born to the tribe."

Early travelers in the colonies have declared that the Indians
had no conception of the meaning of private ownership or sale
of land. The colonists themselves presently realized this, and the
expression "buying" the land gradually gave way to that of "making presents" to the Indians.

And these payments, whether expressed as payments for land
or as presents, were, in the last analysis, for the sole purpose of
securing safety for the settlers from being scalped or otherwise
murdered by the irate natives who were being driven from their
habitations. Without this protection the lords proprietors would
have had difficulty in inducing colonists to cross the ocean to
settle on their land grants.

Because the word "purchase," to indicate consent by the
Indians for others to occupy the land, is fixed in common usage
it is so used in this writing.

Contrary to the contention of the British government (and
to popular belief) that the Indians had no fixed habitation, Sir
William Johnson, Indian agent in the Mohawk Valley and fully
competent to speak on the subject, wrote in 1764 to the Lords of
Trade: "Each Indian nation is perfectly well acquainted with its
exact original bounds; the same is again divided into due proportions for each tribe and afterwards subdivided into shares to
each family, with all which they are most particularly acquainted.
Neither do they ever infringe upon one another or invade their
neighbors' hunting grounds."

That the Cherokees, in Carolina, had a permanent abode is
evident from their holding at the period of the American Revolution the same lands as they had held eighty-three years previously
at the time they sent a deputation to Charles Town. [126]

Governor Kieft of New Netherland demanded some tribute of

furs from neighboring Indians "whom he had defended against their Indian enemies," and threatened, in case of their refusal, to "employ proper measures to remove their reluctance." [16]

To execute this threat, Kieft conceived the atrocious Pavonia, New Jersey, massacre, an account of which has been left us by De Vries, "the only man who durst go among the Indians." [16] De Vries enjoyed a high reputation for veracity, [49] and was a directing mind of the Dutch regime.

"It was two nights in February, 1643, that the soldiers executed their foul deeds . . . At midnight I heard loud shrieks. I looked towards Pavonia. I saw the flash of the guns and heard the yells and clamor of the Indians who were being butchered in their sleep. About day the soldiers returned to the fort, having murdered eighty Indians. Children were butchered in the possession of their parents and their mangled bodies thrown into the fire or water. Some were thrown into the river alive and when parents rushed to save them, the soldiers prevented their landing and let them all drown together. Those who escaped to the bushes, making their appearance in the morning to beg some food, were killed in cold blood."

Though De Vries had many losses by the Indians he had a good opinion of them, and said: "They will do no harm if no harm is done to them."

The council of eight, composed of representative citizens at Manhattan, addressed a memorial to the company in Holland, drafted by Andries Hudde, town surveyor, saying: "All right-thinking men have known that these Indians have lived as lambs among us, until a few years ago, injuring no man, affording every assistance to our nation. These hath the Director [Kieft], by various uncalled-for proceedings, from time to time, so estranged from us, and so embittered against the Netherland nation."

Lord Halifax declared that the Indians in New York, and in the Ohio region, had been systematically defrauded of their hunting grounds and cheated in trade; and that their lands had been occupied by settlers before making terms with the Indians.[a]

The same may be said of the early treatment of the natives in Virginia and South Carolina. In Maryland, instead of paying

[a]N. Y. Col. Doc.

them, Calvert took their lands, placed a tribe on a reservation and obliged them to pay land rent to him as owner of the land. Yet there was scarcely any Indian trouble in that colony.

General Sam Houston, a pioneer, and later, governor of Texas and United States Senator, said in 1846: "I have never known a treaty made with an Indian tribe first infracted or violated by them."

A federal commission to negotiate a treaty with California Indians declared, in 1851, that by far the greatest share of the Indian troubles could be traced to white aggression. [61]

Colonel E. Walters, for twenty-seven years the government public auctioneer of oil leases of Indian lands in Oklahoma, who has lived all his seventy-two years among the Indians, has said: "The Indians are the best and most honest race in the world. I can say more for the Indians than I can say for my own white people."

During the nineteenth century the government made treaties with the Indians by which they were moved to other locations where they were promised they could remain "so long as the stars shone and water ran." Few decades passed however, before they were again shunted farther west to approximately worthless lands.

The white population so increased and occupied the land that the natives were, year by year, driven inland from the tidewater region, away from the source of their food supply of fish, oysters, clams, crabs and water fowl and towards the domains of enemy tribes. Is it to be wondered at that they made an occasional attack on the whites who then designated them bloodthirsty savages? It is needless to suggest what the white race would have done under reversed circumstances. Land surveys presaged to many chiefs the taking of their lands by the white race.

Growing contempt by some of the whites toward the natives, ill usage, cheating by white traders, debts for goods sold at exorbitant prices with land subsequently taken in payment, naturally engender resentment. Gradually, a deep grudge was created in the Indian's mind, and presently he sought revenge in attacks on white settlers.

Unfenced growing corn of the Indians was often ruined by

stray cattle of the Dutch. The Indians sometimes killed the cattle, which led to reprisals. An Indian war began in 1641, and, except for five months, continued five years and threatened to terminate the existence of New Netherland.

Sale of weapons to the Indians had been forbidden. This was observed at Manhattan, but the white traders among the Mohawks disregarded it. Governor Kieft counseled extermination of the Indians, and, in two years, 1,600 were killed.

The English of Plymouth Colony, when Indians declined to sell them corn, took it from them by force, just as the English were doing in Virginia. When the natives at Plymouth threatened retaliation, Captain Miles Standish "dealt so fatally with some of them that the survivors remained pleasantly tractable for a considerable time."

Three years after the English settled in Connecticut a force of English, with Indian allies, made a surprise night attack on the Pequot Indians near Stonington, and as cited in the chapter on Connecticut, exterminated the entire Pequot nation and appropriated their land.

Dutch settlers complained to Director-General Stuyvesant that: "We are usually and every year full of apprehension that the natives, by the murders they commit because they have not been paid for their lands, may commence a new war against us."

In all the wars in which the Indians were involved with the English and Dutch it may be fairly doubted whether the Indians were in a single instance the aggressors.[b]

Jeremiah van Rensselaer, a Dutch patroon, wrote that the Esopus Indian War was started by the Dutch who shot an Indian, and that "the cruelty of the natives towards the whites, will, when traced, be discovered in almost every case to have been provoked by oppression and aggression." The Esopus war in 1652 was the outcome of Thomas Chambers settling on a large tract of land in that section. In the militant contest that followed "the Indians were forced by the Dutch to directly depart thence without being permitted to return to plant."

Soon after the location of the first English settlement in Carolina the Spaniards on the south incited the Indians to resist the

[b]Scharf. Hist. West Chester County

English encroachments on their lands. These intrigues continued many years, resulting in frequent hostilities and the killing of many hundreds of whites and natives.

The French persuaded the Indians to join them in what became the French and Indian War against the British by the promise that their lands, taken by the whites, would be restored.

An Onandagas chief, Outreonti, in conference at Albany with Governor Dongan's envoy in 1684, said: "He who made the world has given me the land which I occupy. I am free." [16]

Outstanding Indian warriors resisting encroachment of the whites were Philip, Pontiac, Tecumseh and Black Hawk. The last named, in his Life, dictated by himself, said: "My reason teaches me that land cannot be sold. The Great Spirit gave it to his children to live upon and cultivate as far as is necessary for their subsistence; and so long as they occupy and cultivate it, they have the right to the soil."

Tecumseh, generations after great harm had been and continued to be done, is recorded, on August 12, 1810, as having said: "The land belongs to all for the use of each. No party has the right to sell, even to each other, much less to strangers. The only way to stop this evil is for the red men to unite in claiming a common and equal right in the land, as it was at first, and should be yet, for it never was divided."

President Hayes in his annual message to Congress in 1877, said: "They [the Indians] have been driven from place to place. In many instances when they had settled down upon land assigned to them by compact and began to support themselves by their own labor, they were rudely jostled off and thrust into the wilderness again. Many, if not most, of our Indian wars have had their origin in broken promises and acts of injustice upon our part."

The chairman of the South Dakota State Planning Board, Mr. W. R. Ronald, was quoted in 1936, as saying: "The greed of the whites has known no sense of justice to the Indian, with the result that he has been shunted along from one region to another until now, in South Dakota, which has a large share of the Indians living in this country, he is expected to make a living from the very kind of land that the federal land-use section of the government is buying from whites because such land cannot support them."

No Indian policy which recognized that the Indians had any rights had ever been satisfactory to the American settlers. From the time the first colonists landed on the Atlantic seacoast until the first federal Indian reservation was opened in Oklahoma, the procedure has been the same. The white man wanted the Indian's lands and was going to have them. If his policy of intrusion aroused the red man to resentment and to reprisal, extermination of the red man was considered justified. [161]

As a rule the Indian was unprepared to cope with the pressure put upon him. Thus, partly by legal means, partly by fraud and graft, the Indians were stripped of their lands. This process was hastened by the discovery of oil on land on which they had been placed. The rights of civilized Indians were no more respected than those of "wild tribes." The land was there and the white men were determined to get it. In these circumstances there could be only one result.[c]

In consenting to white occupancy of the land, for whatever pay they could get, the natives had in reality lost nothing the white man would not have taken anyway. [4]

The firm hold that the lords proprietors had on the monopoly of land is treated in the chapters on the different colonies.

For the United States Supreme Court, in the first important case before it dealing with Indian title to land, Johnson *vs* McIntosh, Chief Justice Marshall delivered the opinion covering some sixty pages, all summed up as follows: "The Indians were admitted to be the rightful occupants of the soil with a legal as well as a just claim to retain possession of it and to use it according to their own discretion; but . . . their power to dispose of the land at their own will to whomsoever they pleased was denied by the original fundamental principle that discovery gave exclusive title to those who made it.

"In the United States the rights of European discoverers having been succeeded to by the states or by the general government, the Indian title to the land is a right of possession and occupancy,

[c]Stanley Vestal

the fee being in the general government or in the state where the land is situated if it is one of the thirteen original states.

"A title to lands under grants to private individuals, made by Indian tribes or nations to the west of the River Ohio, in 1773 and 1775, cannot be recognized in the courts of the United States."

A New York decision, Seneca Nation *vs* Christie, declared: "The Indians were held to be incapable of alienating their lands except to the crown or to royal grantees, and all purchases made from the natives without such consent were regarded and treated as absolutely void."

Chief Justice Depue of the New Jersey Supreme Court, in 1892, in the case of the City of Newark *vs* George Watson, ruled: "By the law of nations, established by the consensus of all civilized nations and by the common law, title to the soil is obtained by discovery or conquest. By the English common law the title to lands in this state was vested in the English crown, and it is a fundamental principle in the English colonial jurisprudence that all titles to lands within this colony passed to individuals from the crown, through the colonial or proprietary authorities."

5

Manors

THE KING, pretending to hold the land from the Great Proprietor of all the Earth, made grants of large areas to some favorites, who made sub-grants to others; of whom some were designated the Lord of the Manor, with power to rule, establish courts-leet and courts-baron, to govern, control and direct the churches, the religious services, the patronage of every church on the manor, and the disposition of "deodands"—a peculiar perquisite.

The court-leet was held by the steward of the manor for the punishment of petty offenses and the preservation of the peace. He also took view of frank pledge, a pledge of surety for free men; a bond or pledge that he shall be forthcoming to answer every violation of the law.[a]

A court-baron—the court of the baron—or lord of the manor —was incident to every manor, to be held by the steward, for redressing misdemeanors and nuisances therein and for settling disputes among the tenants relating to property.[b]

No new manors were created in England after the prohibition of subinfeudations by statute in 1290.[c]

Subinfeudation under feudal law was the granting to another, on rental, of part of the land held from a superior lord. Feud means land held of a superior on condition of rendering him service.[d]

[a]Blackstone Commentaries
[b]Bouvier, Dictionary of Law
[c]Washburn, Real Property
[d]Hedge, Feudal Society

Serfdom disappeared to a large extent in England with the Tudors, but the lordships and manors set up by royal authority and power in the vast forests of America, three and a half centuries after they were prohibited in England, represented the same spirit and possessed cruel powers.

Each of the many manors established in New York and Maryland by British proprietary grants was organized in strict conformity with the principles and theory of the feudal form of government prevailing in Britain, as represented by the crown. The manors were but an intended link in an imperialistic chain binding the province by feudal shackles to the throne of England and designed to halt any movement in the colonies for a more democratic form of government. [100]

The decline of the manor and of feudalism meant only, as someone has said, that exploitation of the subjugated peasants was now carried out by the lords, not through forced labor, but by making serfs into land-rent payers. [55]

While land was granted as manors in New York, Pennsylvania and Maryland, and in the form of baronies in South Carolina, it was only in Maryland, and to a limited extent in New York, that they persisted long enough (other than in the exacting of land rent by the land-holder) really to justify the name. These survivals are treated further in the chapters on those colonies.

6

Indented Servants

INDENTED SERVANTS as a factor in the formulation of Colonial America's land policy and material advancement, should not go unnoticed in the study of this subject. Without them development of the seaboard regions, especially Virginia, Maryland and South Carolina, would have been greatly retarded.

The Beards [10] wrote: "It is probable that one-half of the immigrants before the Revolution, certainly outside of New England, were indented servants and Negro slaves," while John R. Commons is quoted as saying it is probable that one-half of all the immigrants during the Colonial Period landed as indented servants.

The name is derived from the practice of tearing in two parts with jagged edges the contract of servitude; the master and servant each keeping one part.

With the beginning of the cultivation of tobacco in Virginia in 1612, a demand soon arose for laborers. The feudal land system of England, as has been traced, caused England to be overrun with idle, able-bodied men and women. Many of them were willing to go to America to escape their deplorable condition but were without means to pay transportation.

The Virginia Company devised the plan of sending such men and women who would agree to work for a planter for a certain number of years. The period of indenture was usually about four years but this often was unduly prolonged. Upon arrival of a servant, a planter would pay the company a sum sufficient to cover the charge for transportation. Presently shipmasters in general engaged in the business on the same terms.

It was not uncommon for people in London and Bristol to make a business of luring young persons aboard ships for transportation to the colonies. Adults and children were often kidnapped to be sold as indented servants notwithstanding an act of 1670, which made such kidnapping a crime punishable by death.

At that time there were three hundred crimes in the calendar for which capital punishment was inflicted. This was so harsh a penalty for the smallest offense that transportation to America as indented servants was a compromise on the part of humane judges.

However, many who were of good social connections, but without funds, volunteered to go as indented servants. Many captives taken in factional wars in England and Scotland were exported to Virginia and South Carolina and sold as indented servants.

The purchasers of indented servants had a legal property in them during the term for which they were bound. They could be sold or bequeathed for the duration of the unexpired term; and like other chattels, indented servants were liable to seizure for debts of the master. Their status during the period of their servitude was in effect the same as that of Negro slaves, and they were at times subject to as harsh treatment. To desert, was punishable in Maryland by death. In Pennsylvania, when indented servants were levied on for the militia, Benjamin Franklin tells us, "a ferment ensued and the assembly indemnified the owners at a cost of near £3,000."

A common practice of wealthy residents of Britain was to purchase land in Virginia and Maryland and send indented servants to work on land so purchased; the greater the number of servants sent, the greater the area of land the buyer was entitled to receive, upon paying land rent to the overlord.

As years passed and the Atlantic seaboard country became more populous and prosperous, some men of wealth in Virginia and Maryland who were able to acquire more land than they could put to use became ready buyers of indented servants. With the increase in the number of Negro slaves, towards the time of the Revolutionary War, the demand for indented servants decreased.

It was the cheap labor of these indented servants and Negro slaves that led in Virginia and Maryland to acquisition of large tracts of land on which to produce tobacco cheaply. This was the foundation of large landed and, consequently, aristocratic families.

The masters fed and clothed their servants. At the end of his term a servant was supposed to be given two suits of clothes, a set of tools necessary for his trade, and some money called "freedom dues."

Many servants at the expiration of their terms of service became farmers or artisans, either in the locality where they had been living, or elsewhere. In the Middle Colonies some became substantial citizens, while others, unable to obtain land, became just "poor whites." In the South it was difficult for any of them to rise in the social scale.

7

Religious Liberty Overstressed as Motive for Migration

DESIRE for religious liberty being more exalted than economic necessity as a motive for emigration, religious liberty has been widely given as the reason for the rapid settlement of America. This is so to a very limited extent. Those colonies which had been the most noted as havens of religious tolerance became the most intolerant.

In the 1600's there was rabid intolerance in England towards those who did not adhere to the Established Church. A sect of Separatists from the Church of England was so hounded by religious intolerance that some of them decided to seek habitations outside of England.

English settlement in Virginia had begun to be advocated and the first English colony was just then being sent there. But the Virginia Company was sponsored by people high in the councils of the Established Church, which made that opening unacceptable as a location for the Separatists.

So, in 1608, a year after the first English settlement in Virginia, some of the Separatists group departed for Holland and lived there eleven years enjoying religious liberty. During those years Dutch ships were making voyages between Amsterdam and the Hudson and Delaware Rivers, and the Separatists learned from these sailors of the broad expanse of land in America uninhabited by white people and apparently free to settlement.

The Thirty Years' War of opposing religious forces in Europe broke out in 1618. This, with prospects of free land, prompted the Separatists, together with some of their brethren who had remained in England, to go to America. They landed at Plymouth, Massachusetts in 1620, and became known in American history as the Pilgrim Fathers.

In the grant by James I of land in New England to the Plymouth Company (not the Pilgrims) restrictions were placed upon Roman Catholics.

Other groups, known as Puritans, followed the Pilgrims to Massachusetts nine years later, partly, as noted in the chapter on New England, because of failure of their efforts to reform the Established Church, and partly to obtain land. Still others came, or were sent, as indented servants seeking escape from the economic and social distress resulting from feudal landlordism in England.

Fourteen years after arrival of the Pilgrims the population of Massachusetts was estimated by John Winthrop at four thousand; an average increase of only 285 persons per annum—though most of the increase came during the last four years of that period.

How many of these came seeking religious freedom is not known, but because a person needed to be orthodox in religion, and to have a taxable estate of £20, only one person in six had the right of franchise.

According to Bradford and Winthrop, both the Pilgrims and Puritans migrated to Massachusetts to better their condition by getting land. The inference is that only a small percentage of the settlers came to America to find religious freedom.

When Roger Williams was banished from Massachusetts he made a settlement at Providence, Rhode Island, in 1636 and proclaimed religious liberty for all sects. Population increased slowly, and to the displeasure of Williams, land grabbing, rather than religion, soon became the absorbing passion.

In 1643 the House of Burgesses of Virginia passed a stringent law requiring of all persons a strict conformity with the worship and discipline of the Church of England, the established church of that colony. This act was put into vigorous execution, and some Puritans from England who had been settled on the Nansemond River for twenty-two years were stopped from preaching and driven out, some of them settling on the Severn River in Maryland, and others in Massachusetts.

In 1659, during Berkeley's administration, Virginia enacted heavy penalties against Quakers, and in the eighteenth century Baptists were persecuted.

There was a belief that Maryland, established in 1634, was to be a refuge for Roman Catholics, and that adherents of all religions would be welcome. Of the more than three hundred original settlers, including priests, sent to Maryland by Calvert, the Roman Catholic lord proprietor, it is recorded that the large majority of them were Protestants. This fact is further indicated by the record that of twelve who died on the voyage, only two professed Catholicism.

Eleven years later it was estimated that three-fourths of the population of Maryland was Roman Catholic, but as years passed there was a greater influx of Protestants than of Catholics.

Four years afterwards, that is, fifteen years after the first settlement, Calvert, fearing loss of control of the government through the increasing number of Puritans, had the assembly pass the much-praised Toleration Act of 1649 providing religious toleration for all who professed belief in the Trinity. Refusal to believe was punishable by death. For the jeopardized Jews, it was restricted religious liberty.

The year following their arrival, the Puritans, who had been driven from Virginia and settled in Maryland, complained that their conscience would not allow them to acknowledge authority of the Calvert Catholic proprietary and they started a rebellion.

They convened a general assembly to which Roman Catholics, either as members or electors, were declared to be ineligible. The assembly repealed the Toleration Act of 1649 and enacted another providing "that none who profess and exercise the Roman Catholic religion can be protected in the province."

By this act the Roman Catholic Church suffered greatly. Chapels and mission-houses were broken into. Three of the Jesuit priests fled to Virginia and kept in hiding for some years. Only one priest remained in Maryland.

In 1658, although three-quarters of the members of the Maryland assembly were Puritans, the Calvert government was restored upon recognition by Cromwell, and the Toleration Act of 1649 was re-enacted. But twenty-seven years later the Protestant assembly passed "protective" acts against Catholics. Seven years afterward a tax of forty pounds of tobacco (the currency of the province) was levied on all voters, rich and poor alike, regardless of their church affiliation, for support of the Church of England in Maryland. After being in effect eighty years, Charles Carroll of Carrollton, a Roman Catholic, led a legal assault against this illogical tax.

To regain the government of Maryland, of which Calvert had been again deprived, Benedict Calvert in 1715 renounced the Catholic faith and that year a Protestant assembly disenfranchised Catholics.

In the grant of all the land in Maine and New Hampshire to Gorges and Mason in 1639, confirmed by Charles I, it was provided: "Our will is that the religion now professed in the Church of England, and Ecclesiastical government, shall be for ever hereafter professed throughout the province."

At about that time whole towns moved from New England to New Netherland to enjoy among the Dutch that religious liberty denied them by their own people. But thirteen years later a proclamation, issued by Governor Stuyvesant at Manhattan, declared that "the public exercise of any religion but the Dutch Reformed, in houses, barns, ships, woods or fields would be punishable by heavy fines." And Quakers were being persecuted. Even after the American Revolution, John Jay, subsequently governor of New York and Chief Justice of the Supreme Court, moved in the New York State Constitutional Convention that Roman Catholics be denied citizenship and the right to hold land. The motion was rejected.

Quakers went from England to Barbados, whence two of their number, Anne Austin and Mary Fisher, went to Boston in 1656. There they were arrested and jailed, and for fear they might proclaim their "heresies" to the crowd outside the prison, the windows were boarded up. There was, as yet, no law against Quakers, but a council declared their doctrines blasphemous and devilish. Their literature was burned, and after five weeks in jail the prisoners were put aboard a ship and returned to Barbados.

The following year the New England colonies passed a law

to banish Quakers, and in Massachusetts death was the penalty if they returned. One of the Quaker women did return and she, with three other Quakers, was hanged on Boston Common. In New Hampshire the penalty was a choice of imprisonment, banishment, whipping or branding.

President Oakes of Harvard, in a sermon in 1673, said: "I look upon unbounded toleration as the first-born of all abominations."[a]

In Carolina, notwithstanding the fact that the greater part of the inhabitants were not adherents of the Church of England the lords proprietors in England in 1672, ordered that the Church of England should be the ruling religion in Carolina. Thirty-two years later the assembly enacted that all members of the assembly should be members of the Episcopal Church. Liberty of speech, in pulpit, assembly and the community, was practically denied.

The East Jersey assembly, in 1681, ejected one of its members as being a Roman Catholic.

Aside from Rhode Island, the sections of America having the widest recognition of religious liberty were those under the direction of William Penn. During the six years preceding his obtaining the grant of Pennsylvania in 1681, Penn had been successfully establishing Quakers and religious freedom in West Jersey. He afterwards restricted religious liberty in Pennsylvania, where only those who professed faith in Jesus Christ could become free men capable of voting or being elected to public office. Thus Penn, as Calvert had done in Maryland, discriminated against Jews and other religious sects.

Queen Anne, when appointing her cousin Lord Cornbury as governor of New York and New Jersey in 1702, declared there should be "liberty of conscience for every one except Papists." The governor, however, imprisoned Presbyterian ministers and confiscated their meeting houses in New York; and the New York assembly passed a law condemning to death all Roman Catholic priests found in the colony.

The royal charter of Georgia in 1732 restricted settlement of the province to Protestants.

Even the Pilgrims, Puritans and Quakers, an infinitesimal

[a]Felt, Eccl. Hist. New England

number of all who migrated, while expressing religious fervor, were not disassociated from a desire for land.

An insight into the cause of the distressing poverty and man's inhumanity to man in Europe clearly shows that poverty emanated from feudal landlordism, and this being stabilized as it was, relief was possible only through emigration. America offered the only escape.

I believe it will be recognized that during more than two centuries the compelling cause of the mass movement of people seeking homes in the savage-infested wilderness of America was the desire for material betterment of themselves and their children through access to land.

Assigning a desire for religious freedom as largely the reason for peopling America, has been overstressed.

8

Virginia

JAMES I, King of England, claimed as his personal domain, which he could bequeath to his successors, or otherwise do with as he pleased, all the land in America between the French settlement on the St. Lawrence and the Spanish settlement in Florida. [145]

The first Virginia charter, issued by James I on April 10, 1606, granted to Sir Thomas Gates and three others named, "and any others whom they join with them, to be called the first colony [known as the London Company], all the lands, woods, soil, havens, ports, rivers, mines, minerals, marshes, waters, fishings, commodities and hereditaments whatsoever for fifty miles north and fifty miles south from the seat of their first location in America [which was subsequently made at Jamestown, Virginia], and directly into the main land for one hundred miles, with all the islands within one hundred miles between 34° and 41° north latitude [between Wilmington, North Carolina and Long Island Sound]."

Included in the charter was a similar grant to Thomas Hanham, of Plymouth, England, and three others named, to be called the second colony (known as the Plymouth Company) of an equal area between 38° and 45° north latitude (between the present Virginia-Maryland boundary line, across the Delaware peninsula, and the eastern boundary of Maine).

Inasmuch as these areas overlapped, it was provided that "neither shall locate within a hundred miles of the other that first begins their location."

The grants cited: "They shall order the search for gold, silver and copper, giving to us our heirs and successors the one-fifth part of such gold and silver, and one-fifteenth part of all copper found. Authority is granted to capture any persons, ships or goods which shall be trafficking without license within the limits of said plantations. Upon petition, we shall grant unto such persons and their heirs and assigns, as either council shall nominate, all the lands and tenements which shall be within that colony."

Those to whom the grant was made solicited subscriptions to stock in the company at its par value of £12, 10*s* per share. A widespread promotion for sale of the stock was developed, the venture even being advocated from church pulpits on the plea of advancing religion by christianizing the aborigines. It was believed that not only gold, but iron and copper would be found to replace imports of those metals from Spain and Sweden respectively; also that wine and silk produced in America would relieve dependence on France and Persia for those commodities; and that dependence on the Baltic countries for naval stores would be similarly relieved.

A satire, "Eastward Ho," by Ben Jonson and associates, when produced on the stage excited the public imagination. In it one of the characters declared: "I tell thee gold is more plentiful in Virginia than copper is with us; and for as much red copper as I can bring I'll have thrist the weight in gold. All the dripping pans there are of gold; all the chains for chaining the streets are massive gold, all prisoners are fetterd in gold; rubies and diamonds are gathered on the seashore. Why man!"

The promotion not only brought subscriptions for the stock, but a great desire by many to emigrate. The stock was subscribed for by more than one thousand men and women, many in high places, and by merchants, professional men, tradesmen and land speculators.

The following January 1, 1607, three ships of the London Company, in command of Captain Christopher Newport, sailed from London with colonists, stated by various writers as 105 and 143 in number, but which Captain John Smith, one of the colonists, reported "to the number of 100."

By prevoyage agreement all products of labor during the first seven years were to be pooled for the entire colony. This communist principle induced hundreds of unemployed in England presently to go to Virginia, or to be sent there as indented servants.

Each emigrant was to receive, at the end of the seventh year, a share of stock in the company and every shareholder was to receive a grant of land in proportion to the number of shares held.

When the colony was scarcely more than a year old stockholders in England began clamoring for profits from their supposed Eldorado. They demanded a piece of gold, and threatened to forsake the settlers as "banished men" unless a cargo of goods worth £2,000 sterling was sent.

In May, 1609, James issued a second charter [145] to the London (Virginia) Company, enlarging the grant, and separating it and the Plymouth Company, designating the former as "The Treasurer and Company of Adventurers and Planters of the City of London for the First Colony in Virginia." The Plymouth Company, under this charter, was not developed, and all attention was centered on the first (London) company.

James expanded the area granted the company from ten thousand square miles to more than one million square miles. Its bounds were to run two hundred miles north and two hundred miles south of Point Comfort (approximately between Wilmington, Delaware and Wilmington, North Carolina), and in depth all the land from sea to sea, north and northwest (which became the basis for Virginia's claim to the land north of the Ohio River) and all the islands within a hundred miles along the coast of both seas, together with all soils, ports and mines. This territory was made over to the sole use of the company and their assigns for ever, with authority to distribute and assign the lands therein granted.

James also increased the number of grantees, designated as adventurers to persons, including by name, 8 earls, 12 lords, 106 knights, 1 bishop, 1 divine, 3 ministers, 57 captains, the mayor of London, the sheriff of London, 28 esquires, 4 doctors; among all of whom there were more than one hundred who then were, or had been, members of parliament. There were also included fifty-six trade guilds.

To conclude the record of Virginia charters: James on March 12, 1612, added to the grants all those islands lying within three hundred leagues (nine hundred miles) between 30° and 41° north latitude (between Florida and Long Island Sound). This included the Bermuda Islands. George, Lord Archbishop of Canterbury, was added as an adventurer. Lotteries were authorized in England for the benefit of the plantation. Complaint was made against persons who had gone, or been sent, to Virginia and surreptitiously returning maligned it.

Shortly after the English migration to Virginia began, Philip III, King of Spain, wrote his ambassador, Zuniga, at London, "You will report to me what the English are doing in the matter of Virginia. Thereupon it will be taken into consideration here what steps had best be taken to prevent it."

In October, Zuniga had an audience with King James to endeavor to persuade him to recall the Virginia settlers, and send no more there; that Spain claimed all that country. Following this, Zuniga wrote the King of Spain: "It will be serving God and your Majesty to drive these villains out from there [Virginia]: hanging them."

Zuniga, the following March, again wrote his king advising of an intended voyage of English to Virginia, saying, "It seems to me necessary to intercept them on the way." Philip wrote Zuniga: "Report when they will depart, with what force, and what route they will take. You should act with great precaution with the Baron of Arundel." (Arundel was afterwards father-in-law of Cecilius Calvert.)

Philip, in June 1611, wrote his new ambassador at London: "I command you to send from England, two Catholic men whom you can perfectly trust, aboard the first British vessel that may sail to Virginia, directing them to bring to you an exact account of all that is going on there."

Philip himself evidently initiated a voyage of discovery because, just two months later, Governor Dale in Virginia advised London that: "A Spanish caravel came into our river fitted with a shallop to discover the river and creeks, and anchored at Point Comfort. Three Spaniards were sent ashore into the fort there, demanding a pilot to bring their caravel into the river. The caravel departed, leaving the three Spaniards, who I have here as prisoners." Evidently Spanish spies.

George Calvert, in August 1612, wrote Philip protesting against Zuniga tarrying in England after his mission had ended.

The same year the Spanish ambassador in London wrote his king: "A ship has arrived from Virginia, and well-informed think that the business does not grow, but rather diminishes; that forty or fifty of the English have married women of the savages, and that the women whom they took out from England have gone among the savages and they have received and treated them well—that a zealous minister was seriously wounded in many places because he reprimanded them."

The dire reports from Virginia of deaths and starvation caused many subscribers to the stock of the company to refuse to pay further instalments due, and suits were brought against them. To obtain funds, the company sold the Sommer (Bermuda) Islands for £2,000 to 120 of its members in England. To procure additional badly needed funds the company held a series of lotteries in London, with a first prize of £5,000, but gradually, over a period of years, this source of revenue petered out.

Cultivation of tobacco began in 1612, and within four years the demand in Europe became so great that the colonists devoted all their time to its cultivation to the exclusion of everything else. They even gave guns to the Indians with which to kill game to supply the settlers with meat, while the settlers grew and cured tobacco. Tobacco growing was exhausting to the soil and necessitated constantly taking up more virgin land; the used land was, however, suitable for growing wheat and corn.

The previously fixed seven year era of communism in the colony was terminated by limitation under Dale in 1614. He leased to each of the colonists, many of whom were indented servants whose terms of servitude expired that year, three acres to cultivate at an annual rental, variously stated as two-and-a-half, and six, bushels of corn, payable into the community storehouse. In addition, the lease called for one month's work not in seedtime or harvest, for the commonwealth. These terms produced an era of energetic activity of which the social effect was marvelous in the reduction of idleness, poverty and crime.

To induce men of family to migrate to Virginia, Dale offered them a house and twelve acres free of rent, food for one year, and implements and domestic animals, if they would grow exclusively wheat, corn, roots and herbs.

The company, as a reward for services, allotted Captain John Martin ten shares, entitling him to a thousand acres, which he selected at Martin Brandon, on the James River. "He was to enjoy his lands in as large and ample manner as any lord of any manor in England." This caused great complaint and the first contest for title to land in America. After prolonged controversy a new deed was offered him in substitution: this he declined to accept until nine years afterwards. [17]

The town of Henrico, named for Prince Henry, was located by enclosing with a stockade seven acres on a peninsula seized from the Indians. The houses were partly of brick and more than half of the population lived in that section. When Dale left in 1616, there were four communities in the region, including Jamestown, Hampton (the oldest continuous English settlement in America, near Old Point Comfort), and Dale's Gift, across the bay at Cape Charles. [112]

The council of the company in England announced: "For that part of the country fit for plantation, we intend, God willing, to begin a present division of land by lot to every man that hath already adventured his money or person: for every single share of £12, 10s, fifty acres of land, till further opportunity will afford to divide the rest, which we doubt not will bring at least two hundred acres to every single share. But this present division is to be only in the land lying along the King's (James) River on both sides, and about the town erected. The holder may dispose of his lot, or go there to possess it, or send families to cultivate it, as many do for half the clear profits." This was the beginning of land tenantry and share-cropping in America.

Surveyors were sent to Virginia to make maps and allotments to the shareholders, such allotments to be capable of transfer as an estate of inheritance. To prevent fraud, deeds were not valid until ratified by the quarter-court, a committee of the board of directors of the company in London.

Captain Christopher Newport, who was prominent in the settlement of Virginia, made five voyages transporting settlers during a period of five years. He was presented by the company with thirty-six shares of stock entitling him to 3,600 acres. He later entered the East India service and died aboard ship in 1617. His widow was granted 3,500 acres. For a time the company shares had a value and were frequently bought and sold. [17]

Samuel Argall was granted land, and arrived in 1617 as deputy-governor. He was recommended by Sir Robert Rich (later Earl of Warwick, who became prominent in making land grants in New England). Argall promptly began to appropriate for himself all the movable property of the company and when he departed two years later nothing much remained.

The company treasury in London was exhausted by 1618, and £16,000, instalments on stock subscriptions, remained unpaid. Suits were begun, but with small results.

A grant of 200,000 acres on the James River, near the mouth of the Chickahominy River, was made to a group of adventurers, and on it 300 tenants were afterwards located. Other grants of large area were made, but only one such was developed by the grantee. [112]

Slaves were first brought to Virginia in 1619; and though the ship was Dutch, there was suspicion that Argall, the late governor, and his ship the "Treasurer," were concerned in the transaction. Notwithstanding all his roguery, Argall was knighted three years later.

George Yeardley, son of a poor merchant tailor, was knighted and sent to Virginia as governor in 1619 to replace the rascally Argall. In accordance with instructions, he inaugurated the first representative assembly in America, which met at Jamestown on July 30.

Grants of land in fee simple became more general and included grants to the early settlers. The assembly petitioned for a resident treasurer to collect land rents, and for rents payable in tobacco which was the currency of the country because there was no coin.

Berkeley's Hundred, 4,500 acres on the upper James River, was granted to five prominent men in England as a first dividend on their stock holdings of forty-five shares. In a feudal manner, the company held land for its absentee shareholders. The purpose was to realize profits from the labor of their tenants and from increase in land value.

When private ownership of land in fee simple became more general, Yeardley was instructed by the company to set aside land at Jamestown, Charles City (City Point), Henrico and Elizabeth City. Three thousand acres were to be for the support of the governor, 1,000 acres for the ministers, 10,000 acres for endowment of a proposed school for Indians, 1,000 acres for the master of the school, 1,200 acres for the superintendent of the company lands, 1,500 acres each to the treasurer of the company and high marshal, 500 acres each to the secretary of the company and the physician, and 300 acres to the vice-admiral.

These were set aside to be inseparable from the office held, and to assure payment of salaries. But as they were valueless without men to work on and produce from them, a certain number of tenants were assigned to each tract, at an annual rent of half the crop.

As it is not possible to develop a colony without women, the company annually for several years sent properly chaperoned marriageable women as prospective wives. To recoup the expense of transportation, each suitor to be accepted, had to pay 120 pounds of tobacco. The company offered married tenants twice the area of land that it offered unmarried men. Ninety maidens were sent in 1619 and the following year a hundred additional were sent.

Planters appealed to England to send charity youths who were a burden on the English parishes. In response, several hundred children, many of them orphans, were sent as apprentices for seven years. After the first seven years they were to become tenants for seven years, and were then each to be allowed twenty-five acres and a cow, at 6d land rent.

The first general clause in grants of land, in 1620, was: "To all . . . know that I, Sir George Yeardley, governor, by virtue of the great charter of Orders and Law agreed on by the treasurer, council and company of adventurers and planters for the first Southern colony of Virginia, according to authority granted them by his majesty under the great seal, and by them dated London, 18th day of November, 1618, and directed to myself and the council there resident, doe, with the approbation of the council, who are joined in common with me, give and grant to, etc."

After the company treasury became exhausted, it issued what were designated as "bills of adventure," at £12, 10s each, which was the same as the par value of the stock. These bills entitled the holder to an allotment of a hundred acres and other emoluments and, in effect, constituted a preferred stock. Many purchasers of these bills associated together in obtaining vast areas of land to be held on speculation, and for rent to others. From some such, Smith's Hundred and Martin's Hundred resulted.

Combinations of shareholders holding two hundred shares were entitled in the initial division of the land to twenty thousand acres and to twenty thousand additional acres when, and if, the first division of land was settled upon.

William Claiborne, aged thirty-eight, son of Sir Edward of Westmoreland, and afterwards prominent in Maryland in opposition to Calvert, was sent in 1621 to Virginia as surveyor to lay off land which was being granted. His compensation was £30 per annum, and house rent.

A grant of a large tract of land on the Nansemond River was made in 1621 to Edward Bennett, a wealthy London merchant, who sent a group of Puritans to Virginia. The company shares, par £12, 10s, were that year being offered in London at £10.

Notwithstanding that tobacco had become the all-important commodity of export, King James opposed the use of it, declaring it a "smoke weed," displeasing to him, and scandalous unto the plantation and unto the whole company.

The company granted licenses to fish in the ocean between 33° and 45° north latitude (between the Santee River in Carolina, and the eastern boundary of Maine), with the right to use land for drying nets.

The company refused to recognize that the aborigines had any right of ownership or occupancy of the land. The company agents were continually driving them from their established locations and preempting the land to distribute to holders of bills of adventure and stockholders.

Brick was being exported from Virginia to Bermuda in 1622, at 18s 8¼d—a fact which would tend to disprove that buildings in Virginia or Maryland were ever constructed of English brick. The colony exported lumber, furs and tobacco in payment for English goods brought in at high prices.

The company leased land to some tenants at an annual rental of twenty bushels of grain, sixty pounds of tobacco, and one pound of silk. In such leases three or more tenants were obliged to live together, and were each individually bound for the entire rent. Some who were sent over by associations of stockholders were obliged, after clearing the land of heavy timber, to pay a land rent of one-quarter of the product of their labor.

In the early 1620's the company and the settlers were again in fear of an attack by the Spaniards. Since there were no defenses, efforts were made to have Jamestown abandoned and a settlement and fort located in a more suitable place. The company was unable to provide for a fortification, and there were no guns or munitions. An appeal was sent to England for old firearms from the Tower of London and this was complied with.

A demand was made upon the company by the settlers that land be granted in smaller tracts to secure more concentration and closer settlement of people for defense.

The Indians, realizing from the frequent arrivals of the English that they had come to stay and would, unless prevented by starvation or force, drive the natives farther from their fishing and hunting grounds, in March 1622, armed partly with English guns, made a concerted attack on all the white settlements along the James River. As soon as possible thereafter the English made reprisals on the natives, which brought peace for many years.

Within a year after the massacre, sixteen ships, chartered by holders of bills of adventure arrived bearing eight hundred settlers, as tenants. Unpaid subscriptions of the company stock now amounted to £15,000.

Nicholas Marlier (Martin), an ancestor of George Washington, was the first grantee of the land on which Yorktown is now situated. [151]

During the first seventeen years the colony spread along both sides of the James River, almost as far as the present location of Richmond; and on the north, to the York River. The sparse settlements lacked concentration of population for defense, and the practice of granting land in large tracts to absentee holders was severely condemned after the massacre. But protests against this policy were of no avail. The apparent policy of the company was to dispose of all the land possible to appease demands of shareholders for land dividends and increase land rents, regardless of the safety of the settlers.

Factional differences, disputes, strife and slander within the company, political entanglements in England regarding the company, and the growth of popular government in Virginia, prompted King James in 1624 to force a revocation of the company charter. After a strongly waged contest in England, the Lord Chief Justice declared the charter null and void. Thereupon James appointed Sir Francis Wyatt royal governor with a council of eleven members.

Stith, a Virginia historian, contended that the charter rights of the company had not been legally annulled.

James assured the company shareholders that their vested interest in land would not in the slightest respect be infringed; that his intention was to alter the charter only as to form of government, with the preservation of the land privilege of every holder. The following year he again so assured them.

The land grantees included a great array of noblemen, guilds and bishops, including the Archbishop of Canterbury. To have revoked the land grant, which the company was attempting to monopolize while making use of only a very small area about Jamestown, would have been considered an outrage on the recently acquired vested rights of these nobles and bishops. They wanted to hold the territory for themselves and their heirs to use to exact ground rents from succeeding generations.

Maintenance of the private land privilege was subsequently confirmed by the succeeding king, Charles I. As further evidence, for a long time after revocation of the charter, shares in the company were received in payment for land.

It is roughly estimated that the proportion of shareholders who went to Virginia to live, those who sent others as tenants or indented servants, and those who sold their shares, was about equal.

There were several ways of acquiring land. In the initial division of the land a shareholder was entitled to a hundred acres for each share held. If he placed settlers on it he was entitled to an additional hundred acres in the second division. If of record prior to the dissolution of the company, he was exempt from paying the land rent of 12*d* per fifty acres, but not if before that year he had acquired fifty acres by "transporting himself or others into Virginia at his own charge."

The Indian massacre of 1622, together with the revocation of the charter, caused abandonment of the project for a college, and the ten thousand acres of land which had been allotted for that purpose became subject to disposal by the king.

Taxes could not be levied without approval of the assembly. A tax of 2*s* per hogshead was levied on tobacco and another on indented servants and slaves. Prior to revocation of the charter, land rents were payable to the company. After that time, they were payable to designated collectors for the king; and although the king's personal revenue, they were for a while applied to local public uses.

William Claiborne, the surveyor, for defeating the Indians on the Pamunkey River in 1629, was granted a tract of land there. As a barrier against Indian raids, fifty acres were offered to each person who would locate on the outer fringe of the settlements.

The Virginia assembly in 1634 complained that Governor Calvert, although he had been in Maryland less than five months, was interrupting trade. The lords of the council in England wrote that the farmers in Virginia should enjoy their lands and trade with the same freedom and privileges as before revocation of the charter.

To the Virginia Council's protest of the grant to Calvert of the land in Maryland, all formerly included within the Virginia grant, King James gave the excuse: "There being land enough for many thousands, and work is more easily overcome by a multitude of hands and assistants." [108]

This controversy led, as an outgrowth of the Claiborne fight for Kent Island in the Chesapeake, to a revolution in Virginia. Governor Harvey, of Virginia, abetted Governor Calvert and was seized and deported to England, but through the intercession of Cecilius Calvert was returned to Virginia.

Yearning for a close monopoly of all the land between Carolina and Long Island Sound, the respective governors of Virginia, in 1623, 1631, and 1635, sent expeditions to the Delaware to drive out the Dutch, who were supposed to be there trading with the Indians. In the second of these expeditions all the Virginians were killed by Indians, and the other two also proved futile, as shown in the chapter on the Delaware Region.

A grant of eighty thousand acres in Martin's Hundred was made in 1635 but, as usual, settlement there was sparse. A grant of eight thousand acres in Barcley Hundred was made the following year by an association of adventurers to William Tucker and associates.

Jerome Hawley, one of the councillors of Maryland, was made treasurer of Virginia. His instructions were to examine all Virginia land grants and demand thereupon a yearly rental for use of the king. [108]

Ever eager for more emoluments, although already granted all the land of Maryland, Cecilius Calvert proposed in February, 1637, that he be made Governor of Virginia, at a salary of £2,000 a year. Despite his plea that he could advance the king's service in that colony, his bid was rejected. Calvert had hoped that as governor of Virginia he could stifle the opposition which had arisen there against the granting to him from the Virginian domain, of all the land in Maryland.

Land rents of one shilling per fifty acres on land granted by the company were not to begin until seven years after the date of each grant. Actually, no serious attempts were made to collect the rents until 1637. At that time, all grantees were directed to pay rent to the king's collector either in coin, which was very scarce, or in tobacco at 3d per pound (the price of tobacco was later reduced to 2d per pound).

These land rents were almost impossible to collect for the reason that forfeiture of land could not be forced, owing to popular opposition. The office-holding class, including governors, strenuously resisted breaking up speculative landholding. The seven year provision was revoked by Charles II, and the revocation was afterwards confirmed by James II since it induced speculators to take up large tracts of land and hold them out of use. A moratorium on rent was found to be injurious to the development of the colony, just as a low tax on land values is today injurious to the development of any community and state.

Large numbers of English gentry settled on the Eastern Shore; the first deed for land there was recorded in Accomac County, in 1638. [170]

English girls continued at that date to be imported into Virginia for wives for the planters. The cost of their transportation, which the planters had to pay, had declined to one hundred pounds of tobacco, selling at three pence per pound; equivalent to £1, 5s.

Francis Wyatt, again governor, in 1639 granted land at the direction of the king.

Richard Lee, of Shropshire, England, with seventeen indented servants, in 1640, was the first of the family to locate in Virginia. He acquired a thousand acres of land between the York and Potomac Rivers, and became the largest individual landholder of his generation in that colony.

Charles I, in October, 1643, granted letters of marque to Governor Calvert in Maryland to seize all ships belonging to Virginia. Whereupon the British Parliament, in opposition, appointed the Earl of Warwick as governor of the colonies, and commissioned eight vessels, one in command of Ingle, to transport ammunition, clothing and supplies to the Chesapeake. The following April a fight occurred on the James River near Newport News between a twelve-gun ship of the adherents of King Charles and two vessels of the parliamentary forces.

Fighting between the English set the Indians a bad example which prompted them to massacre all the settlers they could reach. In this second Indian massacre three hundred whites were killed. [108]

A treaty of peace with the Indians, two years later, provided, as did every treaty ever made between Europeans and Indians, for relinquishment of their land. The Indians were driven, in this instance, to north of the York River, which restricted their marine food supply.

Revenue collected from rents, and from land granted by the king since revocation of the company charter was appropriated as the personal property of the reigning monarch. In 1645, however, it was ordered by the assembly that the revenue from land rents should be disbursed for such purposes as the assembly should order. Later a portion was appropriated for building William and Mary College. But diversion by the assembly of any part of the revenue for a public purpose was by sufferance only.

Appropriation of the rent of absentee-held land by the public treasury for public purposes, instead of allowing it to be privately appropriated, was a logical policy. Had this been continued through the centuries to the present time, Virginia would have a large, continuing public revenue, with a greatly reduced tax burden and, in all likelihood, no state of municipal debts. Furthermore, by this discouragement of speculation in land values industrial and social welfare would have been advanced far beyond what they are now.

About 1646, as a precaution against the aborigines, land continued to be granted at outlying points to persons who agreed to maintain an armed force for defense. Captain Thomas Rolfe, son of Pocahontas, was granted four hundred acres at Fort James on the Chickahominy River; Captain Roger Marshall six hundred acres at Fort Royal; and Captain Abram Wood six hundred acres at Fort Henry, the present site of Petersburg.

The old problem of non-payment of land rents again came before the assembly in 1648. The treasurer was given authority to levy upon the property of delinquents, but political influences were so powerful in favor of holding land for the anticipated increment that collections continued slow until the latter part of the century, when more regularity was enforced.

The great lack of geographical knowledge in the province is indicated in a pamphlet printed forty-two years after the first settlement. In it is expressed the "Hope soon to discover a way to China. The question is, how broad is the land from the head of the James River?"

In 1649 Charles I was beheaded. Charles II claimed the throne.

In 1650, while in exile, he gave two thousand acres in Virginia to one of his Scotch servants by the name of Prodger. Presumably, Prodger was to pay the usual annual land rent to the crown, beginning after the seventh year.

William Byrd, as a young man and heir of a large tract of land, located in Virginia in 1653, the first of the name in the colony. On part of his land the city of Richmond was afterwards founded.

The English law principle of primogeniture, which grants the father's land to the eldest son, was then respected in Virginia, but not altogether effectively.

In 1653, the assembly, anxious to place a military force in the Roanoke River region as a protection against Indians, offered, regardless of who owned the land, ten thousand acres in fee simple to any association of persons equipped with guns and ammunition who would settle there.

A poll tax enacted in 1657 on all men, including indented servants, was the general method of providing public revenue. The tax on these servants was a property tax payable by their owner.

It may be of interest to note that Colonel John Washington, forty-four years of age, a man of wealth and influence, the great-grandfather of George Washington, came to Virginia in 1657.

After the defeat at Worcester of the adherents of Charles II, Charles was again a fugitive, and Chief Justice St. John, head of affairs under Cromwell, caused Parliament to pass the celebrated Navigation Act of 1651 which proved so harmful to the southern colonies, and led to war between the Dutch and the British.

The act provided that all commodities to or from the English colonies in America, and even some commodities traded between the colonies, should be carried in ships built and owned in England or the colonies. Of the ships' crews, three-fourths should be English subjects. The duties imposed by the act were payable in England.

The effect was to prevent Dutch ships, theretofore important carriers to and from the colonies, from entering American ports, and cut off except through England, with duty added, the important and lucrative export of tobacco to the Dutch market.

Holland vehemently objected, and to enforce its objection, built 150 ships of war. During the following two years, these ships, commanded by van Tromp, fought several desperate battles with the British fleet under Blake.

Upon the restoration of Charles II, in 1660, the act was made even more drastic; five different times during the next sixty-two years, additional specific commodities were added to the restricted list.

These acts, particularly hard blows to the growers of Virginia tobacco, were the incentive for developing New England shipping in illicit commerce. To evade the restrictions of the act, southern growers sent their products to New England ports, whence they were illegally shipped in fast New England vessels to Portugal and other foreign countries.

As a consequence of the act, the Dutch developed tobacco culture in Sumatra, their East India colony, in competition with Virginia, just as the artificially controlled high price of cotton in the United States in the 1930's was to induce all other countries possible to promote cotton culture and permanently compete with American growers.

Sir William Berkeley, the long-time governor, was sent to England by the colonial assembly to protest against enforcement of the navigation act. He failed to effect any change, but returned the following year with grants of land for himself. [169]

Colonel Edmund Scarborough was a leading planter and merchant on the Eastern Shore of Virginia and Maryland. As the king's collector of land rents he was an important personage in that section. Berkeley held 79,041 acres in the adjoining counties of Accomac and Northampton, and three thousand acres in the disputed territory between Virginia and Maryland. [170]

The Indians in Accomac County, on the Eastern Shore, complained that they had been deprived of their lands to such an extent that they were in straitened circumstances. [170]

Another war broke out between England and Holland in 1664, which continued three years and during which the British captured New Netherland. In the closing year of the war, a Dutch squadron of men-of-war sailed into the Chesapeake and captured twenty-six English vessels, including one man-of-war. The Dutch scuttled most of the prizes and returned to Flushing, Holland, with eleven tobacco-laden ships.

Eight years afterward, England, joined by France, warred on Holland. A Dutch fleet of nine men-of-war took two British warships in the Chesapeake, sank or captured several merchant vessels there, and proceeded to New York, which they recaptured from the British. Both these wars, which were caused by restrictions on international trade, produced economic distress in Virginia.

Not until sixty-three years after the first settlement at Jamestown had the English made any exploration beyond the Alleghenies to learn the nature of the country, or to find the much hoped for opening to the Pacific Ocean. [5]

Universal suffrage in Virginia was abandoned in 1670 when an act of assembly established a property qualification for voting. "None but freeholders, landholders and housekeepers shall hereafter have a voice in the election of burgesses." This disfranchised the majority of the people. [5]

Governor Berkeley in 1671 said: "I thank God we have no free schools nor printing, and I hope we shall not have these hundred years; for learning has brought disobedience and heresy and sects into the world, and printing has divulged them and libels against the government. God keep us from both."

Land rents, and the holding out of use, by private appropriation, of vast areas of land, were a constant cause of dissatisfaction among the settlers, as they were in all colonies. These grievances, and the hardships resulting from the navigation acts, caused a period of hard times in the 1670's, which resulted in Bacon's rebellion.

Nathaniel Bacon was a young cavalier twenty-nine years of age, a lawyer educated at Cambridge, son of an English gentleman, and member of his majesty's council in Virginia. He suddenly appeared as a leader and aroused the people of the York peninsula and contiguous country in a rebellion of the poor against the large landholders. Bacon declared: "All the power and sway is got into the hands of the rich, who, by extortionate activities, having the common people in their debt, have always curbed and oppressed them in all manner of ways."

He opposed the recent enactment of a property qualification for voting, and the poll-tax, which "taxed both rich and poor alike," as a cruel injustice and declared that "every man should be taxed according to the tracts of land he holds."

At the head of one thousand men of Virginia and Maryland, he moved against Jamestown, burned it, and inflicted widespread damage. In due course a regiment of British soldiers arrived in Virginia to put down the rebellion.

Governor Berkeley hanged so many of the rebellious, including his appointee, Governor Drummond, of North Carolina, that King Charles, when he learned of it, exclaimed: "The old fool has hanged more men in that naked country than I have hanged for the murder of my father." The rebellion terminated the following year with the death of Bacon. Universal suffrage was restored, and some other causes of the rebellion were afterwards removed.

John Bland, a wealthy London merchant interested in the Virginia trade at the time, recognized taxation as an outstanding factor, and said: "All inequalities in taxation might be eliminated by adopting a land tax, which seems to be the most equitable tax, and will generally take off the complaint of the people, although perhaps some who hold greater proportions of land than they actually plant will not like it."

When the people of Warwick County asked that "all persons may be rated and taxed according to their land value," the king's commissioners, who were investigating the matter, replied: "That is a thing to be wished but never to be granted them, since the common usage always has been taxing by the poll." The commissioner's belief that, "whatever was good enough for grandfather is good enough for us," is one hardly conducive to social progress and welfare.

King Charles in 1684 forbade use of printing presses in Virginia, and the same year ordered that land rents be collected in coin, not tobacco. There was no coin in the colony, and the landholders petitioned the governor, Lord Howard, to be permitted to pay in tobacco.

Throughout this period, "squatting" on unused land—that is, locating on land which one neither owns nor rents, was a common practice. In course of time this brought numerous disputes as to land titles. In 1684 many such squatters petitioned that their holdings be made legal. To this the king assented upon condition that the tenants pay, in coin or tobacco, an annual land rent of one shilling per hundred acres. The sheriff, who collected the rent, was to receive 10 per cent for collecting. In default of payment, the land was to revert after three years to the king.

Many grants of land had been made with the proviso that they must be settled upon within three years. Also, land in rent default for three years after the seventh year was to revert to the king. Many tracts did so revert, and were granted to others.

The assembly enacted that a person who had been for two years in occupancy of land which should have reverted to the king, but which had not reverted, could have title thereto by paying a hundred pounds of tobacco for each fifty acres, and annually thereafter the usual land rent.

The following figures are given by Bruce, [20] and quoted by Fiske, [48] as the maximum size of any land grant made to individuals during the years stated (on some the nearest occupant was often two or more miles distant):

1632	350 acres
1634	5,350 acres
1635	2,000 acres
1636	2,000 acres
1637	5,350 acres
1638	3,000 acres
1640	1,300 acres
1641	873 acres
1642	3,000 acres
1643	4,000 acres
1646	1,200 acres
1647	650 acres
1648	1,800 acres
1649	3,500 acres
1650	5,350 acres
1651–5	10,000 acres
1656–66	10,000 acres
1667–79	20,000 acres
1680–89	20,000 acres

Numerous other grants of smaller acreage were made each year.

Of £4,375 collected in land rents during the six years preceding 1692, only £1,985 were expended for public services in Virginia.

Let us revert momentarily to the defunct company. To induce increased immigration and thereby increase the company revenue from future land rents, the company, prior to 1618, announced an addition to the then existing methods of taking up land by shareholders and buyers of bills of adventure. The company would issue what was designated, "a Head Right," for each human being coming, or being brought, to Virginia. Head rights were issued not only to those coming to settle, but to whoever paid for the transportation of another person, including indented servants and Negro slaves.

These rights were exchanged by the holders for tobacco, and the tobacco grower, in turn, presented them in payment for more land; each right being accepted by the company for fifty acres, on which the annual land rent was to begin seven years after date of the deed.

But the privilege was soon abused by connivance of shipmasters bringing in indented servants and Negro slaves. Captains of arriving ships would apply for, and get, rights on all their passengers and the crew; and each one of the white passengers and crew would do likewise for themselves.

Clerks in the land office presently began to graft by issuing for a few shillings rights for fifty acres to all applicants. Colonel Ludwell, a member of the council, was entitled to 2,050 acres on forty-one head rights, but by adding a cypher to each figure on his certificate he received 20,500 acres.

As the object of the company was to dispose of land, the local agents were not particular as to the method of disposal. The more land granted, the greater the prospective revenue from land rents.

The consequence of all these head rights was that vast areas of land were granted in large plantations to tobacco growers, or to speculators whose sole object was to sell or rent it to others. Increasing population made tracts valuable before the land rent became due at the end of the seventh year.

The Beards [10] said: "The land office of Virginia was a sink of corruption, and all the governors owed their appointments to politics and intrigue." Commenting further on the governors: "Lord Delaware, with the pomp of an Oriental potentate; Dale, hard, brutal and efficient; Argall, a petty tyrant who robbed the settlers and cheated the corporation; Yeardley, a liberal gentleman who applied himself for the most part in planting tobacco; Wyatt, during whose five years' service the colony passed from the company to the crown."

New arrivals coming to create homesteads, and indented servants wanting land at the expiration of their services, found that land along all the streams (in that densely wooded country, the only means of travel and communication) had been appropriated, either by large plantation owners, or by speculators. Shut out from temporarily rent-free land on which to apply their labor, newcomers were forced to become tenant farmers, share croppers, or laborers for others. Under these conditions head rights became less valuable.

Evidently, considerable skepticism prevailed for many years regarding the validity of land titles acquired through head rights. So uncertain were holders that requests were repeatedly made to the successive kings to confirm them. In 1625 King James I gave them his approval; two years later King Charles I, then reigning, further confirmed them; four years later he confirmed them a second time, and two years after that, confirmed them for a third time; and in 1662 Charles II confirmed them.

By the end of the seventeenth century head rights had ceased to be used, and land grants were made at the land office on payment of a fee, on land rent of 5s per fifty acres, payable in coin or tobacco; the rent to begin at the end of the seventh year. Head rights were never used in the "Northern Neck" region of Virginia.

Robert Beverley, a Virginia historian, wrote in 1705 of the people of Virginia as "not minding anything but to be masters of great tracts of land"—lords of vast territory. Thirty-one years later, his son, Colonel William Beverley, acquired a grant of 118,-491 acres in the Shenandoah Valley.

By 1718 nearly three million acres had been granted. Great opposition was made by speculating officials and politicians to collection of land rents, or the making of rent-rolls. Governor Spotswood and associates took up 85,027 acres prior to 1723. [12]

Some Germans, who squatted on land in the Shenandoah Valley and made improvements, were afterwards obliged to buy the land of a Welshman who had obtained a grant of it in 1730. Thomas Lee promoted a rapid influx of Germans into Northern Virginia and the Shenandoah Valley. Always anxious and eager to acquire land to the westward, he obtained 4,200 acres in the present Fauquier County, and several thousand acres in adjoining Loudoun County, in which Leesburg is situated. [4]

Richmond was planned in 1737. There was no public school in Virginia until 1728, no newspaper published until 1745, and few roads until 1750. With these backward social conditions, land-grabbing, land speculation and other forms of gambling, were diversions of the gentry. Virginia declared the region northwest of the Ohio River to be part of Virginia, as the county of Illinois.

Benjamin Borden, an Indian trader from New Jersey, obtained grants of 600,000 acres in the Shenandoah Valley in 1734 and 1739. In the same region, Yost Heydt, from York, Pennsylvania, was in 1749 granted 140,000 acres on which he settled a hundred German families. Title to this land was disputed by the Fairfax family for the next thirty-seven years.

James Patton petitioned the Virginia council for "200,000 acres on three branches of the Mississippi, and the waters thereof, on which I propose to settle one family for each 1,000 acres." [4] Subsequently the council granted him 100,000 acres in the Woods and Holston Rivers region in southwestern Virginia, and promised an additional 100,000 acres as soon as he had settled 100 families on this grant. The Ohio and Loyal Companies entered caveats (warnings) against Patton. [4] Such grants illustrate the lavish manner which prevailed in the giving away of large areas of land on the promise of only the most meagre use of them. Land speculation was actively promoted to the economic and social injury of continuing generations.

At the same session in which the Patton grants were put through, the council made to its president, John Robinson, a similar grant on the Greenbrier River in present West Virginia, from which he formed the Greenbrier Company. [4]

In 1754 the government in London directed that a thousand acres in Virginia be granted to settlers west of the Alleghenies, free of land rent for ten years. This was revoked nine years afterwards when settlement west of the Alleghenies was forbidden.

People of tidewater Virginia took little interest in the French and Indian War in the 1750's, because they realized the war was for the profit of a few land speculators. [1]

The Father of our Country was quite as much interested in land grabbing and speculation as were many other leading citizens. Land was plentiful, and obtainable for the asking by men of influence. They saw no harm in the practice, just as many otherwise righteous citizens of today see no harm in it. Only since population has increased, and the demand for desirable urban land for acutal use correspondingly increased, has the harm of land grabbing, in the form of slum-housing and the high price of land, become apparent to those who study the effects of it.

George Washington, in 1767, then aged thirty-five years, wrote his friend and associate, William Crawford: "Any person who neglects the present opportunity of hunting out good lands and in some measure marking and distinguishing them for their own (in order to keep others from settling them), will never regain it; if therefore you will be at the trouble of seeking out the lands, I will take it upon me the part of securing them as soon as there is a possibility of doing it . . . By this time it may be easy for you to discover that my plan is to secure a good deal of land." He advised him to carry on his operations "Snugly under pretense of hunting game." [1]

Five years later Crawford wrote Washington: "There will be no possibility of taking up such quantity of land as you want near Fort Pitt, as there is such numbers of people looking for land, and one taking each other's land from him. As soon as a man's back is turned another is on his land. The man that is strong and able to make others afraid of him seems to have the best chance as times go now."

The Virginia Council, in 1773, ordered that squatters should have preemption rights to four hundred acres of land on which they had settled, but unless the settler held a soldier's claim, he was to pay £3 per hundred acres to the land company in which some, if not all, members of the council were shareholders.

No other Virginian could rival Dr. Thomas Walker of Albermarle County, a conspicuous land speculator of the time, in his powerful connections in tidewater Virginia. Walker effectually dominated the land speculation interests of the colony. He was the active head of the Loyal Company, [1] which is treated in the chapter on Kentucky.

Most of the revenue collected from land rents in Colonial Virginia, beginning in the eighteenth century, was sent to England. £7,420 was sent in 1775. A gateway leading to the House of Parliament in London was paid for by Virginia land rents.

That part of Virginia between the Potomac and Rappahannock Rivers, from their sources to the Chesapeake Bay, designated as the Northern Neck was, during the Colonial Period, so apart from the James River region that it is here treated separately.

Charles II, while a fugitive prior to the restoration in 1660, granted all the land in the Northern Neck to: Henry Jermyn, as Lord Hopton; the Earl of St. Albans; Lord Culpepper; Lord Berkeley; Sir William Morton; Sir Dudley Wyatt and Thomas Culpepper. They were to pay Charles one-fifth of all gold and one-tenth of all silver discovered.

By 1673 some of these grantees had died, and a new grant was then made to Lord Culpepper, "one of the most cunning and covetous men in England," and Henry Bennett, Earl of Arlington, father-in-law of the king's son by Lady Castlemaine. Charles gave them for a term of thirty-one years "all the dominion of land and water, called Virginia"; they were to pay him an annual rental of 40s.

Culpepper and Arlington's grant gave them the right to grant land anywhere in Virginia, and to confirm former grants, to establish counties, towns, parishes, churches, schools; appoint sheriffs, ministers and other officers; establish fairs, markets, manors and manorial courts for their profit.

It included not only all unallotted land, but all land which had been long cultivated by the hard-working settlers, from whom they were to collect land rents. They might even review the title to land which had been already granted to the settlers. They rented or sold to immigrant settlers and absentee speculators portions of the unallotted domain, to their own profit.

Hopton and Arlington were two of the very few men who had collaborated with Charles in, and knew of, the iniquitous secret treaty of Dover, between Charles II, King of England, and Louis XIV, King of France. In the Dover treaty, Charles, among other things, transferred Dunkerque to Louis. A year after this grant, Arlington, who as secretary of state, had been unscrupulous and self-seeking, fell into disgrace by being impeached by the House of Commons for corruption, betrayal of trust and embezzlement. Nevertheless, Charles, ever trustful of his friends, afterwards appointed him Lord Chamberlain.

Culpepper was, by order from London, to use revenue from land rents to erect a fort on a site which he might select (although thirty-four years previously, the assembly had optimistically enacted that land rents were to be appropriated only by the assembly). The assembly petitioned the king, in 1675, to buy the Northern Neck for the colony, but this was disregarded.

Culpepper, acting through his agents, granted land in the Northern Neck at 5*s* per hundred acres up to six hundred acres, and at 10*s* in excess of that acreage. This resulted in concentration of large tracts in private ownership. One Fitzhugh held twenty thousand acres, and another speculator, Hayward, thirty thousand acres.

The grant to Culpepper created so much discontent in the colony, during the succeeding eight years, that the king revoked the right to collect the land rents. In consolation for the revocation, the British government granted to Culpepper a pension of £600 a year for twenty years, and the government ordered that hereafter no private grant for collecting land rents should be made; that they should be used solely for general purposes.

Culpepper was recalled as governor-general in 1683, and was succeeded by Lord Howard, as lieutenant-general; but the following year Charles confirmed Culpepper in the possession of all the land in the Northern Neck.

By the terms of the grant, the entire Neck region was to be put to use within twenty years, but this provision was afterwards recognized as practically impossible of fulfillment and, in 1688, it was revoked by James II, then ruling, and the entire Neck was granted to Thomas, second Lord Culpepper.

All land in the Neck not disposed of by Culpepper passed, by dower with his daughter Catherine, to Thomas, Lord Fairfax, Baron Cameron. [169]

Early in the eighteenth century Fairfax was selling land in his domain at 5s per hundred acres, in tracts under six hundred acres, or at half the rate of crown lands. On larger tracts the rate was 10s per hundred acres. [20] At the same time the governor of Virginia, regardless of the Fairfax sales, was granting land to settlers in the same region.

Fairfax came to Virginia in 1735 with an order from the king restraining the governor from making further grants. Eleven years afterwards he became a resident of Virginia, and died there in 1782, willing his land to a nephew, Rev. Denny Martin Fairfax, a British citizen. [12]

After years of building up a strong fortification of precedents and manipulating a legislature, John Marshall, Chief Justice of the United States, and his brother James, managed to get legal hold of the much-coveted Fairfax estate by a decision of his own court, handed down by an associate justice whose fraudulent Fletcher and Peck case had been decided favorably by Marshall four years previously.[a]

The Provincial Assembly of Virginia ordered the landholders in the Northern Neck to pay their land rents to the public treasurer, but a large sum in past due rents was paid to the Fairfax executors. [12]

The land remaining in Fairfax possession passed to Albert Kirby Fairfax, Virginia born twelfth Baron Fairfax, a citizen of England, to whom the occupants in Virginia must pay land rent.

Large landed estates were established by primogeniture and entail prior to the American Revolution, at which time Jefferson introduced a bill in the Virginia assembly to abolish entail. It was bitterly opposed and nearly defeated. [73x]

The Virginia convention, at the outbreak of the American Revolution in 1775, condemned the land policy which Governor Dunmore had announced . . . the eminent domain of the crown in American land was denied, and it was argued that the land ultimately belongs to the people, or to their local governments. [1]

[a]Myers, Hist. U. S. Supreme Court

In May, 1776, just prior to the Declaration of Independence, the Virginia assembly took over the crown's control of the land and the right to collect land rents. Three years later it levied taxes for the new state, in lieu of land rent, which had been collected by the crown and sent to England.

The Provincial Assembly of Virginia offered land, in 1778, at £40 per hundred acres, with no limit on the area to any one purchaser. It was estimated that this price, the 2s annual land rent having been abolished, was about equivalent, in the then depreciated currency, to the old colonial price of 10s per hundred acres. [1]

In 1784 all unallotted land in Virginia became the property of the commonwealth under the laws of escheat and forfeiture. Now the State offered land at £25 per hundred acres on the eastern waters—tidewater region—and at auction in York and Elizabeth Counties, except at Point Comfort (on which suit was to be brought for any unpaid rent).

Absentee holders of large areas of land acquired for speculation realized, after the American Revolution, that the anticipated public demand for land was not appearing. With no prospect of profit from unearned increment in land value, they abandoned much of their holdings to the Commonwealth of Virginia.

In the early days of the colony, when there appeared to be more land than would ever be used, the extravagant granting of land to be held unused on speculation seemed to be not harmful. However, as time passed, and population increased, the demand for land broadened.

Land along the streams, which were the only highways to market, having been privately appropriated and held largely unused, new arrivals, native youths, and freed indented servants were forced to locate on uneconomic locations, to the detriment of the material and social welfare of themselves and the colony.

While a condition of the grants was that they must be settled on within three years all sorts of subterfuges were practiced to circumvent that wise provision. Often it was complied with by merely erecting a shack on a large tract, or planting a few acres of corn, each to be afterwards neglected. Because so many persons of influence, including government officials, were holding land out of use on speculation to forestall the next generation, forfeiture of such land was seldom ordered. Thus, as in our own times, nefarious practices were countenanced if backed by powerful influences.

Not until eighty-five years after the first settlement, was definite notice given that such land would be forfeited unless settled upon within three years. By that time great harm had been done to generations of native born, and of freed bond servants, who had sought, and been denied, land on which to locate and earn their living within convenient distance of the market for their produce; with the result that these were forced to become tenants of absentee landholders at rack rents, share-croppers, laborers on plantations, or shiftless whites.

Enormous importation of Negro slaves, which afforded more cheap labor, brought large profits from tobacco, for which there was a constantly increasing market. This encouraged the expansion of plantations into thousands of acres, each under one ownership.

Through wealth produced on these plantations, resulting from the land system and slavery, the large landholding families became powerful and their social life aristocratic. Sons and daughters of these families married those of other families of like station, and thus concentration of land and wealth in individual holdings went on apace.

The mere existence of indented servants, landless free men, and Negro slaves, shaped the future social and economic conditions of the commonwealth. With these elements the society became one characterized by large landed proprietors and hordes of landless people, the latter earning but a scanty living; by poverty, bad housing and human wretchedness; by large public debts, and heavy charges for the resulting poverty and crime.

Similar conditions and influences prevailed later throughout the cotton- and tobacco-plantation regions of the Southern States. Without such conditions these states would have become the homes of small landholders earning a decent living. And, what is more, the underlying cause of the war between the states would not have existed.

9

Massachusetts, New Hampshire, Maine
and New France

THE voyages to the New England coast of Bartholomew Gosnold in 1602, and of Bartholomew Gilbert and Martin Pring the following year, and that of George Weymouth two years later, and the voyages of the French fishermen to the adjacent waters, awakened in England and France an active interest in acquisition of land and colonization in America.

Weymouth gave to Ferdinando Gorges, governor of Plymouth, three of his kidnapped Indians, from which gift Gorges became interested in America.

On April 10, 1606, King James I granted to Thomas Hanham, of Plymouth, England, and three others named (the group known as the Plymouth Company), the land between the latitude of the present Virginia-Maryland boundary across the Delaware Peninsula, and the eastern boundary of Maine. However, the Virginia Company, whose charter was granted the same day, had the right to occupy the southern part of the Plymouth grant.

Under this grant to the Plymouth Company, the moving spirits of which were Gorges and Sir John Popham, Chief Justice of England, colonization was attempted along the New England coast.

They sent ships with colonists to Maine in 1606. One ship, with Captain Thomas Hanham and Martin Pring and Gorges' three Indians, sailed in October, and arrived at the Sagadahoc River (which is the lower reaches of the Kennebec River) four months before the first Virginia colonists arrived in the Chesapeake. The other ship, the "Richard," fifty-five tons, under Captain Henry

Challons, with twenty-nine Englishmen and two Indians, proceeded by way of the Canary Islands and was captured by the Spaniards in the West Indies and taken to Bordeaux.

The first ship remained at the Kennebec until the following spring, awaiting arrival of the "Richard," and then returned to England. Except for the capture of the "Richard," Maine, instead of Virginia, would have been the seat of the first permanent English settlement in America.

A vlei-boat, the "Gift of God," commanded by George Popham, brother of the Chief Justice, and a ship, the "Mary and John," four hundred tons, commanded by Raleigh Gilbert, nephew of Sir Walter Raleigh, sailed from Plymouth, England, in May, 1607, with one hundred and twenty persons, being about the number in the first Virginia colony which sailed four months previously.

Both these commanders were included as grantees of land. They formed the first settlement in New England, August 19, at Sabine, now part of Phippsburg, at the mouth of the Kennebec River.

They built a fort which they named St. George, and equipped it with twelve pieces of ordnance; built therein fifty houses, a church and a storehouse. They also built a pinnace of about thirty tons.

Popham died and was buried at Sabine. More than half the voyagers returned to England the following December, leaving forty-five in the colony.

After existing for a year on the Kennebec, the settlement broke up, some returning to England and others going to Virginia.

One French mariner had made forty voyages to America before the English settled at Jamestown in 1607, their first settlement in America. [5]

Champlain returned to the St. Lawrence in 1608, where he found a party of Basques trading with the Indians. He founded Quebec, and the following year explored Lake Champlain. With occasional trips to Paris, he lived in Canada until his death twenty-seven years later.

A party of Frenchmen from Port Royal, Nova Scotia, sailed to the rivers St. John, St. Croix, Penobscot and Kennebec in 1611. After inspecting the fort which had been erected and abandoned by the English, at the mouth of the Kennebec, the French affixed to it a cross. [72]

The ship "Jonas" sailed from Honfleur, France, in 1613, with forty-eight persons taking horses, cattle, tents and munitions, and intending to found a Jesuit settlement on the Penobscot River. A prolonged dense fog prevented this, and they sailed to Port Royal. After five days there they went to Mount Desert Island, and landed at Saint Sauveur, Somes Sound, Frenchman's Bay. [72]

An English sloop of war of fourteen guns, from Jamestown, in command of Captain Samuel Argall, was just then making its annual trip to the fishing banks for a supply of cod. Following instructions of Governor Thomas Dale of Virginia, to keep a lookout for, and expel, any French settlements, he put in at Mount Desert. Discovering the French ship there, he fired a heavy volley on the ship, which was returned; but taken by surprise and unprepared for defense, the French surrendered after one man was killed and four wounded.

This was the first blow, in time of peace, and started a series of wars in America between England and France, which continued in America intermittently for 150 years, costing the lives of thousands of French and English and a countless number of Indians. [72]

Argall was subsequently accused by the French of having taken their ship, horses and cattle, and of plundering the Frenchmen of everything in their possession, even their clothes. He inhumanly put fifteen Frenchmen adrift in a small boat. They reached Nova Scotia and were afterwards taken to France. Fifteen others, who were ashore at the onset of the attack, later joined those in Nova Scotia. The remaining fifteen Argall took to Virginia.

The following October, Dale ordered Argall to return to Maine and Acadia, taking his French captives with him, and to destroy all the French settlements. One of Argall's ships carrying the French priest, Biard, became separated from the other in a storm, and was obliged to make for the Azores, then to England, whence the Frenchmen were sent to France. [72]

Nevertheless, the French continued to claim the region, maintaining trading stations and missionaries, and cultivating friendly relations with the Penobscot Indians.

France made a claim on England for the loss caused by the raids of Argall: for the value of the ship captured, for the horses and for great quantities of train and whalebone. The claim included the sum of a hundred thousand livres to reimburse Madame La Marquis de Guercheville, who had financed the settlements thereabout. [17]

Ferdinando Gorges in 1614 sent Captain John Smith, recently of Virginia, to explore the New England coast with two ships. Smith scanned the shore from Penobscot Bay to Cape Cod, locating for a while on Monhegan Island, where he built seven fishing boats. Meanwhile Adrian Block, the Dutch explorer, was sailing from Manhattan to the eastward through Long Island Sound, putting in at all rivers and bays en route, and discovering Block Island.

In July Smith sailed for England with one ship. The captain of the other ship, which was left on the coast, entrapped twenty-seven natives aboard, carried them to Malaga, and sold them as slaves to Spaniards. The free natives naturally retaliated on later-arriving English. [16]

Gorges, the following year, fitted out another vessel in command of Smith [16], but it met with mishaps and returned to England. [72] The two Weymouth Indians captured by the Spaniards were that year returned from England.

An excellent map of the New England coast, made by Smith in 1616, stands as a milestone in American cartography; upon it he placed the name of New England, the first map to bear that name.

Smith was subsequently to write: "In neither of those countries [Virginia and New England] have I one foot of land nor the very house I builded, nor the ground I digged with my own hands, nor ever any content or satisfaction at all, and though I see ordinarily those two countries shared before me by them that neither have them nor know them but by my descriptions." [62]

The prospective rise in value of land in Virginia from tobacco growing quickened Gorges and his associates to obtain from the king a new charter to replace the defunct Plymouth Company grant. [16]

Some of the English Separatists who had been living in Holland for eleven years, and had learned of America from Dutch sailors, determined to go there. Accordingly, after long negotiation to procure funds for such an expedition, Thomas Weston organized a group of seventy merchants in England, who subscribed to about seven hundred shares at £10 each. [62] Land in the Delaware Bay region was obtained from the Virginia Company, which had been granted that region. [47]

The colonists were to engage in farming, fishing, building and trading. Every person over sixteen years of age of those who went, was to receive a share of stock. Children between ten and sixteen years were each to have half-a-share. The entire group bound themselves to work seven years and apply their net earnings to a common fund. At the end of seven years this fund was supposed to repay the loan.

After many false starts in two ships, which proved unseaworthy, 102 of the migrants finally got under way in the 180 ton ship, "Mayflower."

Owing to storms, or poor navigating, instead of making land at the Delaware Capes, they came to shore in Cape Cod Bay, December 29, 1620, and dropped anchor at the present location of Provincetown. That location being so exposed to north and northwest winds, they sought the west shore of the bay, where they made a settlement and named it Plymouth.

However, after a wretchedly uncomfortable, disease-engendering voyage of three thousand miles in winter weather over a watery waste, they found there ahead of them an absentee landlord—the reorganized Plymouth Company (Council of New England)—holding title to all the land in New England by grant made by King James I of England while the Pilgrims were voyaging westward.

They subsequently were permitted to occupy some land—without title being granted them.

The Plymouth Company (not the Pilgrims), was reorganized in 1620 as, "The Council Established at Plymouth in the County of Devon for the Planting, Ruling and Governing of New England in America"; it became known as the Council of New England.

Following are excerpts from the grant which King James I made on November 3, 1620, to forty favored Englishmen [145]:

"We ordain that all the American continent between 40° and 48° N. [Philadelphia and Bay of St. Lawrence], from sea to sea, shall be the bounds of the second [the New England] colony and that it shall be called New England in America. [Virginia was called the first colony.]

"And we ordain that from henceforth there shall be for ever in our town of Plymouth [England] one body corporate which shall have perpetual succession which shall consist of forty persons for the planting and governing of New England and by the request of said petitioners we hereby appoint the following:

"Lodowick, Duke of Lenox, lord steward of our household; George, Lord Marquis Buckingham, our high admiral of England; James, Marquis Hamilton; William, Earl of Pembroke, lord chamberlain of our household; Thomas, Earl of Arundel; Robert, Earl of Warwick; Earl of Bath, Earl of Salisbury, Earl of Southampton, Viscount Haddington, Lord Zouch, Lord Sheffield, Sir Ferdinando Gorges, Sir Francis Popham, Sir Thomas Gates, Sir George Somers [and twenty-four others named].

"And we grant all the fisheries, mines and minerals as well royal mines of gold and silver, and quarries and other jurisdictions, royalties, privileges and franchises upon the main land and islands adjoining, *provided* they are not actually possessed by any other Christian prince, to have and hold the aforesaid lands and continent, and to profit therefrom, for ever to be holden of us and our successors; yielding and paying to us, our successors, one-fifth part of the gold and silver which may be found.

"And further we authorize said council shall from time to time distribute and convey such portions of lands hereby granted, respect being had to the proportions [investment of each] of the adventurers."

The capture of unlicensed ships and goods was authorized, "one-half of the value to go to the council and one-half to us." (There were restrictions as to Roman Catholics.)

"And we covenant that if the council at any time shall conceive a doubt concerning the validity of this grant or desire to have same renewed or confirmed by us or our successors we or our successors will forthwith make and pass under the great seal of England such further and better assurance of all the lands, royalties and privileges aforesaid granted or intended to be granted."

Bancroft [5] remarked: "Estimated at more than a million square miles, and able to support more than two hundred million people—given to forty individuals!"

This grant was opposed by the Virginia Company, which caused a delay of two years in beginning of operation.

The company announced that each stockholder was to pay in £110, but "only persons of honor or gents of blood would be admitted, except only six merchants to be admitted for services in trade and commerce." It purposed making a profit by grants of land to applicants, one such grant being to The Governor and Company of the Massachusetts Bay in New England, and to others as hereinafter related.

The grant of land in the Delaware region for the Pilgrims was obtained from the Virginia Company by John Pierce of Plymouth, England. As soon as Pierce learned the settlement at Plymouth was north of 40°, outside the Virginia Company area, he procured of the Council of New England, located in England, for himself and associates, land where the Pilgrims had located, at an annual land rent of 2s per hundred acres. This created him a landed proprietor. [112]

The grant to Pierce was the first one made by the Council of New England. It established no boundaries, but allowed a hundred acres for each person who should remain in the settlement three years. Pierce equipped and sent two expeditions to take possession of the Plymouth grant, but neither reached America, and he sold his claims for £500. [62] Governor Bradford afterwards wrote: "Pierce mente to keep it to himselfe and alow us what he pleased to hold of him as tenants."

The Mayflower colonists, seven years after they arrived, bought of the London merchants for £1,800 the seven hundred shares of stock for which the merchants had subscribed to send the Pilgrims to America. They were enabled to do this by granting a monopoly to Governor Bradford and seven others—the monopoly of trading with the Indians.

The colony was thus released from communism, and land was then allotted to the individual settlers, though titles were never ratified by the crown. Each person was allotted one acre, and a few years later an additional twenty acres. Meadow lands were declared as commons, for the free use of all.

Governor Bradford said the experience with communism in Plymouth taught that self-interest checked "those most able and fitte for labour without advantage otherwise."

The Mayflower colony was founded by the common people, and was ignored by the crown and the Church until seventy-one years later, when it was suppressed by the crown and absorbed by the Massachusetts Bay Company.

The monopoly conferred upon the Council of New England was immense. Without the leave of the council, not a ship might sail into a harbor between Newfoundland and the latitude of Philadelphia. To protect its monopoly, like all subsequent colonial lords proprietors, the council did not permit settlers to trade with the Indians. Not a skin might be purchased of the Indians, not a fish might be caught on the coast, except upon license granted and payment of 5 per cent toll on all fish caught, not an immigrant might tread the soil. And the right was held to capture any vessel poaching thereon without a license from the council.

To avoid conflict with Spain, France or Holland, a proviso in the grant excepted, please note, all territory "actually possessed or inhabited by any other prince or state." The Dutch were then there.

Not only did the Council of New England hold all the land, but it had a monopoly of the ocean bordering thereon, just as to-day holders of title of beach-front land along the seashore of northern New Jersey exercise a monopoly right; erecting wire fences, and charging a fee for the privilege of bathing, or of even wetting one's feet, in the Atlantic Ocean.

A contention arose between Ferdinando Gorges and the London (Virginia) Company as to the monopoly rights of fishing along the coast; some contending that the sea was as free as air.

[112]

Conflicting grants of land in Massachusetts, New Hampshire and Maine, were sometimes unscrupulously made by the Council of New England. Boundaries were ill-defined, which resulted in quarrels and fights. [47]

The Indian population in Massachusetts was estimated by Gookin to have been thirty thousand, prior to the plague, which killed a very large proportion of them shortly before the arrival of the Mayflower colony.

Williamson, in a *History of Maine,* said the European population of Maine in 1620 was twelve hundred distributed as follows: Piscataqua 200, Saco 175, Casco and Brunswick 75, Kennebec 100, Sagadahoc, Sheescot, Pemaquid, St. George and islands 500, and York 150.

The council made a formal complaint against the Dutch at New Netherland, whereupon the English government for the first time distinctly asserted the unlawfulness of the Dutch occupation. [16]

The region between Cape Cod and the Chesapeake was unexplored by the English, and almost unknown to them, until the Englishman, Dermer, sailed into New York Bay through Long Island Sound in 1619. [16]

At the request of King James I, the Council of New England in 1621 made a grant of land to Sir William Alexander, Secretary of State for Scotland, secretary to James, and later to become Lord Stirling. Under this grant, Alexander claimed he was entitled to land in Maine, between the St. Croix and Kennebec Rivers.

Ferdinando Gorges and John Mason, both of London, president and secretary respectively of the Council of New England, on August 10, 1622, granted to themselves jointly, their heirs and assigns for ever, all the land between the Merrimac and Sagadahoc (Kennebec) Rivers, to the farthest heads of said rivers and beyond—to a point not clearly discernible. There were many settlers in Maine when this grant was made. [169]

Joint ownership was apparently not satisfactory, and this grant was replaced by separate grants to each [145] of land within certain defined areas. On November 7, 1629, they, as officials of the council, granted to John Mason, his heirs and assigns, all the land between the Merrimac and Piscataqua Rivers, to the heads thereof, including all minerals, fishings and jurisdictions, together with all islands within fifteen miles of the coast; he to pay to each, the council and King Charles I, one-fifth of all gold and silver discovered.

This grant was modified about five years later, to include additional land . . . together with all land rents for ever, reserving for his majesty, King Charles I, one-fifth of all gold and silver obtained.

The King in 1639 confirmed to Sir Ferdinando Gorges, knight, his heirs and assigns, a grant of all that part of New England between the Salmon Falls and Kennebec River, from the ocean to the heads of each; and also the north half of the Isles of Shoals, and all the islands within fifteen miles of the main land, and the islands of Capawock (Cape Poge) and Newticum (one of the Elizabeth Islands).

"And we ordain that the land aforesaid shall be called the Province of Maine, together with the fishing and whales, also all royalties of hunting and all mines of gold and silver and other metal, and ambergris, which shall be found, and all patronage and advowsons of all churches erected and to be consecrated according to the ecclesiastical laws of England . . . To be held of us our heirs and successors . . . yielding and paying to us our heirs and successors, one-quarter of wheat and one-fifth part of the gold and silver found, and one-fifth part of the yearly profit of pearl fishing.

"And we grant all treasure trove, chattels of felons and felons themselves, waifs, estrays, pirates goods, deodands, fines and amerciaments of all the inhabitants.

"Our will is that the religion now performed in the Church of England and Ecclesiastical government shall be forever hereafter professed throughout the province. We grant power to establish a government, erect forts, cities, boroughs and markets. Any want of certain bounds or situation of the province, latitude or misnaming of places or lands shall not invalidate this grant."

It is interesting to know something of these two men, and of the influences which caused them to be granted an empire within New England. Sir Ferdinando Gorges, soldier of Elizabeth, friend of Raleigh, was a follower and favorite of Essex, and fell with him, but was later restored to favor and appointed governor of Plymouth, England. His interest in land in America was awakened when Weymouth presented him with three kidnapped Indians. He never was in America.

John Mason was a London merchant who was in the navy during the war; he was made governor of Newfoundland and came to America. He returned to England and was elected a member of the Council of New England.

It was said that Mason had no religious scruples to interfere in the manner of his acquiring land. [7] Neither Mason nor Gorges would recognize any right of the Indians to land. [5]

Robert Gorges, son of Ferdinando, and a shareholder in the Council of New England, was sent to America in 1622 to prevent fishing, except by those who paid a license as provided by the grant of the fishing monopoly. He "found the fishermen stubborn fellows and too strong for him," and he soon returned to England. [169]

He had a tract of land ten miles along the coast, and thirty miles inland, on the northeast side of Massachusetts Bay, granted to him by the council, partly in consideration of his father's services to the company.

Thomas Weston, who had arranged the financing of the Pilgrims' migration, obtained a grant of land near the site of the future town of Weymouth. He sent sixty men to the mouth of the Quincy River. There they built a trading post which later failed. [62]

In 1623, in payment for Monhegan Island, the first bill of exchange in America was drawn by Abram Shurt for £50, upon a firm in Bristol, England, in favor of Ambrose Jennens of London. [72]

People from Plymouth and Dorchester contended for land on Cape Ann, and the Mayflower settlers located outposts on Buzzards Bay and on a grant made to them along the Kennebec River.

A grant of six thousand acres and an island near the mouth of the Piscataqua River was made by the council, in 1622, to David Thompson, a Scotsman. Associated with him in the speculation were three merchants of Plymouth, England. Thompson came to New England some months later and made a settlement at Little Harbor (Portsmouth) probably the first settlement in New Hampshire. The following spring, Gorges and Mason sent over some fish mongers and others to settle at Little Harbor, some of whom, including Edward Hilton, settled at Dover Neck. A few years later, Gorges and Mason, officials of the council, granted to themselves surrounding land, a part of which they later sold to some merchants of Bristol, England. In 1632 they sold the remainder, presumably, to Lord Say and Sele, and to Lord Brook and his associates. [169]

So many grants were made about the mouth of the Piscataqua River that it is difficult to define their boundaries. Grants were made at the mouth of the Saco River, on which Saco and Biddeford are situated. Others were the Muscongus grant, thirty miles square along the seacoast between the Penobscot and Muscongus Rivers, and the Laconia grant, stretching along the coast between the Kennebec and Cape Porpoise and forty miles inland. [112]

Captain Christopher Levett, of Somersetshire, England, a member of the council, obtained for himself a grant of six thousand acres of land, to be located at his pleasure. He sailed from England and in 1623 arrived at the present site of Portland, where he was welcomed by the native chief and urged to settle there, which he did. [80]

This area was, however, within the territory which Gorges and Mason, as officials of the council, had granted to themselves only nine months previously.

The council in 1623 divided, as the first dividend to its remaining twenty members, the land between Cape Cod and the Bay of Fundy; at a drawing by lot at Greenwich, in England, on Sunday, at which the king was present. [169]

In the drawing, the Earl of Arundel drew the eastern-most part of Maine; Sir Robert Mansell drew the Mount Desert region; the Earl of Holdernesse drew the Casco Bay (Portland) section; the Earl of Warwick obtained Cape Ann; the Earl of Buckingham got southern New Hampshire; Dr. Gooch received Cape Cod, and Gorges drew the prize of Boston harbor and its abutting land. [112]

Captain Wollaston arrived in 1625 with a group of indented servants, and located on the site of Quincy, but afterwards carried the servants to Virginia and sold them.

The earliest permanent settlement in Maine seems to have been at Pemaquid, in 1625, or the following year.

The Company of New France was organized in 1627 as a land-holding and trading company, composed of one hundred associates, of whom Richelieu was the head. The whole of New France, from the Arctic circle to Florida, and from Newfoundland to the source of the St. Lawrence and its tributary waters, was conferred on the Company for ever, with sovereign powers. The king of France gave two ships of war, armed and equipped. [114]

Thenceforth there were numerous French voyages to the St. Lawrence until the French had well-established settlements and forts, not only along the St. Lawrence but along the Great Lakes and the entire course of the Mississippi River and its tributaries. [47]

Supplying the Indians with firearms was forbidden in New Hampshire, as in most colonies, and an English trader from Massachusetts, who had done so, was arrested and sent to England. [7]

A grant of land, [145] and a charter to the Governor and Company of Massacusetts Bay in New England (Massachusetts Bay Company) were issued by the Council of New England, on March 19, 1628, to Sir Henry Roswell, Sir John Young, Thomas Southcott, John Humphreys, John Endicott and Simon Whetcomb, their heirs and assigns and associates for ever. The grant included all that part of New England lying along the Merrimac and Charles Rivers, from the Atlantic Ocean to the South Sea, and all islands in both seas. All jurisdictions and rights, all mines and minerals were ceded; yielding and paying to King Charles I, his heirs and successors, one-fifth of all gold and silver discovered.

It was provided, as in the original grant of 1620 to the council, that if any part of the land granted was "actually possessed or inhabited by any other Christian prince or state, the grant should be utterly void." This grant included all the land between Esopus, on the Hudson River, and the Mohawk River, then in possession of the Dutch, and it conflicted with the grant to Gorges and Mason in 1622 and with a grant of three hundred miles square to Robert Gorges, subsequently compromised.

Charles I on March 4, 1629, confirmed the grant by his father James I, November 3, 1620, to the Council of Plymouth for New England (Council of New England), and the grant by the council to the Massachusetts Bay Company, just cited. To the latter he added the names of Sir Richard Saltonstall, Theophilus Eaton and eighteen others. [145]

The Massachusetts Bay Company, composed mainly of Puritans, was not dependent on capital from London investors, as had been the Mayflower colony nine years previously. It included some men of landed estates in England, some wealthy merchants, as well as members of professional classes, scholars and yeomen in the eastern counties of England. [10]

The company on August 20, 1629, voted to remove the seat of government from Plymouth, England to Massachusetts. The management of the company was to be by a governor, deputy-governor and eighteen directors. John Winthrop, forty-one years of age, a lawyer and landed proprietor from Groton, in Suffolk, was elected governor. A committee was appointed to consider the distribution of land.[a]

A few weeks later the regulations were submitted and accepted. Provisions were made for land to be granted to adventurers (investors) and to others settling in the colony.

John Endicott was selected to lead a party of sixty, taking the charter with him. John White, Puritan rector of Trinity Church, Dorchester, was of the party. Upon arrival in September, 1629, they united with the existing colonists and founded Naumkeag (Salem). Endicott served as governor until the arrival of Winthrop the following June.

During 1629 six ships arrived with 300 men, 80 women, 26 children, 180 indented servants, 140 head of cattle, 40 goats and abundance of arms, ammunition and tools. The leader of this company was Francis Higginson.

At Salem, a committee adopted a plan for dividing or allotting land, so as to "avoid all contention twixt the adventurers." In

[a] Mass. Col. Rec.

some places it was allotted by vote in town meeting, or by committees. Consideration was given to needs, and the ability to use the land. To later arrivals the allotment to each was to be reduced to fifty or one hundred acres. [63]

If the town plan had been made, and known publicly, no one was to build elsewhere. It was ordered that town lots of half-an-acre could be had in Salem by any who wanted them. Fifty-acre tracts were also allotted to shareholders, and a similar acreage to each member of a family that had come at its own expense. [112]

Winthrop was selected to lead a migration consisting of "Puritan gents and yeomen families" with their indented servants and cattle. With him was Thomas Dudley, later governor of the colony. They sailed from Plymouth, England, in April, 1630, with four ships, including the "Mary and John" of four hundred tons. During the voyage of ten weeks, "there was preaching and expounding every day."

No fewer than seventeen ships arrived during 1630, with sixteen or seventeen hundred immigrants, mostly from the western England counties of Devonshire, Dorsetshire and Somersetshire. [142] This migration to America, in two years, was the largest of any in a like period until a century later, when William Penn settled Pennsylvania.

They first located at Salem, but soon thereafter Endicott sent fifty persons to begin a settlement at Charlestown. The following September they founded Boston, where William Blackstone, an English clergyman and recluse, had previously erected a cabin on the Shawmut Peninsula, since called Boston. Samuel Maverick, son of an English clergyman was located on Noddle's Island, East Boston, and Thomas Walford, a blacksmith, was located on land at Charlestown.

Gorges claimed all these as his agents, and as was usual everywhere, payment was demanded for the right to locate there the future New England metropolis. Many settlements were made thereabouts which—strange to say at that early day—are stated to have failed because of "ungovernable persons, the very scum of the land."

It would seem that up to the time of the transfer of the company to America, a division of the land was contemplated. But the rules for allotting land had been in force for some time when Winthrop came. After his arrival the company no longer acted as a land company or sought to profit by its landholdings. But as population increased, it was more difficult to obtain land because those who had early become possessed of it exacted ever-increasing prices from later arrivals.

The first grant of land, made to any one person, appearing in the records of the Bay, was one of six hundred acres made in 1631 to John Winthrop, the only entry for that year.

The settlers had dwellings of their own, a varied diet, few wants and rarely much education, but they had the great satisfaction which comes from hard, productive work, victory over nature, and, by reason of some land being obtainable, increasing opportunities for themselves and their children. [63]

The Mayflower colony held, by a grant from the Council of New England in 1628, the land along the Kennebec River, but the boundaries had never been clearly defined. A confirming grant, issued by the council in 1630 (but never confirmed by the king), read, in part:

"The council do give and grant to William Bradford and associates, heirs and assigns . . . the space of fifteen English miles on each side of the Kennebec River. Yielding and paying to our sovereign lord the king, his heirs and successors, for ever, one-fifth of all gold and silver discovered; and one-fifth part to the council."

Eleven years later Bradford and his associates surrendered a portion of this land to the freemen, and sold to Tyng and others for £500 one tract extending eight miles inland, which became known as the Kennebec purchase.

John Gorges, in 1629, tried to assert the validity of the claim of his late brother, Robert, by executing conveyances covering portions of it. One of these was made to John Oldham. Gorges further maintained that he retained possession of the country through the presence of his brother's tenants, Blackstone, Maverick, Walford and others, on the shore of the bay. [47]

To the chagrin of the land proprietors, the early immigrants in Maine, instead of taking up land for farming, found it more profitable to apply their labor to the fur and fishery trades, but even these occupations involve use of land.

At first, all islands were reserved for the public benefit, to be let and disposed of by the governor, and accordingly many leases of islands were made to individuals. But in time, at the urge of land grabbers and speculators, the islands were granted like other lands; though some were granted only for life, at an annual rental.

John Stratton, claiming residence in New England for three years, was in 1631 granted land at Cape Porpoise, Maine. A grant of twenty-four thousand acres on both sides of the Acomenticus River, in Maine, was made to several persons, including Ferdinando Gorges, three years of age, a grandson of Sir Ferdinando. [169] Ten years later, part of the area, the present location of York, was chartered as the city of Georgeana, the first incorporated city in America. [72]

Roger Williams, a Welshman about thirty years of age, arrived in Massachusetts with his wife in 1631. Williams, "Lovely in carriage," "Godly and zealous, having precious gifts," had a degree from Cambridge. He had been a student in the law office of Sir Edward Coke, who had assisted in his education. [5] He was seeking a refuge from the autocratic rule of the later discredited and beheaded Archbishop Laud, ecclesiastic servant of Charles I.

Two years after his arrival Williams became pastor of a church at Salem. He wrote a pamphlet in which he took the broad ground, ethically sound, that the true and ultimate source of title in land in America was not the royal grant of some intruder like a so-called Christian king, but the Indians; [47] that "to rely upon a title to land derived from the crown was an usurpation, and a sin requiring public repentance."

He advocated equal protection of all forms of religion, separation of church and state, and other religious reforms. He again renewed his attack on the royal charter of Massachusetts, particularly "that part respecting the granting of land," and of which he complained in a letter to the king. [124]

Williams was charged with "teaching publicly against the

king's land grant, and that our great sin is in claiming right to the land thereby." [112] In consequence of this he was summoned before the court and was condemned by a council of clergymen. Having been sentenced to banishment, and on the verge of seizure for deportation to England, Williams, in the midst of bitter cold and snow in January, left Salem to seek a home in the Narragansett country. His activities there in founding a state are related in the chapter on Rhode Island.

The settlers at Massachusetts Bay denied any claim of Gorges to the land in Maine, and in 1632 he appealed to the privy council in England. [63]

In all the colonies a grant of land was often made as an inducement to erect a mill or perform other public service. After the first few years there were such grants as that to a Mr. Eaton, a teacher, "on condition that he continue his employment with us for life"; to E. Rawson, that "he go on in the business of powder"; to Stephen Day, "for being the first that set up printing"; to Goodwin Stowe, "for writing the laws"; to John Winthrop Jr., "on condition of his establishing salt works"; to Governor Endicott, "on condition that he set up copper works"; to others for establishing iron works and mining. Three to five hundred acres were given to different persons for ordinary civil services. [42]

The French claimed all the land in Maine, at least as far west as the Kennebec and Androscogin Rivers. The English would not admit the French claim to extend south of a line drawn through Houlton, Mount Katahdin and the north shore of Moosehead Lake. This English claim was based on the grant of King James I: "We give them all the land up to 45°N. which do not actually belong to any Christian prince." But at that time the French were in possession of the region south of 45° (the parallel which is ten miles north of Bangor).

Reports that the French were, in 1633, attempting colonization of the coast to the eastward, excited apprehension. It was decided that a settlement should be begun at Agawam (afterwards named Ipswich), thirteen miles north of Salem, "lest an enemy, finding it void, should take it from us."

The Council of New England had, by this time, granted the

entire territory between the Piscataqua and Penobscot Rivers. Settlements which had been made prior to the Gorges grant were respected.

Gorges took the northernmost Isles of Shoals and made them a part of Maine: Mason took the southernmost islands and annexed them to his province of New Hampshire. [79]

The council, about 1633, granted to former Governor Craddock a large area which extended "a mile from the riverside in all places." They also made two other grants of five hundred acres each, besides that of Taylor's Island.

New grants were exempt from payment of public charges (taxes) for a variable number of years up to six, or even more.[b] This made easy the holding of land out of use, forcing others who needed land on which to live to go farther afield from the protection of the settlements—which was the cause of many murders by Indians.

Furthermore, the exemption from taxes encouraged taking up more land than was needed for use, and holding it for an increased price from settlers as they came in needing land.

Naturally, many grantees neglected to improve their land, and presently it was ordered that if any large grant were not improved within three years the court might dispose of it.[c] But this was generally disregarded.

The population of Massachusetts was estimated by Winthrop, in 1634, at four thousand. About three thousand settlers arrived the following year. So much land had been granted and held unused by absentees that the pressure for land to use began to be felt. New arrivals were obliged to locate in the interior, or along the remote seacoast. This began on an extensive scale within fourteen years after the arrival of the first settlers, and was thereafter practically continuous.

Gorges sold to Mason a tract three miles in breadth along the northeast side of the Piscataquay River, from its mouth to its source. [7]

The southern part of the Isles of Shoals, held by Mason, became important in fisheries. The population increased to about

[b]Mass. Col. Rec.
[c]*Ibid.*

six hundred, which was greater than at any other settlement, and title to the island became of substantial value.

The first settlers in New Hampshire and Maine were from Devonshire, Cornwall, Bristol, and Dartmouth, and other southwestern parts of England. [80]

The Plymouth Company (Council of New England) had been accused in England of maintaining a monopoly in land which led to adverse conditions. Sir Edward Coke, preceptor of, and undoubtedly prompted by, Roger Williams, declared in the House of Commons that the company is "a grievance of the commonwealth, for private gain." To which Gorges, a foremost member and beneficiary of the company, hypocritically replied that it was undertaken for the advancement of religion. After repeated hearings in the House of Commons, in 1635, the charter was declared forfeited.

Unlike the land of the Virginia Company charter, which, upon forfeiture eleven years previously had been appropriated by the king, the land of the New England Council was not forfeited. The company, in preparation of dissolution, distributed among its remaining eight members, original grantees, the residue of its land which lay along the coast and extended, generally, sixty miles inland. The company then surrendered its worthless charter.

In this, with previous distributions, Gorges and Mason, and some influential nobles at court, including Salisbury, Sterling, Arundel, Lennox, Pembroke and Buckingham, were allowed to parcel out among themselves a large part of the land in New England. [112]

Gorges was governor-general of New England, but he sent a nephew, William Gorges, to govern, who remained less than two years. [5] Gorges received from Charles I confirmation of his grant, and undertook the organization and settlement of the province of New Somerset, or Maine. [24]

With the death of Mason in 1635, and the aging of Gorges, several settlements along the coast north of Massachusetts were without adequate government, and Massachusetts, upon invitation of some of them, took over the government.

Three of the grantees of the Council of New England were apparently without interest in the land which had been allotted them as dividends. The other five continued to meet, no longer as a corporation controlling the territory and government, but as absentee landholders desiring to obtain confirmation by the king of title to the lands granted them. Lack of geographical knowledge of the country prevented distribution of all their land, and such afterwards-discovered land again came into possession of the crown. The indefinite, or lack of, boundaries were, in the words of Sullivan, the historian, "but a course of confusion."

Upon these grants, about which there was so much dispute, rests the title of a great part of the land in New England. These grants are the fundamental documents, upon which were based the right to occupy and dispose of land. The grants were vague, and often in conflict. Few of the land titles in New England were legally correct. [63]

The territory under jurisdiction of the Massachusetts Bay Company included not only the original grant to the company but, during the more important part of its history, the territory of Maine under its various names, and of Plymouth; and also, for a time, the southern part of New Hampshire.

The town of Malden was granted one thousand acres for the use of the ministry for ever, but this was exceptional.

Some English peers, including Lord Say and Sele, and Lord Brook, became interested in obtaining land in America. As an inducement to come to America they exacted that the court (the legislative body) should consist of two branches, an upper and lower house, in the former of which they should have seats. This was granted, but the colonists objected to and defeated the proposal of an hereditary nobility in the province. [5]

Water-power was not recognized as subject to absolute private property. Sawmills and grist-mills were regarded as quasi-public utilities. [63]

In 1637 a committee was chosen to supply land to those who might want and deserve it. Fitness to receive land rested upon the ownership of common stock in the Massachusetts Bay Company, ability to improve the land, and the area already held.[a]

The court declared that the Indians had a natural right to only that land which they could improve, and that other land was open

[a]*Op. cit.*

to those who could and would use it. John Winthrop said: "It would be very prejudicial to the commonwealth if men should be forced to go far off for land while others had much and could make no use of it more than to please their eye with."

Disregard of this broad principle has created most of the world's economic and social welfare problems.

"Like Roger Williams, or worse," as the perplexed Winthrop exclaimed, was Anne Hutchinson, "of ready wit and bold spirit." In 1637 Mrs. Hutchinson, and Wheelwright, who was pastor of the church at Braintree, were brought to trial for expounding perplexing religious views, and were condemned to banishment. With her husband, they went to New Hampshire and founded Exeter. Winthrop wrote: "Mr. Wheelwright being banished from us, gathered a company and sat down by the Falls of Piscataqua, called their town Exeter, and bought land of an Indian, and then wrote us that they intended to lot out all these lands in farms, except we could show a better title."

Because of the rigorous climate they abandoned Exeter. Joining with others of their sect led by William Coddington, they settled for a while at Narragansett, as related in the chapter on Rhode Island.

Governor Dudley in 1637 received a grant of one thousand acres in Massachusetts, and the following year there were fourteen grants averaging 372 acres including one of fifteen hundred acres. [42]

Beginning in 1638, and continuing for many years, the peltry trade was farmed out for a fixed sum per annum, probably much as the Alaska seal catch was granted by the United States government after acquiring Alaska.

The number of Indians in Massachusetts at that time, in the opinion of Dr. J. G. Palfrey, the historian, did not exceed fifty thousand, of which one-half were in the Connecticut and Rhode Island regions, including eight or ten thousand Narragansetts, of whom one-fifth were fighting men.

A committee was appointed to report on all applicants for land, and in 1639 there were twenty-three grants, averaging 360 acres each. There were more than one hundred grants by the court to other individuals; the largest being 3,200 acres to the executors of Isaac Johnson, in consideration of his large "adventure" (investment) in the stock.

There were granted to Mr. Saltonstall, 3,200 acres; to Mr. Nowell, 2,000 acres; and to Mrs. Winthrop, 3,000 acres. John Winthrop received 3,000 acres which had been conquered from the Pequots. [42] By this time the immediate wants of the leading men for land had been satisfied, and all others were referred to the promoters of the various towns to which the court had granted land.

At Rowley, the inhabitants labored in common, there being no individual landholders since the land was owned by the community. After five years, about 1639, this plan was abandoned. [158]

In Salem there were large areas of common land such as there had been in England. In such commons, ten or more fields were fenced and cultivated by numerous individuals or families. One field in Salem contained 600 acres and another 490 acres. The larger field was continued in cultivation until after the Revolutionary War. There were similar commons in most other towns.

Boston voted in 1640 to admit a carpenter named Palmer as an inhabitant, "if he can get a house, or land to set a house upon." In Charlestown John Greenland had a similar experience. [158] It seems ridiculous that, within only twenty years after the first white settlers arrived, all the land at Boston should have been privately appropriated. Certainly it could not have been occupied.

Meadow, pasture and plow lands were often held in common. At first, cultivation of land held in common was on a much larger scale than it was at a later day; the diminishment was probably owing to private allotments and fencing. [42]

The fathers of New England in the early days evidently intended, by the distribution of land, that every industrious man should have the means of obtaining an adequate share of the comforts of life. [89x]

Aside from grants of large areas by the king to court favorites, there was no land granted free in New England except that granted by the court, or later, by the court to town promoters, who distributed small patches to only the very earliest settlers. All subsequent settlers had to buy land of the town promoters.

The usual procedure for starting new towns was: The court granted to a group of promoters the site for a new town, and the promoters subscribed a small sum for promotion to attract settlers to help create land value. After allotting a plot to each settler attracted, the promoters retained the remaining land, which became the promoters' profit.

In general, a tract six miles square was thought the best size for a settlement. Some were eight miles square, which the court thought large enough for sixty families, and which would have given them more than one square mile each. [42]

Egleston [42] clearly defined the status of these proprietors: " 'Commoners' were originally those to whom the court had made a grant of land in common for settlement. But the term 'proprietors' was also used with the same meaning as 'commoner' and became the legal term." Though probably not so intended, or even contemplated when this method of allotment was inaugurated, the proprietors in time assumed a vested privilege in the land, remaining unallotted, in that, "the right of a commoner, or proprietor, might be conveyed or inherited like other land. The commoner was not necessarily an inhabitant, nor entitled to vote in the town. Nor need a town voter be entitled to a voice in the control of the common lands, or any right to them whatever. The town promoters and the political community were distinct bodies. Separate records of these proprietors' meetings are very generally found in the older towns, where they form legal evidence of title."

There was no uniform rule, and land was variously distributed in different towns, and even in the same town. In a few towns, the least share was half as much as the greatest, or the poorest man received half as much land as the wealthiest. In others the smallest share was only one-third, or even one-tenth, as much as the largest. In some the inequality was much greater. [89x]

Some of the leading men of Ipswich were, in 1635, allowed to send settlers to form a settlement in Newbury. In 1641 the court granted land at Charlestown to seven promoters. The settlers there, comprising about sixty families, received tracts of varying sizes. "The poorest men and families received twenty-five acres upland and six or seven acres of meadow."

In Lancaster, in 1654, the promoters decided to limit allotments to thirty-five families, who were to become townsmen. Lots were laid out equally for the most part, among rich and poor, "partly to keep the town from scattering too far, and partly out of charity and respect to men of meaner estate. Yet that equallitie, which is the Rule of God, may be observed, we agree that in a second division and all other divisions of land, he that now hath more than his estate deserves, shall have so much less, and he that hath less shall have more." [110]

The earlier settlers in New England were able to get small patches of free land; which was preferable to the obligation imposed upon the settlers in all other colonies to pay to some lord proprietor, living beyond the sea, a perpetual land rent on all land obtained. Nevertheless, qualifications for obtaining free land in New England were shamefully restricted by the proprietors, or promoters, in most towns.

The area of land already held and taxes paid elsewhere, the amount invested in the new promotion, and the "quality" and qualifications of the applicant, were paramount factors in the distribution of free land in the new towns.

Such were the conditions at Springfield, Northampton and Ipswich, and the rule almost everywhere. At Barnstable one-third of the land was granted on that basis. The remaining land seems to have been allotted one-third to all equally, and one-third to those over twenty-five years of age. At Hadley, forty-eight promoters subscribed £50 to £200 each, and after a small allotment of land was made to each settler, including minors over sixteen years of age, the remaining land was divided among the promoters in proportion to their subscriptions.

Those under sixteen years of age, when they reached manhood, were obliged by those of the preceding generation who had become possessed of the land to pay for the right to produce and earn their living on unused land. And that uncivilized practice is universal today.

Roxbury promoters, sending settlers to Woodstock about 1661, agreed that if thirty men should go there and settle, they should have one-half of the land in one tract eight miles square, at their selection, together with £500 to be laid out in public buildings to create a town.° The promoters were to retain the other half of the land.

In Dedham, married men received twelve acres each, unmarried men eight acres, although a certain few were allotted more. Keeping up the town promotion business, the proprietors of Dedham in 1661 sent men to found the town of Wrentham, and later exacted of the settlers who went there £160 in payment for the land on which they had settled.ᶠ

At Haverhill in 1663, it was voted that "he that is worth £200 is to have twenty acres, and every one under that sum to have acres proportionably." Fishers' Island was, in 1668, granted to John Winthrop, Jr., at an annual rental of one lamb, payable to the Duke of York, and the island was held by his descendants for nearly two centuries. [16]

The division of upland, meadow, marsh and rocky land in any equitable manner was most difficult, and resulted in widely separated strips of land of varying quality being in one ownership. Consolidation of these tracts occurred gradually through purchase or marriages.

Distribution of the common land might have been made to better advantage, to both the community and the individuals, by allotting tracts of land at an annual ground rent to the community. In that way he who wanted a choice tract would pay more rent than he who had a poorer tract; besides, had the rental charge been subject to increase as population made the land more valuable, speculation would have been discouraged and a revenue brought into the community treasury in lieu of imposing taxes to provide funds for schools, highways, and bridges. Duxbury did do this to some extent.

As the inhabitants of a town increased, the proportion of landless increased, and they actively resented this concentration of the common and unallotted land in the possession of a relatively few promoter-proprietors, who quite obviously formed a limited and privileged class. [172] Control of land acquired a monetary value in these growing towns and became an object of desire both to those already owning land and to those who had sought it. The

°Ellis, Roxbury
ᶠAnnals of Dedham

proprietors soon discontinued allotting to new arrivals the privilege of participation of ownership in the commons. After a time free land was denied, and a price put upon all land, payable to the promoter-proprietors or their heirs and assigns. [112]

In Watertown, as early as 1635, it was ruled: "No foreigner coming into the town, or any family [the younger generation] arising among ourselves, shall have any benefit, either of commonage, or of land undivided, but what they shall purchase."⁵ In the name of greed, surrounded by unused land, they denied free land to their own children who wished to start their own homes. Thus arose on a continent where for centuries there has been unlimited unused land, the existence of an ever-increasing horde of landless people, the major cause of poverty and crime.

At the end of twenty years, the nineteen original promoters in Dedham, or their heirs, voted to discontinue allotting free land and exacted payment by new settlers. There then arose as in most towns, a dispute between the promoter-proprietors and heirs and the settlers, as to the division of the unallotted land and the monetary spoils. The court (council) had granted land from the public area to the town promoters without cost, and the question was raised: to whom belongs the land remaining ungranted by the promoters and their heirs?

The heirs and assigns of the original grantees claimed they were the sole proprietors. They were thus, in a small way, like unto the Calverts and the Penns. The opposition contended and maintained for two generations, and with reason, that the land had been granted by the court to all the original and future inhabitants collectively. [112]

Of the people of the old towns soon after their settlement, a much greater proportion were free-holders and independent farmers, than at any subsequent period. [89x] Land tended to concentrate in fewer hands, owing to the desire to reap the unearned increment in land value arising from increase in population—with what disadvantage to the rising generation we have already seen.

As a mutual protection against the claims of the Dutch, the threats of the French, and the danger from Indians, the four

⁵Bond, Watertown

New England colonies—Connecticut, New Haven, New Plymouth and Massachusetts (which included New Hampshire and Maine)—in 1643 formed a confederacy of the United Provinces of New England.

One article of the confederation read that: "The spoils of war on the Indians, whether it be in lands, goods or persons," were to be proportionally divided among the confederates. [16]

The expenses of war charged to each colony were based upon the proportion of its number of males between the ages of sixteen and sixty. The confederation continued for half a century until the British government terminated it. [71]

The confederated colonies contained thirty-nine towns, with a population estimated at 24,000. [47] The population of all Massachusetts was estimated at 26,000.

The Mayflower colony at Plymouth had, about 1630, established a trading post at the mouth of the Penobscot River, and another at Machias, near the extreme eastern edge of Maine. (Much of the information here given pertaining to the conflict over these settlements is from Osgood.) [112] There was a French trading post at the mouth of the St. John River, directed by Charles de la Tour, sanctioned by the Company of New France, and another, in competition, across the Bay of Fundy, at Port Royal, in command of D'Aunay Charnisay, under authority of the King of France.

The French had continued to assert that the bounds of New France extended west and southwest to the Kennebec River. Charnisay captured the Plymouth settlement at Machias, and three years later preempted the one on the Penobscot. He also captured and imprisoned LaTour.

LaTour, upon his release, went to Boston for help and proposed that he would assist the Plymouth people in recapturing their post. Some Boston merchants organized a filibustering expedition of four vessels and seventy men, and with the tacit consent of the Massachusetts officials sailed for Port Royal. In the encounter, three Frenchmen were killed and movable property captured. The expedition returned to Boston, and the Plymouth partners sold their claim against Charnisay to some venturesome mariners.

The following year LaTour organized an expedition at Piscataqua, and with about twenty men proceeded to attack Charnisay, at Penobscot, occasioning further loss of life. Subsequently, a Massachusetts vessel and the LaTour fort were captured by the Charnisay forces, and all the garrison executed, except LaTour, who escaped. In 1645 a treaty of peace was agreed upon.

Sir Ferdinando Gorges died in 1645, but the government in his interest continued at Saco and York. [112]

Gorges had held all the land between the Piscataqua and Kennebec Rivers in Maine, but did very little as lord proprietor. Upon the death of royal grantees of land there generally resulted much confusion about land titles and boundaries, which led to prolonged and expensive contentions. [63]

In Maine, the transplanted feudalism of Gorges, and the large grants from the Council of New England, were looked upon with disfavor by the people of the colonies, and were with difficulty maintained among them. These large grants were doubtless an injury to the provinces, hindered their development and, to a great extent, left them wastes. [42]

During his later career, Gorges was an advocate of the feudal type of colony, and could he have had his way, would have firmly established it in New England. [112]

Stuyvesant, the governor of New Netherland, in a letter to the New Haven authorities in 1647, claimed as part of New Netherland all the land between Cape Henlopen, Delaware, and Point Judith (which the Dutch called Cape Cod—the present Cape Cod, the Dutch called Cape Malabarre). Eaton, at New Haven, declared the Dutch director to be a disturber of the peace, "making unjust claims to our lands and rivers." [16]

Upon dissolution of the Laconia Company, shareholders brought suit between themselves and litigation continued several years. [169]

The British Navigation Act of 1651 injured Dutch commerce and the Virginia tobacco growers, but inadvertently helped build up a merchant marine in New England to carry contraband goods to Europe in swift vessels.

After appropriating the land of the Indians, the Massachusetts court enacted that land might be allotted to Indians who adopted civilized customs.

The Sagamore of Nashaway having died, the selectmen of Lancaster in 1654 appointed a committee of two to go to the tribe to persuade them to appoint as the new sagamore one whom the selectmen favored.

There were repeated conflicts in Maine between the English and French and their respective Indian allies. The English attacked the French at the Penobscot and St. John Rivers in 1654. Nova Scotia was taken and in a few weeks the French were subjugated.

Thomas Mayhew, a Watertown merchant, in 1641 bought Martha's Vineyard, Nantucket and the Elizabeth Islands [112] of the Earl of Stirling, to whom they had been granted without cost.

Governor Winthrop, in behalf of the Massachusetts Bay Company, claiming that the northern limits of its royal grant extended to Casco Bay (Portland), took possession of New Hampshire and Maine in 1643 and retained them for nearly forty years, until 1679.

Cromwell, as Lord Protector, apparently considered himself the owner of the land in America in as complete a way as the king previously had been. In 1656 he granted Nova Scotia to Sir Charles St. Stephen, Thomas Temple and William Crowne, for a payment "yearly, and every year, to us and our successors, twenty beaver skins and twenty mouse skins." [6] Thirty-five years previously, at the request of King James I, Nova Scotia had been granted by the Council of New England to Sir William Alexander (Earl of Stirling).

Massachusetts claimed all land from the Atlantic to the South Sea (Pacific Ocean), north of 42° N. latitude, its present southern boundary. It granted land opposite Fort Aurania on the Hudson River, near Albany, to a number of English traders. Stuyvesant vehemently objected; the outcome is noted in the chapter on New York.

A proclamation by King Charles in June, 1664, ordered people of Maine to recognize the rights to the land of Gorges' heirs, and Gorges' grandson was appointed collector of land rents. But his effort at collection proved futile. With land obtainable at low rental without payment of purchase-price, any one physically able could go and dig and hew a living; beggary was unknown, theft was rare.

While the French had, by 1671, established missions or forts along the Ohio and Mississippi Rivers, and about the Great Lakes as far west as Sault Ste. Marie (more than a thousand miles from the Atlantic seaboard), the English colonies, which were more than twenty times as populous, had no foothold beyond the sparse settlements contiguous to the Atlantic seaboard.

Bancroft [5] cites the presumed population of New England, in 1675, as 55,000 whites, and barely 30,000 Indians.

Brodhead [16] said: "Philip, the youngest son of Massasoit, and now sachem of the Wampanoags along the eastern and northern shores of Narragansett Bay, incensed at the arrogance of the English, revolted against the whites. The Puritan colonists had generally disregarded the feelings of the Indians. As the Puritans had already exterminated the Pequots, or sold them as slaves, so they now doomed to extinction or bondage the other natives of New England whose lands they coveted.

"Philip saw that the Europeans had crowded his people into narrow necks of land where they were jealously watched—especially about Bristol and Tiveton, in Rhode Island.

"Knowing of the kindness of his father, Massasoit, to the English, the pride of the aborigine was wounded. Their hunting grounds and parks became cultivated or used for grazing by the English.

"Cautiously visiting the neighboring tribes, he urged them to drive out the destroyers of their race. The Narragansetts were won to the task and preparations made secretly for a rising of the natives in the spring.

"They gathered seven hundred warriors within one stronghold near Bristol. In July, 1675, occurred the Indian massacre at Swazey, near Hope. In one engagement, nearly one thousand Indians and two hundred English were killed and wounded."

Philip's war extended from Connecticut and Rhode Island into Massachusetts and New Hampshire, at Exeter, Berwick, Dover and Lancaster. Dartmouth was beset. One hundred and fifty

Indians surrendered upon promise of amnesty. The Plymouth authorities sold them into slavery. [63]

One Laughton, from Piscataqua, or that vicinity, enticed aboard his vessel some Indians from about Cape Sable and sold them as slaves. [72]

In midsummer the next year, Philip and forty-three of his warriors were captured and executed, and the war terminated. One-half of the Indian population of twelve thousand, and nearly one thousand white men, were killed; twelve towns were destroyed, and more than forty others, including Providence and Warwick, were the scenes of fire and slaughter. [49]

Most of the Indian warriors were slain, or surrendered. Some captives were sold as slaves, but in the absence of additional buyers, some of the natives were set ashore on strange coasts and abandoned. A few were carried to the foulest of medieval slave marts, Morocco, where their fate was doubtless wretched enough. [49]

Scarcely had the red warriors ceased fighting when they suddenly realized that the English meant to exterminate them and take their lands, and they were finally compelled to submit to the power of the white man. [7]

Henceforth, the Indian figures no more in the history of New England except as an ally of the French. From central and southern New England he disappeared for ever as a power to be reckoned with. [49]

In Maine, the natives were doing great mischief. Fort Charles, with seven guns, was built at Pemaquid in 1677. No one could trade with the Indians there except through a permit from Governor Andros, who had arranged a peace.

Edward Randolph, a cousin of Robert Mason, was appointed by the Lords of Trade in London to investigate conditions in the American colonies, and arrived in Boston in 1677. The following year the king appointed him collector and surveyor-general there. He urged the Board of Trade to order collection of land rents, as revenue, and to compel the colonies to submit to royal authority.

Under Cromwell's rule, Massachusetts had extended its sway over Maine. Colonel Nichols and his commissioners, on instructions of Charles II in 1665, revoked it. Three years later, after the commissioners had gone home, Massachusetts took possession again. [49]

The High Court of Chancery in England rendered a decision that the acts of Massachusetts in taking military possession of Maine were illegal; that the province had descended as a fief to the heirs of Gorges. Thereupon, young Ferdinando Gorges, grandson of the first grantee and proprietor, offered to sell Maine to King Charles, who wanted to bestow it upon the Duke of Monmouth, his favorite son by Lucy Walters. [49] However, the French occupied the land west of the Penobscot, and claimed as far west as the Kennebec. [5]

Governor Leverett of Massachusetts bought for his province the Gorges claim of Maine, paying £1,250 cash. The king resented this vehemently, and demanded cancellation and refunding of the money. Massachusetts refused, with the result that the Massachusetts charter was annulled by a decree in chancery in 1683, and a viceroy was appointed by the king. [49]

In Newbury in 1679, as related by Osgood: [112] "It was voted that if ever the town commons of seven thousand acres be divided, every freeholder should have a like share. But several persons dissented. Seven years later it was voted that every freeholder should receive five acres in the commons. Fifteen dissented, but it was carried by a majority of five. Before the year ended this majority vanished and it was resolved that, in the division of the seven thousand acres only one-half should be divided equally among all, while the other half should be shared by those who, during the past two years, had paid taxes; and in proportion to the amount of taxes each had paid. The gradual breaking down of the majority vote for equal division causes wonder as to what kind of persuasion was used to effect it."

In Massachusetts and Connecticut towns, the general rule was that no person would be received as an inhabitant unless he was "well recommended as to character and of a non-contentious disposition," so great was their desire to avoid schisms. "To such, a house lot would be granted, but unless built upon within one year it would be forfeited."

Reviving a projected settlement begun fifteen years previously,

Worcester was planned in 1684. It was divided into 480 lots, of which 400 were to be taxable, and 80 free of taxes. The tax-free lots, except a few for certain public services, were donated to the agent for procuring the grant. Two hundred lots were apportioned to the promoters, and two hundred were to be sold to settlers and speculators.

The Duke of York's land rents at Pemaquid, Maine, were in 1684 ordered to be collected. Land being plentiful, Massachusetts gave land in sizeable tracts to certain men, merely because an ancestor had rendered some service to the colony.

After an existence of fifty-six years, the charter of the Massachusetts Bay Company was revoked in 1684, and Massachusetts became a royal province, with a governor appointed by the king, and all its unallotted land reverting to the king. Seven years later, a new charter was granted.

Governor Dongan in New York, representing the Duke of York, made extravagant grants to his favorites of land in the eastern part of Maine, the land rent payable to the Duke.

Charles II died in 1685, and his brother James, the Duke of York, came to the throne as James II. The following year James commissioned Sir Edmund Andros to succeed Dongan, and to become governor-in-chief over his "Territory and Dominions of New England in America." These included Massachusetts Bay, New Plymouth, New Hampshire and Maine, to the river of Canada (St. Lawrence), and from the Atlantic to the western ocean, with all islands. Andros was to govern with a council of forty-two of the principal landholding inhabitants. Two years later Andros' commission was enlarged to include Rhode Island, Connecticut, New York, and East and West Jersey. "We grant you full power with the advice and consent of our council to agree with all inhabitants concerning such lands as are or shall be in our power to dispose of, and under such annual land rents to be reserved to us."

Andros arrived in Boston from England in December, 1686. His salary of £1,200 was to be paid from the royal treasury until sufficient revenue was collected in the colonies. [12]

Landholders in Massachusetts asked that each county should have in the council a counselor who must be a large landholder, and that no law be passed without the consent of a majority of these counselors. This proposition, if accepted by the king, would have placed the colonial government in control of a local aristocracy of landholders. [16]

Andros announced that upon land granted but not yet royally confirmed, an annual land rent of not less than 2s 6d for each hundred acres was to be paid to the king. Settlers felt keenly the injustice of being obliged, after years of hard toil in establishing a farm, to pay part of the proceeds of their labor to a profligate king across the ocean. [63]

At a crowded meeting at Salem in 1688, the Rev. Francis Higginson, who fifty-nine years previously had led a group of Puritans to Massachusetts on the promise of free land, said: "The title to the land was derived by the people from God. As the crown had no claim to the lands before the English came, it could not subsequently confer any right to them." To which Andros exclaimed: "Either you are subjects, or you are rebels."

In a three volume compilation of his researches, Doyle [40x] wrote: "Andros was authorized to grant land on quit-rents. Some colonists foresaw that this was intended as a comprehensive claim to the land in New England. The theory accepted by the crown was that no claim to land based either on a grant from the Massachusetts Company or on purchase from the Indians was valid, and that no New England settler had ever acquired a legal title to his lands.

"It might be that the Massachusetts charter had been overthrown in due course of law, and that with it perished all those political rights to which it had given birth. It might be that no settler in New England had acquired a title to his land which could be recognized as valid by English law. It was contended that a corporation could not create a corporation, and that therefore no town in New England had any legal status" [by which it could grant land]. And yet, titles to a great part of the land in New England rest upon town grants.

At the first rumor of the abdication of King James, and that the Prince of Orange had landed in England, a flame burst forth in the American colonies. In Boston the people assembled in arms in April, 1689, and those "public robbers," as Andros and those under him were designated, were made prisoners as Andros, disguised as a woman, was attempting to escape. His land policy was one of the chief causes of his overthrow.

Major Waldron, at the behest of the Boston troops, committed an act of treachery towards the Indians when he invited them in 1676 to a peace conference, and without warning, slaughtered or hanged large numbers of them, and sold two hundred into slavery. The Indians brooded over this for thirteen years, and then, prompted by a raid made by orders of Andros on the home of a French baron, de Castine, who had married a squaw and was beloved by the Indians, ferociously attacked the English, tortured many, and sold the English captives as slaves in Canada. [7]

With the cession of Nova Scotia to France by the treaty of Ryswick in 1697, the French became firmly established in Maine as far west as the Kennebec River. After the Peace of Utrecht in 1713, which ended the War of the Spanish Succession to the detriment of France, the Indians sought the friendship of the English, and there was a rapid increase in English settlements in Maine. However, the French in Nova Scotia continued as a menace to English occupation east of the Merrimac River.

So little value was placed on land of the Boston peninsula by the first settlers that they did not trouble to make an Indian purchase until Governors Dudley and Andros were disturbing the colony. Whereupon, Charles Josias, grandson of the old chief, was sought and in 1708 he signed a deed for the land to the colonists, which was accounted a valid Indian title. [158]

Until late in the 1600's and early 1700's there were continual disputes and litigation about titles to land in New Hampshire and Maine. These disputes were the cause of intermittent wars between the English settlers and the French and Indians during nearly forty years.

In a tract printed in Boston in 1716, was recorded: "Though this country be large, and much good land in it, which for want of people cannot be improved in many generations; yet a shame it is to say, this colony cannot provide themselves necessary food.

"In the first settling of this country, land was easy to be attained, and at a low price, which was an inducement to multitudes to come over as indented servants; but now the land being so generally taken up, few come over that can live elsewhere . . . If the country should put a tax upon such tracts of land as lie convenient to settle upon, in order to make the holders willing to throw them up to the country, such yearly tax would be more justifiable, and more equal, than to tax a poor man ten shillings, that has much ado to live; those estates being valued worth hundreds of pounds by the owners thereof, who keep only in hopes that as other places hereafter shall be settled, they may advance upon the price. And in the meantime their poor neighbors must pay perhaps a greater tax than would be put upon him in the most arbitrary kingdom in Europe."

A letter from Major Sewall, a prominent man in Salem in 1717, to J. Dummer in London, shows how English capital was induced to engage in American land speculation more than two centuries ago:

"Sir: . . . We have a deed of conveyance from the native Indian proprietor thereof, and pray you to inform us whether you think a confirmation thereof might be obtained from the crown, whereby persons that are able would freely disburse for the settlement . . . Pray sir, give me a line on this head. We would willingly part with some few guineas rather than fail to help forward therewith, and take you in as a proprietor, equal with us, if your phancy leads you thereto. Our lieutenant-governor, your brother, is chosen one of the council."

Sixteen Scotch-Irish families settled at Londonderry, New Hampshire, in 1719, and these attracted 120 Presbyterian families from the north of Ireland the following year.

Barstow [7] said: "The Indians complained that they were cheated in trade. Avarice often led the English to obtain Indian deeds to land by deceit, and when they got the Indians drunk their land could be taken without an equivalent.

"Having no records, the new generations of Indians knew nothing of any land transactions in years past, and declared the former sachems had no right to sell the birthright of the younger generation.

"The English declared war against them as rebels, and in making peace styled them as British subjects. The French, on the contrary, did not declare the Indians to be subjects of France. They left to all the tribes their native independence, and seldom sought to obtain their lands. The French sent them missionaries, which the English never did.

"When the English mistreated one of their favorite French missionaries, the Indians sought revenge in a frightful war which lasted four years, at the end of which the Indians were defeated, and driven to Canada. The English appropriated the conquered lands, large tracts of which were granted to those who had fought in the war and to descendants of all the previous wars."

The English in New Hampshire and Massachusetts in 1725 offered £100 paper for each Indian scalp, and many were taken. [49]

At Penacook, New Hampshire, on the Merrimac River in 1725, each settler paid the province £5 for his right to land. If he failed to clear and fence one acre within a year he was to forfeit £5 "to the community of settlers." Land was also granted for establishing needed industries. [158]

With the increase in population in Massachusetts, the consequent inevitable increase in price of land made its appearance in 1711. Three acres of woodland was quoted at £15 "silver or paper." At Hadley in 1722, meadow land was 2s 6d to 3s per acre, in silver. Six years later these lands were 7s to 8s per acre. There was a marked movement by individual speculators in Boston, Salem and other towns to buy wild lands in the new towns and in the commons of the old. [158]

Some fortunes began, in 1726, to be gained by increase in value of large bodies of land. [63] In Massachusetts, four acres and three roods of woodland sold in 1737 at £25, and six and one-half acres pasture near a village, at £32. These prices merely reflect the effect of increasing population in creating land value.

Projects for new settlements were continually being formed by town promoters, and an avaricious spirit of speculation in land prevailed everywhere in New Hampshire; but large areas of the best land remained unused, and the real prosperity of the country was thereby diminished. [7]

Prior to the purchase by Massachusetts of the Gorges claim to Maine, the Massachusetts colony was striving to extend its boundary into that region. To render Gorges unpopular, the Massachusetts government supported the theory that the Indian right to land must be superior to the Gorges', or to any grant conferred by the Council of New England. Consequently, purchases of land from Indians became frequent, and were regularly upheld by the Massachusetts courts, a policy advocated by Roger Williams a century previously, and for which he was banished from the province. Such purchases became so extensive that the government in 1731 forbade all purchases from Indians without license of the legislature, and declared all deeds taken without such license to be null and void.[h]

New Hampshire became a royal province in 1741, with Benning Wentworth as governor; previously the governor of Massachusetts had acted also as governor of New Hampshire. As governor of the combined provinces he had made grants of the site of Concord, over which there was a struggle for forty years before it was decided in favor of the Massachusetts group of grantees. [172]

John Mason at the time of his death was negotiating for royal confirmation of title to his New Hampshire grant, but the grant was never confirmed by the king. He had not made any improvements on any of the land he held, or held jointly, except on the Laconia grant.

Barstow said of Mason: "His darling scheme was the introduction of the feudal system into New Hampshire; by which his family were to be the lords, and the people tenants on the land, with land rents and feudal tenure." [7]

Mason had sent seventy settlers to settle on his New Hampshire grant, and upon his death he was indebted to them. They demanded payment and, upon default, certain lands were seized and divided among them. [62]

Mason bequeathed all his land to his grandchildren, John and Robert Tufton, who for years thereafter distressed the homesteaders.

Mason's widow sent Joseph Mason to New Hampshire in 1651, with power to dispose of land. Mason brought suit against one Leader, for trespass in erecting a sawmill, and he asked "jus-

[h]Sullivan, Land Titles

tice" from settlers who had settled at other places on the land. He made public protest against the action of Massachusetts in extending its government over the Mason grant, but that colony apparently gave it no attention. [112]

Upon the death of the widow a few years later, Robert Tufton, then the executor and sole heir, came over and instituted suits against occupants of the land. The court decided that a portion of the land proportionate to Mason's expenditures, with the privilege of the river, should be laid out to the heir. Tufton, a strong supporter of royalty, considering it useless to apply to Cromwell for relief, gave up the remainder as lost to him. But at the Restoration of King Charles II, Tufton, who had taken the surname of Mason, determined to make another attempt to recover the vast region by appealing to parliament for redress. The attorney-general, Sir William Jones, reported that Mason had a good and legal title to the province of New Hampshire. [7]

Robert Mason, in 1661, obtained a decree which upheld his title to all land in New Hampshire. Massachusetts opposed it but, in 1674, the crown's attorney reported in favor of Mason's land rights. [12]

Three years later the Lord Chief Justices of England decided that Massachusetts had no right of jurisdiction over New Hampshire, and that the title and jurisdiction were in the crown, subject, however, to the vested rights of John Mason in the land.

Titles to land in New Hampshire, which had been granted by the Massachusetts Bay Company, were set aside. This decision, for many years, rendered land titles uncertain in both New Hampshire and Vermont. [42]

New Hampshire, comprising the four towns of Exeter, Hampton, Dover and Portsmouth, after being under the jurisdiction of Massachusetts for thirty-eight years, was in 1679 made a royal province. This marked a definite triumph for Mason. [12]

The government which was established favored the claim of Mason to the land. This was repugnant to the people; they viewed it as the triumph of a vested interest. It was difficult for them to see how a piece of parchment, taking precedence of contract with the natives, and of rights defended at the price of blood, should give title to vast tracts along the Piscataqua and Merrimac

Rivers. But this government had kindled new hopes in the breast of Mason. [7]

Mason came over the next year and began to push his claims. He offered to waive all rent arrears if the settlers would promise to pay a land rent of 6d in the pound on the annual value of all land which the settlers had improved and cultivated. The settlers, citing fifty years' occupancy, objected. Judgments were invariably in favor of Mason, but useless, because of local opposition. [12]

Citing that while the land in New Hampshire had been granted to Mason, the government thereof had not been granted to any one, Charles II appointed John Cutt to govern as president of a council of ten. At the same time, he called upon the settlers to pay to Robert Mason an annual rent of 6d in the pound (2½ per cent) on the value of all buildings, gardens, orchards and other improvements which they themselves had created; failing which, such settlers would be referred to the privy council in England.

After two years of administration by Cutt, Mason became dissatisfied with the government, and to bribe King Charles to appoint Cranfield as royal governor, Mason surrendered to the king one-fifth of his prospective land rents. But after Cranfield was appointed, to hasten his claim to the land and the land rents, Mason bribed the council to make an annual payment to Cranfield of £150. Subsequently, to protect itself against Mason's machinations, the council voted to pay Cranfield £250 per annum.

The next year a settler, Edward Gove, leading a body of men, marched from town to town in New Hampshire calling for reformation of the government. He was arrested, convicted of high treason, and sent to England, where he was imprisoned in the Tower of London. [7]

The governor called upon the inhabitants to take out leases, with land rent to Mason. This was rejected, and Mason threatened to seize the land of the principal settlers, but the people were determined not to submit. [7] Lawsuits about land became numerous. Mason having mortgaged his land, was unable to find a buyer. [5]

Like many royal grants of land in America to speculators in England, the Mason land remained unused for a long time. This was a common practice in all the colonies, notwithstanding stipulations that land granted must be put to use.

Forty-four years after the death of Mason, his heirs were still suing to obtain possession of the land which by that time, due to the increase in population, had assumed some value. [169]

Colonel Samuel Allen, a London merchant, bought the Mason claim to the province for the equivalent of $1,250, and became governor in 1692, but the active ruler was his son-in-law, John Usher.

Governor Bellomont in 1700 declared Allen's title defective, and brought charges that Allen had tried to obtain royal confirmation of the title by bribery. Allen litigated about it until his death in 1715. [107] Thirty years afterwards, 124 years after date of the original grant, a new generation of heirs having arisen, they revived the claim.

After being in controversy for 147 years, the claims were sold to twelve persons in Portsmouth, designated as the Masonian proprietors, who began exacting land rents of the settlers.

Lands throughout New Hampsire and Vermont were settled and granted without regard to Mason's claim.

In 1752 a party of English went to the location of present Charlestown, New Hampshire, to lay out a township. The Indians objected that the English were carving out more land than they could cultivate, and threatened hostilities. The Indians felt themselves the rightful lords of the land, and clung to the hunting grounds of their fathers. [7]

With sullen discontent, successive generations of Indians during the preceding century had seen the rapid spread of English settlements. The English cut the forest, erected mill dams, sawmills and forts, regardless of ill effects on the game and fish—the food of the Indians. Hunting grounds were growing narrower, and their game fled at the repeated sound of the woodman's axe. Indian minds began to be haunted with melancholy forebodings of eventual dispossession. They resented these encroachments and asked the English to set a boundary beyond which they would not go, but the English were determined to take all the land and refused. [7]

Urged by the French, the Indians began hostilities, and fell upon the frontier settlements. English prisoners taken by them were sent to Montreal, where they were sold as slaves at good prices. The war soon became part of the French and Indian War.

Louis XIV in 1688, ignoring the grant made eighty-five years previously by a predecessor, Henry IV, gave Mount Desert Island, Maine, to Sieur de la Mothe Cadillac as a fief.

After driving out the Dutch at New Netherland in 1664, the Duke of York confirmed individual land grants made by the Dutch, but a successor, King George III, a century later, ignored that policy when he gave Mount Desert Island purportedly for inducing settlers to Maine, to Sir Francis Bernard, late governor of Massachusetts.

With the American Revolution, the island became the property of Massachusetts. Shortly after that war, Bernard's son, claiming that he had been loyal to the colonies, was given the west half, and Marie de Cadillac, granddaughter of the previous grantee, was given the east half.

The town promoters of Augusta, Maine, in 1761, to induce settlers, and for personal profit, divided nine hundred acres into lots. They retained four hundred acres for themselves, and to help run up the price of lots offered five hundred acres to whoever would come and settle there. [50]

Massachusetts in 1762 sold at public auction nine townships, and land in the Berkshires.

War between England and France, in both America and faraway India, continued for many years during the middle of the eighteenth century, with France gaining dominion over nearly all of India.

The French had a strong foothold in America until a short while before their surrender in 1763. Their strength had its origin when Samuel, Sieur de Champlain, in 1608 founded Quebec, where Jacques Cartier had made and abandoned a settlement seventy-four years previously.

The exhausted condition of the French treasury at the close

of the French and Indian War, due to unwise measures to meet expenses, presently caused discontent among all classes of French society. Public clamor arose against the authority and prodigality of the king's courtiers under Madame de Pompadour.

Riots ensued in both Paris and the provinces, and the government was even accused of kidnapping children for transportation to New France, in America. Louis XV, satiated with pleasure, and indifferent to the State, depended solely on those who could amuse him, of whom Madame de Pompadour was the chief. The command of armies depended on her favor, and Queen Maria Theresa of Austria addressed de Pompadour as "My Cousin." [58]

The Duke of Cloiseul, elevated by Madame de Pompadour to the ministry of War and Marine, in 1759 gathered a fleet of twenty-one vessels, and prepared to attack the English. But the English destroyed the fleet before it had well got into action. England was now triumphant on every sea. [58]

Replying to desperate appeals from Montcalm in Canada for reinforcements, Cloiseul wrote: "I am very sorry to have to send you word that you must not expect any reinforcements . . . There would be great fear of their being intercepted by the English." The necessity for peace was beginning to dawn upon Madame de Pompadour's little cabinet. [58]

That year the French were overcome by Wolfe on the Plains of Abraham. Quebec, all Canada, the Great Lakes and the trans-Appalachian regions became British by the treaty of Paris in 1763, and shortly after, the Quebec Act extended jurisdiction of Canada to include the Ohio and Mississippi regions and all conquered territory.

The French were among the bold pioneers of civilization in America, but they were hampered by wars in Europe and in India, which prevented rendering support in America. Very much as the Swedish military campaigns in Europe during the previous century were outstanding causes of Sweden losing New Sweden on the Delaware, so were the French military campaigns in India an outstanding cause of France losing New France in America. Two years after losing New France by the surrender at Quebec, France lost India by the surrender of Pondicherry.

Squatters in Maine, when complained against in 1778, wrote the court saying: "Opening the wilderness and turning the desert into wheatfields, while it supports individuals, is of great advantage to the public." They appealed for grants of land at fair prices. The land in Maine was held by various interests—absentees, individual proprietors, townships, corporations and the Province of Massachusetts. The township of Framingham, Maine, was divided into lots of 200 and 250 acres, the former given to settlers and the latter retained by the proprietors. [50]

Land in Maine was given freely to those who induced settlers to come there. During the Revolutionary War settlers were arriving there in large numbers, without making application for land.

The proprietors in Maine were required by the court in 1785 to allow every settler fifty acres free of charge, to include what improvements the settler had made, and the right to buy fifty acres additional at not exceeding 3s (75¢) per acre. Henry Rust, of Salem, in 1787 bought of Massachusetts six thousand acres in Maine, and sold them in small tracts to settlers at 50¢ per acre. [50]

For having represented the colony in London during the Revolution, Massachusetts granted to Arthur Lee, of Virginia, six thousand acres east of the Saco River.

General Knox had title to the land in what is now Knox and Waldo Counties, Maine, on which five hundred squatters had located. After the Revolution, the courts sustained the claim of ownership of land by Knox and other proprietors, but directed that each settler should be allotted a hundred at $2.25 per acre. The settlers had either to agree to the price and terms for the land, or go elsewhere. Some moved to uneconomic locations, but many remained on the land for a long period of time, using force to maintain their possessions. [50]

10

Connecticut

THE first European to discover and sail up the Connecticut River was Adrian Block, a Hollander, who is supposed to have sailed in 1614 as far as the site of Hartford. The Dutch traded on the river eighteen years before the river became known to the English.

DeRasiere, a Dutch captain from Manhattan, in 1627 told the Pilgrims at Plymouth of the fertile Connecticut Valley, and invited them to come there, but they rather discourteously declined the invitation, informing the captain that the Dutch had no right in that country. They deferred for six years acting upon the suggestion. [142]

Robert, Earl of Warwick, President of the Council of New England, on March 19, 1631, granted to William, Viscount Say and Sele, Lords Brooks and Rich, Sir Nathaniel Rich, Sir Richard Saltonstall, George Fenwick and others to the number of eleven (designated as lords and gents), and their heirs and assigns and associates for ever: "All that part of New England in America which lies and extends from Narragansett River the space of forty leagues (120 miles), upon a straight line near the seashore to the west and southwest, from the Atlantic Ocean to the South Sea, and all islands, mines and minerals; and north and south in bredth, reserving for his majesty his heirs and successors, the one-fifth of all gold and silver found."

Johnson [87] said: "The foundation of the claim of the Earl of Warwick to this territory is mythical. The grant to Say and Sele shows no title on the part of the grantor and is merely a quit claim."

The Dutch acquired an Indian grant of land at Saybrook, at the mouth of the Connecticut River, the year after the grant by Warwick, on which they erected the Arms of The Netherlands. They also acquired a tract of land along the river at the present site of Hartford where, in 1633, they erected Fort of Good Hope and equipped it with two cannon.

John Winthrop in October, 1633, sent the bark "Blessing" from Massachusetts on a voyage through Long Island Sound to New Amsterdam for trade, and to show to the Dutch governor, van Twiller, Winthrop's commission signifying that the King of England had granted the river and country of Connecticut to certain of his subjects. When the commission was shown him, van Twiller stated that the land belonged to the West India Company by prior discovery, occupation and grant of the States General, and requested the Plymouth people to defer their pretense of claim to Connecticut, and refrain from settling there until the King of England and the State General should agree about their boundaries so that they "as Christians might dwell together as good neighbors in these heathenish parts." [16]

William Bradford and Mr. Winslow, of Plymouth, went to Boston in 1633 to confer with the Massachusetts men about their joining them in going to the Connecticut Valley. Governor Winthrop afterwards said: "There was a motion to set up a trading-house there to prevent the Dutch who were about to build one . . . but being three or four thousand Indians there we thought not fit to meddle with it."

Winthrop stated that subsequently four men went overland to Connecticut in September, 1633, to trade, and that at a session of the general court at Newton, Massachusetts, the subject of the migration to Connecticut was long and earnestly discussed. Among the principal reasons for the removal were "the fruitfulness of the river valley with its great meadows."

Migration overland by people from Dorchester started in the autumn, taking horses, cattle and swine. The trip took two weeks of weary traveling. Household goods had been sent by water. The weather was stormy, some of the vessels were wrecked or frozen in the river, and the food supply ran short. [142] The Dorchester expedition probably reached the site of Hartford ahead of the Holmes expedition, which went by sea from Plymouth at about the same time.

Motives for the migration were also political. Men were dissatisfied where only one in six had a vote. The Warwick grantees were preparing to take possession at the mouth of the river; so it was "reluctantly consented to," on condition that the new colony should continue within the jurisdiction, and be a part of Massachusetts. [142]

The colony had much livestock. Wood said: "They had 1,500 head of cattle, 4,000 goats, and swine innumerable." Nine years later there were 1,000 sheep.

The Dorchester party which included people from Watertown and Newton, entered upon the Great Meadow and apportioned it in sites, to which they first gave the names of the Massachusetts towns from which they had come, but the present names were afterwards substituted. The Watertown group located at Wethersfield, the Dorchester group at Windsor, and those from Newton at Hartford. [87]

William Holmes of Plymouth, with his company, having a commission from the governor of Plymouth, in September, 1633, took to Connecticut on board a large new boat the frame and material for a house. He found the Dutch were at Hartford and had made a fort, and planted two pieces of cannon. The Dutch forbade Holmes going up the river, stood by their cannon and ordered him to strike his colors, or be fired upon. He disregarded the Dutch command and was fired upon. But he proceeded and erected his house on the west bank of the river, near Windsor, and fortified it with palisades. Governor Wolcott said this was the first house erected in Connecticut, though the Dutch erected a trading-house there at about the same time, which they called the House of Good Hope. The Dutch sent a force of seventy men to drive Holmes away. He was so well fortified and vigilant that they attempted to checkmate him by making another location higher up the river. [148] But about this time smallpox broke out among the Indians. [142]

The Dutch were striving to protect their monopoly of the beaver trade with the Indians, said to amount to ten thousand skins per annum. The English sometimes sent to England in a single ship £1,000 worth of otter and beaver skins.

The epidemic of smallpox, which killed 950 Indians out of 1,000, removed the last Indian from the meadows in Windsor and rendered these meadows, "the lord's waste," and a land where the pioneers could raise food. [142]

The English having at length obtained a foothold on the Connecticut River, the towns of Massachusetts soon rang with the fame of the fertility and "excellent meadows" of that valley; and consequently these lands became an object of great desire and competition. [111] More settlers came from Cambridge, Watertown, Dorchester and Newton and other places and found homes along the river.

A provisional government for Connecticut was under a commission from the general court of Massachusetts, instituted in 1635 to eight persons who had resolved to go to Connecticut. Rules and ordinances were enacted, including regulation of land allotments.

The ship "Abigail" arrived at Saybrook on October 5, 1635, with John Winthrop, Jr., Sir Henry Vance and Rev. Hugh Peters representing "the lords and gents." Young Winthrop promptly tore down the Coat of Arms of The Netherlands which the Dutch had placed there three years previously.

Sir Francis Stiles, who was sent out from England largely at the expense of Saltonstall, arrived at Windsor by boat with twenty men, soon after the Dorchester pioneers had reached there.

Saltonstall came to New England with Governor Winthrop, in 1630, and returned the next year. He later sent his sons Richard and Robert. The latter died in Massachusetts and, among other property, left two thousand acres at Warehouse Point, near Windsor. [142]

Saltonstall had planned laying out sixteen hundred acres. He offered to buy the buildings which the Dorchester party had erected, but they refused to sell and move out. His party, led by Stiles, was crowded to the extreme north end of the meadows and these meadows were the only land fit for immediate cultivation.

There was intense animosity along the Connecticut River between the Plymouth people and the Dorchester people. William

Bradford, Miles Standish, John Alden, Thomas Prince, William Brewster and John Howland, of Plymouth, gave power of attorney to William Holmes "to enter and seize all those our lands upon the Connecticut River known by name of Windsor and Hartford, and hold them, and also our indented servants, and chattels, and to dispose thereof."

In the spring of 1636 John Winthrop, Jr., who had been appointed by the "lords and gents" partly as governor of Connecticut (though never so acknowledged by the three Connecticut towns), went up the river from Saybrook to arrange the difficulties between the pioneers under Stiles and the Dorchester people.

Springfield, Massachusetts, was settled in 1636, by Mr. Pynchon of Roxbury, and continued for two years under the Connecticut government. [148]

In less than four years after arrival of the first settlers on the Connecticut River, all the land in the immediate vicinity was privately appropriated, and as new settlers came in needing land, the inevitable speculation in land developed. New arrivals had to pay others for a place on and from which to live.

The Plymouth colony in 1637 reserved forty-three and three-quarters acres in the Plymouth Meadow. On the same date it is recorded that Thomas Prince sold an equal acreage of meadow, and forty acres of upland at Hartford, to inhabitants of Windsor for £37 10s, payable three months hence. About the same time, fifteen-sixteenths (94 acres) of the Plymouth lands were acquired by the Dorchester people. [142]

Thomas Ford, of the Dorchester party, became the owner of large tracts by original grants, including thirty-two acres which was half of Pine Meadow, and most of the site of Windsor Locks. Hundreds of acres were granted him on the east side of the river, and he bought many acres from others. [142]

The three independent settlements in Connecticut were the nucleus of the Connecticut colony. In the fourth year they consisted of 160 families, comprising 800 persons.

The locations of New London, Groton and Stonington were considered the habitations of the Pequot Indians.

Barely more than three years had elapsed after the Massachusetts people had settled in Connecticut, at Hartford, Windsor and Wethersfield, when, joined by settlers in Massachusetts, they declared a war of extermination against the Pequots.

After a night spent in prayer, an English force of ninety men led by John Mason (not he of the New Hampshire Grant), together with twenty led by Underhill, plus sixty Mohican Indians under Uncas, and four hundred other Indians under Miantonomo, proceeded to Mystic River, near Stonington. At dawn they fell upon the Pequots and exterminated them by sword and fire, burning their village. No quarter was given or mercy shown. There were six hundred Indian warriors, women, old men and children killed, and two hundred taken prisoners. Two Englishmen were killed and twenty wounded. Those natives who escaped were pursued, and a remnant hunted into "a most hideous swamp." All this was done in less than an hour. [16]

About thirty Indian prisoners were taken offshore in a boat and drowned. Some fifty others seem to have been reduced to bondage, and were distributed among the English. Some were sold as slaves in the West Indies. An aboriginal nation had been almost exterminated; their coveted land won. Comparative peace reigned for thirty-eight years, but the seed of enmity in the Indian tribes was sown for ages. [16]

Winthrop recorded: "There was a day of thanksgiving kept in all the churches for the victory, and for other mercies." Captain Mason wrote: "Thus the Lord was pleased to smite our enemies and to give us their land for an inheritance." Washington Irving, in *The Sketch Book,* gives a vivid account of this massacre.

Laborers being in demand, as is invariably so where land is easily obtainable, Hugh Peters, a prominent citizen, wrote Governor John Winthrop, Jr., that he had heard of a dividend of women and children from the Pequot captives, and would like "a young woman or girl, and a boy"; another wrote that slaves were needed to improve the country.

The general court ordered that men be sent to settle on the land conquered from the Pequots, and hold it for the colony. [112]

The people of Windsor, Hartford, and Wethersfield in 1639

"conjoined" themselves (Springfield declining to join) to be as one public state or commonwealth. They established a general assembly or court, to make laws for their government and dispose of lands, and from then on the assembly exercised that power.[a]

This was the beginning of the organization of Connecticut. Their "Fundamental Orders" were the first written constitution creating a government known to history. [10] The general court legislated not only concerning the colonist but acted also in settling affairs between the Indians. [112]

The general court enacted that land already measured out should be recorded, and that no inhabitant should make sale of his house and land without first offering it to the town in which it was situated.[b]

So rapidly did their settlements increase in population that, six years after the Massachusetts people arrived, Hartford contained more than one hundred houses. [111]

The fort at Saybrook was planned and commanded by Lion Gardiner, an engineer who had served in Holland under the Prince of Orange. He disapproved of the Puritan policy respecting the Pequots. Johnston [87] rightfully said: "The English settlement at Saybrook rested on a paper title which rested on nothing and was never perfected. The other settlements had not even a baseless paper title to rest upon. Both were perfect examples of squatter sovereignty." Egleston [42] in confirmation said: "The settlers of the river towns had no right of jurisdiction other than that of occupancy, purchase from Indians, or conquest such as in the Pequot Massacre. Their policy seems to have been to dispose as quietly and cheaply as possible of the claims of such as challenged their land titles, into the exact nature of which they were not disposed to provoke too close an investigation." However, from these "rights" emanated the present titles to land in Connecticut.

A party of English from Yorkshire, Hertfordshire and Kent, led by Theopholis Eaton of Oxfordshire, and Rev. John Davenport, a famous divine, arrived in Boston in 1637.

[a]Conn. Rec.
[b]*Ibid.*

Eaton had been a London merchant, a deputy governor of the East India Company, had lived in India three years, and was a large landholder in England. Other settlers with him possessed wealth; all had an urge to grab more land in America than they could use, to be held idle until the continuing stream of settlers had run up its price.

In the spring of the following year they settled on a tract of land eight by five miles in area, which they named New Haven. They had no grant of land, but made terms with the Indians, and began to distribute land among those of their group. Eight years later the Dutch governor protested against the English settling in the area, which the Dutch called Red Mount, claiming infringement of the rights of the States General. [148]

Each settler was to receive two-and-a-half acres, partially in upland and meadow, and partially on the neck. Those who invested £100 in the venture received twenty acres in upland. [158]

Eaton, the chief promoter, had 963 acres, with land rates assessed at £10, 13s, while John Brackett had 25 acres with £2, 6d rates. Every landholder was to pay his proportion of all public charges, and was to expect land in all subsequent divisions.

Being accustomed to good houses in England, Eaton built a house with nineteen fireplaces, and Davenport one with thirteen fireplaces.

Some of the New Haven and Wethersfield people founded Milford, where they acquired a large tract of land from the Indians for some merchandise of small value.

About the same time, some people arrived from Surrey and Kent in England, and settled at Guilford, where they obtained, in like manner, a tract of land ten by thirteen miles in area. Everybody received land, on which he must pay his proportion of all expenses. But in anticipation of an unearned increment in land value, to accrue to the promoters from an increase in population, no one was permitted to invest more than £500.

Stamford was founded two years after Guilford. The people of Milford "sequestered" a belt of land around their town two miles wide, and divided the land among the settlers in the manner usually practiced in New England, according to the area of land each recipient already held.

Another trick widely practiced in land distribution in New England is illustrated by the division of land at Milford in 1805 (being one-and-two-thirds of a century after the founding of the place), when allotments were made to heirs based upon the list of landholders and the area held by each 119 years previously; the object being to confine grants to the descendants of the first families—thereby shutting out subsequent arrivals and their descendants, and tending to form a landholding aristocracy.

Land was often granted to soldiers, and to others who had rendered some public service. The assembly in 1696 granted six miles square of the conquered Pequot lands about Voluntown to Thomas Leffingwell, John Frink and others who had served in the Pequot Massacre. [148]

Sir William Boswell, British ambassador to Holland, advised the English to "crowd on, but without hostility, crowding the Dutch out of those places which they have occupied."

The English were so strong in numbers in Connecticut, three years after they arrived there, that they denied to the Dutch, the first European settlers, all title to any possessions on the river. The English government attempted to justify the encroachments by saying that though the Dutch had been in possession several years, they had done nothing to improve the country, and that "it was a sin to leave such valuable lands uncultivated, when such fine crops could be raised from them." [111]

The above plea, if admitted, would afford a justification for any one settling on unused land anywhere, the action being construed as fulfilling a law of nature.

O'Callaghan [111] wrote: "It is not easy to discover on what ground the Dutch were regarded by the English, or by their historians, as mere intruders. The Dutch had made the effective discovery of, and established themselves along, both the Hudson and Connecticut Rivers, before these rivers were known to the English. They had obtained a grant from their government before the date of the grant to the English, which had as good a right to grant lands discovered by their subjects as any other state. After trading with the Indians for several years, the Dutch acquired of them a tract of land and built a fort and trading house before the country had been taken possession of by the English. The people of the Plymouth and Massachusetts colonies, when they attempted to drive the Dutch from Connecticut, came without a shadow of title from the Council of New England under which they professed to claim.

"It might have been expected that when the English had settled in America they would, in gratitude for the hospitality which they had experienced from the Dutch during their sojourn of eleven years in Holland and Zeeland, have left New Netherland unmolested. But self-interest entirely eradicated sentiment of justice and gratitude from their hearts. They did not consider whether they had any legal title, or the fact of prior discovery, chartered conveyance, and possession, by the Dutch."

The distribution to individuals by the general court, in 1640, of land at Pine Meadow (Windsor Locks) was in accordance with the sum invested by each person in the general fund, raised before the settlers left Massachusetts to meet the expenses of the migration. Governor John Haynes, of Hartford, received ten acres. When land had been allotted to the first settlers as needed, for cultivation, pasturage, fuel and timber, the remaining land was held in common by the town, and later granted by vote, as needed. What remained was granted to those on the tax list, the allotment being based in proportion to the wealth and the amount of taxes paid by each. In 1752, about 130 years after the first settlement, a committee of proprietors distributed nearly all the remaining land in the town among the heirs of the original proprietors. These heirs were largely lineal descendants of the first settlers. [142]

Mathew Allyn and the Wolcotts were recorded as holders of lots north and south of the Plymouth reservation. Allyn, in 1640, bought all the land reserved by the settlers from Plymouth. [142]

Governor Haynes, in 1640, had 30 acres meadow, 150 acres home lot and woods, and 284 acres on the east side of the river, all appraised at £140. At his death, thirteen years later, it was inherited by a man in Boston, who sold it fifteen years afterwards to Henry Wolcott. Many of the Saltonstall party bought lots at Windsor. From the early days, mortgages were given, a practice which facilitates hoarding land for speculation. Taxes were paid in farm products. [142]

The four towns of New Haven, Milford, Guilford and Stamford united, in 1643, into the "republic" of New Haven. A constitution was adopted and courts established. Only church members could vote, which disfranchised more than one-half in New Haven, and nearly half in Guilford. [47]

Massachusetts, having joined in the conquest, laid claim seven years afterwards to a part of the Pequot lands, and George Fenwick asserted this claim was of great consequence to "the gents" interested in the Connecticut grant. [148]

Fenwick, one of the surviving grantees of the discredited Warwick grant of 1631, threatened to sell to the Dutch the fort at Saybrook and lands at the mouth of the river, or to levy a tax on all exports and imports passing through. He proposed to the Connecticut court that they buy his rights and privileges.

Thereupon an agreement was made between Fenwick and representatives of the jurisdiction of the Connecticut River, by which, "Fenwick conveys the fort and munitions at Saybrook. All the land upon the river shall belong to the said jurisdiction of Connecticut, and such lands as are yet undisposed of shall be ordered and given out by a committee of five, of which Fenwick is always to be one. All the forementioned grants the said Fenwick doth engage himself to make good to the jurisdiction aforesaid. Also promises that all lands from Narragansett River to Saybrook shall fall under the jurisdiction of Connecticut if it come into his power. The parties authorized by the general court of Connecticut agree that for ten years there shall be paid to Fenwick or assigns: for each hogshead of beaver down the river 20s; each pound of beaver traded within the limits of the river, 2d; each bushel of corn or meal out of the river 2d per bushel," there were also many other articles upon which duties were levied. Fourteen months later this agreement was amended, by which Connecticut was to, and did, pay Fenwick or assigns £180 per annum in produce for ten years. [148]

Fenwick seems to have been somewhat of a highbinder in his asserted private ownership of the mouth of the river.

Abram Pierson, a minister in Yorkshire, England, came to

Boston and later located himself at Southampton, Long Island, whence he went with his congregation to Branford, Connecticut.

Isaac Allerton (1588–1658) was one of the English who had settled in Holland and came to Plymouth in the "Mayflower." He became possessed of land in Rhode Island and Maine, was one of the leaders, and the deputy-governor and agent for the Plymouth Colony in England. In 1646 he located at New Haven, and traded with the Dutch and Swedes on the Delaware.

The great influx of English people into Connecticut, while the Dutch population remained static, resulted in 1650 in a treaty at Hartford between the two nationalities, whereby Stuyvesant practically abandoned all claim to New England. Therein it was agreed: That upon Long Island, the territory lying east of a line run from the westernmost part of Oyster Bay, in a straight line to the sea, should belong to the English; the western part to the Dutch. The line between Connecticut and New York was to begin at the west side of Greenwich Bay, about four miles from Stamford, and was to run north twenty miles, its continuance to be fixed by agreement between the two governments of the Dutch and New Haven (provided that said line came not within ten miles of the Hudson River). Greenwich, subject to future consideration, was to remain under the Dutch.

This caused the English about Hartford to become aggressive and violent. Four years later they even appropriated, and held by force, land which the Dutch settlers had made ready for planting, whereupon the farmers came to blows. The court at Hartford ordered and declared that the "Dutch House of Hope, with the lands, buildings and fences thereto belonging, be hereby sequestered."

Governor Winthrop, of Connecticut, was, in 1661, sent to Europe to make representations against the Dutch and French. The eventually discredited and beheaded Archbishop Laud opposed his proceedings, and caused Winthrop to be imprisoned as a Separatist, but he was released.

The Dutch West India Company directors, mistrusting Winthrop, with whom they had conferred at Amsterdam, instructed Stuyvesant to "explore his mind," and if possible effect a definite settlement with Connecticut. Stuyvesant went to Boston, and met the commissioners of the United Colonies, but could reach no agreement with them about their encroachment upon the Dutch domains. [16]

The Connecticut committee asserted: "The Dutch West India charter is only a charter of commerce." This prompted Stuyvesant to write to the Amsterdam Chamber, requesting that the original charter should be solemnly confirmed by a public act of their High Mightinesses, the States General, under the Great Seal, "which an Englishman commonly dotes upon like an idol." They promptly complied with this request, declaring that the charter authorized the company to plant colonies in any unoccupied parts of America, from Newfoundland to the Straits of Magellan, and particularly in New Netherland. [16]

Through the influence of Lord Say and Sele, and other friends of the Connecticut colony at the court of Charles II, the people of Connecticut, on April 23, 1662, obtained from the king a grant of all the lands embraced in the original grant to Lord Say and Sele and others, of March 1631. The grant, of course, included the location of the New Haven colony. [145] This gave the Connecticut settlers the first authoritative title by a potentate to lands in Connecticut, and was the basis on which they claimed land west of the Alleghenies.

Excerpts from the grant read: "We do give and grant unto said Governor [Winthrop] and company [naming nineteen persons] and their successors, all that part of our dominions in New England bounded on the east by the Narragansett River, and on the north by the line of Massachusetts Plantation; and on the south by the sea, . . . to the South Sea on the west, with the islands thereunto adjoining, together with all the lands, havens, ports, rivers, mines and minerals within said tract. To have and to hold the same unto the said governor and company, their successors and assigns for ever, upon trust, and for the benefit of themselves and their associates, freemen of the said colony, *their heirs and assigns,* to be holden of us, our heirs and successors, yielding and paying to us the one-fifth part of all gold and silver which shall be there gotten . . . And they shall have perpetual succession, and possess lands, and the same to lease, grant and dispose of."

The expense of getting the grant, including sending Governor Winthrop to England, was £1,300.

Two years afterwards, on March 12, 1664, King Charles granted to his brother James, Duke of York, all the land between the St. Croix River and Pemaquid, Maine, and between the west side of the Connecticut River and the east side of the Delaware: he also granted James the Hudson River, Long Island, Martha's Vineyard and Nantucket. [145] This grant included within the boundaries named all the region occupied by the Dutch. Also included was a part of the Connecticut grant extending to the Pacific Ocean, which Charles had only two years previously confirmed to Winthrop and associates. This grant to James was further renewed to him by the king ten years later, after recovery of the region from the Dutch.

In the final distribution of land by the Council of New England in 1635, James, Marquis (afterwards Duke) of Hamilton, was granted land between the Narragansett and Connecticut Rivers. This was four years after the aforesaid grant of the same territory by the Earl of Warwick.

Heirs of Hamilton endeavored, thirty-three years later, and again nineteen years after that, to set up their claim in opposition to the Connecticut grant of 1662, but it was barred by Prescription.

An agreement between Governor John Winthrop and John Clarke of Newport, in 1663, terminated the controversy regarding the boundary between Connecticut and Rhode Island. The line was decided upon as being at the Pawcatuck River, though to act in accord with the royal grant, they violated a geographical fact in pretending that the Pawcatuck River was the Narragansett River. The boundary on the west, between Connecticut and New Netherland, was still undetermined.

In a controversy between Lyme and New London in 1664 over the land claimed by both, it was decided that, rather than go to the expense of litigation, the difficulty be settled by a fist-fight by two champions from respective towns. Lyme won, and took possession. [29]

The general court, in 1664, gave liberty to Governors Hopkins and Haynes to dispose of the lands upon the Tunxis River, near Windsor, to such of the inhabitants of Windsor as they should judge expedient. [148]

When Connecticut and New Haven united in 1665, the general court became the general assembly, and adopted resolutions dissolving the New Haven colony. The Rev. Davenport became disgusted at the union of the Connecticut colonies, and moved to Boston. The people of Branford also were so displeased that the Rev. Pierson, and almost his entire congregation, went with Robert Treat to found Newark, New Jersey. This left the town almost without inhabitants for the next twenty years. [148]

The allotting of land in many places in New England was proportionate to what each person invested in the adventure of making a new settlement. In fact, making these new settlements became what would be designated today as a racket, with some aspects of a lottery.

A grant of land eight miles square, for a settlement at Woodstock, was made in 1683 to a group of promoters in Roxbury. Such grants to make settlements at different locations became a source of profit to the promoters.[e] A group was formed in Farmington, which created twenty-eight shares for the promotion of a settlement at Waterbury. [148]

The English slaughtered five hundred Indians near Stamford, in 1675, which "ranked with the massacre of the Pequots thirty-eight years previously."

Notwithstanding priority of the Connecticut grant of 1662, just cited, to that to the Duke of York, Governor Andros asserted the Duke's claim to all that part of Connecticut west of the Connecticut River. [148]

With the number of settlers and the demand for land increasing, land value increased. At Hartford, Windsor and Wethersfield, meadow land in tracts of fifty and sixty acres, was held at £5 to £7 per acre, pasture land £3, 6s, 8d, and woodland at 11s. [158]

It was common for land to be forfeited if the grantee did not build a dwelling within one year.[d]

With the population increasing, the English increased the re-

[e]Ellis, Roxbury

[d]Bronson, Waterbury

straint upon the Indians. Reservations were established and the Indians were confined to them. In 1659 a tribe was reservationed at Bridgeport. Eight years later, two thousand acres between Groton and Ledyard were set apart as an Indian reservation, and sixteen years still later, another tribe was confined near North Stonington. The English forbade Indian pow-wows and worship of "false" gods. [112]

The general assembly, in 1685, "granted the promoters of the town of Windsor [fifty years after it was founded] all those lands unto . . . and the rest of the said present proprietors of Windsor, their heirs and successors and assigns for ever, paying to our sovereign lord the king, his heirs, successors and assigns, his dues [one-fifth of the gold and silver discovered], according to the charter." Signed: "Robert Treat, Governor."

In 1686 there were granted to 12 promoters, 15,100 acres in Windham County. Massachusetts people planted the first colony in that county, and Connecticut people soon followed. Sir Robert Thompson, of England, held the land on which Thompson, Windham County, is located. [142]

Sir Edmund Andros was, in 1688, made governor of New York as well as of New England. He went to Hartford to seize the Connecticut charter, but was foiled in the attempt. He declared that the Indian land titles of the colonists were of no value; that Indian deeds were no better than "the scratch of a bear's paw."

By his actions, settlers who had improved and cultivated their land during fifty or sixty years' occupancy were obliged to take out new deeds, and pay an increased annual land rent to the Duke of York. In some instances a fee of £50 was demanded, as a perquisite to Andros. Those who demurred had their land confiscated and deeded to others.

The general assembly, in 1693, granted to a group of promoters a township, six by eight miles in area, on which Danbury was afterwards founded.

The assembly in 1696 granted six miles square of the conquered Pequot lands about Voluntown to Thomas Leffingwell, John Frink, and others who had served in the Pequot Massacre. [148] Many tracts of land were given to Yale College.

The assembly, in 1703, enacted that all the land in the townships already granted should remain, with all the privileges and immunities therein granted, in fee simple to the promoter-proprietors, their heirs and assigns for ever. [148]

The people were thus for all future ages alienated from the land, except by purchase from those who had been born earlier and got possession of it.

Some of the prominent citizens of the colony, including Captain John Mason, in scheming to possess a large tract of land conquered from the Pequots, became malcontents and appealed to England against the colonial assembly. Litigation continued seventy years, when it was finally disposed of by King George III.

A tract of 2,400 acres in Windham County, which had been sold several times by, and to, speculators, brought, in 1711, £312.

A boundary dispute between Connecticut and Massachusetts was disposed of, in 1715, by Connecticut receiving 105,793 acres in the disputed region. This was sold at public auction to twenty-one speculators from Massachusetts, Connecticut and London, England for £683, about 3¢ per acre.

Five years later Connecticut sold sixteen thousand acres at auction to a small group, one of whom was Roger Wolcott, a well-known Hartford land speculator, for £510, or about 16¢ per acre. [172]

With the increase in population and continued land speculation, land prices increased. Seven-and-a-half acres of meadow land at Hartford were sold at £8 per acre; land in "the second meadow" at £2, 10s per acre, and a tract on the "copperhills" at 2s per acre. [158]

Litchfield was founded by speculators in 1720, when a tract nine by ten miles in area was laid out into sixty-four allotments, of which sixty-one were sold at auction. Willington was laid out the same year, on a tract five by seven miles, and sold for £510. [148]

Captain Jeremiah Fitch, of Norwich, had acquired a claim to a large tract at Coventry. He was legally opposed, and judgment given against him, whereupon he was imprisoned, but his neighbors stormed the jail and released him. [142]

There was continuing active demand for land for homes, but

since all land about the settlements was held by speculators for higher prices, incoming settlers and the maturing younger generation were forced to far-off regions. At Windsor, a "right" in a large tract of remote land was, in 1725, valued at 3s 4d per acre. [158]

The township of Mortlake, afterwards annexed to Pomfret, was granted by the assembly in 1726 to one Blackwell, of England, who, contrary to expectations, held it unused for a considerable time. He sold it to Governor Belcher of Massachusetts, who also neglected to settle it, whereupon the assembly wisely annulled the grant. [148]

To avoid having the lands of the colony grasped by Sir Edmund Andros, the English governor, the assembly conveyed certain large areas of unallotted land to the towns of Hartford and Windsor for safekeeping. After the danger of appropriation by Andros had passed, the towns, when called upon to return the land, refused to do so and proceeded to sell allotments for their own benefit. [148]

This was compromised, in 1729, by the two towns returning less than one-third of the land to the colony; the towns retaining 291,806 acres, which they sold. The land returned to the colony was later distributed, mostly among influential citizens, in proportion to their wealth, to land already owned, and to the amount of taxes paid by each on the tax list of nine years previously; [142] a policy adverse to democratic principles, or fair dealing.

New Fairfield was laid out in 1730, into fifty-two allotments and four hundred acres were allotted to each of the twelve promoters designated as the original proprietors, their heirs and assigns, and a hundred acres for the first minister. [148]

At Torrington 20,924 acres were, in 1732, granted by the assembly to 106 promoter-proprietors. At Barkhamsted 20,531 acres were granted to a group of promoters, and at Colebrook 18,199 acres were likewise granted to seventy-nine persons. The last named tract was not surveyed and laid out until twenty-eight years afterwards. [142]

The assembly enacted, in 1737, that land on both sides of the Housatonic River should be divided into fifty-three rights, and fifty rights sold at public vendue. Every purchaser was obliged to build and finish a house, at least eighteen feet square, and subdue and fence at least eight acres within three years after purchase, and pay the taxes. [148]

Cornwall township of 23,654 acres was laid out in 1738 in fifty-three allotments or rights. The rights, averaging 446 acres each, sold at £50 per right, or about 54¢ per acre. [148]

Norfolk township of seven by nine miles was, in 1754, divided among fifty promoters, each of whom was to help create land value by settling a family on each right within three years. [148]

Land in New Haven was in 1774 offered in tracts of a hundred to a thousand acres, at £5 per hundred acres—12*d,* or 24¢, per acre. It was sometimes sold at auction at a minimum price of one-half that. [50]

A Windham County group organized the Susquehanna Company, in 1753, and applied to the assembly for a quit-claim for land in the Wyoming Valley, Pennsylvania, extending along both sides of the Susquehanna River. Connecticut claimed this as part of the grant by the Earl of Warwick in 1631, confirmed by Charles II in 1662; but nineteen years afterwards, Charles granted this same land to William Penn.

About two thousand Connecticut people went to the Wyoming Valley in 1778, and fought for possession of the land. During the American Revolution, British soldiers and Indians fell upon and killed about three hundred of the Connecticut settlers, in the historic Wyoming massacre. The survivors fled back to Connecticut. Some details of this tragic and prolonged controversy are given in the chapter on Pennsylvania.

The new state of Connecticut in 1786, by intercession of the Continental Congress, relinquished its claim to the Wyoming Valley and all western land north of the Ohio River, excepting 3,366,921 acres in northeastern Ohio which were reserved by it. Ten years afterwards it sold nearly three million of these acres, at 36¢ per acre, to the Connecticut Land Company, composed of forty-eight speculators, mostly in Connecticut. The company opened offices, conducted a sales campaign, and sold the land to settlers and speculators, mainly the latter. Oliver Phelps, a merchant and land speculator of Windsor, was the leader, largest stockholder, and general manager. Phelps had earlier been in the forefront of a similar promotion. [142] Notwithstanding his extensive land-jobbing, Phelps died a relatively poor man.

During the Revolutionary War, some people in different Connecticut towns suffered losses from depredations by the British. As an indemnity, the legislature divided several hundred thousand acres in its Western Reserve in Ohio, among the sufferers, at an appraised value of $1.50 per acre. Some of the recipients settled on their tracts, while others sold, or allowed their tracts to go for taxes. There was so little value to land without population that, at the present site of Sandusky, a holder of fourteen hundred acres there exchanged his allotment for a horse.*

*Bailey, Danbury

11

Rhode Island

GOVERNOR Bradford of the Plymouth colony, seven years after their arrival, in 1627, requested the Dutch to forbear trading with the Indians of Narragansett and Cape Cod Bays. The Dutch replied they had traded there above twenty-six years, by authority of the States General and Prince of Orange. Bradford asserted that the English had traded in those parts forty years, by grants from Queen Elizabeth. [111] There is no record to sustain either of these claims.

Roger Williams, having been condemned by a court of Massachusetts ministers, for heresy and preaching against the royal land system, as stated in the chapter on Massachusetts, was sentenced to banishment. On the verge of seizure for deportation to England, in January, 1636, he sought the wigwams of Massasoit and Canonicus, whom he knew, and of whose language he had some knowledge.

He there found the earlier mentioned William Blackstone, formerly of Boston, apparently the only European in the Narragansett region, who, to escape their religious tyranny, had left Massachusetts upon the arrival of the Puritans.

With no charter or documentary authority from any white man, Williams went into the wilderness to found a government of religious and soul liberty. [158]

Upon his own testimony, his benevolent intentions were in behalf of the Indian occupants of the land, rather than in behalf of any of his countrymen, and to found "a shelter for persons of distressed conscience." He even added, more explicitly, that he "desired not to be troubled with English company, but out of pity I gave leave to several persons to come along in my company," they being Harris, Smith, Angell and Wickes.

Canonicus and Miantonomo gave verbal assent to Williams to occupy the land. After a winter of great privation in the forests, Williams and his companions founded Providence.

The following year, Canonicus granted Prudence Island in the bay to Williams and John Winthrop. Williams soon disposed of his half-interest to Richard Parker of Boston, a partner of Winthrop; Winthrop gave his half to his son Stephen, who sold it three years afterward for £50 sterling. [124]

Under sentence of banishment from Massachusetts, Anne Hutchinson, and some adherents of her religious sect, left Massachusetts in March, 1638, in quest of a location on Long Island Sound, or the Delaware.

Calling en route on Williams at Narragansett, they received a suggestion that they locate on Acquidneck Island, on which Newport is now situated, which they did. Through Williams, the Indians gave them permission to occupy the island, in consideration of receiving forty fathoms of "peage," equally divided between Canonicus and Miantonomo. Ten coats and twenty hoes were judiciously distributed to the natives, who "shall remove themselves off the island before next Winter." [159]

Thirteen new arrivals came in August and were admitted. They made a settlement on the upper part of the island, which they named Pocasset (Portsmouth). [159] Mrs. Hutchinson, after the death of her husband four years later, left Rhode Island with her children, and settled west of Stamford, which was supposed to be in New Netherland. The following year she and fifteen others were murdered by Indians.

The Indian sachems granted to Williams, as a gift, the Providence and Pawtucket tracts, afterwards designated as the Providence Purchase. [124] The following October, Williams donated this land to the "Towne Fellowship," composed of himself and twelve others.

In the deed by Williams, the granting clause read, "I, Roger Williams, do freely and fully grant and make over equal right and power of enjoying and disposing of the same lands purchased of Canonicus and Miantonomo unto the loving friends and neighbors [designating them, including himself, by name] and such others as the major part of us shall admit into the same fellowship of vote with us." [124]

Presently others were admitted to the Fellowship, increasing the number to fifty-four. Land was assigned to each individual member; five acres for a home lot, six acres for cultivation, and the right to additional land to make up a hundred acres.

A board of five men of the Fellowship was appointed, "to be betrusted with disposal of land," and was to: "give every man a deed of all his lands lying within the bounds of the plantation, to hold it by for after ages," subject, however, to forfeiture, if not put to use within a specified time.

At Pocasset, a six-acre lot was assigned to each proprietor, but new arrivals were charged 2s per acre. As in Providence, it was provided that, "every man having a house lot should plant, fence or build thereon within one year, or he should lose it." [124]

The grant of land to Williams by the Indian sachems gave the right of pasturage of cattle along the upper reaches of certain streams; the provision reading: "up streams without limit . . . for use of cattle." As the population increased, and land consequently became more in demand, at increased value, William Harris and some of the fellowship proprietors, hungering for more land than they could possibly use, claimed such land "up stream" in fee simple. Williams protested on behalf of the Indians, saying: "That monstrous bound or business of up stream without limit was not thought of." [112]

Thwarted by Williams in his illicit land grabbing, Harris allied himself with Connecticut people who were endeavoring to get possession of all the land in the entire Narragansett country. [159]

Previous to the settling of Newport, nine hundred acres had been "laid forth by the Acquidneck government unto William, Samuel and Francis Hutchinson, and the same is still, [in 1640] granted them and their posterity." [124]

The increasing acquisitiveness of absentee landlordism on Acquidneck Island is apparent in the repeal, only three years after its first settlement, of the order of two years previously, that land allotted must be used within one year, or forfeited. With the revocation of this wise provision, it was ordered that, "all men's properties in their lands of the island . . . shall be such and soe free that neyther the state nor any person shall intrude into it . . . and that this tenure and propriety . . . shall be continued to him, or his; or to whomsoever he shall assign it for ever."

Williams was sent to England in 1643, where he obtained, from the Board of Commissioners, a charter of government for Rhode Island in which boundaries were partially defined. But the charter did not include any grant of land.

Fiske [47] said: "This board, the same year, granted to Massachusetts, all the territory on the mainland of Narragansett Bay; and the following March incorporated the townships of Newport and Portsmouth, together with Providence, into an independent colony. Just how far it was intended to cancel the Williams charter nobody could tell, but it afforded conflict of claims."

Williams, returning from England, arrived in Boston in September, 1644, with the Rhode Island charter. His safe conduct through Massachusetts was ordered by the Earl of Warwick, head of the Commission of Foreign Plantations. Thus he was enabled to pass through Massachusetts to Seekonk—the spot of his first location. [124]

The Providence colony comprised the proprietors (of the Fellowship), additional settlers, and those admitted to be freemen. In 1645 they adopted the name Rhode Island. Each one of twenty-eight persons received "a free grant of twenty-five acres, with the right in the commons according to their proportion of land," and those newly admitted agreed "not to claim any right to the purchase of said plantations, or to vote, until we shall be received as freemen."

The United Colonies of New England, which refused to admit Rhode Island as a member, in August, 1645, made war on the Narragansett Indians, and forbade conducting any government of Rhode Island under the charter granted to Williams. [78] The other colonies regarded Rhode Island as an outlaw for discrediting the royal land grants.

John Smith, one of the original settlers in Providence, received a grant of land on which to erect a mill. [159] The land system of Providence, by distribution of free land, afforded the early settlers an opportunity to become independent.

But all these early land grants were based only on Indian grants, and not on a British monarchial grant. These settlers and their heirs became involved in litigation and great trouble, after the grant by Charles II in 1663.

Samuel Gorton, a London clothier and irregular preacher, arrived in Massachusetts with his wife in 1637, and presently settled in Plymouth, whence he was the following year banished for expressing his opinions on interpretation of the Scriptures. [124]

In snow knee deep, the Gortons made their way to Portsmouth, on Acquidneck Island. After two years there, falling out with some of the people, he was banished, and went to Providence. There his reputation had preceded him, and he was refused admittance as an inhabitant.

Meanwhile, however, he had converted some people to his religious views. In a controversy which had arisen between the landed proprietors and the landless, he denounced the highhanded encroachment on the public domain, and there was some bloodshed. Thereupon, he moved to Patuxet, within the jurisdiction of Providence, where he acquired land and commenced a settlement. [124]

Some contentious members of the Fellowship, led by William Arnold, in their greed for a larger proportion of land, in January, 1641, induced Saccononocco, a local sachem, to make to them a grant of the same Patuxet tract which, five years previously, the chief sachems had granted to Williams, and was by him transferred to the Fellowship. [124]

The Arnold faction placed themselves, "their families, lands and estates," under the government of the Puritans of Massachusetts Bay—an action the Puritans were happy to accept. Because of this, and because they denied to later arrivals the privilege of the common lands, Gorton quarrelled with the Patuxet proprietors. [124]

Thereupon, Gorton and his followers migrated farther south along the bay to Samoset, where they obtained from Miantonomo a concession of land, made to Gorton and ten others, and began there a settlement which they named Warwick. This tract, from Warwick Neck to Gaspee Point, extended twenty miles inland. [124]

At Warwick, speculation in unused land was not tolerated, as "lots granted must be built upon within six months or revert to the town."

The Atherton group, speculating in the purchase and sale of Indian lands, also participated in the opposition to Gorton. [78] The Gortonists were summoned to Boston to answer trumped-up charges, and were told that if they refused to comply they would be "fitted for the slaughter." [78]

A body of forty white men and Indians was ordered by Governor John Winthrop of Massachusetts to proceed to Warwick to arrest the Gorton settlers and bring them to Boston for trial. [78] The Gortonists withstood the onslaught for several days and frustrated the attempt to set fire to their blockhouse.

To avoid bloodshed, Gorton and nine followers then agreed to go to Boston under safe convoy, but soon found they were prisoners, and that the Massachusetts invaders sent by Winthrop had robbed them of all their cattle. [78]

Upon reaching Boston, Gorton was imprisoned and put on trial for his life. After five months he was released, but not allowed to go to his Warwick home, or to remain within the jurisdiction of Massachusetts. Going thence to Portsmouth, from which he had been previously banished, he was elected a magistrate. [78]

Meantime, the Atherton coterie, with help from Governor Winthrop, had made progress towards gaining possession of the land at Warwick. To checkmate this, Gorton in 1664 obtained a commission from the Narragansett Indians to submit themselves to the British government. This action was hastened by the outrageous murder of their chief Miantonomo, by the Mohicans, with the consent of Winthrop and the Massachusetts elders, whom the Narragansett Indians now feared. [78]

A meeting was held at Portsmouth, in 1644, to protest against that system of close ownership of the common lands by which a relatively few persons were able to appropriate a vast area, as at Providence, and from which Gorton had suffered so much. Gorton called "for a new disposal" (redistribution) of lands which had been allotted. This was objected to by Elder John Brown of Plymouth, "as if some had too much and some too little, and for no respect of persons, and their lands to be laid aside for after ages—a most vile end." It has been just this "laying aside" of unused desirable land, preventing its use by the rising generation, except by mortgaging their future earnings to pay a speculative price, that has been the basic cause of vast unemployment, widespread distress, and social unrest.

Shortly after the meeting, Gorton, with Randall Holden and one other, sailed from Manhattan in a Dutch ship bound for England by way of Holland. Upon arrival in England they applied for, and obtained from the Earl of Warwick, a grant of the land at Warwick, which guaranteed them possession against all claimants. Holden returned with the grant in 1646. Gorton returned to Warwick two years later. [78] He had an order for his safe conduct through Massachusetts, which was also to protect him in the possession of Shawomet. [47]

Pomham, the local chief, and some of his tribe, lingered about until he was paid £30 in wampum to move away. Gorton died in 1677.

In 1650 it was enacted that, thereafter, land in Providence would be allotted to those who were received as inhabitants, at one shilling per acre for a house lot, and 6d per acre for additional land not exceeding twenty-five acres, and that a charge would be made for pasturage on the commons. [159] This was twelve years after the distribution of free land through the Indian grant, and shows the stimulating effect of additional population in creating land values.

Disputes prevailed in Providence for many years between the original proprietors of the Fellowship, under the gift by Williams, and the later-admitted small landholders. Williams sided with the small holders, who contended that the grant by him to the twelve proprietors of the Fellowship was in trust for the community, while some of the proprietors clung to the idea of private ownership of the bulk of the land for themselves. In transferring the land to the Fellowship, Williams had not created a trust, but he felt it a moral duty to accommodate with land all who came as settlers. [159]

There existed in Providence, by reason of the Fellowship, the very conditions needed for the development of a landed aristocracy. That, in fact, is what resulted from it, in spite of many protests, and efforts at resistance.

The original grantees of the Fellowship, each of whom received a hundred acres, subsequently admitted certain other members, each of whom received twenty-five acres. Staples [141x] said the whole number never exceeded one hundred and one persons. Their successors in the Fellowship were their heirs. Outsiders could become landholders, but they could never become one of the inner council of the Fellowship proprietors, who controlled the land privilege and government. Thus were developed, in conflict with each other, on the one hand an aristocracy based on land, and on the other, a class equally desirous of representation in the government, but studiously kept from attaining the privilege of proprietors. [51]

In 1718, connection between the proprietors of the Fellowship, and the other freemen was severed. Six years later, the Fellowship divided among themselves all the land remaining unallotted therein.

There was a large immigration of Jews from Lisbon to Rhode Island, in 1655. [159]

John Hull and others, of Boston, acquired an Indian grant of land, south of Wickford, known as the Pellaquamscutt purchase.

The Atherton Company was formed in 1659, with Humphrey Atherton, of Boston, John Winthrop, Jr., Edward Hutchinson, Jr., Richard Smith and others, mostly Massachusetts men. They obtained an Indian grant to a large tract north of Kingston. [112]

Elisha Hutchinson, William Hudson, Major Atherton and their associates acquired of the Indians a tract of more than five thousand acres on Boston Neck, above Wickford. Large tracts about Narragansett Bay were held by others on Indian grants. [148]

The Commissioners of the United Colonies, being opposed to Rhode Island, and playing into the hands of the Atherton Company, imposed a heavy fine upon the Niantic Indians, for an infraction by certain members of that tribe. Whereupon, for profit regardless of ethics, Humphrey Atherton and John Winthrop, Jr., proposed to the Indian sachems that they would pay the fine if the natives would give them a mortgage on their lands in the southwestern part of Rhode Island. This they did, and six months later the land grabbers foreclosed, and took the land. [63]

The location of Westerly was, in 1661, acquired of the Indians by Stanton and others of Newport. [159] Massachusetts and Connecticut people laid claim to land which had been settled on by Rhode Island people. Some of the settlers were arrested and taken to Boston, where they were imprisoned until they paid a fine. The Rhode Island authorities arrested some of their own citizens who favored the Connecticut claimants. [159]

Some Connecticut people obtained from the king, in 1662, a grant of all the land in Rhode Island, but it caused so great a protest by Rhode Island people that it was promptly revoked. Massachusetts and Connecticut officials continued to claim the land west of Narragansett Bay.

One year previous to the grant by Charles II in 1663, confusion in land titles in Rhode Island had become so great that a law was passed vesting the fee in whoever, having possession, should record his claim within thirteen months, if on the spot, or within two years if elsewhere. [3]

Dr. John Clarke being in England representing Rhode Island obtained from Charles II a grant of the Rhode Island land and government, dated July 3, 1663, from which the following are excerpts: [145]

"We do ordaine for us our heirs and successors that Roger Williams, William Codington, Benedict Arnold, Samuel Gorton [and twenty-two others named], and all others who shall be admitted and made free of the company, shall be for ever hereafter a body corporate and politique by the name of The Governor and Company of the English Colony of Rhode Island and Providence Plantations, in New England in America: and they and their successors shall have perpetual succession, and to possess lands and the same to lease, grant and sell and dispose of at their pleasure. There shall be one governor, one deputy-governor and ten assistants, to be elected out of the freemen of said company who shall apply themselves to care for the affairs of and concerning the lands herein granted. Benedict Arnold is appointed the first and present governor.

"And further for us our heirs and successors do give and grant unto the said governor and company and their successors all that part of our domain in New England containing the Narragansett Bay and country, and parts adjacent [bounds as at present], together with all lands, ports, rivers, fishings, mines, minerals, quarries and all other commodities, privileges and franchises whatsoever within said bounds (including Block Island), to have and to hold the same unto said company for ever upon trust for the use and benefit of themselves and their associates, freemen of said colony; their heirs and assigns.

"It shall not be lawful for our Rhode Island colony to invade the Indians within the colony. And it is declared unlawful (they having subjected themselves unto us, and being by us taken into our special protection) without the consent of the governor and company of Rhode Island for other colonies to invade or molest the Indians or any other inhabitants within the Rhode Island colony.

"Paying to us and our heirs, the one-fifth part of all gold and silver obtained; any late grant to the Connecticut colony to the contrary notwithstanding." The population of Rhode Island at that time may have been 2,500.

This grant gave all the land, water and minerals in Rhode Island to the twenty-six named, and all others they might admit to the company, to have and to hold unto the said company for ever upon trust for the benefit of themselves and associates, freemen of the colony.

All Rhode Island colonists were not legally freemen. The grantees named being freemen, this might have been interpreted as indicating that the grant was for the twenty-six named, together with any other freemen they might admit to the company.

However, it seems to have been interpreted as for the benefit of all in the colony, which showed more magnanimity than was ever shown by the royal grantees of land in other colonies. The

Rhode Island charter existed until it became the oldest constitutional charter in the world.

It was both a land grant and authority for establishing a system of government. A general assembly established under it confirmed, in 1682, being nineteen years after the initial settlement, titles to land in Newport, Providence, Portsmouth, Warwick and Westerly which had been previously obtained by Indian grants. Subsequently, early Indian grants in other towns were similarly confirmed.

From this it can be seen that Indian grants alone did not give legal title. Nor have they given legal title anywhere in the United States.

The general assembly stood for the public welfare in respect to land grants in Rhode Island, where Calvert, Penn, Carteret and other royal grantees stood for their personal profit in land grants in their respective proprietary colonies.

The provision in the Rhode Island charter by Charles II respecting protection of the Indians is exclusive with Rhode Island as amongst all the American colonies, and in all probability stemmed from the incessant advocacy by Roger Williams of friendship for the Indians. Such provision does not appear in the grant made by Charles of Connecticut the year previously, or to the Carolinas only three months previous to that of Rhode Island, or in the grant of the vast territory he made to the Duke of York the following year, or by the duke for New Jersey that same year; or by any other British monarch at any time.

Submission of the Narragansett Indians to the British crown apparently did not include submission of the Wampanoags under King Philip.

An "incursion and invasion of Indians" caused the council in Providence to appoint twenty prominent citizens, to command ten men each, to "scout, kill and destroy" them—those natives whom they had driven from their land and thus forced to desperation.

The war between Philip and the white settlers in and beyond Rhode Island, thirty-one years after submission of the Narragansetts, was the most frightful of any of the Indian wars in New England.

Within less than half a century after a wilderness had become a fixed settlement of English pioneers, a monetary value to land developed and squabbling about land ownership increased. There were disputes about titles in Providence and Pawtucket which caused suits, counter-suits and writs of ejectment. Improved land was held at £2 and £3, and unused land at 3s per acre. [12]

The general assembly enacted, in 1684, that all unallotted and common land within Portsmouth and Newport should be deemed to be the property of every freeman of said towns, subject to grant by the freemen in their public meetings. [124]

Upon revocation of the Edict of Nantes large numbers of Huguenots fled to the American colonies, and forty-five such families located at East Greenwich in 1686, on land held by the Atherton Company. Disputes about land titles, however, caused them to go elsewhere; [159] possibly because the Atherton Company held land only by Indian grant not yet confirmed by the assembly.

Sales of land at Pawtucket were made in 1716 at £3 per acre. [159] By 1724, being eighty-eight years after its settlement, practically all the land in Providence except a few desirable sites had been distributed. [124] The smaller landholders—mechanics and tradesmen—were disfranchised unless they possessed land valued at £200 or had an annual income of £10. [28]

Quoting Channing: [28] "The Narragansett country was the scene of the rivalries of two land companies and, besides, for half a century, it was a bone of contention between Connecticut and Rhode Island people. The first land speculators in the field were originally five in number—John Hull, of Boston, among them. They were, with that exception, Rhode Islanders, and they acquired Indian rights to the land about Pettasquamscot Rock with the full countenance of the Rhode Island authorities. Owing to the number of Indians whose consent was necessary they did not obtain a complete Indian title until 1660.

"The second, and most important company was composed of Humphrey Atherton of Boston, John Winthrop, Jr., of Connecticut and associates, who, with few exceptions, were all absentees—residents of Massachusetts or Connecticut.

"Atherton acquired of the Indians the lands about Smith's

trading house in Wickford, and a large tract through foreclosure of the Indian mortgage [previously mentioned]. Due to jurisdiction over the Narragansett country being claimed by both Rhode Island and Connecticut, a long and bitter contest ensued over the first of these purchases.

"But both purchases included the lands bought of Hull and associates and, after much dispute, the matter was amicably settled in 1679. According to a reliable tradition, the Smiths (father and son) owned at one time a tract of land nine miles by three miles, while Thomas Stanton is reputed to have acquired 'a lordship' of some four and a half by two miles and Colonel Champlain, a neighbor of the Stantons, owned two thousand acres. Tracts of five, six and even ten miles square existed.

"The Pettasquamscot purchasers seem to have sold their lands in moderately small parcels. Towards the middle of the eighteenth century land was acquired in one way or another by William Robinson, who is said to have held several thousand acres, while Robert Hazard is estimated by a descendant to have had as much as twelve hundred acres.

"As showing the iron grasp of the landed aristocracy on the government, the real estate of a debtor residing in Rhode Island could not be attached for debt. If a man died intestate his entire realty descended to his eldest son."

12

Vermont

JACQUES CARTIER, seeking a northwestern passage to the East Indies, sailed up the St. Lawrence River in 1535, to the present site of Montreal.

Sixty-eight years passed before another explorer, Samuel Champlain, aged about forty-two years, arrived in the St. Lawrence and, five years afterwards, in 1608, founded Quebec.

At the solicitation of a party of sixty Indians, Champlain and two Frenchmen, in twenty-four canoes, went on an expedition against the Iroquois, and to see the great lake told of by the natives; to which lake Champlain gave his name. They came to battle, supposed to have been near Ticonderoga, and the French used their arquebuses with deadly effect.

The French, in 1665, were the first settlers in Vermont. The King of France, in 1676, authorized grants of land in Canada which also extended into Vermont, and were based on the old feudal system of France; the seignior owing homage to the crown, and the tenants rendering fealty to the seignior. This system continued for 178 years, not being abandoned until 1854. [36]

Some of these grants were made to eminent French officers, without payment to the crown, but if they were not used they were to be relinquished. There were but few real settlements beyond the range of the guns of some French fortress—on the plea that settlers could not be obtained because of fear of Indian raids. [36]

Governor Fletcher, the royal British governor of New York,

in 1696 made to Godfrey Dellius, minister of the Dutch church
at Albany, and Commissioner of Indian Affairs, a grant of 840
square miles of land in New York and Vermont, for which
Dellius had obtained an Indian grant.

The Earl of Bellomonte, who succeeded Governor Fletcher,
regarded such large grants as an impediment to the settlement
of the country. He had the grant annulled, and Dellius suspended from the ministry, for "deluding the Mohawk Indians
in obtaining the grant." [39]

The general court in Massachusetts, claiming the land in 1716,
granted a hundred thousand acres in the southeastern part of
Vermont, but no use was made of the land until eight years
later, when a settlement was made at Fort Dummer, now Brattle-
boro. [27]

The Massachusetts court ordered the laying out of some townships in Vermont, six miles square, to be opened to the settlement of sixty families. Each settler was required "to build a
house at least eighteen feet square, and fence, plow and stock
five acres within three years." [36]

The French, in 1731, made a settlement in Vermont, at Addison
on Lake Champlain, opposite the village of Crown Point, which
the French had also established. Fort St. Frederic on the west
shore of the lake was, in 1742, considered the strongest French
fortress in America, with the exception of the one at Quebec. [36]

During the middle eighteenth century many persons began
coveting land in the Vermont region, which was claimed by the
officials of Massachusetts, New Hampshire and New York, the
last named asserting that its boundary, by grant of Charles II
to the Duke of York, extended east to the Connecticut River.

The grant by Charles II to the Duke, of all the lands between
the Connecticut River and the east side of the Delaware, was
inconsistent with the charters which previously had been granted
to the Massachusetts and Connecticut people, and it would not
bear strict examination. But upon this inadequate and blunder-
ing transaction of Charles the New York officials founded a
claim and hope of obtaining the lands in Vermont. [164]

New Hampshire claimed all territory to a line drawn north

and south twenty miles east of the Hudson River, north of the northern boundary of Massachusetts.

In 1749 Benning Wentworth was the royal governor of New Hampshire. A notorious land grabber, with an unbounded craving for land, he asserted the claim of New Hampshire to the Vermont region by making a grant of land six miles square, on which Bennington is now situated, twenty miles east of the Hudson River, and six miles north of the Massachusetts line.

This grant was divided into sixty-four equal shares or "rights," of 360 acres each, the grantees residing mainly in Portsmouth— the seat of government. None of them is known to have moved to Bennington. The first settlers to get land on which to build were obliged to buy of these speculative shareholders, and then to begin a lifetime of the severest toil and almost incredible hardship, to establish farm homesteads. Wentworth granted fifteen other townships, prior to interference of the French and Indian War.

After their defeat in 1654, the French abandoned their settlements in Vermont and about Lake Champlain, and retreated to Canada. Colonel Philip Skeen, a British officer, held large tracts of land granted to him along the lake. During the war, numerous bodies of troops passed and repassed through the fertile valleys of Vermont. Upon cessation of hostilities the soldiers, to whom the land had been promised as a reward for services in conquering the country from the French, were forgotten in the hasty covetousness of an avaricious governor. [7]

Wentworth, to protect his monopoly by means of strengthening his claim to Vermont, as against the claim of New York officials, began making grants with indefinite boundaries to both speculators and settlers.

In each of these numerous township grants, he reserved five hundred acres for himself. These reservations, and his fee of about $100 on each grant, brought him a large fortune.

Pioneers from Massachusetts, Connecticut and New Hampshire began settling in Vermont without license. There were vast areas of equally good land lying unused in all those colonies, but they were held by speculators at a purchase price which very few pioneers were able to pay. The settlers became so numerous that they formed towns, and obtained charters from the New York authorities, who coveted the fees for making land grants in Vermont.

Wentworth made not less than 129 township grants of land now in Vermont, mostly after the French War. They included: three tiers or rows of townships laid out along the west side of the Connecticut River for sixty miles; three tiers along a line approximately twenty miles east of the Hudson River, as far north as Poultney; and two tiers from this point north along the east shore of Lake Champlain, to the town of Highgate. [172]

The township grants were divided by the promoters into shares, each share representing 250 acres: one share to each grantee or promoter; two shares, equal to five hundred acres, for Wentworth; one share for the Incorporated Society for the Propagation of the Gospel in Foreign Parts; one share for a glebe for the Church of England; one share for the first settled minister, and one share for the benefit of a public school.

Other grants of six miles square, containing 23,040 acres, were issued divided among sixty-four shares, each representing 360 acres. Conveyance of the land to the individual shareholders was by drawing of lots—which assigned the portions to the holders and "to their heirs and assigns for ever." These proprietary shares were purchasable, much as stock in a corporation is purchasable. They were highly prized and became an object of speculation.

In some grants, a condition was that every grantee, his heirs and assigns, was to cultivate five acres for every fifty acres in his share, within five years, on penalty of forfeiture and regranting to others. But this was not enforced. The reason for these exactions was that the presence and activity of people would naturally enhance the value of the land, to the benefit of each other.

At the end of ten years, every landholder was to pay an annual land rent of one shilling per hundred acres. To whom this was payable, or for what purpose, is not clear, but it went, probably, to the public treasury. Before the rent-paying date arrived, the original land speculators had mostly disposed of their holdings, to settlers, or other speculators.

The grant by Wentworth, in 1761, of the town of Windsor, was obtained through the influence of Colonel Josiah Willard, who was a famous land speculator and absentee landholder in at least eighteen townships in New Hampshire and Vermont. There is little to show that the original grantees of Windsor had any desire to put to use the lands granted them. There is, however, much to show that they were mainly interested in holding the land as absentee proprietors, until the increase in population increased the demand for, and value of, the land, so they could sell at a profit. The records show that only nine of the fifty-nine grantees took any active part in the organization, and only three of them settled in Windsor. [172] Speculation dominated the situation.

Title to the land in Windsor was later disputed, which led to a long contest, compromised after eleven years by obtaining a grant from the New York authorities. To obtain this grant, the funds to pay the fee of approximately $2,300 demanded by the corrupt New York officials, were advanced by two men in New York. One of them received three thousand acres, or one-eighth of all the land in the township, and the other, eleven hundred acres; at an average cost of 56¢ per acre.

To check Wentworth and intimidate the settlers, and to reap the fees for making land grants, Cadwallader Colden, acting Royal Governor of New York, claimed jurisdiction as far east as the Connecticut River.

The Board of Trade and Plantations in England, in 1764, ordered that the eastern boundary of New York should be at the Connecticut River, in accordance with the grant by King Charles II to the Duke of York, ninety years previously. Whereupon, New York declared all the grants made in Vermont by Governor Wentworth of New Hampshire to be illegal. This brought forth a bold proclamation by Wentworth, a royal governor himself, that the aforesaid grant by King Charles to the Duke was obsolete.

The first grant issued by New York officials for land in Vermont was that of 1765, to twenty-six persons for twenty-six thousand acres at Princeton, on which fifty families had settled under a New Hampshire grant.

Most of these New York grantees were "dummies," and within three weeks, all but one had conveyed their holdings to three well-known land speculators. During the same year, Lieutenant-Governor Colden of New York granted ten thousand Vermont acres in one tract, and 151 military patents covering 131,800 acres. These grants took in portions of the grants previously made by Wentworth. Following these grants, Colden, in about one year, granted to various persons 603,000 acres in Vermont. [36]

The speculative craze for land in Vermont had become so intense by this time that, on September 27,1766, three Americans—Benjamin Price, Daniel Robertson and John Livingston—to obtain what would pass as tokens in the prevailing land gamble, paid to the heirs of M. Pierre Raimbault, 90,000 livres (equivalent to about $18,000) for the absolutely valueless grant of the seigniory of La Maunadiere made by the King of France ninety years previously. The seigniory fronted twelve miles on Lake Champlain and extended fifteen miles inland: on it, Burlington is now situated. [35]

Some of the Wentworth grantees of Vermont land sent three agents to England to seek of the king protection from the New York officials. As a result, Lord Shelburne of the Board of Trade, in 1767, wrote Governor Moore of New York that the king commanded that no new grants be made by New York officials in the disputed territory, "until you receive further orders." But the governor's term expired and his successor disregarded this order. Making grants at $2,000 to $2,500 for each township, was a lucrative business for the New York officials. [27]

The question of the validity of grants caused prolonged litigation in which ejectment proceedings were instituted by New York officials in 1770. Grants, including large areas to speculators, continued to be made by officials of both New York and New Hampshire, of the same land which each had granted to others.

In October, 1769, New Hampshire settlers resisted New York grantees, and two years later, to enforce the claim of New York, the sheriff and the militia were ordered to eject the settlers on the Vermont land granted by Wentworth. This move met with armed resistance, led by Ethan Allen (the first appearance in

Vermont history of this afterwards celebrated hero of the Revolutionary War). New York officials offered £15 reward for his capture. [164]

Nevertheless, Royal Governor Dunmore of New York made numerous grants of land in Vermont, aggregating 511,900 acres during 1771. The following year, two agents were appointed by Wentworth grantees to go again to London to petition the king to confirm the New Hampshire grants. [36]

Governor Tryon of New York, in one year, made grants in Vermont aggregating 542,450 acres, principally to his friends and dependents. These included judges of the courts, members of the colonial assembly, and prominent lawyers—all of them holding the land unused, until an increase in population should create a demand for it at increased prices. This, together with the large fees to the New York officials for deeds, accounts for the persistent claims of New York officials to the Vermont region.

The New York governor wrote the Board of Trade in London that the Board's restrictions against New York making grants in Vermont were "repugnant to the claims of persons who, from their numbers and connections, have a powerful influence" [36], and that, without any right whatever, people are swarming over the land between the Connecticut River and Lake Champlain. [50]

Colden again became royal governor of New York, and in three years granted 379,100 acres in Vermont. Ethan Allen and his cousin, Remember Baker, speculated in land, and in 1773 "acquired forty-five thousand acres fronting on Lake Champlain, and sundry lesser parcels," which they advertised for sale. In 1776 they held 60,829 acres, valued at $297,408.[a]

In 1774 agents of a group of farmers in Scotland arrived in America, for the purpose of buying land for a Scotch settlement. After inspecting land in several colonies, they bought seven thousand acres at Barnet, in Vermont, paying 14*d* (28¢) per acre. [36]

John Witherspoon, a Scotsman, and President of Princeton College in New Jersey, was quite a land speculator. In 1792, he exchanged 12,057 acres in Nova Scotia for 8,045 acres near Rye-

[a]Pell, in *Ethan Allen*.

gate, Vermont, where he already had 2,760 acres. It was a period of wild land speculation, in which all classes were engaged. [36]

The ouster proceedings continued until 1775; there were riots, culminating at Westminster in the killing of one man, and wounding of several others. But just then came news of the battle at Lexington, and the beginning of the American Revolution, after which the controversy about land grants was put aside. [164]

In addition to Wentworth's personal holdings of sixty-five thousand acres, he distributed numerous town lots and acreage tracts to members of his family, to friends, to high public officials and to other prominent personages, including a great many citizens of New York, some of whom were already large landholders in the latter province. Colonel Benjamin Bellows held between eight and nine thousand acres of land in Vermont and New Hampshire, including Bellows Falls. Vermont grants made by royal and vice-royal governors of New York, before and during the Revolutionary War, aggregated 2,418,710 acres; [36] totaling 40 per cent of the area of the state.

Robert Livingston of New York, who held thirty-five thousand acres of land in Vermont under a New York grant, was the presiding judge at the trial of suits to eject the Vermont settlers. The judge's brother-in-law, Duane, counsel for the plaintiff to oust the settlers, was largely interested in Vermont land through grants by New York officials, the title to which depended upon the decision in this suit. [36] Ethan Allen was an agent of the defendant settlers. Judgment was rendered against the settlers.

Names of many well-known New York families of today, such as van Cortlandt, De Lancey, Livingston, Schuyler, Stuyvesant, Teneyck, Jay and others, appear in the New York grants of Vermont lands. [36]

The ascendancy of these families in wealth and influence can be attributed to the land privilege, through which, in colonial days, they acquired choice locations of land at little or no cost. Constantly increasing population and development of the country made the tracts more valuable; and their estates were consolidated through intermarriages.

For many years before the American Revolution, the Vermont

region was known only as the "New Hampshire Grants." A convention in June, 1777, adopted the name Vermont.

Thomas Chittenden, first governor of the State of Vermont, was an active land speculator in at least forty-two town proprietaries created by the new state legislature. [172]

The remaining ungranted land was, by authority of the legislature, offered for sale. Companies of speculators formed to buy it were composed of stockholders in all parts of New England, and from as far away as Maryland.

Land speculation interfered with the success of colonization, and delayed actual settlement. [36] But land speculation, while it brought fortunes to a few, had repercussions for many in the usual disappointment, disaster and financial loss during years succeeding the boom collapse. Land was often sold at a fraction of a cent per acre at tax sales, for nonpayment of taxes.

13

New York

THE earliest recorded discoverer of the Hudson River was Jean Giovanni da Verrazzano, a Florentine, in the ship "Dauphine," in 1524, on a voyage of discovery for Francis I of France.

For many years following, Frenchmen sailed up the river as far as Albany, where they traded with the natives for peltries, and probably met other Frenchmen from Canada.

In July, 1609, the French explorer, Champlain, discovered the lake given his name, two months before Hudson sailed into the river to which his name is given.

Henry Hudson, an Englishman, had been in the employ of some British adventurers in a search for a northwestern passage, but the search having failed, his services were terminated. He went to Holland, and was engaged by the Dutch East India Company to go on a voyage of discovery to America. He was provided with the yacht, or vlei-boat, the "Half Moon," a Dutch vessel of forty lasts, with a crew of sixteen to twenty men of Dutch and English nationality.

A vlei-boat had two masts, and was so named from being built expressly for the difficult navigation of the Vlei and Trexel waters. A "last" was equivalent to two tons. [16]

He made the American coast, north of the Chesapeake Capes, and anchored in the Delaware Bay; thence to the Hudson River, which he entered on September 2, 1609.

The knowledge gained by Hudson on this voyage was afterwards transferred to the United New Netherland Company, organized in 1616, and then to the Dutch West India Company, chartered in 1621.

Returning to Holland, Captain Hudson put in at an English port and was there commanded not to leave England, but to serve his own country. The "Half Moon" was detained in England for eight months.

The following year, a Dutch vessel was sent to the Hudson with merchandise to trade with the Indians for furs, which proved profitable.

Broadhead [16] rejects the story that Argyle of Jamestown stopped at Manhattan Island in 1613, and found Dutch occupants, whom he ordered to leave the country.

A number of Dutch merchants petitioned the States General of the Netherlands, in 1614, for the privilege of making four voyages to America, agreeing to report any discoveries. License was granted.

Five vessels were fitted out by merchants of Amsterdam, and all arrived at Manhattan. Some sailed up the Hudson and found an old fort just below the site of Albany, on Castle Island, which had been erected by Frenchmen. After repairing it, and naming it Fort Nassau as a compliment to the family of the stadtholder, they equipped it with a dozen cannon and manned it with as many men.

One of the vessels, in command of Adrian Block, sailed easterly through Long Island Sound, and discovered the Connecticut River and Block Island. In another one, the "Fortune," Captain Cornelius Jacobson Mey sailed to the Delaware. He then with others—except Captain Hendrickson, who remained to make further explorations—returned to Holland, where they awakened interest in American trade.

Dutch merchants again petitioned the States General, and were granted the privilege of forming themselves into a company, "to exclusively navigate to the said newly discovered lands lying in America between Virginia and New France, between 40° and 45° North [Philadelphia and eastern Maine] for five voyages within three years."

Captain Thomas Dermer, an Englishman, employed by Sir Ferdinando Gorges and others, grantees of the land in New Eng-

land, on an exploring expedition of the New England coast
sailed through Long Island Sound into New York Bay in 1620,
in a small pinnace of five tons. It is asserted by those who dispute
that Argyle visited there seven years earlier, that Dermer's was
the first English vessel to put in at New York.

William Usselincx, a prominent Antwerp merchant, went to
Amsterdam to organize a West India Company to trade with
America. But the twelve years' truce between Holland and Spain,
the latter then mistress of the seas, proved an obstacle, until termination of the treaty of limitation, in 1621.

A Dutch charter, good for twenty-four years, with the privilege
of renewal, was granted that year to the Dutch West India Company, for the exclusive trading privilege with the Western
Hemisphere, and for making settlements in New Netherland,
the name the Dutch gave the North American region they were
exploring. The board of directors, denominated, "The College of
XIX," consisted of nineteen members, representing stockholders
in five cities.

The States General agreed to "give them for their assistance,"
sixteen ships of war and four yachts, to be manned and supplied
by the company. Anyone, anywhere, could subscribe for the
stock, and so eagerly was it sought that the subscription books
were closed within three weeks. [16]

This was the first Dutch company to combine trading and
colonization. The States General invested a million guilders
(guilders rated at 40¢), on the same basis as other subscribing
stockholders.

Quoting the Beards: [10] "There was no mistake about the
purposes of the West India Company, the principal object of
which was to earn dividends by trade; to carry on large mercantile operations in the Atlantic basin; prey upon Spanish commerce; conquer Brazil; carry slaves to American planters; reap
profits from traffic in furs and establish settlements."

On complaint of the Earl of Arundel, King James I, claiming
possession of America between Georgia and Maine, both inclu-
sive, remonstrated with the Dutch against Dutch vessels going
to America.

The only settlements the English had made in America, up to

that time, were one at Jamestown, Virginia, in 1607; one on the Kennebec River, Maine, the same year, which did not survive; and the Mayflower colony at Plymouth, Massachusetts, in 1620.

In 1623 the company sent the ship, "New Netherland," in command of Captain Mey, on an expedition to the Hudson and Delaware Rivers, with settlers and articles of trade.

A French vessel was found to be in the Hudson, and Captain Mey urged her departure. This year he moved the fort from Castle Island to Fort Orange. He served as the first director-general of New Netherland, for one year, and was succeeded by William Verhulst.

A contention arose in 1623 between the Dutch on the Delaware River and the English from Virginia (at this time the English had little, if any, knowledge of the Delaware). The Privy Council in England wrote the British ambassador in The Netherlands: "Whereas, his Majesty's subjects have many years since taken possession of the whole precinct and inhabited some parts of the north of Virginia (by us called New England) of all which countries his majesty hath by patent granted the quiet and full possession to particular persons," and the Dutch were asked to stop activities there and to forbid further settlement.

However, the Dutch claimed they had discovered the North (Hudson) and South (Delaware) Rivers, and besides, were occupying a region which had been left open by the English in the grants made to the two colonies in Virginia and Massachusetts. Confident of their superior strength in any maritime encounter with the English, the Dutch continued to develop their trade with the Indians, and fortified Manhattan Island, unconcerned at the English protests and the demand that they desist.

From this and other evidence, it will be seen that from the first the right of the Dutch to make settlements and to trade in America was disputed by the English, but constantly maintained by the Dutch.

David Pietersen de Vries, of Hoorn, tried in 1624 to obtain a French commission to trade in furs on the American coast, but was prevented by the Dutch West India Company. [128] In the Company's affairs in New Netherland he afterwards had an active part.

Peter Eversen Hulft, of Amsterdam, in 1625 shipped to New Netherland, at his own expense, horses, cattle, swine, and sheep, with seeds, plows and other implements for farming. The population of New Netherland was then two hundred. [128]

Peter Minuet, a native of Westphalia, arrived in Manhattan as the Dutch director-general in May, 1626, in the ship "Sea Mew," which was bringing a party of Walloons from Belgium and France. The Walloons settled on Staten Island, but afterwards moved to Long Island.

Minuet gave the Indians some miscellaneous merchandise, valued at sixty guilders (about $24), for the right to *occupy* the island, which contains twenty-two thousand acres. This transaction, which was made fifty-six years before the widely proclaimed purchase of land of the Indians by William Penn, has been repeatedly publicized as a purchase by the Dutch of all Manhattan Island for $24.

Early travelers and settlers in America have repeatedly stated that the Indians had no conception of private ownership, or purchase and sale, of land. It is thus inconceivable that they were, by that transaction, selling their birthright to the land in perpetuity. The prevailing belief that Manhattan Island was bought for $24 is fallacious, and the later occupancy of it by the white race was an assumption consummated by force. All existing land titles in New York run back to that force.

Having thus taken control of the land, the company in Holland, to attract settlers, offered all the land a settler could cultivate, at an annual land rent of one-tenth of the produce of the land and one-tenth of the increase of all livestock.

Two hundred acres would be allowed on those terms as a perquisite to any one bringing five persons of more than fifteen years of age. The company stipulated that land for the settlers must be leased or bought of the company, and not of the Indians. It could be assigned and willed by the settler, and must be used, or else forfeited. Forfeiture for non-use was a wise precaution which, had it been continued, would have been of incalculable benefit to each succeeding generation, down to the present time.

The company, with headquarters in Holland, soon found that

piracy upon Spanish vessels burdened with gold from Mexico and Peru, and upon Portuguese vessels with rich cargoes from India, promised quicker profits than trading with Indians, and colonization in America.

The Dutch in 1628 captured Spanish fleets, including nineteen galleons, from the Isthmus, and brought all except two vessels safely to Holland; the booty being valued at twelve million guilders. In two years they captured 104 Spanish prizes, and, in one year, paid 50 per cent dividends.

Nevertheless, the Indian fur trade in America was profitable to those who pursued it, and the company sent some ships to New Netherland for that purpose.

That the Dutch were energetic traders with the Indians is shown by the cargo of the ship "Arms of Amsterdam," which, four months after arrival of the Minuet colonists, sailed for Holland with 7,246 beaver skins, 853-1/2 otter skins, 81 mink skins, 36 wildcat skins and 34 muskrat skins. [115]

A close connection was maintained between the West India Company and the States General in Holland. Laws for New Netherland (America) were made chiefly by the Amsterdam Chamber of the Company in Holland, and were administered by Minuet, assisted by a council of five settlers appointed from Amsterdam.

Finding that few settlers were going to America, the States General at Amsterdam, in 1629, required of the West India Company that it expedite colonization in New Netherland.

One group of the directors advocated privateering and the peltry trade with the Indians as promising large dividends, while another group urged establishment of settlements at their own expense, provided they were granted certain "freedoms, or privileges." Thereupon, the College of XIX in Holland, approved by the States General, in 1629 revised the company charter to be the charter of "Freedom and Exemptions."

The charter created, from among the larger stockholders of the company, patroons, who were privileged to become large landholders within the jurisdiction of the company in America. The company reserved the right to the land and, from time to time, allotted to patroons large areas, with the minerals, rivers, and privileges of fishing, fowling, grinding of grain, and other rights, in consideration of the patroon transporting to the Hudson or Delaware, without four years, fifty settlers over fifteen years of age. Each patroon was to have as his "absolute proprietary," as an "eternal heritage," a tract of sixteen English miles along any navigable river, or eight miles on each side thereof, and "so far into the country as the situation of the occupier will permit." They were each empowered to hold civil and criminal courts, and to act as judges within their colony, and were legal heirs of all who died intestate in their respective patroonships. Patroons had many other feudal privileges.

Every adult settler was required to swear fealty to his patroon, and was bound to pay to the patroon an annual land rent in money, or one-tenth of the products of his labor; to obtain a license to hunt and fish; to have his grain ground at the patroon's mill; and to offer the sale of this grain first to the patroon. The patroons thereby completely controlled the immigrants they sent over and made them American serfs.

None of the colonists under the patroon, "either man or woman, son or daughter, man-servant or maid-servant," was allowed to leave the service of his patroon during the period for which he might be bound to remain, and the company in Holland pledged itself to do everything within its power to apprehend and deliver up every such colonist. [16]

The company reserved for itself the Island of Manhattan. This charter established a monopoly in land, as the previous one had in trade, and put the Hudson River largely in possession of those patroons who were favorites of the company officials. [16]

The company land policy chiefly concerned two types of grants: lordly patroonships of immense size, open to stockholders of the company, which offered unusual advantages to persons of great wealth, and smaller grants to the less opulent. [125]

For the benefit of the company's shipping, all industrial production was forbidden in the colony, on pain of banishment. No one was allowed to hold any lands that had not been previously derived from the company. [125]

Rich directors, forestalling humbler settlers, made prizes of the most valuable land, and with the company's policy of prohibiting manufacturing or other industrial enterprises, people had little inducement to emigrate to a new country against such heavy odds. [16]

It was provided that the patroons must deal with the Indians for the land which they acquired. [16]

The patroons were exempt from paying to the company for eight years any duty on imports, and their colonists were free from provincial taxation for ten years, other than the 10 per cent land rent to the patroon.

Pamphlets were printed and circulated in Holland and adjacent countries to induce immigration. But the policy of the patroons was so illiberal, and the people so disinclined to emigrate, that few settlers were attracted. [125]

Introduction of the feudal system into New Netherland was the most unfortunate result of the charter. [16]

Kiliaen Van Rensselaer, a diamond merchant in Amsterdam, and one of the directors of the West India Company, received a grant of land forty-eight miles by twenty-four miles in area, extending along both sides of the Hudson River, about Albany; being almost all of Albany and Rensselaer Counties, and part of Columbia County, for which he made terms with the Indians. He became patroon of the manor of Rensselaerwyck. He never came to America, being always an absentee holder. He sent some colonists, mostly well selected, and well provisioned with cattle and implements. But during the first sixteen years, only 216 colonists had been sent.

All settlers were bound under oath not to purchase any peltries of the Indians, under forfeiture of their goods and wages. Such privilege was expressly vested in a patroon, by the sixth article of the charter. [111]

A flour mill and a sawmill were early supplied. Colonists were required to pay certain rents and dues, "as may be defined by custom, contract or lease." The patroon did not sell land, whether wild or improved. He granted it only by lease, to be held so long as the land rent was paid. Some land was leased on one-third to one-half the produce. Some settlers rented bare land for a term of years, and erected buildings thereon, to become at the end of the lease the property of the patroon—a practice which, in addition to an annual land rent, continues in the City of New York, and some other places. For renewal of a lease there was paid, in one cited case, in addition to the customary tenth, six hundred guilders annual rent, and a quantity of butter, called toepact. [125]

Kiliaen van Rensselaer died in 1646. His vast land area was held intact by succeeding generations of the family for more than two centuries. He had been interested also in a patroonship in Delaware.

Minuet was recalled in 1632, and dismissed. He was eminently just, honorable and sensible, and friendly with the English in New England, who objected to the Dutch settlement. [47]

The Dutch ship, in which Minuet was returning to Holland with five thousand beaver skins for account of the company, was forced by stress of weather to put into Plymouth, England, and was there seized on the charge of trading in countries subject to his Britannic majesty. Directors of the West India Company presented a memorial to the States General for presentation to the King of England, in which they "attributed the seizure to the intrigues of the Spanish ambassador at London," and set forth the right of the West India Company to their North American possessions. The directors urged on the States General the propriety of instructing their ambassador at the British court to demand the release of the ship and goods, for, they reasoned, the natives of America are free; subject neither to the King of England, nor to their High Mightinesses, and at liberty to trade with whomsoever they pleased.

They insisted it was contrary to all law and reason for any power to prevent subjects of others to traffic in a country of which it never took actual possession, and title to which it never obtained from the right owners, the natives, either by conquest or purchase. Much less was it lawful to set up a claim to lands the propriety of which "the subjects of their Dutch High Mightinesses have obtained, partly by treaty with the Indian proprietors of the land, and partly by purchase."

The directors of the company demanded particularly that the States General maintain their sovereignty, the freedom of the seas, and the validity of those contracts which were entered into with distant Indian nations who, by nature, were independent of all, and had not been subjected to any power by conquest.

Copies of this vindication of the company's rights were ordered by the States General to be sent to the Dutch ambassador in England, who was at the same time informed that it was the determination of their High Mightinesses to maintain the right of the West India Company to trade with New Netherland.

A reply on the part of Charles I and the Lords Commissioners of England, in support of the British claim to lands of which the Dutch now had possession in North America, said: "It is denied, first, that the savages were possessors, *bona fide,* of those countries so as to be able to dispose thereof either by sale or gift, their habitations being changeable, uncertain and only in common. Secondly, it cannot be proved, *de facto,* that all the [Indian] nations of said countries were parties to the said pretended sale . . . His Britannic Majesty's interest will not permit him to allow them to usurp and encroach on one of his colonies of such importance."

This does not seem to have brought any rejoinder from the Dutch, other than that they continued to press for release of the vessel—which later was granted "without prejudice to his Britannic Majesty's rights."

Wouter van Twiller, a clerk in the company's office in Amsterdam, who had married a niece of Kiliaen van Rensselaer, and whose sister was married to one of the van Rensselaers, was appointed governor of New Netherland. He arrived in New Amsterdam in April, 1633, in the warship "Southberg," of twenty-one guns, and a crew of fifty-two. There were about 104 soldiers, the first military force to appear in New Netherland. [47]

Van Twiller, having power as governor-general to grant land, granted to himself and his friends in the council the best land in the colony, including Governor's Island, and two islands in Hellegat. [111] He and some of his associates obtained between ten and fifteen thousand acres in Brooklyn, and he became the largest landholder in New Netherland. [16] He granted to Roelot Jansen, sixty-two acres on Manhattan Island, north of Warren Street, which became immensely valuable. For private profit, large quantities of land on which numerous villages could have been established were granted. [111]

The patroons were granted large areas of land, but they sent scarcely any settlers. The fur trade was so profitable, and so many of the company employees, in defiance of regulations, were enticed to engage in it, that Negro slavery was early adopted.

The company itself introduced some settlers, but few remained. Had it filled the country, as did the English, with thousands of hardy pioneers, transported cattle, and encouraged towns, instead of building solitary forts to serve as rendezvous for lazy Indians and a few isolated settlers or traders, things would have been different. A disposition prevailed among almost all the employees of the company, to enrich themselves at the expense of their employers. Foreign companies never advanced the settlement of America. [111]

With English settlements on the north, and Swedish settlements on the south, progress of the Dutch colony was slow. The States General, after a gesture of taking over the province, demanded a more vigorous policy in colonization. [125]

The Dutch, by reason of their settlement at Fort Orange (Albany) on the Hudson, Saybrook and Hartford on the Connecticut, and their fort and previous settlement on the Delaware, claimed, as New Netherland, all the land and water in the intervening territory, extending from the mouth of the Connecticut River to Albany, and thence to the Delaware Capes.

De Vries returned to New Netherland in 1638, with several immigrants who settled on his land on Staten Island. But the colony was molested by Indians, and De Vries himself settled on sixty acres along the Hudson River, fifty-two miles above Fort Amsterdam.

At Rusdorp, Long Island, it was ordered, "no one shall ingross into his hands two home lots, and if any doe contrary, they shall sell one of ym to such person as the town shall approve." [158]

William Kieft, an active, inquisitive and rapacious person, succeeded van Twiller as governor. [16] He arrived in 1638, on a man-of-war "carrying two metal, sixteen iron and two stone guns." During his administration of nine years Kieft expanded the Dutch area into the Connecticut River Valley, and on Long Island west of Oyster Bay. He granted land near Corlaers Hook, on Manhattan, to Andries Hudde.

The patroons, desiring to enlarge their "privileges," presented to the States General demands that they be allowed to monopolize more land, be vested with larger feudal powers, be supplied with convicts from Holland as servile laborers, and with Negro slaves, and that all "private persons" and poor immigrants be forbidden to take up land except from patroons. [16]

These grasping demands of the patroons were offensive to the States General. But reserving them for future consideration, the council determined to open up free competition, with certain reservations, for trade in New Netherland. Public notice was given by the Amsterdam Chamber that all persons of friendly countries might freely convey to New Netherland, "in the company ships," any merchandise and domestic animals, paying to the company import and export duties of 10 to 15 per cent.

The company, in 1638, abolished the monopoly of trade which it had enjoyed for sixteen or seventeen years, and the prohibition against manufacturing; and other new regulations were established. The only exclusive privilege retained by the company was the right to carry settlers and supplies. No person was, henceforth, allowed to hold any land which had not been derived from the company. Land granted by the company "shall remain the property of the grantee, his heirs and assigns, provided that he shall pay the company the tenth of all produce therefrom, including livestock, after it shall have been four, afterwards ten years, pastured or cultivated. Failing to pay, the land shall be forfeited with a penalty, for which his successors or assigns shall be holden." [111]

Farms, fully equipped with improvements, implements and livestock, were offered on six years' lease, at a yearly rental of a hundred guineas ($40) and eighty pounds of butter. This encouraged immigration.

Now that there was easier access to land, New Netherland became filled with life and activity. Some wealthy men arrived from Holland; some also, as their terms of service expired, came from tobacco plantations of Maryland and Virginia, and intro-duced cultivation of tobacco. Farmers also came from Europe, until eighteen nationalities were represented. [111]

Cornelius Meylyn, an Antwerp merchant, who had been in New Netherland and returned to Holland, obtained from the directors, while in Holland, an order for Staten Island. He re-turned to New Netherland with his wife, children, servants and a thousand guilders ($400). In 1642 letters-patent for a patroon-ship of all Staten Island, except the bouwrie of Captain De Vries, were issued to him. [111] But an Indian war dashed his hopes, and seventeen years later he sold out to the company. [125]

Following is the form of deed to land by Kieft, in 1638: "We, the Director and Council of New Netherland, residing on the Island of Manhattan in Fort Amsterdam, under authority of the High and Mighty Lords, the States General of the United Netherlands, and the General Incorporated West India Com-pany, at their chambers at Amsterdam: By these presents do publish and declare, that pursuant to the Liberties and Exemp-tions allowed on the seventh day of June A.D. 1629, to Lords Patroons, of a lawful, real and free proprietorship, we have granted, transported, ceded, given over and conveyed, and by these presents We do grant, give over and convey to, and for the behoof of ——————, a piece of land containing ——— morgens, situated . . . on condition that he, and his successors, shall acknowledge their High Mightinesses, the managers afore-said, as their sovereign lords and patroons, and shall render at the end of the tenth year after the actual settlement and cultiva-tion of the land, the just tenth part of the products with which God may bless the soil, and from this time forth, annually."

Prosperity prevailed. Bouwries were located, and the number of them increased from seven to more than thirty, "as well stocked with cattle as any in Europe." [16]

A bouwrie was a farm on which a family lived. A plantation was land which was partly cultivated, but on which no one dwelt. [111]

Numerous Dutch grants were made to adopted citizens, among them two hundred acres opposite Coney Island to Anthony Jan-sen, a French Huguenot, and another to George Holmes (who four years previously had led the English expedition from Virginia against the Dutch on the Delaware) for joining his former companion, Thomas Hall, who had previously deserted the English expedition. [16]

Eleven years after the charter of Freedom and Exemptions was granted, it was revised, and the size of the land grants was reduced to four miles along any navigable river and eight miles into the interior. These charters created class divisions and, through them, there was transplanted from Europe to New Netherland a system of "feudal land tenure." Consequently, a landed aristocracy arose, with all its feudal honors, and with feudal burdens upon those then living, or who might later come within its sphere.

Ownership of many of these large patroon tracts in New York State was confirmed by the English governors, after the English took possession of the country, thus continuing this feudal land system.

Some Connecticut people, in 1640, acquired Indian rights to land at Southold, on Long Island.

At the request of Charles I, the Council of New England, in 1635, granted all of Long Island to William Alexander, Earl Stirling, the secretary of state for Scotland. Shortly thereafter, Stirling gave a power of attorney to James Farrett to dispose of his land, in whole or in part, as would most conduce to profit. Pecuniary gain, to obtain wealth without work from absentee landholding, was the base motive.

Fellow countrymen in Scotland were reluctant to migrate, and English settlers were drawn from New England. Farrett made grants on land-rent terms. In one case, the annual rent for eight square miles was four bushels of best Indian corn. All traces of these grants have disappeared. [24]

Farrett selected for himself Shelter Island and Robbins Island, in Peconic Bay. Previous to Farrett's arrival, Lion Gardiner, the Dutch commandant at Saybrook, had procured from the Indians what is now known as Gardiner's Island, being three thousand acres, and this was confirmed by Farrett at a land rent of £5 annually to Lord Stirling.

Farrett later visited Manhattan and, in the name of Lord Stirling, boldly laid claim to all Long Island. He placed a party of settlers from Massachusetts on land at Manhasset, whereupon, Kieft sent a sergeant and twenty soldiers to arrest them for tearing down the Arms of The Netherlands. After a hearing at Fort Amsterdam, they were released.

Farrett was determined to sell land on Long Island, and relocated the Manhasset colony on a tract between Shinnecock Bay and the easternmost end of Long Island, extending from the Atlantic Ocean to Long Island Sound; the consideration was £400.

Lord Stirling died heavily in debt, shortly after the unsuccessful attempt of Farrett to take possession of the western portion of the island. Farrett, as agent, then gave a mortgage of £110 on all the remaining land, payable in three years. The mortgage not being paid, the land was forfeited in 1644 to some men in Connecticut. [24]

Stirling's widow, Maria, determined, notwithstanding, to maintain her title, gave a power of attorney to Andrew Forrester of Dundee, Scotland. With this power of attorney, she sent him to America, commissioned as governor of Long Island. Stuyvesant, who had succeeded Kieft, ordered his arrest and sent him to Holland. The ship putting in at an English port, Forrester escaped and did not renew the claim. [111]

Following the Restoration of King Charles II in 1660, Henry, the fourth Earl of Stirling, revived his inherited claim to Long Island. Two years later the Duke of Clarendon negotiated a purchase of the territory for the Duke of York, for £3,500, which, however, the duke never paid. In lieu, twenty-eight years later, he granted the earl a pension of £300 per annum, to be paid from the surplus revenue of the province of New York. But there was no surplus revenue. Attempts to renew the Stirling title and claim continued during the nineteenth century but always met with failure. [24]

Gardiner held his island for twenty-four years, at an annual rent of £5, payable to the estate of Lord Stirling. After the English conquest of the Dutch in 1664, his son David held it of the Duke of York, first at £5 annually, then for a lamb, and in 1686 it was confirmed to him by Governor Dongan, as a manor. A rent in money continued to be paid the duke until 1789, except during the American Revolution.

About three centuries after Gardiner obtained possession, the island, abounding in game, was, in 1927, under lease as a game preserve. In that year, a descendant of Lion Gardiner sold the island to Jonathan T. Gardiner, receiving in payment a purchase-money mortgage for $345,000; an accretion in value created, not by the Gardiners, but automatically, by the mere increase in population and development of America. This, and all similar accretions rightfully belong to the public, and should be paid into the public treasuries.

The land between the Harlem and Bronx Rivers was taken up by Jonas Bronck in 1641.

The population of New Amsterdam, in 1643, was possibly twenty-five hundred persons. Allowing four hundred additional about Rensselaerwyck and a few towns on Long Island, the entire population of New Netherland, aside from Delaware totaled about three thousand, made up of eighteen nationalities. [111]

A tract at Throgs Neck was, about 1643, settled by thirty-five English families, led by John Throgmorton.

The West India Company stated that the country had, from 1626 to 1644, cost the company more than half a million guilders, over and above the returns from there. Nevertheless, they were "hopeful of the future." [111]

Kieft granted land to the town of Gravesend, Long Island, in 1645. The following year he was removed as governor and sailed for Holland, but the ship, with eighty persons, was lost.

The Dutch military operations in Brazil ended disastrously to the Dutch in 1643, and they retreated to the Island of Curaçao, whence 130 soldiers were sent to Manhattan. The company became bankrupt.

Rev. Francis Doughty, one of the first Presbyterian ministers in America, [60] while preaching at Cohasset, Massachusetts, in 1642, was dragged from the assembly, for venturing to assert that "Abraham's children should have been baptized." He thereupon moved to New Netherland, and founded Maspeth, near Newtown, Long Island, where Kieft had granted him and his associ-

ates thirteen thousand acres. This settlement was shortly thereafter destroyed by Indians. Doughty afterwards returned there,
and would not permit any one to build, except upon extraordinary terms of purchase or rent.

Several Negroes and their wives, originally captured from the
Spaniards, were, during 1644 and the following two years, manu-
mitted for long and faithful services. They were granted land,
but were bound to pay to the landholder, yearly, twenty-two
bushels of corn, wheat, peas or beans, and one fat hog; failing
to do so, they would lose their land and be returned to their
former servitude. But all children born to them, before or after
their freedom, were to serve the company as slaves. The deten-
tion of the children in slavery was highly disapproved of by the
people, who considered it a violation of the law of nature. [111]

The price of a Negro at that time is stated as having averaged
between the equivalent of $100 and $150, though, only ten years
previously, the price was stated as forty florins, or $16.

The rich and fertile lands of Katskill were, in 1646, granted
by Kieft to Cornelius Antonissem van Slyck, of Brooklyn, in perpetuity, in consideration of his having brought about a general
peace with the Indians thereabouts, and his ransoming of prisoners from the Indians. For similar services, Kieft had granted to
Adriaen van der Donck a large tract, bounded by the Hudson
and Bronx Rivers and the Sawkill and Spuyten Duyvil, on which
Yonkers is located. But it was held unused on speculation many
years.

Van der Donck wrote an enticing description of New Netherland which was circulated in various parts of Europe, and attracted settlers from different countries, including England, and
also from some of the American colonies.

The right of pasturage on unused land was practiced in New
Netherland.

Isaac Jacques, a French Jesuit, and the first Roman Catholic
priest in New York State, wrote of New Netherland in 1646:
"This country is bounded on the New England side by what
they call the Fresch [Connecticut] River which serves as a
boundary between them and New England. The English settlers, however, come very near to them, choosing to hold land

under the Hollanders, who provide them with horses, cows and provisions, repayable at ease; and as to land, after ten years he pays the West India Company the tenth of the produce which he reaps. The English exact land rent, and would fain be absolute.

"Rensselaerwyck is a fort on the west side of the Hudson River [Albany] where there are about one hundred persons and some twenty-five or thirty houses. In the principal house lives the patroon's agent. Houses are of boards. A sawmill saws pine lumber. They found some pieces of good land, cleared by the Indians, in which they sow wheat and oats for beer, and for their horses, of which they have many."[a]

General Peterus Stuyvesant, who had been appointed director-general of New Netherland, Island of Curaçao, Buenaire and Aruba, arrived in North America in May, 1647. He was a Frieslander, son of a clergyman, and had been trained in military service. While governor of the Dutch colony in the West Indies, three years previously, he had lost a leg in an unsuccessful encounter of the Dutch with the Portuguese, on the Island of St. Martin. Sculptors and painters of more recent times have been puzzled as to whether it was the right or left leg.

At the beginning of Stuyvesant's administration, there were between 250 and 300 men in, and around, New Amsterdam and Rensselaerwyck, capable of bearing arms. This would indicate a population of two thousand. [111]

"A fourth-part of the city of New Amsterdam consisted of grog shops and houses where nothing is to be got but tobacco and beer." Drunkenness and broils were of common occurrence. The people were "approaching a savage state." The church, which had been commenced five years previously, remained unfinished. Director Kieft had applied to his own use public funds which had been appropriated to aid its completion. Money subscribed for a school house was misappropriated. Such was the state of affairs when Stuyvesant assumed the government. [111]

The country between Rensselaerwyck and Manhattan, on both sides of the river, then remained a wilderness, and most of the lots already granted in New Amsterdam remained in their virgin

[a]Jacques Papers

condition. All lot holders were directed to improve them within nine months, or, in default, they would be assigned to those who would improve them. [111] It was ordered by the governor and council that no house should be roofed with straw or reeds, and no chimney be made of shingles or wood.

The Thirty Years' War in Europe, ended by the treaty of Munster in 1648, forever rid Holland of the domination of Spain.

Lord See and others, in 1649, bought a tract of thirty thousand acres, including land on which Easthampton, Long Island, is situated, and four years afterwards built a house there.

A convention of settlers at Manhattan petitioned for a "suitable burgher government," and for the right to trade along the entire Atlantic coast, and to the West Indies and Europe. The directors, sitting in Holland, resented this attempt to shake off their rule, and declared they must have recourse to God, to nature, and the law. They instructed Stuyvesant "to proceed against such malignants in proportion to their crime."

Within two years after the arrival of Stuyvesant, there was public complaint that, "director-general Stuyvesant was everything; that he governed the country, had breweries, several shops, was part owner in ships and a trader in both lawful and contraband goods." A memorial was addressed to the States General pleading that they take the province under their safeguard. The administrations of both Kieft and Stuyvesant were severely criticized. [16]

The pledge which the patroons exacted from the colonists, not to appeal from their individual judgments to the court of New Netherland, was held to be a crime.

Mulford [105] wrote: "The principal directors of the West India Company, in the character of patroons, secured almost a monopoly of the land. To the mass of actual settlers nothing whatever was given. The charter allowed a kind of feudal or manorial rule, by which the colonists would be held in a state of complete dependence. No provision was made for the division of lands, either present or prospective. The people sent by the patroons were regarded, and were to be controlled, by the owners of the land as a servile class. They were to become American serfs. No plan could have been devised less calculated either to benefit adventurers, or to promote the interests of the province. By this mistaken policy the foundation was laid for social and civil distinctions which have not been effaced to the present hour, and which have always continued to act as a cause of irritation and a bar to general improvement.

"The charter gave liberty to private adventurers to select land. Yet these individuals were subjected to many disadvantages when acting by the side of the patroons who, from their special privileges, were enabled to exert a controlling influence."

Proposals were made, in 1650, to convey from Holland to New Netherland three or four hundred orphans, and "every person seemed inclined to proceed thither." Already two hundred farmers and field laborers had embarked and "six times that number" were ready to accompany them, but there were no ships. A vessel was chartered to carry two hundred. The company offered to transport families to America who were unable to pay passage, to be re-paid in double the amount in four years. [111]

All the inhabitants of the United Provinces and neighboring countries were free to proceed to New Netherland and obtain there, "under land rent or feudal tenure in fee," as much land as they could cultivate, provided they entered on the improvement within a year, or in default, be deprived of it. [111]

Edmond Wood and others, in 1650, acquired of the Indians land extending across Long Island, on which Islip is situated, and also land in other parts of the island. Three years later, the Rev. William Leverich and others obtained Indian consent to about twenty thousand acres at Oyster Bay; the object being an extensive land speculation.[b]

Contracts for land on Manhattan Island had become so frequent that, to guard against fraud, it was ordered that all sales of land should be void unless approved by the director and council.

An agreement made at Hartford, in 1650, between the Dutch and the English settlers on Long Island, stipulated that a direct line, run from the westernmost part of Oyster Bay to the ocean, should be the bounds between the English and the Dutch. The eastern part was to belong to the English, and the western part

[b]Armbruster, Hist. Long Island

to the Dutch. The bounds on the main land were to begin at the west side of Greenwich Bay, about four miles from Stamford, and so run north twenty miles, provided that the line come not within ten miles of the Hudson River.

Beeren Island, in the Hudson River below Fort Orange, was in 1650 fortified by the agent of the Rensselaerwyck patroon, who exacted a salute and toll of five guilders from all passing vessels. But the Amsterdam Chamber notified the director-general that the river must be kept open for free trade. [16]

Jean Baptiste van Rensselaer, recorded as a younger half-brother of the patroon, and agent of the estate, appears to have been the first of that family to visit America. He issued an order, in 1651, that all the inhabitants of his patroonship should take the oath of allegiance to the patroon and his representative.

The first English Navigation act, passed in 1651, deprived the Dutch of a large part of their shipping and caused great hardship, especially to the Virginia tobacco growers, as two-thirds of the trans-Atlantic carrying trade had been hitherto in Dutch vessels. This was largely the cause of the war between England and Holland, which began the following year, and interrupted Dutch immigration to New Netherland.

Notwithstanding that all persons were forbidden by the company to buy land of the Indians on pain of forfeiture, Indian grants were being acquired in the wilderness, not for improvement but for speculation, to be held at ransom against later arriving settlers.

Some of the Rensselaer settlers, desiring to escape the feudal restrictions of the manor, settled on an Indian tract near Esopus, in 1652. The same year William Beekman purchased Corlears Hook for 750 guilders ($300).

During the first five years of Stuyvesant's administration, not a single bouwrie was planted on Manhattan. Large tracts of land were granted to favored persons, to the great injury of the province. [16]

To check the increasing desire for large tracts of land, to be held unused on speculation, the company issued new regulations. Recent purchases of land from the Indians, made by van Twiller and others on Long Island, by van Slechtenhorst at Katskill and

Claverack, and by van der Capellen about Navesink, were declared void. [16]

The land rent of a tenth of the produce, which became applicable after the land had been in cultivation for a decade, attracted little attention from either the authorities or the landholders, until the time drew near for its collection, in the early 1650's. When collection was attempted, the thrifty pioneers found many arguments for delay. Population being sparse, and unused land plentiful, the returns were meager.

New Amsterdam (Manhattan) was granted municipal status in 1653. By means of a loan—the first public debt contracted in the Dutch provinces—the city was partially enclosed. The Wall Street wall was finished, but the fort was still unrepaired. [111]

To repay this loan, an annual surtax of twenty stivers was levied on every morgen (two acres) of arable land, in addition to the regular tenth. Subsequently the land speculators brought about a reduction to ten stivers, by levying 5 per cent per annum on rents of houses [112]—which was a retrogression in tax policy to the disadvantage of householders.

A convention of delegates from several towns was held at New Amsterdam to set forth the will of the people. The demands of the convention were met by threats of arbitrary punishment by Stuyvesant. "We derive our authority," he said, "from God and the West India Company. The company," he added, "has no regard to the will of the people, and let them no longer indulge in the visionary dream that taxes can be imposed only with their consent." This detached the people from their government, and afterwards reconciled them to submitting to English jurisdiction.

During the Cromwell government in 1654, a treaty of peace at Westminster terminated the war between Holland and England, and virtually conceded New Netherland to Holland.

During the attack of the Dutch on the Swedes along the Delaware, in 1655, the Indians made war against New Netherland, provoked because a squaw was killed in New Amsterdam for stealing peaches. It extended to Pavonia, Hoboken and Staten Island; being a repetition of the experiences at Pavonia twelve years previously.

Thomas Pell, an Englishman, without asking permission of the government at New Amsterdam, in 1655, acquired land of the Indians at about what became Pelham Manor, and began to colonize. Stuyvesant protested, and ordered Pell to "depart with your people, servants, slaves, furniture, cattle, implements and every article of property you and your nation have brought hither, or take the consequences"; to which Pell gave no heed.[c]

The Dutch, after the conquest of the Swedes, had besides New Amsterdam, two settlements on the Hudson River, Oostdorp in Westchester, eight villages on Long Island, and the entire Delaware River below the Schuylkill.

Vigorous efforts were begun in June to collect the tenths. An ordinance warned people who, "by patent or deed are liable for tenths," not to move their crops from the harvest field without first compounding for them with the provincial officials; or otherwise be subject to arrest.

Directors of the company were disinclined, after 1657, to make grants like the Rensselaerwyck patroonship.[d]

The Indian massacre of 1655 was a blow to Staten Island and adjoining New Jersey. Van der Capellen was, however, determined not to abandon his claim to the island. To remove any dissatisfaction among the natives, a treaty of peace was made and the island was purchased anew for ten guns, ten staves of lead, thirty pounds of powder, also shirts, stockings, kettles, cloth and other merchandise. [111]

When the directors at Amsterdam learned of this, they instructed Stuyvesant to declare the sale null, to obtain a transfer of the land from the savages to the company, and reconvey to van der Capellen as much of it as he might require, which was one-third of the island.

Land between Gowanus and Conyen (Coney) Island, which was granted in 1652 to Cornelius vanWerckhoven, of Utrecht, Holland, and had been abandoned after his death, lay waste for five years until his executor applied for its erection into a town. This was done and the name "New Utrecht" given it. The inhabitants declared they needed meadow land near Coney Island,

[c]Hartford Records
[d]N. Y. Col. Doc.

which was granted, and after dividing it into twenty-four parts, the twenty-four settlers there, who already had land, drew lots for it. [44] This division promoted land speculation and, after three years, the place contained only twelve houses.

The director and council in 1658 formed the village of New Haerlem in the northern part of Manhattan Island, allowing each inhabitant about forty-two acres for tillage and about fourteen acres of pasture land, subject to a land rent payable to the company after the fifteenth year. [111] The southern boundary was, roughly, a line drawn from the Hudson River just above Grant's Tomb at 129th Street, southeasterly to the East River at the foot of East 74th St. Andreas Hudde married, and was granted land there. [120]

To reduce the number of vacant lots in New Amsterdam, an annual surtax of the fifteenth-of-a-penny was levied in 1658 on the value of unimproved land in the city. [112] A tax of twelve stivers per morgen (two acres) was the same year levied on land, for support of a minister. Stuyvesant announced: "All who do not consent to this order are to dispose of their property and quit the town." [111]

The Massachusetts colony, whose charter was granted eight years later than that of the Dutch West India Company, claimed in 1659 the land in New York north of 42° N. lat. (on a line with the southern boundary of Massachusetts), from the Atlantic to the Pacific, and granted land opposite the Dutch Fort Orange (Albany) to several English inhabitants in that region.

They proposed making a settlement for trading with the Indians. To circumvent them, Stuyvesant bought the land of the Indians and wrote the directors in Holland to send immediately a colony of Polish, Prussians, Lutherans, Dutch or other Flemish peasants. The English, exercising influence in Holland, sought the right of passing along the Hudson River. But Stuyvesant remembered that twenty-three years previously the English had asked, and been granted, free passage along the Fresch (Connecticut) River, past the Dutch fort at Saybrook. Acting with that permission, the English finally usurped not only the beaver trade but the entire river and, after a while, all the land between the Connecticut River and Manhattan Island. Stuyvesant was determined to oppose a repetition of that game.

The general court at Boston sent commissioners to Stuyvesant, to whom they described their bounds, and claimed the upper Hudson, "though the Dutch perhaps may have intruded within the same." They asserted their intention to settle on the land therein not actually in possession of the Dutch. Stuyvesant reminded them that, "the Hudson was discovered by Henry Hudson in the *Half Moon,* in the service and at the expense of the Dutch East India Company in 1609, which transferred it to the West India Company in 1623—two years before Charles I ascended his throne; that it had been navigated by the Dutch for more than fifty years; that the States General had granted a patent to the West India Company, with power to make grants to their subjects; that the government of Massachusetts had forgotten either accidentally or deliberately to mention the date of their patent, but it is well known from history that the late English monarch from whom they claim a patent did not grant their patent until eight years after the Dutch grant. The appellation of 'intruder' can consequently, with more justice, be applied to those who themselves now endeavor to intrude within the Dutch limits, and who 'intruded' and settled between the Fresch and Hudson's Rivers, on Dutch territories, secured by Dutch forts, many years before one single Englishman had possessed any land between those two rivers."

Stuyvesant added: "The Dutch cannot grant to Massachusetts or to any other government any title to trade on their rivers, or a through passage thereon, without a surrender of their honor, reputation, property and blood, their bodies and lives." The revolution in England, which restored the Stuart monarchy, interrupted further contentions.

A number of children from orphan asylums in Holland arrived in New Amsterdam in 1659, and were "bound out" for from two to four years, at from forty to eighty guilders a year. [111]

There seem to have been no Europeans at Esopus until 1652. Seven years afterwards Dutch soldiers killed some Indians there, which led to retaliation. Ensign Smith, with forty soldiers, went into the interior, where he captured twelve natives and took a quantity of grain and peltries. Following the example of the New England people twenty-three years previously, Stuyvesant ordered the prisoners to be transported to the West Indies and sold as slaves. The remaining red men never forgot their exiled people and exacted severe retribution. When hostilities finally ceased, terms of peace provided, as was usual in peace treaties between Europeans and the natives, that "all the lands of Esopus" were conveyed to the white race. The aborigines were forced farther into the interior, remote from their marine food supply.

A grant of Coney Island was made in 1661 to Dirck de Wolff, an Amsterdam merchant, to make salt, but operations had scarcely begun when the settlers at Gravesend, who had recently drawn from a hat deeds to the unused island, destroyed the salt works, to the public injury. Several Frenchmen began that year the settlement of what is now Bushwick, in Brooklyn. [111]

Melyn surrendered to the company, for fifteen hundred guilders, all his rights as a patroon on Staten Island. The company also bought all the claims of van der Capellen to Staten Island, by which the Company then became possessed of the entire island. [16] By these transactions, Staten Island became disenthralled from feudal lords for the remainder of the Dutch rule. [111] Thereupon the company made grants to various persons, among them several French Waldenses and Huguenots from Rochelle.

Some of the land grants made in New Netherland by the Dutch, mostly for large areas, and some farms and lots, are listed by O'Callaghan. [111]

John Scott, a bold, unscrupulous adventurer, who had been dismissed from the English royalist army for misdemeanor, and afterwards was on the Cromwellian side, later migrated to Connecticut. [47] The Restoration of Charles II had attracted to England several prominent American colonists, among them, this John Scott. Scott petitioned the king to bestow upon him the government of Long Island, of which he claimed to have "purchased of the Indians near one-third part of the land." The application of Scott for possession of the island is probably what prompted the Duke of York to purchase Long Island of the Earl of Stirling at that time.

Scott returned to America in December, 1663, and was received with favor at New Haven. The people endeavored to engage his assistance in procuring for them a patent for the lands they had so often striven to possess at Salem on the Delaware. But Scott's main object now was to promote his personal interests on Long Island, on which two-thirds of the people were English. [148] Some of the towns there invited him to "come and settle" their troubles, and empowered Scott "to act as their President."

At the head of 170 men, Scott set out to reduce the neighboring Dutch villages; and many Dutch families were obliged to abandon their homes. [16] However, upon charges being brought against him by Governor Winthrop in Connecticut, he was arrested and imprisoned. But more of him later.

The West India Company directors in Holland expressed a desire in 1664 to obtain a cession of the Mohawks' lands in New York; "by which our English neighbors would be prevented from dispossessing the company of its immense beaver trade."

While wampum was almost exclusively the medium of exchange, beaver skins were the standard of value in New Amsterdam, just as tobacco was the standard in Maryland and Virginia.

Holland was crowded with refugee Huguenots, Waldenses, Norwegians and Germans. Many of the better class from Rochelle were desirous of emigrating to New Netherland at their own expense, and large sums were appropriated for vigorous prosecution of colonization.

Stuyvesant stated that the company had expended on the province 1,200,000 guilders more than it had received; an increase in the deficit of 800,000 guilders in the foregoing twenty years. The population of New Netherland in 1664 was "full ten thousand." New Amsterdam (Manhattan), with an air of prosperity, contained fifteen hundred, composed mostly of Hollanders, Walloons, Waldenses, Huguenots, Norwegians, Swedes, and English. [16]

While Stuyvesant was endeavoring to stay the encroachments of the English settlers from New England, the internal conditions of New Netherland were becoming more and more alarming. The colony now appeared to be in such jeopardy that a "Landtdag" was summoned, composed of elected representatives.

To strengthen the fort and increase the military force and to "instil fear into any envious neighbors," a public loan of nearly thirty thousand guilders was subscribed at 10 per cent.

An Indian attack at Wiltwyck, near Kingston, in which seventy Indians were slain or captured; an expensive Indian war; the invasion of Dutch territory by people from Connecticut; the revolts of English villages on Long Island; and the exhaustion of the public treasury showed the situation was perilous.

The West India Company, then in bankrupt condition, alarmed at rumors of pending English aggression, called on the City of Amsterdam, Holland, for assistance, and on the States General for three hundred soldiers and a ship of war. But van Gogh, the Dutch ambassador at London, reported that King Charles constantly protested that "he would not in any way violate his aliance with the Dutch," and the States General, wishing to give no undue umbrage to England, refused the company's request. [16]

There were great possibilities for profit from speculation and rents in American land grants by royal favor. Charles II had granted to Sir George Carteret and seven other favorites all the land in the Carolinas. Preferring to have a grant in which there were fewer associates with whom to divide the profits, Carteret may be presumed, from later developments, to have made a proposal to Charles' brother, James, the Duke of York, a proposal which aroused the avarice of the duke, and which, in its execution and high-handed effrontery, has no parallel in Colonial American history.

Immediately upon the Restoration of Charles II in 1660, the duke was made Lord High Admiral of the Navy. George Carteret, who had sheltered Charles and his large following on the Island of Jersey during his banishment, was knighted and appointed treasurer of the navy. James controlled the ships, Carteret controlled the funds which paid the sailors and bought the supplies—a happy combination for the proposed venture—and as Carteret had a way of juggling his accounts which later caused him to be expelled from the House of Commons, the cost could be easily hidden.

The duke had various motives actuating him to fall in with

the proposal. He disliked the Dutch. He had been libeled in Holland, and the libelers were not punished as promptly as he had desired. He was also, as governor of the Royal African Company, pecuniarily interested in the slave trade in competition with the Dutch, and his company had, in time of profound peace, committed aggressions against the Dutch on the African coast "without any shadow of justice."

In the combined circumstances, it can be easily and logically surmised that Carteret, having a longing desire to possess that inviting territory now comprised within New Jersey, and which was then a part of New Netherland, proposed that James obtain from his brother Charles a grant of all the land in America north of Delaware Bay. When obtained, James was to grant to Carteret that portion of it which lay between the Hudson and the Delaware; James to retain all the remainder, which included all New York, Long Island and part of New England. This, Carteret could show him, could be granted to others, at an annual land rent, and thereby secure to James a princely annual income to be paid by the Dutch and other settlers.

The followers of Charles, needy and unscrupulous, could be depended upon to endeavor for selfish purposes to excite the prejudices of the new monarch against the Hollanders and represent them as hostile to British settlements in America.

Since James, like his brother Charles, was always sorely pressed for funds to maintain his libertine existence, it can be readily imagined that the proposal made a strong appeal to him.

So it was to such a man, of such principles, that Charles II in 1664 made a grant of all the territory between the eastern boundary of Maine and Pemaquid (near the Kennebec River), and between the Connecticut River and the Delaware Bay. A large part of the grant was at the time, and long had been, in possession of the Dutch, and another part he had, only two years previously, granted to Winthrop. But Stuart kings repeatedly disregarded royal grants of land in America made by themselves, or their predecessors, when they wished to advance the interests of some new favorite.

Bancroft, [5] the historian, said: "To satisfy the greediness of favorite courtiers, Charles II, in 1663, narrowed the limits of

Virginia by giving to eight favorites the immense Carolina grant. In 1664, he gave to his brother James all the land in Maine between the Pemaquid and the St. Croix, and in defiance of his grant to Winthrop in 1662, and the possession of the Dutch, and the rights of ten thousand inhabitants, gave to the duke, and by the duke to his favorites, the fine country from the Connecticut River to the Delaware Bay.

"Without revoking the grant of Nova Scotia to Sir Thomas Temple, he restored Acadia to France. Prince Rupert and his associates were endowed with a monopoly of the regions on the Hudson Bay. In 1677, the proprietary rights of New Hampshire and Maine were revoked, with the intent of acquiring them for the Duke of Monmouth, his reputed and worthless son, who was later to die on the scaffold.

"He granted Pennsylvania to Penn. From Nova Scotia to Florida, with few exceptions, the tenure of every territory was changed. Nay, further, the monopoly of the trade with the coast of Africa was given to a company in which he himself was a shareholder.

"Charles II gave away a large part of a continent. Could he have continued he would have given away the World."

The duke having obtained the grant, the next move was to obtain possession of the land. With that object James assembled a squadron of four men-of-war, with a crew of 150 sailors and 300 soldiers, and sent it on a voyage of conquest to appropriate the land which the Dutch had been occupying along the Connecticut, Hudson and Delaware Rivers for more than half a century.

So certain were James and Carteret of the success of the venture that, on June 23 after the squadron had sailed and was on the high seas, James executed a deed of all New Jersey to Carteret and their mutual friend John, Lord Berkeley, who was on the Admiralty Board with James. They evidently thought Berkeley would be a conciliating influence in their behalf should any embarrassing question arise.

The squadron, in command of Hugh Hyde, the duke's brother-in-law, comprised the frigate "Guinea" of thirty-six guns; the "Elias," of (variously stated) thirty to forty-two guns; the frigate

"Martin," of sixteen to eighteen guns; and the "William and Nicholas," a transport, of ten to sixteen guns. It set sail from Portsmouth with orders to assemble at Gardiner's Bay, and to proceed thence "to reduce the Dutch to an entire obedience."

In the expedition were: Colonel Richard Nicolls, groom of the bed chamber of the duke, who was to act as governor of the conquered territory, Sir Robert Carr, Sir George Cartwright and Samuel Maverick, Esq., who were to act as commissioners to take possession of the country. Further, letters were sent to the governors of the English colonies of Massachusetts, New Haven and Maryland, enjoining their assistance.

Men of influence and power like Nicolls had attached themselves to Charles and James during the years preceding the Restoration of Charles.

After putting in at Boston, where they tarried for a month taking on supplies and five hundred New England volunteer troops, the squadron proceeded, and at the end of August anchored inside Coney Island. A few days later two of the ships were moved near to Governor's Island, and two were anchored in the river above the fort.

Three companies of soldiers led by Nicolls were landed on Long Island. Joined by Captain John Scott (who had been released from prison in Connecticut), commanding a troop of horse, and by Captain John Younge, with a company of infantry of about sixty men, they proceeded to co-operate with the fleet.

All approaches by land and water between the city and outlying settlements were blockaded. Farmers were prohibited from sending food to the city and coasting vessels were captured. The "Gideon," a Dutch ship, which some months previously had been sent to Loango, Africa, for slaves, was in the harbor with 290 slaves of both sexes, one-quarter of which were to be sent to New Amstel on the Delaware.

The stone fort contained twenty cannon and 150 trained soldiers. It had been built only as a defense against Indians and was not intended to stand against a civilized force. In a Dutch population of fifteen hundred, not more than three hundred men capable of fighting could be raised on Manhattan, and there was only one day's supply of powder in the fort.

Nicolls demanded surrender. The citizens, who were dissatisfied with the Dutch Company for not affording better protection, implored surrender, as there was "no hope of relief, and impossible to make headway against so powerful an enemy."

Stuyvesant replied to Nicolls, maintaining the Dutch title by first discovery, uninterrupted possession, purchase of land from the native owners, and the recognition of the sovereignty of the States General by the articles of peace with England only ten years previously. But Nicolls declined discussion and told him the question of right did not concern him; that was to be considered by the King and the States General. He meant to take the place. [16]

Terms of surrender were agreed upon which provided that: "all people shall continue free denizens and shall enjoy their lands, houses, goods and ships wheresoever they are within this country, and dispose of them as they please." The fort and all Manhattan were surrendered.

Cartwright was sent to, and took, Fort Orange (Albany), while Sir Robert Carr was sent to take possession of the Delaware region. On October 1 the whole of New Netherland became subject to the British crown. New Amsterdam became New York, Fort Orange became Albany, New Amstel became New Castle. The captured Dutch soldiers were given by Nicolls to a merchantman, in payment of services, and they were transported into Virginia to be sold as indented servants.

Upon receiving advice of the conquest, Charles laughingly said to Carteret, "How shall I do to answer this to the Netherlands ambassador when he comes?"

"Thus," said O'Callaghan, [111] "was consummated an act of spoiliation which, in a period of profound peace, wrested New Netherland from its rightful owners by means violating all public justice and infrinting all public law."

"In the history of the royal ingrates by whom it was planned, and for whose benefits it was perpetrated, there are," said General Benjamin F. Butler, writing of that time, "few acts more base, none more characteristic."

Mulford, [105] a New Jersey historian, wrote: "In the conduct of the Duke of York there is exhibited a great degree of duplicity or obtusity, or rather a singular mixture of both."

Fiske [47] said: "It would be hard to find any canon of political morality upon which this achievement of Charles II could be defended. The duke was a bigot and despot by natural temper."

Louis XIV, referring to the reply of Charles to the demands of the Dutch of restitution of New Netherland, declared that the reply of Charles was "hard, dry and haughty," and added: "Having examined what the English and Hollanders have written upon the subject, it appears to me that the right of the Hollanders is the best founded; the habitation, joined to a long possession are, in my judgment, two sufficiently good titles to destroy all the reasons of the English." [16]

Van Gogh, the Dutch ambassador at London, in an audience with the king, denounced the capture as "an erroneous proceeding, opposed to all right and reason, contrary to mutual correspondence and good neighborhood, and a notorious infraction of the treaty lately concluded."

The States General represented to the King of France the wrong which the King of England had done them and asked, to no avail, the aid of France, as guaranteed by the treaty of two years previously.

D'Estrades, the French ambassador at The Hague, urged his sovereign, Louis, "to prefer England to the States," because he could thereby "procure the restitution of Acadia from the Penobscot River to Cape Breton, being eighty leagues (240 miles) of coast, and oblige the King of England, by the same treaty, to declare war against the Iroquois, whom the Hollanders have always assisted with arms and munitions against us. By this means Your Majesty would free Canada from the only enemies which she has in that country, and by attacking them on the Canadian side, and on that which the English occupy, they would all be destroyed in a year."

Finding that the designs of Louis on the Spanish Netherlands controlled his actions, the States General informed him that they were ready to adjust their differences with King Charles, by restoring everything they had taken from him, if he would "bind himself to restore New Netherland and other prizes." [16]

Downing of England, answering the Dutch statement, insisted that New Netherland was within the New England grant; that the treaty of 1654 had not cut off the English claim, and, that even if it had, the New England colonies had *jure belli* within themselves without first appealing to England. [16]

The Dutch soon published a "demolition of the Downing memorial." "The English have no other title to the possession of New England than the Dutch have to New Netherland, to wit, the right of occupation, because all those countries being desolate, uninhabited, and waste, as if belonging to nobody, became the property of those who have been the first occupants of them; therefore, a continued possession for such a long series of years must confer on this nation a title which cannot be questioned with any appearance of reason."

The Dutch ordered reprisals against the English in Africa, Barbados, New Netherland and Newfoundland. The West India Company was authorized "to attack, conquer and ruin the English everywhere, both in and out of Europe, on land and water."

Without formal declaration of war, the British seized 130 Dutch merchant vessels in English ports. The British East India Company equipped twenty ships. All fisheries were suspended to supply men for the war vessels, and the king issued a declaration of war against the Dutch.

In New York, Nicolls confiscated the property of all the Dutch who had not taken the oath of allegiance, seizing Blackwell's, Randall's and Ward's Islands. Nevertheless, it was said, the administration of Governor Nicolls was conciliatory and the changes were in no sense disturbing to the colonists.

In the eleven years preceding the surrender, the population of New Netherland increased from about two thousand to ten thousand and of New Amsterdam (Manhattan) from eight hundred to fifteen hundred. A tax was levied for schools, of one-twentieth of a penny on buildings, and twice that on cultivated land.

The Duke's Laws were made by the governor and assembly,

at Hempstead, and later confirmed by the duke. They provided: All tenure of lands was to be from the duke. All persons were required to bring their old deeds and take out new ones from the governor, upon the sealing of which a fee was to be paid. No purchase of land from the Indians was to be valid unless the governor's leave was obtained, and the natives acknowledged satisfaction before him, upon which a grant with annual land rent to the duke was to be made by the governor and recorded in the secretary's office. [16] Suffrage continued to be based on landholding. Holding land in common still obtained and was recognized in the Duke's Laws. [44]

A French expedition from Canada against the Mohawk Indians in New York destroyed their villages and, now, through forced treaties with the confederated Iroquois, the French controlled all the land in central New York. The French were watched as intruders within the province. [16] Subsequently, Governor Andros notified the French governor of Canada that the Five Nations of Indians were British subjects and would be protected as such. [169]

New grants of land were issued by Nicolls during the first two years after the conquest. However, the grant of Haerlem, previously made by the Dutch, was confirmed; the land rent payable to the duke.

Constant and Nathaniel Sylvester, of Barbados, settled on Shelter Island, and for a payment of £150 in beef and pork Nicolls granted them the island for ever, free of all taxes. [16]

The tenure of land was derived from the duke, who would grant land at rents of one penny per acre when the tract was purchased by his agency from the Indians, and 3d per acre when bought of Indians by the colonists.

Governor Nicolls went to Esopus and obtained of the natives a large tract of land, which he offered settlers at an annual land rent payable to the duke, beginning at the end of the fifth year. He granted Randall's Island to Mayor Delavall of New York.

By a general order of the Court of Assizes, at New York, all persons in the conquered territory, including the Delaware region, who held old land grants from the Dutch, and those who had none, were directed to apply at New York for grants under

British authority, paying land rents therefor to the duke and fees to the governor.

The war between England and Holland was concluded by the treaty of Breda in 1667, by which the English title to New York was confirmed. Holland received Surinam (Dutch Guiana) in South America, and the Island of Poleron, near the Moluccas, East Indies.

Nicolls granted an island in New York harbor to Captain Needham, who sold it to Bedloe. Bedloe's widow afterwards sold it to James Carteret, son of Sir George, who had been "elected President of New Jersey." The possession and rights of the patroon of Rensselaerwyck were recognized by Nicolls, but a new grant was not issued until twenty years afterwards.

Sixty-two acres between Warren and Christopher Streets in New York, which had been held by the Dutch dominie, Bogardus, was confirmed to his heirs by Nicolls, and was afterwards vested in the Duke of York. [16]

Nicolls confiscated to the duke the lands of the West India Company on Staten Island. He granted to the soldiers of the garrison at Esopus thirty lots of thirty acres each, to secure their loyalty, and granted to Samuel Edsall land opposite Haerlem which had been granted by the Dutch to Bronck. Nicolls then sailed to England with the good will of all. [16] He was succeeded as governor of New York by Francis Lovelace and, later, by Andros, and then by Dongan.

Several Indian sachems insisted, in 1670, that they were the owners of Staten Island. They were told that their forebears had sold it to the Dutch, but to quiet their claims, Governor Lovelace bought it of them for the duke. Part of the agreement (probably dictated by Lovelace) read: "That they ye said sachems now are ye very true, sole and lawful, Indian owners of the said island, and all and singular of ye premises, as being derived to them by their ancestors." They were given a quantity of guns, powder, lead, and hardware. This was the initial transaction in the alienation of Staten Island from the New Jersey grantees and its attachment to New York.

Peter Stuyvesant, former Dutch governor of New Netherland (1647–64), and conqueror of New Sweden, died in New York in 1672, aged eighty years, and was buried in St. Mark's Church. After the English conquest of New Netherland in 1664, he had been recalled to Holland to explain his surrender, but had returned to New York four years later. He married a granddaughter of Nicholas Bayard, a French Protestant clergyman.

Stuyvesant was autocratic and mistreated those he disliked. [111] He was the most picturesque figure in the history of the Dutch rulers. He was stern, resolute and iron-tempered, and imprisoned two citizens for slander. At the trial he said: "Thou shall not speak evil of the ruler of the people." [120]

As a private citizen he passed the brief remainder of his life on his bouwrie which occupied land between Fourth Avenue and the East River, and Sixth and Seventeenth Streets. Title to an infinitesimally small piece of it, at the northeast corner of Fourth Avenue and Eleventh Street, in 1936, (264 years after his death) was held by Princess Elizabeth de Caraman-Chimay, a descendant of Stuyvesant. To her the United States government paid $134,000, for the right to build a branch post office on the lot. This value, though created automatically by all the people, was paid to the absentee princess by taxes levied on themselves.

A secret treaty between Louis XIV, King of France, and Charles II, King of England, the latter a pensioner of the former, led them in March, 1673, to war against Holland.

The previous December, Cornelis Evertsen of the Netherlands, son of a former admiral, had been sent with fifteen ships to the West Indies, where he was joined by four ships under Jacob Binckes. They then sailed to the Chesapeake, where they captured eight English vessels and burned five.

A sloop just arriving in the Chesapeake from New York was captured. In reply to an inquiry as to the strength of the defenses at New York, the master declared they were very strong, whereupon Samuel Hopkins of New Jersey, a passenger aboard the sloop, said they were very weak, and that the governor was absent in Connecticut.

The Dutch admiral had added to his fleet the captured prize ships, and now had twenty-three vessels, with sixteen hundred men, including seven ships of war. He proceeded to New York to take the place, "which is our own, and our own we will have." Arriving there, the ships fired broadsides at the fort, killing and wounding some of the garrison, whereupon, "the fort fired upon them, and shot the general's ships through and through."

The fort under the English was just as untenable as it was when the English took it from the Dutch nine years previously. Dutch soldiers, to the number of six hundred, were landed at the foot of Wall Street and were joined by four hundred Dutch burghers. [128] In the absence of Governor Lovelace, the commander of the fort surrendered it and its garrison of eighty men.

Thereupon two hundred men were sent up the Hudson in several vessels and captured Albany and Esopus. All the English soldiers there were brought down to New York as prisoners of war. Never before had the bay of New York held so majestic a fleet. The name of New Netherland was restored as far north as Albany, and to the east end of Long Island, and on both sides of the Delaware. The Dutch population was estimated at between six and seven thousand. The name of New York was changed to New Orange, in honor of William of Orange; the name of Albany to Williamstadt, and its fort to Nassau. The former Dutch name of New Amstel, on the Delaware, was restored at New Castle.

Anthony Colve, a captain of infantry, was appointed governorgeneral. In the history of the New Netherland region, the successive conquests by, and of, the Dutch, Swedes and English, resulted in the conquered inhabitants, for the most part, taking the oath of allegiance to the new masters. So, in this case, the major part of the English magistrates, constables and inhabitants in New York, New Jersey and on the Delaware, swore allegiance to the Dutch States General and the Prince of Orange and once more came under Dutch rule.

Lovelace, the retiring English governor, upon his return from Connecticut to Manhattan after the conquest, was arrested for debt resulting from his extensive land speculations; he was indebted to the Duke of York to the extent of £7,000. [16] He was taken to England aboard a Dutch ship.

Possession of Shelter Island by Nicholas Sylvester was confirmed by Colve, as was Gardiner's Island to David Gardiner.

Jeremiah Van Rensselaer was required to obtain from the States General a new grant of Rensselaerwyck.

A treaty of peace between England and Holland in February, 1674, two months before they learned of the Dutch reconquest of New Netherland, provided that whatever countries, towns or forts had been taken by either during the war should be returned. This again put the English in possession of New York, New Jersey and the Delaware, with restoration of the English place-names.

As to why Holland so readily relinquished New Netherland after regaining it, Brodhead [16] said: "The Dutch Republic could not, singlehanded, cope with France and Britain. Peace with the latter had become a necessity. William of Orange felt that, to secure the Republic, Louis must be effectively crippled. Alliances were made between Holland, Germany and Spain against France and England. Spain, however, made it a condition that the Netherlands should consent to a peace with England upon the basis of a mutual restoration of conquests. Political necessity alone could bend the States General to these hard terms.

"When the news of the reconquest reached them they were too deeply committed to recede—and in fact their position otherwise was so weak that they begged Charles to accept the proffered peace."

The duke announced in July, 1674, that his brother Charles II had renewed to him the grant of land in New England, New York and New Jersey. [145] He appointed Major Edmund Andros as governor. Andros arrived in New York with his wife in 1678, after a nine weeks' voyage.

New York then contained twenty-four towns, villages or parishes. The city contained 343 houses, with a population of 3,430, and indented servants were in demand. A merchant having £500 or £1,000 was thought substantial, and a planter worth half that in movables was accorded rich. [16]

Penn was, in 1680, making his application through the Duke of York for the grant to himself of all Pennsylvania. His telling the duke of the great profits to be made from land rents in America suddenly awakened the cupidity of the duke, and caused him to realize he was not getting those large land rents from America which Carteret, as an inducement to James to send the squadron to conquer the Dutch, had so glowingly pictured to him.

So in June, James dispatched John Lewin, a London lawyer, to America with orders to: ". . . find out all the estates, rents, revenues, profits and perquisites which in any sort belong to me, and to demand, ask and receive the same, as I am proprietor of said places; the same respecting what land rent every person at all places do or ought to pay, how paid, who has received it for the past six years, what my share, and whether I get it, or who does." By letter, by the same ship, Governor Andros was instructed by James to return to England, which he did the following January first.

Thomas Dongan arrived at New York in 1683, succeeding Andros as governor, with authority to grant land. He was instructed, with advice of the council, to call an election. All acts of the legislature were to be subject to veto by the governor and the duke. Government by landholders was to continue, and as an inducement to acquire land and pay land rent to the duke, landholders alone were to hold public office.

Dongan immediately called for a show of all deeds for land heretofore granted, under threat of expropriating the land for the duke; the object being to exact increased land rents for the duke, and numerous registration fees for himself.

Anthony Brockholls, who was left in charge upon departure of Andros, refused, in 1681, to surrender Staten Island to Philip Carteret, governor of East Jersey. Up to that time no land rent had been demanded, or paid, on Staten Island.

The East Jersey assembly had not included the island in any of the four counties it established in 1683. By February the following year, more than two hundred families had settled on the island. The registrar of land on the island was directed by Dongan to collect the land rents there, and the surveyor-general was ordered to lay out all the land according to each owner's patent. The sheriff was directed to summon before the governor and council all persons there located. [16]

Sir John Werden, secretary to the duke, wrote: "Staten Island, without doubt belongs to the duke, and those who disturb the quiet of possession are certainly very injurious to the duke, and we think have no color for such pretenses." This was written by the duke's secretary, who only the previous year had witnessed the duke's grant to the proprietors of East Jersey of all land west of Long Island, and knew its full intent.

The proprietors of East Jersey, relying upon the duke's grant to them, had meanwhile revived the claim to the island, which they had also bought from the widow Carteret in 1681. Regardless of the provision, "west of Long Island," as one of the outlets of the Hudson River ran around Staten Island, it was "adjudged to belong to New York." [16]

Charles II died of a stroke of apoplexy in February, 1685, and was succeeded by his brother, the Duke of York, as King James II.

Trumbull [148] said of the new king: ". . . . he was an obstinate, cruel tyrant, destitute of all the principles of true honor, faith, justice, or humanity. He wantonly trampled on the constitution, laws and liberties of the nation; and, with his ministers and officers, in an unrighteous and merciless manner, shed the blood of his subjects, and wreaked his vengeance on all who made the least opposition to his lawless proceedings. The most humble petitions; arguments from reason; charters; the most solemn compacts and royal promises, from justice, humanity, or any other consideration, which a subject could plead, had no weight or influence with him."

There had been no land office in New York, New Jersey or Carolina. Deeds were issued by the governors, secretaries and surveyors-general. Dongan insisted that, without exception, all deeds recorded during his administration should contain a land-rent provision. Rents in Manhattan were payable in money, but in the country in wheat, fish, or other commodities. At first rents were payable to the duke but, later, to him as king.

King James, who was pecuniarily interested in the Royal African Company, one of the purposes of which was to ship Negro slaves to America, ordered that there be no trading from New York to any part of the African territory of the company. Fearing that the printing of pamphlets might foment the spirit of liberty, he ordered that no printing press be set up in any of the provinces, without a license from the respective governors. At the same time James abolished the New York assembly, which he had granted three years previously, and vested all legislative power in the governor appointed by him, and in his council. [16]

Dongan confirmed the Nicolls' (previously Dutch) grant to the New Haerlem landholders, but at an increased land rent. [120] In 1925, 267 years after the original grant by Stuyvesant, about two hundred descendants of the original New Haerlem landholders organized to seek title to twenty-five hundred acres in the tract.

For £500 paid to him, Dongan granted a charter to the city of New York in 1686, in which the city was granted, "all the waste, vacant and unpatented lands on Manhattan Island, reaching to low water mark."

Major Edmund Andros was knighted, and appointed by James, in 1686, as captain-general and vice-admiral of New England, with headquarters at Boston. Two years afterwards, New York and New Jersey were added to his jurisdiction; Andros succeeding Dongan.

The Iroquois, or Five Nations, a confederation of the Mohawks, Oneidas, Onondagas, Cayugas and Senacas which occupied land in upper New York, is supposed to have been formed about fifty years after the discovery of America. They were joined in 1711 by the Tuscaroras, driven from Carolina; forming the Six Nations.

James determined to maintain the claim asserted by Andros and Dongan that the Five Nations were British subjects, and in 1687 ordered that they be protected against the French in Canada. The agents of King Louis insisted that the Iroquois had, by treaties in 1665 and 1666, declared themselves French subjects and that the French had taken possession of their land in New York province.

At Montreal in 1688 the Oneidas, Onondagas and Cayugas rejected Dongan's assumption that they were British subjects. They declared they had always resisted his pretensions and wished only to be friends of both the French and English equally, without either being their master. They gave as their reason that they "held their land directly of the Supreme Being and had never been conquered in war." Thus the Iroquois asserted their independence of both French and English, and preserved northern New York from annexation to Canada. They only desired the return of their twenty-eight countrymen, prisoners in France; most of whom were returned a year later. [16]

In August, Andros went from Boston to New York, assumed the governorship and remained two months. He required all deeds and wills to be recorded in Boston. Arbitrary taxes were imposed and the common lands were encroached upon. All deeds for land were inspected and land rent increased, payable to the duke, with excessive fees exacted for himself.

The following year Andros, upon learning in Boston that King James had abdicated, tried, disguised in female attire, to escape to Europe in a frigate, but was arrested and imprisoned, and afterwards sent to England.

All the land in the province of New York, granted to James by his brother Charles, was held as his personal property, and subject to disposal by him. After his abdication it passed to his daughter, Queen Mary, and after her was held by her sister Queen Anne, and by succeeding British monarchs.

In the war which Louis XIV declared against England in 1689, and which continued eight years in an unsuccessful endeavor to regain the British crown for James II, an English governor of New York, Benjamin Fletcher, who had arrived in New York in 1692, launched the Iroquois thunderbolt against Canada, one of the most frightful Indian incursions known to history. [49]

A Continental Congress, the first such congress in America, was convened in New York by Jacob Leister, in 1690. For another reason, Leister was later hanged.

Governor Fletcher in 1695 confirmed to Colonel Nicholas Bayard title to 620,000 acres about "Skohere," with an annual land rent payable to the duke. Bayard had bargained for this land with six drunken Indians, giving them rum and other goods. Grants of such large acreage diverted settlers to other colonies. [12]

The next year the governor granted to Godfrey Dellius, a clergyman of Albany, a tract of land twelve by seventy miles in area along the Hudson River above Saratoga, extending into present Vermont. This was declared to be extravagant and three years later it was revoked. [164]

There was no effective system for collection of land rents during the seventeenth century, and few rents were paid. Juries refused to convict delinquents. In 1699, future rents were fixed at 2s 6d (30d) per hundred acres. [12]

English royal governors having an insatiable yearning for fees, Dongan and his successor, Fletcher, renewed previous Dutch grants of extensive areas of land as manors. The manors comprised almost all the land along the Hudson River between Manhattan Island and Albany, and on Staten Island, and the south shore of Long Island.

The grant of the manor of Rensselaerwyck, of seven hundred thousand acres, by the West India Company to van Rensselaer in 1630, was renewed by Dongan, who granted him one court-leet and one court-baron and authorized him to "destrain" for all land rents; to appropriate all estrays, wrecks, deodans and goods of felons forfeited within the said lordship. Included also were the post fines, advowson and right of patronage of all and every church erected within the said lordship. He was authorized and empowered to "choose" deputies to sit in the general assembly. This was the model of most of the English manorial land grants subsequently made in the province of New York. The grant of this manor was further confirmed by Queen Anne in 1704, at an annual ground rent of fifty bushels of wheat payable to her.

Upon van Rensselaer relinquishing to the king his claim to the townsite of Albany and the surrounding territory extending sixteen miles into the country, Dongan, on promise of £300 being paid him, issued a charter to Albany. [16]

A large tract about Yonkers, which had been granted by the Dutch to Adriaen van der Donck, was in 1658 willed by him to his wife. Ten years later three hundred acres of the tract were sold for £5 and a horse. Subsequently a portion of it was erected by Governor Lovelace into the manor of Fordham. The residue of 7,708 acres was sold to speculators.

Stephanus van Cortlandt in 1685 gave seven Indians some rum, guns and other articles of small value, and obtained from them, "the true and rightful owners," Indian consent to use a large tract of land in what is now Westchester, Putnam and Dutchess Counties. Upon this, Governor Dongan, representing the Duke of York, made to van Cortlandt a confirmatory grant of this land, with all manorial privileges, including the right to send a representative to the assembly after the lapse of twenty years.

The fees to Dongan, for the north half alone, are said to have amounted to three hundred Pieces of Eight. The land in this grant, on both sides of the Hudson, together with Iona Island in the river, was erected into the manor of Cortlandt and later confirmed by King James. Van Cortlandt died leaving twelve children who intermarried with the large landholding families of De Peyster, van Rensselaer, Skinner, Bayard, and De Lancey. [III] A portion of this land descended to Jacobus van Cortlandt, grandfather of Chief Justice Jay, and probably a part of it descended to the chief justice.

Frederick Phillipse, "the richest man in New York," and his son Philip, obtained the assent of the Indians to possession of the land between Spuyten Duyvil Creek and Croton River, a tract twenty-two miles wide which included the Pocantico Hills region. A portion was granted by Governor Dongan in 1686 to Phillipse and, seven years later, another portion was granted by Governor Fletcher to Phillipse as "the manor of Phillipsborough," with feudal appendages of court-baron and court-leet. [III]

Robert Livingston, town clerk and receiver of the king's revenue at Albany, was granted by Dongan, under hand and seal, "to be kept by Robert Livingston, his heirs and assigns for ever," a territory of 160,240 acres on the east side of the Hudson River just below the van Rensselaer patroonship. The tract stretched from a point opposite Catskill to one opposite Saugertieskill, and Livingston was granted manorial privileges similar to those granted van Rensselaer, including one court-leet and one court-baron. This made him one of the largest landholders in New York. [16]

Although Livingston had given the Indians only the meager payment usually given to Indians, the grant was worded to read, "the said Livingston has been at vast charges and expense in purchasing said land of the Indians."

Livingston was a younger son of a poor exiled clergyman. In currying favor with one official after another he was unscrupulous, dexterous and adaptable, and changed his politics with change of administration. [107]

His son Robert married the daughter of Henry Beekman, who had been granted by Fletcher a tract sixteen miles in length in Dutchess County, and another tract twenty miles along the Hudson, extending eight miles inland. [107] Combining his wife's inherited lands with his possessions, he became the reputed largest landholder in New York.[*]

The Livingstons always had immense political power, and it was alleged in the press that the lord of the manor "bought" that notable privilege. It was the powerful and corrupt Livingstons who installed John Jay as Chief Justice of the United States Supreme Court—to be a protector of the absentee landholding privileges. [21]

Myers, in his *History of the Supreme Court,* said, "The large landholders and the politico-capitalists of both political parties stood staunchily together. Both indiscriminately joined in granting to each other great tracts of public lands and company charters."

Thomas Chambers came to New Netherland as a farmer, under the patroonship of van Rensselaer, and occupied the alluvial tract on which Troy now stands. In 1652 he moved to Esopus, where he accumulated, by commercial and other speculation, large areas of land. Twenty years later the English governor, Lovelace, of New York, erected Chamber's great tract of land about Kingston into the manor of Fox Hall. Dongan confirmed this grant fourteen years later and invested the manor with power to hold court-leet and court-baron; and also granted all waifs, estrays, felons' property, etc., to the lord of the manor, with the right of advowson and patronage to such church as he might establish on the land. The confirmation did not include the privilege of representation in the assembly. Chambers

[*]Nat. Cycl. of Amer. Biog.

established an intricate and continuing entail by which the manor was to be kept entire. In time the manor itself became "a waif and estray." The name disappeared. [111]

Governor Dongan, acting for the duke in 1684, granted to John Palmer 4,500 acres on Staten Island, as the manor of Cassiltown, which James II enlarged three years later to 5,100 acres.

Owing to the uncertainty then existing as to whether Staten Island was in New Jersey or New York, the grant was recorded in both provinces. It contained the usual manorial rights, except representation in the assembly.

The Duke of York, through Andros, had in 1676 granted to Christopher Billop 922 acres on the southern end of Staten Island, on which Tottenville is now situated. Eleven years later, as James II, acting through Dongan, he confirmed it, and increased the grant to sixteen hundred acres as the lordship and manor of Bentley, giving to Billop and his heirs and assigns complete manorial privileges, and creating him lord of the manor. This tract, along with most other manors, was confiscated as property of Tories during the American Revolution and sold at public auction. The manor, reduced to 1,078 acres, but with improvements, sold for £4,695.

Governor Nicolls had, in 1666, granted to Thomas Pell a tract of land about eight miles square, fronting on Long Island Sound, and including the bays, islands and seas; extending from East Chester River (in the present Pelham Bay Park) to Larchmont. Twenty-one years later James II, through Dongan, confirmed this grant to John Pell, nephew and legate of Thomas. It included many of the same privileges that were contained in previous manorial grants.

The British monarchs, William and Mary, through Governor Fletcher, in 1693 granted to William Smith, Chief Justice of the Province, a tract of land fifty miles long on the south side of Long Island. It was set up as the manor of St. George, with powers incident to an English manor, including one court-leet and one court-baron. Smith forced the town commissioners of Southampton to accept £10 for the greater part of the forty miles of beach. [107]

William III, through Governor Fletcher, made a manorial

grant in 1697 to Lewis Morris, his heirs and assigns, "nephew and heir of the late Colonel Lewis Morris," with the customary manorial privileges and powers, to be known as "The mannour or lordship of Morrisiania." It also granted "all the rights, members, liberties, privileges, jurisdictions, royalties, hereditaments, tolls, benefits, profits, advantages and appurtenances whatsoever to the necks of land within the limits, meadows, marshes, swamps, ponds, rivers, creeks, inlets, islands, fishing and fowling." Apparently William intended that everything worth having should be included.

William III, through Lieutenant-Governor Nanfan, at New York, in 1701 granted to Colonel Caleb Heathcote a large tract of land, with the usual manorial privileges, designated as "the lordship and manor of Scarsdale," for which Heathcote had bargained with some Indians.

Richard Coote, Earl of Bellomont, a friend of William III, was appointed governor of New York, Massachusetts and New Hampshire. The immense land grants of the patroons, and other feudal privileges, disgusted him. He opposed the English land grant policy and proposed it be made illegal for any person in the province to hold more than a thousand acres. [47]

The earl, writing from New York to the Lords of Trade in 1701, said: "Mr. Livingston has on his great grant, of sixteen miles broad by twenty-four miles long, but four or five cottagers, as I am told, men that live in vassalage under him. Colonel Cortlandt has on his great grants four or five of these poor families." Other similar cases are cited;[t] and the earl added that by "intolerable corrupt granting of land of the province, Governor Fletcher got in bribes at least £4,000." [107]

William Beekman, who became a large landholder in New York City, is believed to have come in 1647 with Stuyvesant, who sent him to the Delaware to perform clerical work. In 1658 he was appointed by Stuyvesant as vice-director and governor of "the Company Colony north of the Christina." When the city of Amsterdam, Holland, bought that region, he asked for appointment elsewhere, and Stuyvesant transferred him to Esopus, where he served as sheriff until 1672. The following year he

[t]Doc. Hist. N. Y.

went to New York and became a burgomaster, and then an alderman until 1696. He died in 1707, aged eighty-four years, possessed of large tracts of land in the city, where a street is named for him.

Queen Anne, in 1708, through Governor Cornbury, granted all her landholdings on Staten Island, inherited from her father, James II, to Lancaster Symes, a prominent citizen, commander of the troops, and vestryman of Trinity Church in New York. After that date Staten Island was fully recognized as being within the jurisdiction of New York, instead of in New Jersey; notwithstanding it had been granted by the Duke of York to Carteret and Berkeley; and subsequently purchased from the widow Carteret by the East Jersey proprietors; and granted anew by the duke after the Dutch conquest, to the East Jersey proprietors.

At Kingston there is recorded an indenture, dated August 25, 1709, signed by eight Dutchmen and one Huguenot, reciting that they, with others, had purchased of the Indians a certain tract of land near Hurley (New Dorp), extending south to the New Paltz patent. It refers to a Dutch grant in 1708 to Cornelius Cool and associates, and states that the lands were purchased to serve as commons for wood, pasturage and drift-way (for driving cattle), and that the woodland should be held for ever. By an agreement ten years later, by authority of the governor and assembly of the colony, seven freeholders were appointed trustees, made a body politic, and given power to sell any of the common lands, not to exceed £225 in value.

The Hurley commons were continued, not for ever, but until nearly a century later, when in pursuance of an act lobbied through the New York State legislature, a division of the land was made. This division was based roughly upon the then existing individual holdings within the corporation and length of residence therein, including also non-residents who held land of not less than $2,000 value. The expenses incident to the division were met by levying a tax on lots. [44] This is one more instance of land robbery by law, and of inequitable and unjust distribution.

Cadwalader Colden, surveyor-general of New York in 1732, wrote: "Every year the young people go from this province and purchase land in the neighboring colonies, while much better, and every way more convenient, lands lie useless to the king and country. The reason for this is that the grantees of land held unused are not, nor never were, in a capacity to improve such large tracts. And other people will not become their vassals or tenants, as one great reason for people's (the better sort especially) leaving their native country in Europe was to avoid the dependence of landlords."

In anticipation of the nineteenth-century land reformer, Henry George, he said: "The following proposal seems to me to be most practical, viz., to establish a land rent on all land. The land would, in this case, be sufficient to support the government and if applied to that purpose I believe would give general satisfaction, because it would be as equitable a taxation as could well be contrived, and the taxes would not, as they do now, fall upon the improvements and the industry of the people."[g]

In New York, and in other colonies, when the assemblies refused to vote funds for the governors' salaries, the governor would increase the public revenue by exacting license fees for various occupations. Increasing public revenue by high license fees, to reduce by that much the tax rate on land values, prevails today everywhere.

Three tracts of land of at least one million acres each, and several others of two hundred thousand acres each, were granted about 1750. [10]

All efforts to collect land rents were virtually a failure up to 1761, as only £800 had been collected. [10] No doubt, as Surveyor-General Colden said, the reason was land being held in large unproductive tracts on speculation, with the holders unable to pay. However, during the next thirteen years population increased, which increased the demand for land, with the inevitable result that those who had to have land were obliged to pay increased prices exacted by the speculators. Rents on new grants were increased from 2s 6d per hundred acres, to 4s 2d.

A grant of twenty thousand acres was made in 1765 to King's College (now Columbia University), with a land rent reserved to the king, in recognition of feudal authority. In 1814, the tract

[g]*Op. cit.*

of land in New York City now occupied by Rockefeller Center was granted by the State of New York to Columbia College, which has leased it to Mr. Rockefeller at a ground rent of $3,600,000 per annum. This vast annual land rent paid by Mr. Rockefeller to Columbia University represents the economic rental value of the land his buildings occupy. Fortunately, this rental is devoted to education.

But the economic rent of all the surrounding land of equal value, automatically created by all the people, is being privately appropriated by a relatively few people, at the expense of all the people; and all the people seem too stupid to claim it. They seem content to go on paying taxes from their personal earnings, instead of having this publicly-created land rent collected for public revenue to reduce the general tax levy.

Sir Peter Warren, a British admiral, acquired through marriage with Miss De Lancey of New York a vast tract of land in the Mohawk Valley. He appointed his nephew, Colonel William Johnson, an Irish gentleman, as superintendent of it. [1]

Johnson arrived in New York in 1738 and located on the land, and became British Agent of Indian Affairs in the Northern District. He ruled the valley in a manner that was partially barbaric and partially feudal. [49] He commanded the troops sent to drive the French from Lake Champlain, and subsequently was made a baronet. He was an extensive land jobber, and in 1772 with Lord Dunmore, then governor of New York, and Governor Tryon, his successor, acquired of the Indians a million acres in the northwestern section of the province. [3]

Fort Stanwix, near Rome, at the time of the French and Indian War, and for many years afterwards, was the western limit of English settlements.

Dr. Harry Yoshpe, of Brooklyn College, writing of the confiscation by the government of manors and other land held by Tories in New York, said: "The land held by James de Lancey, a royalist, covering a mile of waterfront on the East River was not seized by the poor yeomen dependents and tenants, which might have marked a substantial gain for social and political equality. Instead, the bulk of the lands fell into the hands of fifteen persons, practically all of them conspicuous representatives of noted mercantile and landholding families. These included the Livingstons, Gouverneurs, Roosevelts and Beekmans, who formed socially, economically and politically, a single privileged ruling class, as against the rank and file of small freeholders, tenant-farmers, shopkeepers, artisans and laborers."

The legislature of the new state government in 1785 passed an act for the partition of lands, by which land in individual ownership became, in course of time, more general.

The land in New York State below a line drawn between Troy and Buffalo, was within the limits of the royal grants to the Massachusetts and Connecticut grantees.

By a compromise in 1786, ownership of a portion of this land was given to Massachusetts, while the sovereignty was given to New York.

Two years later Oliver Phelps, a merchant and land speculator in Windsor, Connecticut; Nathaniel Gorham of Massachusetts, a former member of the Federal Constitutional Convention; and associates; manipulated an act through the Massachusetts legislature by which they contracted to buy of Massachusetts six million acres in the Genesee country in New York for £300,000 (less than 25¢ per acre). This land was in the present counties of Monroe, Ontario, Livingston, Yates, Steuben, Wayne, Allegany, Orleans, Geneva and Wyoming.

It was to be paid for in Massachusetts Consolidated Scrip, then much depreciated in value, which reduced the price realized by the state to a fraction of the sale price. They bargained with the Indians for 2,600,000 acres and opened a land office at Canandaigua. During the following two years they sold about five hundred thousand acres at an increased price to different buyers, and the remaining 2,100,000 acres to another noted land jobber, United States Senator Robert Morris of Pennsylvania.

A rapid rise in the value of the Massachusetts scrip prevented them making payment for the remaining million acres not yet acquired of the Indians, and their contract was surrendered.

The Massachusetts legislature, in 1791, sold its remaining lands in New York State to Samuel Ogden, who assigned his contract to the same Robert Morris. Morris acquired of the Seneca Indians four million acres, of which he conveyed three million acres to

Herman LeRoy, John Linclain and Garrett Boon, in trust, to be transferred to Wilhelm Willinck and eleven other land speculators in Holland, who paid the relatively small sum of purchase money. The remaining million acres apparently were retained by Morris as his profit in the deal. [2]

Robert Morris carried on land operations so extensively on large amounts of borrowed money, which he could not repay, that a court judgment lodged him in jail, where he remained for some years. [21]

Now York State having, on its own account, as distinct from the Massachusetts area, seven million acres of good agricultural land to be opened for settlement, the legislature in 1791 authorized the State Land Commissioners, of which Governor Clinton and Aaron Burr were members, to dispose of it. Instead of dividing and selling it to actual settlers in small tracts, they restricted sales to very large tracts which only speculators could buy.

The commissioners sold 5,543,173 acres at an average of 18¢ per acre. Alexander McComb, through subterfuge, got 3,635,200 acres at 8*d* (16¢) per acre, to be paid in five annual installments, without interest, which gave him time to unload on the settlers and speculators at advanced prices before full payment by him became due. The public wanted to know how McComb got land at only 8*d* (16¢) per acre, while John and Nicholas Roosevelt paid 3*s* (75¢) per acre. It was insinuated that Clinton and Burr and their friends were secretly interested in the McComb purchase. All these buyers were rank land speculators, reaping profits from sales to the oncoming farmers while slowing up land division and settlement by exacting increased prices. Their transactions retarded development of the state.

The Dutch grant of more than sixty acres between Cortlandt Street and Greenwich Village, on Manhattan Island, which had been made to Anneke Jans, was confirmed to her by Governor Nicolls in 1664. Seven years later, five of her heirs sold the farm to Governor Lovelace, who bought so much land on speculation that he overloaded himself, was arrested and became disgraced. Becoming indebted to the Duke of York, the farm was confiscated by the duke, and was known as the duke's farm until 1685, when, with James accession to the throne, it became the king's farm. Queen Anne, after her succession to the crown, possessed it, and conveyed it as already cited.

At the beginning the farm had very little value, but with the increase in population, which creates land value, it became enormously valuable and claimants brought suit. During a period of ninety-seven years, between 1750 and 1847, not less than sixteen or seventeen suits were brought. It was not until nearly two centuries after its original grant that, in 1847, Vice Chancellor Sanford decided that Trinity Church had acquired a valid title to it. [47]

A farm of twenty acres in New York City was bought in 1799 for $2,500, and the buyer, after using it some years, sold it for $10,000. It subsequently came into possession of the Astors, who received a large rental for it as building sites. To obtain a small part of it, as the site for the Empire State Building, the builders were obliged to pay the Astors $15,000,000 cash before a spade could be put in the ground. The interest on this price is being paid by the rents of the tenants of the building, and by the policy-holders of the insurance company that invested in the undertaking.

Of Astor's real estate operations, Myers [107] said: "If we are to accept the superficial, perfunctory accounts of Astor's real estate investments in New York City, then he will appear in the usual eulogistic light of a law-loving, sagacious man engaged in a legitimate enterprise. The truth, however, lies deeper than that —a truth which has been either undiscerned or glossed over by those conventional writers who, with a panderer's instinct, give a wealth-worshiping era the thing it wants to read, not what it ought to know. Although apparently innocent and in accord with the laws and customs of the times, Astor's real estate transactions were inseparably connected with consecutive evasions, trickeries, frauds, and violation of law.

"The Cosine farm at Broadway, 53rd and 57th Streets, west to the Hudson River, was acquired by Astor by foreclosing on a mortgage for $23,000. It is now worth $6,000,000. The Eden farm in the same vicinity, along Broadway north from 42nd Street and slanting over to the Hudson River, was likewise acquired by Astor through his foreclosure of a mortgage for $25,000. This land is now worth $25,000,000."

In the 1830's, J. M. Bixby, a young New York lawyer without financial resources, at the importunance of, and to oblige a friend, reluctantly gave a note for $200, for which he received title to the block of land between Fifth and Sixth Avenues, and 39th and 40th Streets in the City of New York. After two or three renewals of the note he sold part of the land and paid the note. The present value of that land is close to $15,000,000. There have been numerous similar transactions in New York—and to a lesser extent in all cities. [121]

Showing the enhancement in land value in and adjacent to public parks, the land in Central Park, New York City, cost $5,040,000, in 1859. The Park Department now appraises the land as worth $570,000,000, an annual increase of $6,890,000, or 117 per cent *per annum*.

Within a year of the establishment of this park abutting lots trebled in value. For one large tract near the park, for which $40,000 was paid at about that time, $1,250,000 was refused twelve years later [121], representing a private profit created by all the people merely by their presence, and by municipal improvements paid for by taxation. Except for the high cost of land, all cities could have more and finer parks. A drastically increased tax on all land value offers the logical and only possible relief.

Before permission was given to build the Hotel Pierre on Fifth Avenue, New York, the builders were obliged to agree to pay to the Geary Estate $225,000 annual ground rent, and then to pay the taxes on the land, and on the building to be erected.

These double charges of ground rent and taxes proved so burdensome that the hotel was unable to pay them, and went into bankruptcy—a frequent occurrence in stifling private enterprise by private appropriation of the publicly-created ground rent by title holders.

The interplay of the pressure of population; private appropriation of ground rent necessitating taxes on buildings; and the activities of land speculators, create high rents and high land prices—and slums, the locale of most poverty and crime.

Manhattan Island, with a population of 2,000,000 people, with

77,000 separate lots, has about 40,000 title holders. Of these, about 35,000 own single lots. The bulk of the 4 billion dollars of land value is held by about 5,000 persons. Less than 1 per cent of the population have approximately 95 per cent of the land value.

Notwithstanding virtual abolition, after the outbreak of the American Revolution in 1775, of many of the old manorial and patroonship privileges, the small leaseholders could not dispose of their land without paying the landlord a portion (usually one-quarter) of the amount received in the sale. This came to a crisis in 1839, when Stephen van Rensselaer, one of the largest manorial landlords, died, having willed the land on the west side of the Hudson to his son Stephen, and that on the east side to his son William.

The agitation continued for eight years among leaseholders in Albany, Columbia, Delaware, Montgomery, Rensselaer and other counties and culminated in anti-rent riots against feudal landlordism. Tenancy had increased and in the fight against the landlords murders were frequent. With the result: Stephen sold his portion for $2.30 an acre, and William sold his tract for $42,000, and the new state constitution of 1846 abolished all feudal tenures.

An article in the *New York Times,* December 30, 1884, said: "By the constitution of the State of New York, 'all feudal tenures of every description, with all their incidents, are declared abolished,' but as a matter of fact, the incidents of feudal tenure are not abolished. This very cumbrousness and complexity of the transfer of land is one of them, and the right of dower is distinctly another. The common law of England upon the subject of real property is a survival from feudal times, and it has nowhere in this country been completely remodeled in conformity with the needs and usages of an industrial community. There is, by law, a special sanctity attached to ownership of land as compared with that of other property, and the alienation of it is purposely made difficult. In England, this treatment of land still corresponds to a real public sentiment. The owner of land is an object of much more social consideration than the owner of an equal value of personal property. Inasmuch as the 'landed interests' still govern Great Britain, it is to be expected that British laws should make as troublesome as possible the acquisition of 'estates' by new men who have enriched themselves, and who aspire to 'found families.'

"We have abolished primogeniture and entail which are the chief legal supports of the landed aristocracy. But we have by no means got rid in our laws of the feudal habit of regarding property in land as more important to the state than other property, and it is from this habit that the practice of making land less easily alienable than other property proceeds."

Anson Bingham, in the *Law of Real Property* wrote: "The State of New York not only holds the supreme title to all land within its boundaries but so does every other of the original thirteen states, *over and above private titles of every kind and nature.* The present holders of land title in New York, whether or not conscious of the fact, hold their titles in subordination to the absolute title of the state, and can convey only their rights subject thereto . . . *The rule naturally follows that no person can, by any possible arrangement, become invested with the absolute ownership of land . . . Absolute right of land is vested in the State.*"

The constitution of the State of New York, Article I, Sec. 10, reads: *"The people of this state, in their right of sovereignty, are deemed to possess the original and ultimate property in and to all lands within the jurisdiction of the state."*

Notwithstanding this, the tremendous increase in land value in the City of New York all these years, created by all the people, has been allowed by law to be appropriated by those in whose names the land stood registered, and who have done nothing to earn it.

14

The Delaware Region
(Below the Schuylkill)

ALL the land in the Delaware region was included in the grant by King Charles I of England to the Virginia Company, in 1606.

Henry Hudson, an Englishman in the service of the Dutch East India Company, in the *Half Moon,* seeking a northwestern passage, seems to have been the first European to discover the Delaware Bay, in which he anchored on August 28, 1609.

He attempted no settlement, but tarried there a few days making observations and soundings, filling his water casks from some Delaware creek, and for food, catching fish, which were plentiful there at that season. Five days after entering the Delaware he sailed into New York harbor.

The Delaware was named for Lord De la Ware, the Virginia governor, by Samuel Argall of Virginia, who dropped anchor in the bay one day the year following the visit of Hudson. There is no evidence that De la Ware ever saw the bay. [16]

No attempt was made by any one to explore the Delaware until five years after Hudson discovered it, when five vessels were fitted out by merchants of Amsterdam, Holland, to make discoveries in America, as related in the chapter on New York. All arrived at Manhattan, whence, in one of the vessels, the "Fortune," Captain Cornelius Jacobson Mey sailed to the Delaware, and gave his name to Cape May. He then returned with the others to Holland, except Captain Hendrickson, who remained to explore the Delaware River. This Hendrickson did in 1615 or 1616, in the boat "Onrest" (Restless), which he built to replace the one he had lost. It had a keel of 38 feet, length 44-1/2 feet and a beam of 11 feet. He sailed up the river as far as the Schuylkill, and undoubtedly was the first European to sail up the Delaware.

The Dutch West India Company in 1623 sent a vessel, the "New Netherland," with Captain Mey, to the South River (the name the Dutch gave the river subsequently named the Delaware). They arrived in the Delaware and erected Fort Nassau at Timber Creek, on the New Jersey side, about five miles below Camden. This was the first attempt by Europeans at settlement on the Delaware.

When the governor of Virginia, at Jamestown, learned that the Dutch were trading on the Delaware, he sent Captain Jones to "vindicate the exclusive right of the English," but it is recorded that, "by the wickedness of him and his mariners the adventure was lost and the whole project overthrown." The Virginians denounced Jones and asserted that he seemed to have been bribed by the Dutch. As a result serious contention arose between the English and Dutch governments.

Samuel Godyn and Samuel Bloemaert, Amsterdam merchants and directors of the West India Company, through agents sent by them, obtained from the Indians in June, 1629, for "a certain parcel of goods," a tract of land in Delaware, thirty-two English miles along the shore of the Delaware Bay and two miles inland, extending from Cape Henlopen, to Little Creek, opposite Dover. This purchase was ratified by Director Peter Minuet and the Council of New Netherland, at Manhattan, "under the Jurisdiction of their Noble Highnesses, the Lords-States-Generals of the United Netherlands and the Incorporated West India Company, Department of Amsterdam." This gives, the deed read, "Godyn and Bloemaert, or those who may hereafter obtain their interest, full and irrevocable authority and power to hold and possess the land." This was afterwards confirmed by the Chamber of XIX at Amsterdam.

The following year, possession of a tract across the bay, sixteen miles square in Cape May County, New Jersey, was obtained from the Indians for the same patroons.

Immediately upon acquiring the Delaware tract, a syndicate

of several patroons who were favored stockholders of the company was formed in Holland to send a colony to occupy it. They took as a partner and patroon David Pietersen de Vries, "a bold and skilful seaman and master of artillery in the service of the United Provinces," who had two months previously returned from the East Indies.

Among others who joined the syndicate was Kiliaen van Rensselaer, an Amsterdam diamond merchant, and a cormorant for land in America beyond his ability to use.

The colony sailed from the Trexel in December, 1630, in two ships, one of which was captured by pirates. The other one, the "Walvis," with thirty colonists, arrived at the Delaware Capes the following April.

The Dutch fort, Nassau, on the Delaware, erected seven years previously, had been abandoned.

The colonists located a settlement which they named Swaanendael (valley of the swans) inside of Cape Henlopen. They brought cattle, provisions, agricultural implements, merchandise for trading with the Indians, and also brick and other materials for a building which they erected and surrounded by palisades. This is the only specific statement of brick being imported that I have seen in my researches in colonial history.

This was the first white settlement in Delaware but, unfortunately, due to a trifling cause about an Indian tearing down a piece of tin bearing the Coat of Arms of The Netherlands to make a tobacco pipe, the entire colony was murdered. The Indians raised considerable quantities of corn, and, had they not lacked ingenuity, could have made a better pipe of a corn cob, and this massacre might not have occurred.

Some writers have stated that De Vries was in command of the "Walvis," which brought the settlers, but he did not come until twenty months later. Arriving in December, 1632, he found the remains of the murdered colonists. He continued in the Delaware River for some time; went to Fort Nassau, and found it in decay and occupied by some Indians wearing English-made coats. He had the fort repaired.

So uninformed was the governor of Virginia of the geography of "Lord Delaware's Bay," that not until twenty-five years after the settlement at Jamestown did he dispatch a sloop with seven or eight men "to learn if a river flowed into the bay." This was the first attempt of the English to explore the Delaware. [16] They were killed by Indians, and it was the coats of these which the Indians were wearing.

The deplorable massacre of the colony discouraged the patroons from making further efforts at that time to colonize in Delaware. Henceforth, for many years, the Dutch confined their activities along the Delaware largely to trading with the Indians. But for that purpose it was necessary to locate trading-houses at strategic points, and that meant they must have land on which to locate them. And, quite as important, it was necessary to monopolize the land to prevent other nationalities from likewise establishing trading-posts in competititon. This led to continuous fights for monopoly of the land.

Godyn, Bloemaert and van Rensselaer were never in America. They were absentee landholders and their object in acquiring land was to monopolize vast areas and lease it to settlers on a feudal tenure of land rent, payable in money or the produce of the labor of the settlers.

Failing in this at Swaanendael, they sought some method of profitably disposing of their land. Being influential directors of the company, they concluded that the best way out was to unload on the company, which they did six years after acquiring the land, for fifteen thousand guilders (about $6,240). This was the first land transaction in the Delaware region between white people. In the sale, it was stipulated that the right of neither party in a suit pending between the patroons and the company at Amsterdam was to be impaired.

The Calvert grant of Maryland by Charles I, in 1632, included the present state of Maryland and all of Delaware, all of which was part of the Virginia grant of 1606 and 1609. Granting land in America without regard to any previous grant thereof was a common practice of all the Stuart monarchs. But this grant to Calvert excepted any region which was settled and cultivated. This gave rise to continued strife during the next 130 years, between Calvert and the Dutch on the Delaware, and between Calvert and Penn, and their respective heirs.

The Calvert grant was for land, within the aforesaid bounds, which was *hactenus in culta*—in a country hitherto uncultivated. The contention between Calvert and the Dutch hinged on whether Delaware had been "inhabited and cultivated" prior to the Calvert grant. Inasmuch as the massacre of the Dutch settlers at Swaanendael occurred four years prior to the grant to Calvert, and while the settlers were at work cultivating the land, it is evident that the Dutch had the better of the contention.

Charles I of England in 1633 gave to Captain Thomas Younge, a London grocer and a man of influence, a commission to discover and exploit. In July of that year, Younge explored the Delaware River, searching for a northwestern passage to Asia. He is said to have proclaimed the sovereignty of his Britannic Majesty over the region and to have ordered the departure of a Dutch ship, no doubt that of De Vries, which he found near the present site of Trenton.

Notwithstanding that the Dutch colony on the Delaware had been massacred, and the Dutch had no colony on the Delaware, they began actively to pursue the fur trade with the natives along the river, maintaining trappers and traders. These men were instructed to keep a sharp lookout for, and report at once to headquarters at Manhattan, the arrival of any foreign ship.

Valuable fur-bearing animals then abounded, but the only species now remaining is the muskrat, which is still plentiful. It was a low-priced fur until given the name "Hudson seal."

The governor of Virginia, in 1635, sent fourteen or fifteen men to the Delaware River. In command of George Holmes, they were to make another attempt to capture the Dutch fort, Nassau, which, however, was then unoccupied. But Thomas Hall deserted the expedition and went to Fort Amsterdam, where he notified the Dutch and entered their employ. One account cites that a file of Dutch soldiers went to Fort Nassau, arrested the English, and turned them back with the command not to repeat the visit. But Fiske [47] said that, as soon as van Twiller at Fort Amsterdam learned of the English attack, he dispatched a warship to the Delaware and captured the English and carried them to New Amsterdam. De Vries then took them to Point Comfort. There, he found another English vessel just starting for the Delaware, but upon his arrival it desisted in the venture.

The Swedes and Dutch

William Usselinx (1567–1647), a native of Antwerp, was a persistent promoter of foreign trading and colonization companies, and the leader in the promotion of the Dutch West India Company in 1621. Presumably because that company became active in piracy, to the comparative neglect of colonization in New Netherland, in which he was more interested, he disassociated himself from the company. In 1624 he betook himself to Sweden, to endeavor to interest King Gustavus Adolphus in organizing a Swedish company for exploration on the South (Delaware) River.

He so convincingly presented his case that a widespread interest was developed in Sweden, which eventuated in a number of charters being granted.

The Swedish West India Company was granted a charter by Gustavus for twelve years, to begin May 1, 1627, with the exclusive right to trade, make settlements, build castles and cities and administer justice in America, Africa and Magellanica, or Terra Australis. The rights, privileges, duties, exactions and emoluments were as clearly and minutely stated as they might be by learned lawyers and financiers in a charter of the present day: "All vessels taken by the company from pirates shall be for the company benefit, except where they are assisted by government vessels, in which case the prizes are to be divided equally." The government was to subscribe four hundred thousand Swedish dollars and to receive 4 per cent duties, 20 per cent of all precious ores discovered, and 10 per cent of the profits.

Among the subscribers were the king's mother; Prince John Casimir, brother-in-law of the king; members of the royal council; and many civil and military officers of high rank, bishops, clergymen, merchants, country gentlemen and farmers.

Before sufficient capital was subscribed, Sweden became involved in the Thirty Years' War. That, and the death of the king in the battle of Lutzen, in 1632, caused a cessation of public interest in the Delaware project.

Queen Christina, who succeeded her father, is said to have

favored the project. In April, 1633, Oxenstierna, the Swedish chancellor, who was regent during the Queen's minority, signed and made public recommendations of the undertaking which had been prepared by, or for, Gustavus. Meanwhile Usselinx traveled through Europe, endeavoring to enlist interest and financial support.

Peter Minuet, a native of Westphalia, had been the Dutch governor of New Netherland, and upon his recall to Holland, in 1632, was dismissed by the Dutch West India Company. Five years afterwards, he went to Sweden to endeavor to revive the interest of the Swedish government and capitalists, by explaining to them the great profits to be made in the peltry trade on the Delaware.

Again subscriptions to the stock were invited, and many of the nobility became subscribers. The hope that such project would open a market for copper, of which Sweden had a large surplus, helped to bring the promotion to fruition.

Admiral Klaus Fleming, of a wealthy Finnish family, and a Swedish admiral, became financially interested in the undertaking and was appointed director-general. Usselinx was engaged as manager and was to receive 1 per cent of the value of all merchandise exported and imported by the company.

Due to delay incident to the unseaworthy condition of one of the ships, which had to put back three times for repairs, the investment in the first voyage increased as preparations proceeded until it had reached thirty-six thousand guilders when the expedition finally sailed from Goteborg, in November, 1637. In partial extenuation of the unexpectedly large initial cost, the remark was made that, "a good rich Spanish prize will reimburse us."

The ships "Kalmar Nyckel" and "Fogel Grip," heavily armed, set sail with merchandise for the Indian trade. There were about fifty persons aboard, including many petty criminals. Some of the criminals are said to have been bandits, sent to Delaware to serve a term in exile and then to be returned to Sweden. The ships sailed the course usual at that early period, via the Canary and West Indies Islands.

Peter Minuet was in command. Most of the sailors and employees were Dutch. Reaching the American coast, they put in at Jamestown, Virginia, for a few days.

They arrived in the Delaware in the spring of 1638, and settled on Christiana Creek. There they built Fort Christiana, or Christianaham, now Wilmington, the first permanent white settlement along the Delaware.

Arrival of the Swedish expedition was at once reported to Governor William Kieft, director-general of New Netherland at Manhattan, the office which Peter Minuet, the leader of this Swedish expedition, had held only six years previously.

Shortly thereafter, Minuet received a letter from Kieft, in which he said: "The whole South River of New Netherland, both above and below has been for many years our property, occupied by our forts and sealed with our blood [the Swaanendael massacre] . . . We protest against all the evil consequences of bloodshed and worry which our trading company may thus suffer. We shall protect our rights as we find advisable."

Minuet replied that he had as much right to build a fort as the Dutch, and continued to build. He opened trade with the Indians and arranged with the Indian chief, Mattahoon, for permission to occupy the land, for which Minuet gave a copper kettle and some small articles. The chief subsequently said he was promised, but never received, half of the tobacco grown thereon.

When the Swedes arrived, the Dutch had no settlement on the Delaware and were merely fur traders there, though they had the unoccupied Fort Nassau, below Camden. After arrival of the Swedes, they placed a garrison at Nassau.

From that time on, for seventeen years, until the Dutch expelled the Swedes, there was continual strife between them, each one interfering with the other in the fur trade. The Dutch claimed the Swedes had ruined the trade, by which they probably meant that the competition of the Swedes had obliged the Dutch to increase the volume of goods offered the Indians for their peltries. The Dutch often incited the Indians against the Swedes, and induced the Indians to sell land to the Dutch which the Indians had already sold to the Swedes, a common practice with Indians in their land dealings with the whites.

While the Swedes supposed they had bought land from the

Indians, they had really, as in all purported purchases by Europeans of land from the Indians in the early days of colonization, merely obtained consent of co-occupancy of the land. The territory concerned in the transaction was on the west side of the Delaware River, from Cape Henlopen to Trenton Falls, and inland as far as they might wish. Both the English from Maryland and the Dutch asserted their exclusive right to this land, the Indians having sold it to each one in turn.

The Swedes were anxious to establish the doctrine that a land title from Indians was paramount to any other title. Chief Mattahoon said: "All nations coming to the river are welcome, and we sell land to all who ask for it."[a]

Minuet was the first governor of New Sweden, the name the Swedes had given their location. He remained there only three months and departed with the two vessels, leaving twenty-four men on the Christiana. History records that, while en route back to Sweden, he lost his life in a storm at St. Christopher Island, in the West Indies; but Acrelius, who later joined the colony, and who drew from reliable sources, stated that Minuet, after three years at Fort Christiana, died and was buried there. [16]

Minuet was credited with having sagacity and energy. Except for the persistence of him and Usselinx, and especially of the latter, who was never in America, the Swedes likely would never have become a factor in Delaware.

Peter Hollaendare Ridder, variously stated as being a native Swede, Dutch, or of German origin, succeeded Minuet as the second governor. After delay in his departure, he arrived in Delaware in April, 1640, with a company of involuntary emigrants, and was fired on from the Dutch fort, Nassau.

The first Swedish immigrants were as unfitted for the tasks before them as had been the first English settlers at Jamestown. Ridder wrote to Sweden that there was not a man among the settlers who could build a small cottage, or even saw a board. This year thirty thousand peltries were exported to Sweden.

Various privileges were offered by the Swedish Company for the more extensive settlement of the colony. All Swedish subjects were allowed "to establish on the lands of the company as many

[a] N. Y. Col. Doc.

colonies as they may be able, at their own expense, and to use them during certain years of franchise." But, "any one who has purchased land from the savages, or from the company at a just price, and established cultivators, shall possess the same for ever, with all allodial franchises customary. No one, however, can obtain land except by order of the governor."

A Swedish grant was made in 1640 to Henry Hockhammer & Co. (probably shipowners in Sweden or Holland). They were granted as much land as necessary for their purposes, on both sides of the Delaware River, on payment of three florins for each family established in their territory. After ten years, they were to pay in New Sweden, for support of government on the Delaware, 5 per cent on all goods exported or imported. The same year, tracts on the west side of the Delaware, about eighteen English miles above the Christiana, were granted to de Rehden, de Horst and others.

But the promoters of the company found it impossible at that time to induce Swedes to migrate to Delaware. Some Finns were recruited as settlers, and convicts were given the choice of going to Delaware or being hanged. Fortunately for the future well-being of the state, these culprits, though charged with only minor offenses, either died, or were returned to Sweden as soon as their terms of servitude ended. A crime of which many of them were convicted was burnbeating, which seems to have been the burning of grass or other growth to induce greater productivity on land not belonging to them.

The third Swedish expedition arrived in 1641. Colonel Johan Printz, the new Swedish governor to succeed Ridder, arrived in February, 1643, after a six months' voyage over the usual southern course, with the fourth expedition, of two ships—"Renown" and "Fame and Stork."

The instructions given by the regent to Printz before sailing were: "Her Majesty will have the lieutenant-colonel and governor regulate himself upon his voyage and arrival in New Sweden. The Swedish domain extends from Cape Henlopen to Trenton Falls on the west shore, and from Cape May to Raccoon Creek on the east side, which the governor is to keep intact, notwithstanding some English (from Connecticut) have recently settled on the east side at Varkenskill (Salem Creek). The governor is to seek to bring these English under the government of the Swedish crown, and they might also, with good reason, be driven out and away from such place. Should the Dutch undertake any hostilities or attack, be prepared to repel force by force. To treat the Indians with all humanity and respect; to provide a fortress to close up the river; no other subjects to be permitted to trade with the Indians; to encourage and promote agriculture and tobacco, and cattle breeding."

These instructions were penned in the quiet and security of the office of the chancellor at Stockholm, and at a time when Sweden was well on the way to becoming the great military power of the north of Europe. But such instructions, if put into execution, would inevitably result in war and disaster, if not backed by a stronger armed force than Sweden had ever sent to the Delaware.

It is interesting to note the extent of the population on which Printz had to rely for support in carrying out his orders to "shut up the river, drive out the English from Salem, and repel Dutch attacks by force." In 1644, the year in which Queen Christina came to the throne, and just before arrival of the fifth expedition, which increased the colony to 200, the total number of males in New Sweden on both sides of the river was 93; three years later there were 183 persons including children; and five years after that, just previous to new arrivals, the entire population was only 70. From disease, 26 had died in a year. Most of the others returned to Sweden as fast as new ones arrived.

However, in pursuance of his instructions to fortify all important points and "shut up the river," Printz erected Fort New Goteborg, at Tinicum Island, above Chester, and equipped it with four brass cannon. There also he built a handsome mansion. During the year he built Fort Elfsborg, at Elsingboro Point, on the New Jersey side below Salem Creek, which mounted eight cannon and one potshoof; Fort Nya Korsholm, on the Schuylkill; and Fort Nya Wasa on Mingo Creek, the last named to give a more perfect control of the fur trade with the Indians. These, with Fort Christiana, gave the Swedes five forts along the Delaware.

The main object of Fort Elfsborg, aside from "shutting up the river" against others, was to oblige Dutch ships to salute the Swedish flag, in recognition of Swedish sovereignty, which greatly offended the Dutch.

During the first six years of Swedish occupancy, criminals were sent to serve terms in exile, until Printz determined he would have no more of them, and sent new arrivals back without permitting them to land.

Joran Kyn (Keen), a soldier bodyguard of Printz, was granted a large tract of land at the present site of Chester, part of which he cultivated. [3x] Another Swede had a tobacco plantation thereabouts. Indicating the Swedish trading and agricultural activities on the Delaware, the sixth year of the settlement, two ships returned to Sweden with 2,127 packages of beaver skins and 70,421 pounds of tobacco.

Fort New Goteborg, with all its buildings, was burned the next year, and all the powder and goods in store blown up. A servant had fallen asleep, leaving a candle burning. [16]

Andreas Hudde was in 1645 appointed Dutch governor on the Delaware, to succeed Jan Jansen who was charged with fraud and disloyalty. Hudde proved to be more energetic and faithful than his predecessor, and afterwards became a prominent citizen in New Amsterdam.

The Swedes making settlements on the Schuylkill prompted the Dutch to do likewise. Hudde bought of the Indians, and proceeded to build, on land which Printz claimed the Indians had already sold to him. Whereupon Huyden, the Swedish commissary, with twenty-four men fully armed, with fixed bayonets, arrived on the scene. Hudde wrote Printz, complaining of the insults and many "bloody menaces," and said that he himself had purchased the land from the Indians, the real owners, perhaps before the name of South River was ever heard of in Sweden—adding that "tearing down the Arms of the Netherlands was an infringement on the authority of their High Mightinesses the States General, and that of His Highness the Prince of Orange." The messenger who carried the letter to Printz reported that Printz was insolent, threw him out of doors, and took a gun in hand threatening to shoot him.

Hans Jackson, a Dutchman, began to erect a building, but it was destroyed by a son of Printz, who threatened that if he again attempted to build there he would be given a "good drubbing." Thomas Broen, a Dutchman, started a building, but the Swedes, under Sergeant van Dyck, pulled it down. Broen was told if he did not leave they would beat him. Simon Root, and other Dutchmen who were endeavoring to build, were driven away by Lieutenant Swen Schute, and their building torn down. Thus the strife went on interminably.

The Dutch governor continued to grant land to individuals and in 1646 granted to four persons two hundred acres in Delaware, "over against" Reedy Island, with the stipulation that if not cultivated within one year the land would be forfeited. This tract was afterwards forfeited for non-use.

Printz supplied the Indians with guns, with which to kill game for the Swedes, and at the same time wrote to Sweden: "The Dutch destroy our fur-trade with the Indians, strengthen the savages with guns and ammunition and stir up the savages to attack us. They begin to buy land from the Indians within our boundaries which we had bought eight years ago. They see we are weak. A new gristmill has been built; I have caused waterfalls to be examined for a sawmill. We need vessels to trade with the West Indies. We need unmarried women. The freemen desire to know about their privileges and the criminals ask how long they must serve."

The seventh Swedish expedition arrived in 1647 and, the same year, Peter Stuyvesant arrived at New Amsterdam as governor and director-general, succeeding Kieft. He wrote complimentary letters to the governors of Massachusetts and New Haven, desiring to be on friendly terms with them, but at the same time asserting the right of the Dutch to all the land between and along the Connecticut and Delaware Rivers, "as the indubitable right of the States General and the West India Company."

Fort Beversreede (road of the beavers) was built by Andreas Hudde in 1648, on the east side of the Schuylkill, just above the Swedish fort, Nya Korsholm, to which Printz objected. [115]

By the peace of Westphalia, in 1648, ending the Thirty Years' War, Sweden gained, becoming a power of the first class.

Conferences were held in 1650 between Stuyvesant and Printz, and between Stuyvesant and delegates from the United Colonies of New England, for settlement of boundaries of disputed territories. There was no immediate decision; each maintaining his own right to land occupied and denying any right thereto of the respective claimants.

With less than one hundred men, Printz controlled the Delaware River from the Capes to Trenton Falls, on the west side, and to Fort Nassau on the east side. The Swedes forcibly tore down and totally destroyed the houses, country places and gardens on Dutch land, which the Dutch considered disrespect of the States General and West India Company. Printz forbade the Swedes to trade with the Dutch. [65]

Shortly thereafter, a Dutch armed ship from Manhattan arrived in the Delaware and landed two hundred men. Stuyvesant, with 120 men, came over the wilderness from New Amsterdam. He proceeded again to buy land of the Indians on both sides of the river, which Printz claimed the Swedes had already bought, but which the Indians denied.

Stuyvesant, to prove ownership, erected Fort Casimir, at the present site of New Castle, six miles below Swedish Fort Christiana. He equipped Fort Casimir with twelve guns, transferred to it the garrison, and what military equipment remained in Fort Nassau, and abandoned that fort. Thus he practically took control of the entire Delaware region.

The Dutch abandoned Fort Beversreede and concentrated their forces at Fort Casimir, where twenty-two Dutch families located. Printz abandoned Fort Nya Korsholm, the mill and blockhouse at Mondel, and Fort Elfsborg. Great swarms of mosquitoes, which still exist thereabouts, feasted on the garrison day and night.

The "press of business and other obstacles" preventing the government of Sweden from regulating the affairs of New Sweden "as the utility of the company and the interests of the government demanded," the management of affairs on the Delaware was placed in the General College of Commerce in Sweden.

Accordingly, it commissioned John Amundsen Besh, a naval captain, to embark for New Sweden and endeavor to procure every species of advantage to the benefit of her majesty and the Company of the South. At that time more settlers were offering to go than there were ships available.

The site of present Marcus Hook, below Chester, was for past faithful services granted by Printz to Captain Besh, to keep and possess for ever. Although there was no Swedish settlement on the present site of Philadelphia, Printz granted thousands of acres in various tracts there to different Swedes.

Queen Christina granted Tinicum Island, in the Delaware River above Chester, to Governor Printz and "his lawful heirs as a perpetual possession because of his long and faithful services."

This was as far up the Delaware as the Swedes had then settled. It was here that Governor Printz lived and moored his pleasure yacht. The basin is considered the oldest yacht anchorage in America, and is now owned and occupied by the Philadelphia and the Corinthian Yacht Clubs of Philadelphia.

Queen Christina later granted to her new governor, Risingh, and to "his wife and their legal male heirs and their descendants, as much land in the West Indies and in New Sweden as he shall be able to cultivate with twenty or thirty peasants, ceding to him it and all its dependencies in woods, fields, fisheries, rivers and mill sites, as a perpetual property."

Just who gave her, or how she obtained, in far-away Sweden, the right to alienate all this land from future generations who must occupy it, is a question for further consideration.

The Swedes had spread to the New Jersey side and occupied thin settlements between Maurice River and Burlington, but were mostly in Salem and Gloucester Counties. [94] They traded with the Indians for furs, in exchange for hats, cloth, satin, silk and other merchandise. Trade in peltries was prohibited to others than agents of the Swedish company. [16]

Not getting any dividends, and with Sweden at almost incessant warfare in Europe, the company failed to supply arms, livestock and craftsmen, and the needed provisions and merchandise for trading with the Indians. This forced the colony to shift for itself and the settlers became dissatisfied. [130]

There had been no ship from Sweden in six years. The call of

Printz on the home government for soldiers to protect the colony from the growing power, and possible attack, of the Dutch was ignored. After ten years of battling with the Dutch and English, and now weary and mortified at his weak military position, Printz sailed for Sweden in October, 1653, with his wife, four daughters and twenty-five soldiers and settlers, presumably aboard a Dutch ship. His son-in-law, John Poppegoya, was left in command, being the fourth Swedish governor, who served for about eighteen months. The Swedes then had three hundred acres under cultivation.

The Dutch navigator De Vries, satirized Captain Printz as: "a man of brave size, who weighs four hundred pounds and takes three drinks at every meal."

John Risingh was appointed the fifth governor, to succeed Printz. He was instructed to fortify a harbor already established; to extend the Swedish possessions on both sides of the Delaware, but "without causing any breach of friendship with the English or Dutch"; also, if possible, to induce the Dutch to abandon Fort Casimir. His instructions were to use "arguments and serious remonstrances, but without hostility. It is better to suffer the Dutch to occupy the fortress than it should fall into the hands of the English who are more powerful, and of course more dangerous in that country."

Risingh sailed from Goteborg in the ship, "Aren." With him were military officers and troops, a clergyman and more than two hundred settlers. They arrived in the Delaware in May, 1655. This was the first Swedish ship to arrive in eight years and came a year and a half after the departure of Printz.

The Swedish population on the Delaware had, by deaths, desertions to Maryland and Virginia, and from other causes, decreased to less than a hundred. The fresh arrivals infused new life into the colony.

Upon arriving off the Dutch fort, Casimir, Risingh sent about twenty soldiers ashore in a small boat. They were civilly received by Gerritt Bikker, the Dutch commandant of the fort. Disregarding his instructions to gain the fort only by argument and remonstrances, Risingh demanded surrender, and fired two shots at the fort, whereupon it surrendered. The Swedes confiscated everything in the fort and renamed it Fort Trinity, for the day on which it was captured. Most of the Dutch, including Bikker, remained and took the oath of allegiance to Sweden. A few who would not do so were expelled.

Shortly after arrival, Risingh reported to the home government that he had again bought of those thrifty Minqua Indian realtors, land which the Indians had repeatedly sold to the Dutch and Swedes; and, that moreover, the Minqua called themselves protectors of the Swedes. He said, "The Lenni Lennape threaten to kill the Swedes and we must daily buy their friendship, for they are more hostile than heretofore. A great part of the people here are lazy and unwilling Finns. There are 368 Swedes and Dutch on the Delaware." This presumably included the Finns, who had come with the Swedes.

He further reported: "At Christiana six or eight houses are now built. The land is practically clear of Hollanders. Would be well if the same could be said of the English. The English in Maryland draw our Swedish people to the Severn River, and ruin our trade. It is necessary that no land be assigned to any one unless he uses it efficiently. Otherwise, land of the company, or land which belongs to the Indians, is given away. I have caused fields adjoining Christiana to be divided into lots. [106] Some Dutch farmers should be sent. Saltpeter could be manufactured, and a powder-mill established." Whether or not Mr. du Pont de Nemours ever heard of this suggestion, Wilmington became the explosive-producing center of America.

Peace between England and Holland was agreed upon in 1655, the same year that the Swedes invaded Poland and Axel Oxenstierna, the Swedish chancellor, died.

Risingh's capture of Fort Casimir aroused the fighting spirit of the directors of the West India Company in Holland and, now that the war between England and Holland was ended, they issued orders to Stuyvesant "to exert every nerve to revenge the injury, and not only to recover the fort but to drive the Swedes from every side of the river. Those Swedes who desire to settle under the Dutch government shall be allowed to do so."

They provided him with vessels, materials and soldiers, and ordered him to "press any vessels into his service that might be in New Netherland." Stuyvesant went silently though actively to work to prepare a fleet and armaments.

The expedition, consisting of seven warships and six hundred or more men, sailed to the Delaware and anchored above their former Fort Casimir. Stuyvesant, who was with the expedition, announced that the Dutch "claimed the whole river and all Swedish territory thereon"; and Schute was called upon to surrender. Meanwhile all trails leading from the fort were occupied by Dutch soldiers, who raised breastworks. The next morning Schute signed terms of surrender. He and twenty others took the oath of allegiance to Holland and remained in the country.

Having taken this fort, the Dutch then proceeded to attack Fort Christiana. They methodically erected numerous batteries, until they had the fort invested on all sides, and their armed ships anchored in the Christiana at the mouth of the Brandywine. These batteries spread over land in the present Wilmington.

The fort had a force of only thirty men and very little powder. There were many parleys between Stuyvesant and Risingh, but Stuyvesant had his orders to drive the Swedes from the Delaware and he meant to do so. Failing to influence Stuyvesant to desist, Risingh, on September 15, surrendered.

Risingh, in his remonstrance, accused the Dutch of "breaking open our houses; plundering all the settlements on the west side of the river; violently tearing women from their homes, and whole buildings destroyed; killing our cattle, goats, swine and poultry; and plantations destroyed.

"Higher up the river they plundered many, and stripped them to the skin. At New Goteborg they robbed Mrs. Poppegoya (daughter of Printz), and many others who had collected all their property together there. The whole country is left so desolate that scarce any means are remaining for subsistence of the inhabitants."

Swedes who would not take an oath of allegiance to the Dutch were sent to Europe, on the ships "Spotted Cow" and "Bear." For the conquest, Stuyvesant was commended. He was instructed to place Fort Casimir in a state of defense.

The Swedes lost the Delaware. The Dutch thus gained the

monopoly of the land and the fur trade on the Delaware. The Dutch attack was waged by the most powerful fleet and army ever engaged in battle on the North American continent. The terms of surrender are given by Ferris [45] and by Acrelius.

The Dutch, no doubt, would have striven to drive out the Swedes much sooner, except that the Dutch men-of-war had been engaged during the previous two years in a naval war with England over the English navigation act of 1651. Further, the arrogant intrusion of the English on the Dutch settlements in Connecticut, and the unjustifiable massacre of Indians by the Dutch, under Kieft, at Pavonia, New Jersey, and at Esopus, New York, prevented the Dutch at New Amsterdam from giving military attention to the Delaware. And the great distance from St. Mary's (along the Potomac) to the Delaware, together with their own troubles on the Chesapeake, probably accounts for the Calverts in Maryland not making a determined effort to pursue their claim to the Delaware territory.

Shortly after the Swedish surrender, the Swedish ship, "Mercuris," with 130 settlers, the tenth and last Swedish expedition, arrived in the Delaware, causing consternation among the Dutch, as well as the Swedes who were left there. The captain, being forbidden to land the passengers and cargo on the Delaware, proceeded overland to Manhattan to see Stuyvesant. While he was absent, John Poppegoya and Swen Schute, disregarding their recent oath of allegiance to the Dutch, sailed the ship, with a number of Swedes and Indians, past Fort Casimir and landed her passengers and cargo at Marcus Hook, below Chester. The ship returned to Sweden.

Eight years after the Dutch conquest of New Sweden, some Swedes in Sweden fitted out an expedition for the recovery of their former territory on the Delaware. The expedition, commanded by the Swedish Vice-Admiral Lechelm, who had been to New Sweden, consisted of the frigate, "Falcon," of thirty-two guns, and a yacht of eight guns, carrying two hundred or more soldiers in addition to the crew. The expedition ran aground three times at different points in European waters, at the last of which the yacht and all her stores were abandoned and the venture was given up. At that time, both Dutch forts were in a condition of decay and with but few pieces of cannon. Had the Swedes arrived, the Dutch could not have withstood them. Besides, the disaffected Swedes and Finns then on the river far outnumbered the Dutch and naturally would have sided with their countrymen. Delaware would then again have come under the crown of Sweden.

The Swedish ambassador at The Hague made repeated demands for the restoration of New Sweden and nine years after the conquest, addressed their High Mightinesses at Amsterdam maintaining their rights on the river, and deploring the acts of the Dutch, saying: ". . . His most sacred majesty hopes that the West India Company shall be constrained to render restitution. For, had the crown of Sweden acquired Nova Suecia justly? Was the same in lawful possession thereof?"

The difficulties arising from the seizure were not settled until, twelve years after the conquest, a treaty provided that the controversies between the Swedish Company and the Dutch should be examined and satisfaction given.

Inasmuch as the territory had been before that time wrested from the Dutch by the English, it is unlikely that Sweden, or the Swedish Company, ever received any redress. After making settlements, and gaining a commanding position on the Delaware, as they did, the wonder has been that the colony did not have better support from the company and government in Sweden.

Queen Christina came of age and to the throne in 1644, and abdicated ten years later. This was approximately the period of the Printz administration. During that time very few Swedish ships arrived. For long stretches of time, the colony was left on its own resources. No ship arrived between 1644 and 1647, or again until 1653. One ship reached Manhattan in 1649, but was captured by the Dutch.

This neglect practically killed the potentially lucrative Indian trade, in which the colony had made a good start, and closed the door to any export of furs and tobacco to Sweden, which the colony had depended upon to exchange for European goods and other essentials. Without these it could no longer sustain itself or trade with the Indians; in short, on ships from Europe the colony depended for its actual existence.

The lack of support from the home country seems to have been caused by the military aggressions of Sweden in Europe, and by financial prostration resulting from militarism.

When Christina began to reign, 56 per cent of the public revenue was being used for war and military preparation. In that year Sweden began a war on Denmark, which ended the following year with a victory over the Danes, and the treaty of Bromsebro. Immediately thereafter, Sweden re-entered the war in Germany and made a drive on Vienna, which was terminated by the outbreak of an epidemic which drove them back. But the aggression continued until the treaty of peace at Westphalia, in 1648, at the end of the Thirty Years' War.

The loss of men and wealth had been enormous for those times, and was followed by the usual post-war depression and social unrest. Class antagonism became acute in 1650, when the small landholders in Sweden arose and assailed bureaucracy, the aristocracy and the nobility.

Christina was extravagant, spectacular and depraved. Under her government, state lands were allotted to favorites among the nobility and annual rents receivable were hypothecated for quick revenue.

When Gustavus Adolphus died, in 1632, the nobility held one-quarter of the land. When Christina abdicated they held one-half; and public expenditures for the royal court alone were four times what they had been when she came to the throne.

Further, Sweden was surrounded by enemies; all the neighboring countries, Russia, Poland, Denmark and the Germans, were jealous of, and feared, the newly acquired military strength of Sweden, but were ready to attack her at the earliest opportunity. The Swedes were aware of this enmity and felt constrained to hold their ships and man power at home, ready for any attack, rather than send them to far-away Delaware.

Swedish success at arms had made her war-minded and, to indulge her ambitions in Europe, she declared war on Poland in 1655. While she was capturing Warsaw and Cracow in Poland, Stuyvesant moved on New Sweden, which ended the Swedish reign on the Delaware. Sweden lost what might have developed into a Swedish empire in the new world.

New Englanders on the Delaware

The same year that the Swedes arrived in the Delaware, a colony of English settled at New Haven, Connecticut, where they acquired land of the natives.

Although there were vast areas of unused land about New Haven, the early settlers had privately appropriated it and later arrivals had to go farther afield to get land.

Learning that there was no settlement along the South (Delaware) River, in what is now southern Jersey, about sixty persons, comprising twenty families, early in 1641 left the English colony at New Haven to make a settlement on the Varkenskill (Salem Creek), on the New Jersey side of the South River or Bay.

They were under the leadership of Captain Nathaniel Turner, sailing in a vessel commanded by Robert Cogswell. Kieft, the Dutch governor at New Amsterdam, had notice of their coming through the East River. When passing Fort Amsterdam in their slow-moving craft, in a light wind against a headtide they were met by a protest from Kieft, which read: "I, William Kieft, director-general, etc., make known to you Robert Cogswell and your associates not to build nor plant on the South River lying within the limits of New Netherland, nor on the lands extending along there as lawfully belonging to us by our possessing the same long years ago, before it was frequented by any Christians, as appears by our forts which we have thereon; and also the mouth of the river sealed with our blood [the massacre of the Dutch there], and the soil thereof, most of which has been purchased from the Indians and paid for by us, unless you will settle under the States General and the noble Dutch West India Company, and swear allegiance and become subject to them. Failing whereof we protest against all damages and losses which may accrue therefrom."

Notwithstanding, the English proceeded to the Delaware, where they negotiated with the Indians for land and erected buildings, including a trading-house for Indian trade.

Dutch fur traders along the Delaware immediately apprised Fort Amsterdam of the settlement. This brought another protest from Kieft, who claimed it to be within the bounds of New Netherland. It also excited the Swedes and prompted Printz, the Swedish governor on the west side of the river, to buy land of the Indians on the New Jersey side, as far up as Raccoon Creek, below Camden. The Indians, having no conception of what was meant by private ownership of land, sold to Printz the same land which they had sold to the New Haven colonists. Printz sent some armed men to the English settlement with orders to amalgamate the new arrivals with the Swedes or drive them out. He did not, just then, succeed in doing either.

The following year, the New Haven colony extended its operations by building a trading-house on the Schuylkill, a region over which both the Dutch and Swedes had been claiming sovereignty and contending in armed combat. This brought protests against the English from both Printz and Kieft. The latter called a meeting of his council at New Amsterdam which resolved: "Having received unquestionable information that some English had the audacity to begin a settlement on the Schuylkill without any commission of a potentate, which is an affair of ominous consequences, disrespectful of their High Mightinesses the States General, and injurious to the interests of the Dutch West India Company, as by it their commerce on the South River might be eventually ruined; Resolved: That it is our duty to drive these English from thence, in the best manner possible."

Accordingly, Kieft issued instructions to Jan Jansen Van Ilpendam (called by the English John Jansen), head of the Dutch commissary on the South River. As soon as the yacht "Real and St. Martin" from New Amsterdam should arrive in the South River, Jansen was to embark therein with such a body of men as he could collect, proceed towards the Schuylkill, disembark there, and require the English to show by what authority they dared to make such encroachment upon "the Dutch rights and privileges, territory and commerce." Kieft continued, "If they can show no royal commission, then they are to be compelled to depart in peace to prevent effusion of blood. If they will not listen or submit then their persons are to be secured and brought to New Amsterdam. If the English leave the place you are to destroy their improvements and level them on the spot."

Jansen carried out his instructions and expelled the English from the Schuylkill, as later complained of by the English colony at New Haven. They reported to the council at Boston that the Dutch had, in a hostile manner, burnt their trading-house on the Schuylkill, seized their boat and goods, and for a while kept their men prisoners; they also complained of the ill treatment by the Swedes. The damage to the English was estimated at £500 sterling.

In 1644 an English expedition from Boston to the Delaware, in search of a lake supposed to be the source of the beavers, was fired on by the Swedes. To add injury to insult, Governor Printz compelled the English to pay him forty shillings to cover the cost of the shot he fired at them.

To root out the enemy at its source, Printz attacked the settlers at Salem Creek, burnt down their buildings and made prisoner their leader, George Lambertson and some of his men. Printz, with help from the Dutch, expelled all the English who would not take an oath of allegiance to the crown of Sweden.

The English at New Haven evidently concluded, five years later, that any attempt to make a settlement on the Delaware was hazardous, for at a meeting of the commissioners of the United Colonies of New England, at Boston, it was decided, ". . . considering the present state of the colony, the English in most plantations already wanting hands to work, it is thought fit not to send men to possess and plant on South River or to encourage it and, should any go there, the colony will not protect them."

However, the urge for more land was too great to withstand for long. Two years afterwards, a party of fifty English colonists at New Haven hired a vessel and sailed for the South River— to inhabit land which some of them had acquired from the Indians on the previous expedition. En route, around New Amsterdam, Governor Stuyvesant, who had succeeded Kieft, arrested the captain of the vessel and four others, put them in prison and refused to release them until "they pledged themselves under their hands" that they would not go to the South River. He informed them that if any of them were afterwards found there, their goods would be forfeited and themselves sent to Holland as prisoners. They returned to New Haven at a loss of £300.

Stuyvesant wrote the governor of New Haven, asserting the Dutch right to the South River, and threatened to prevent any English settlement there "with force of arms and martial opposition, even unto bloodshed."

Three years after that episode, still yearning for land on the Delaware, the United Colonies of New England reconsidered their previous decision and became more belligerent. They met at Hartford and wrote Risingh, the new Swedish governor, asserting their ownership and rights to land on the South River.

However, it was decided to take no action at present, but that if within twelve months they sent 150, or at least 100 able-bodied men, with vessels, arms and ammunition "fit for such enterprise," and met with hostile opposition from the Dutch and Swedes, the United Colonies would furnish additional soldiers.

Agitation for making a settlement on the Delaware, to be under the government of New Haven, continued for several years. In 1655 an expedition was proposed, which would take with it two guns, half-a-hundred shot, a proportion of musket bullets, and a barrel of powder.

The increasing strength of the Dutch, who that year drove the Swedes from the Delaware, presumably deterred the sending of the expedition, and that is the last account of any attempt by the English at New Haven to make a settlement on the Delaware.

The Dutch on the Delaware

Stuyvesant, upon obtaining possession of the South River for the West India Company, changed the name of the Swedish Fort Christiana (Wilmington) to Altona. The population was about a dozen families.

He began giving deeds to land about Fort Casimir and by August had given seventy-five. He ordered that convenient streets, four or five roods broad, be laid out and lots fifty feet by a hundred feet be granted to the colonists. This was the beginning of New Amstel, now New Castle.

That year a number of families moved from Manhattan to

New Amstel, and were met by a posted placard, which bore a complaint that: "Lots and plantations in the neighborhood of Fort Casimir lie unused, their proprietors are not residing on the spot; others have taken possession of more land than they can cultivate."

To drive the Swedes from the Delaware, the West India Company had borrowed funds from the burgomasters of the City of Amsterdam in Holland. Being unable to pay the interest on the loan, the company agreed to, and did, in 1657, transfer to that city, in liquidation of the loan, all the land on the west side of South River, from the south side of Christiana Creek to Bombay Hook. This was called the "Colony of the City." All land above the Christiana, to the northern limits of the Dutch settlement, was the "Colony of the Company."

The burgomasters of Amsterdam engaged to be financial fathers to the City Colony for one year and provide everything needed by the settlers going to their colony in Delaware. Every farmer was to have, "in free, fast and durable property," as many morgens of land, both plough land and meadow land, as the family could cultivate in two years; uncultivated lots to be forfeited.

Peter Alrich was appointed to represent the burgomasters and, immediately upon receiving the land from Stuyvesant, Alrich sailed from Manhattan to New Amstel, the future seat of his government. He took with him 60 soldiers and 128 settlers, including 76 women and children, who had recently arrived with him from Holland. Gerritt Van Sweringen, afterwards one of the principal officers in Delaware, was the supercargo of the vessel. Fears were expressed at Manhattan that settlement on the Delaware would be injurious to New Amsterdam.

The burgomasters of the city planned to induce settlement, collect land rents, and develop trade between Delaware and Holland. The annual land rent of one-tenth of the produce was not to begin until the end of the tenth year, when the revenue from the tenths was to be applied to public works and public services.

Public and semi-public buildings were erected within the enclosed square. "At the end of the first year, under the burgomasters of Amsterdam, New Amstel was a handsome little town of about a hundred houses."

The authority to lease land and decide terms of rental was with the vice-director at New Amstel. The burgomasters in Holland sent to Delaware a large number of Waldenses and other colonists, including some orphans; and a considerable number of Huguenots arrived. The orphans were bound out among settlers for two to four years, at from forty to eighty guilders ($16 to $32) a year.

New settlers arriving included weavers, shoemakers, tailors and buttonmakers. Farming proved too hard for them and Alrich complained of the incompetence of the immigrants. He wanted farmers and said the breed of horses was too small for farming. This may have been the breed introduced from Sweden, which were the progenitors of the noted Chincoteague ponies which today roam wild on the Maryland-Virginia island of that name.

Complaints were made to Stuyvesant that Jacquette, the vice-governor of the company colony at Altona, had taken possession of and cultivated lands which had been granted to others, and otherwise broken the law. He was arrested but later released. William Beekman was appointed to succeed Jacquette. Seventeen years later Jacquette was living at Salem, where Fenwick dispossessed him of land which Governor Andros at New York ordered that he be restored.

Some English from Maryland were in 1659 reported as being at Cape Henlopen. Having visions of encroachments on the Delaware by Marylanders, Beekman and d'Hinoyossa, agreeable to instructions, went there to investigate. Knowing well the natural characteristics of Indian realtors, Beekman, to shut out these Marylanders, went prepared to buy again the land which the Indians had twenty-nine years previously sold to the Dutch patroon, Godyn, and which Godyn subsequently sold to the West India Company. Again, ten years after the Godyn purchase, the Indians had sold the same land to the Swedes. They would not have waited that long to make another sale had a buyer appeared.

Beekman took with him some coats, kettles, duffels, knives, corals, looking-glasses and trumpets. For these articles, the Indian dealer in real estate sold to Beekman all the land along the Delaware Bay, between Cape Henlopen and Bombay Hook, a distance of forty-five miles, or half the distance between the Cape and Philadelphia, the purchase extending indefinitely inland.

The West India Company directors were agreeable to giving up their land on the Delaware to the Amsterdam burgomasters because it "must contribute to our security at Manhattan against the English in Maryland. Besides, we may expect a more powerful intercession of the burgomasters through the Netherlands government to obtain from the crown of England the final settlement of the long disputed boundaries between Delaware and Maryland."

Two years after the burgomasters had taken possession, New Amstel was overwhelmingly in debt for public purposes. These were the dark days of colonization on South River. [111]

After two years of paternalism, the burgomasters announced they would no longer continue supplies to the settlers and that the ten years' exemption from land rent was to cease before the period stipulated. This was denounced by the settlers as "gross slavery, and chain-fettering the free spirit of worthy people."

Settlers grew distrustful of the burgomasters in Holland, and besought Alrich to accept what property they had and allow them to depart, but he replied: "You are bound to remain four years." Nevertheless, many went to Maryland, Virginia and Manhattan. The burgomasters relented to some extent and placed the blame on Alrich. Messengers were sent to reclaim fifty of the Dutch colonists who had left for Maryland and Virginia.

Many Finns had come to the Delaware with the Swedes and settled between Marcus Hook and Chester. The Dutch disliked having them so near and made efforts to move them to the present site of Philadelphia, or to Esopus, New York, but they refused to go.

Alrich wrote that the people of New Amsterdam were jealous of the South River development and resorted to practices injurious to that region.

Josiah Fendell, governor of Maryland under Calvert, ordered Colonel Nathaniel Utie and a squad of soldiers to go to the Delaware, at New Amstel, with "a command to the Dutch governor and his settlers to depart from Delaware immediately or declare themselves subject to Lord Baltimore." If they refused he would not be accountable for the innocent blood which might be spilled.

Utie was instructed to "insinuate to the Dutch settlers that if they made application to his lordship, the governor of Maryland, they shall find good conditions for granting them land the same as to all comers." Utie said he wanted the Delaware land to dispose of to Maryland tobacco growers.

Alrich replied: "We have been in possession of this land for thirty-six years, as well as by octroy of the States General and directors of the Dutch West India Company. We are in no wise inclined to commit the least injustice but are very willing to yield to those who have the best right."[b]

To which Calvert's officer said that the land was granted to Cecilius Calvert, Lord Baltimore, and was confirmed by the king himself, and sanctioned by parliament to the extent of 40° North latitude (Philadelphia).

Stuyvesant, at Manhattan, when he learned of this, was angry and censured Beekman for not arresting Utie. Shortly thereafter Alrich was succeeded by Alex d'Hinoyossa as governor. The Dutch military forces were so engaged in a self-imposed conflict with the Indians, at Esopus, that they were unable to send a force to protect the settlers on the South River.

Stuyvesant sent Augustine Herman and Resolved Waldron to Maryland as commissioners to confer with Calvert and Fendell. After a disagreeable seventy-five mile journey in a small leaky boat down Elk River and the Chesapeake Bay to Sharp's Island, where they hired a sailboat, they arrived at St. Mary's along the Potomac.

At the conference, in rejoinder to Calvert's claim that the Calvert grant extended along the Delaware to 40° North, the Dutch commissioners presented a blanket claim which was calculated to give Calvert a solar plexus blow: "Notifying first and foremost the ancient original right and title, the subjects of the High and Mighty States General of the United Provinces, under the proprietary of the lords of the West India Company of Amsterdam, in Holland, have unto the province of New

[b]Pa. Archives

Netherland, latitude between 38° and 42° [Maryland-Virginia line, and Cape Cod]. That their ancient right and title comes first from the King of Spain, whose subjects the Dutch were at the time of the first discovery by Columbus, and who, after the war, Spain gave to the United Dutch Republic of the Seven Provinces all the Spanish rights and title they had conquered and settled in Europe, America and the West Indies, including all the islands and the main continent northerly up to Canada; and on the west, Virginia; Maryland upon the Chesapeake, and New England on the east. Then the French, in 1542, by De Verrazzano, a Florentine, came."

Thinking that broad claim would make Calvert more amenable to rational consideration of the point at issue, Herman continued: "Lord Baltimore had requested of King Charles I a grant of land not yet settled and cultivated, and only inhabited by savages. It included in no way Delaware, and had not even as much reference to it as that which Sir Edmund Ployden formerly subreptively obtained. That river unquestionably was in just and lawful possession of the Dutch, and by them settled full forty years, while Lord Baltimore's patent was not at the farthest more than twenty-four to twenty-seven years old."

Herman traced next the history of the settlement by the Dutch on the South River, from the planting and destruction of Godyn's colony at Horekill (Lewes), to the expulsion of the Swedes in 1655—"against all which no man from Maryland or Virginia ever entered a claim.

"From the discovery of the South and North Rivers by Hendrick Hudson, and first actual possession and settlement by the Dutch in these parts, we have always maintained and defended the river against all usurpers and obstructors and shall do so for ever. Further, any claim by Calvert was disbarred by the thirtieth article of the treaty of peace of Westminster, between Holland and England, by which he was obliged to file before May 18th, 1654, being five years past, any claim he might have had in foreign parts."

Calvert was, of course, cognizant of this fact while urgently contending against it. His claim to the South River was utterly denied.

To give Calvert something more to distract him and still further confuse him, the Dutch commissioners put in a claim for Elk River—because of its flowing from the northeast.

"No man," said O'Callaghan, [111] "can rise from this perusal without being convinced that the independent rank of Delaware in this republic is mainly due, for that good fortune and high honor, to the stand taken by the Dutch in 1659." The State of Delaware should erect a magnificent monument to Herman.

The burgomasters of Amsterdam in September, 1659, appointed a committee in Holland to confer with the West India Company about returning to the company the land the burgomasters had acquired of it, but the company did not want it, saying it had cost them 165,200 guilders ($66,080).

The estimated population of the Swedes and Finns on the Delaware, in 1660, was seven hundred.

Calvert's attorney in England empowered an agent in Holland to demand that the Dutch deliver its settlement on the Delaware to Calvert, who would reimburse them for all costs already undergone.

The Dutch replied, asserting their "right by grant and possession." They were resolved to remain in possession and defend their rights; if Calvert persevered and used force, they would use all the means God and nature had given them to protect their rights and would be innocent of any bloodshed. They insisted that a boundary line be run between Maryland and Delaware, but Calvert did not want any boundary line to separate him from the coveted domain. [16]

The directors at Amsterdam ordered Stuyvesant to oppose the claim of the Maryland authorities to the South River country, "first warning them in a civil manner not to usurp our territory; but if they despise such kind entreaties, then nothing is left but to drive them from there, as our claims and rights on the lands upon South River are indisputable."

Captain Neale was sent from England to America, authorized to levy men and make war upon the Dutch by land and water. The people of both Virginia and New England disliked having the Dutch claimants so near them, but Calvert, being unable to get their help, concluded it was unwise to risk war with the

West India Company, which might result in war with Holland. [19]

The claims of the Dutch and Calvert were brought up in a council in Maryland, in 1661, and doubt was then expressed that New Amstel (New Castle) lay below 40°. It was decided that all further efforts for subjugation of the Dutch should be delayed. Conciliation by Herman may have influenced this.

Although the contention between the Dutch and the English over ownership of the land in Delaware continued almost to the point of militant combat, it did not prevent their entering into commercial transactions.

Sailing up Sassafras River, Governor Calvert met with d'Hinoyossa at the head of Appoquinimink Creek, where a treaty was made with the Indians. The English proposed to deliver two or three thousand hogsheads of tobacco annually to the Dutch in return for Negroes and merchandise brought to America in Dutch vessels. [16]

The burgomasters of Amsterdam granted to Pieter Cornelius Plockhoy, as the leader of a colony of Mennonites, a tract of land at Horekill (Lewes), free of tax for twenty years. They also loaned the colony 2,500 guilders. Rigid conditions were adopted by the Mennonites, among them being: "No clergyman . . . to be admitted; all intractable people—such as Papists and usurious Jews; English stiff-necked Quakers; Puritans; fool-hardy believers in the Millenium, and obstinate modern pretenders to revelation"—were excluded. [16]

There was continual dispute between Beekman and d'Hinoyossa, governors of the respective colonies, the former charging the latter with dishonesty.

A grant was made by Stuyvesant to Beekman, in 1663, of fifty-six acres of land now in Wilmington, covering approximately the area from Christiana Creek to Ninth Street, between Church and Walnut Streets, and also of a small valley of sixteen acres with twelve acres woodland, on the west side of the settlement. Beekman advised Stuyvesant that Fort Altona and the palisades were in a state of decay.

In August, Governor Charles Calvert, with a suite of twenty-six persons, visited New Amstel and Altona, where they were entertained by Beekman. When it was proposed to Calvert to define the boundaries of the two colonies, he replied that he would communicate with Lord Baltimore in England. He desired Beekman to convey his thanks to Stuyvesant for his "offer of convoy and horses" on his proposed visit to Boston by way of Manhattan the following spring.

D'Hinoyossa was then in Holland, where he expressed approval of increased appropriations to stimulate emigration to New Netherland. He reported that the Swedes, Finns and others had 110 bouwries or farms in Delaware, with 2,000 cows, 20 horses, 80 sheep and several thousand swine; that the city already had two or three breweries, and more were wanted to supply the English in Maryland with beer in exchange for tobacco; and that ten thousand furs and other articles could be annually procured from the Indians and exported.

The burgomasters in Amsterdam stated that if more Swedes, Finns and others could be induced to emigrate to South River, the city would advance them the cost of transportation and agricultural implements.

The burgomasters, finding they could not induce the West India Company to take back its colony land, proposed in 1663 (and the proposal was accepted) that the Dutch company transfer to the City of Amsterdam the entire South River area, including both sides of the river.

D'Hinoyossa returned to the South River with 150 colonists and arrangements were made to dispatch another ship. Beekman, in obedience to the company's orders, immediately recognized him as chief of the Dutch in the South River country. In a few days Stuyvesant executed a formal act ceding the land to d'Hinoyossa, as the representative of the burgomasters of Amsterdam. [16]

Stuyvesant felt so elated that he became extravagant in defining the boundaries: "Peter Stuyvesant, on behalf of their High, Mighty Lords, States General of United Netherlands, and Lord Directors of the Council, attest and declare . . . transfers to Hon. Alexander d'Hinoyossa, in behalf of the noble, great and respected Lords, Burgomasters of the City of Amsterdam . . . from the sea upwards, so far as the river extends itself . . .

on the east side three miles [inland] from the river, and towards [on] the west side . . . till it reaches the English [Maryland] colonies, etc. signed and confirmed with our seal in red wax, in Fort Amsterdam in New Netherland, December 22, 1663."

Following this, the burgomasters of the City of Amsterdam announced it would settle four hundred colonists on the South River and intimated it would send a greater number.

D'Hinoyossa was now governor of the entire South River country. He chose as the location of his own residence a spot on the Appoquinimink Creek, where he proposed to build a metropolis and promote commerce with the English in Maryland and Virginia. [16]

Beekman, now out of employment, appealed to Stuyvesant for some official position under the provisional government on the North River, and he was transferred to the Dutch settlement at Esopus, New York, as sheriff. He afterwards moved to the City of New York, where he became an alderman under the English government. He obtained a large tract of land, now the busy part of the city, on which the people who occupy it continue to pay to his heirs and assigns enormous annual land rents, which all the people themselves have created.

The Plowden Grant

Mention of an ineffective grant of land in America by the Viceroy of Ireland, presumably with the sanction of King Charles I, to Sir Edmund Plowden, of Shropshire, England, in 1634, is inserted here merely as an interesting mingling of legend and romance and to depict further the intense desire of Europeans to indulge in land speculation in America.

Plowden, who had served James I, in Ireland, petitioned his son, Charles I, then reigning, for a grant of land in America, but judging from the impossible boundaries named therein, Charles, in a spirit of jest, had the viceroy make the grant, although the viceroy had no power to make grants in America.

The boundaries of the territory granted, which was to be named the palatine of New Albion, seemed to include parts of the land now in New Jersey, Delaware, Maryland, Pennsylvania and New York. Charles had previously granted all Maryland to Calvert.

Plowden promptly began in England to sell, or lease, land in his supposed palatine and to induce migration thereto. He leased ten thousand acres to Sir Thomas Danby, "who hath undertaken to settle one hundred persons, paying one silver penny sterling annually for ever for every person resident on the premises, upon certain conditions." Leases for land, some in south Jersey, were made to others. [65]

It is known that Captain Thomas Younge, having "a commission of discovery" from the king, arrived in the Delaware River with a company of fourteen persons in 1633—which was twenty-six years after the settlement of Jamestown. With him was a nephew, Robert Evelyn, purportedly representing Plowden. Evelyn made a habitation on either the east side, at Pennsauken Creek, or on the west side, near the Schuylkill, where he and his companions lived four years. From there he sent reports to Plowden on the favorable conditions of the country and the promising prospects.

Eight years later Plowden came to Virginia, where he made his headquarters with sixteen followers, and was befriended by Governor Berkeley. The following year he procured a small vessel and sailed up the Delaware, where he saw the New Haven colony endeavoring to make a settlement at Salem Creek, on land claimed by Plowden, the Dutch and the Swedes.

Plowden remained in the Chesapeake-Delaware region seven years, during all which time he was contending with Printz, the Swedish governor, and with Kieft and Stuyvesant, the Dutch governors—claiming all land west of the Hudson River.

Printz reported that once when Plowden was sailing from Virginia to the Delaware, his crew put him ashore, without food, clothes or gun, on desolate Smith's Island, outside the Chesapeake Capes, and that after four days he was rescued by a passing British vessel and returned to his habitation, presumably at Accomac, Virginia.

By that time, his funds becoming exhausted, and his followers deserting him, Plowden returned to England by way of Boston, hoping there to promote the development of his palatine and rehabilitate himself. In an endeavor to do so, he circulated pamphlets to induce purchases or leases of land and migration of settlers. "Anyone investing £500 and agreeing to send fifty settlers could have five thousand acres and a manor with royalties, at 5s annual rent; and whoever is willing to transport himself or servants at £10 a man, shall, for each man, have a hundred acres freely granted for ever." [169]

Falling in debt in England, Plowden was imprisoned, and died a few years after returning there. His claim to the palatine came into possession of his grandson, Francis, whose two brothers went to Maryland in 1684.

Just a hundred years later, and 150 years after date of the purported grant, and after the American Revolution, the desire for land in America continuing strong, Charles Varlo, an Englishman, purchased a one-third interest in the palatine and with his family came to America to assert his claim. He traveled through the presumed domain distributing pamphlets giving documentary evidence of his title and conditions for letting and selling land; and issued a warning against any one buying or leasing land of others than himself.

He learned that the land policy in America had become Europeanized, in that no land was too worthless or too remote to be privately owned, though unused; and that all the land in, and far beyond, the inhabited regions had been parceled out.

He brought suit for possession, but in vain; the judge and jury were landholders, holding title through royal crown grants to British lords proprietors.

British Dispossess the Dutch

The Duke of York's expedition having captured New Amsterdam and Orange (Albany) from the Dutch, in 1664, Sir Robert Carr of that expedition was sent from Manhattan to the Delaware with the following instructions to take New Amstel (New Castle): "When you come to what is possessed by the Dutch you shall send your boat on shore to summon the governor and inhabitants to yield obedience to his Britannic Majesty as the rightful sovereign of that tract of land, and let him and them know that his majesty is graciously pleased that all the planters shall, upon quiet submission, enjoy the peaceable possession of their lands upon the same terms of rent which they do now possess them, only they change their masters, whether they be the Dutch West India Company or the City of Amsterdam."

Upon arrival there, Carr had a parley with Governor d'Hino-yossa and the burghers of New Amstel. After five days' negotiation, the burghers and townsmen agreed to surrender the town, but d'Hinoyossa and the soldiers refused, and went into the fort, Alrich and Van Sweringen going with them. The fort mounted fourteen guns but "was not tenable."

Carr landed his troops and from the ship fired two broadsides into the fort. His troops at the same time made an attack on the fort and took it by storm. The Dutch lost three killed and ten wounded. The British soldiers and sailors then began to plunder.

All the soldiers from the fort, and many of the citizens of New Amstel, were given to a merchantman in payment for services, and were transported to Virginia to be sold as indented servants.

Among the things taken were: all the produce of the land for that year, 100 sheep, 30 or 40 horses, 50 or 60 cows and oxen, a brew house and still, and a sawmill ready to be erected.

One ship was sent to the Horekill (Lewes), seventy miles south of New Amstel, where the crew also plundered the Mennonite settlers of everything.

New Amstel was no sooner surrendered than Robert Carr appropriated to himself the farm and chattels of the governor, much of which he was obliged to give up, while his son, Captain John Carr, took possession of the 150 acre farm of sheriff Gerritt van Sweringen, who had defended the fort. Ensign Stock took all of Peter Alrich's land. Governor Nicolls later made formal grants of these lands to those who had appropriated them, except the Alrich lands, and an island of about sixty acres seven miles below New Castle, which were granted to William Tom "for his good services." They each were to pay to the Duke of York an annual land rent of one bushel of wheat for each hundred acres.

Governor Nicolls confiscated all the land in New Netherland, but allowed land already granted by the Dutch to individuals to be retained by them, upon payment of an annual land rent to the duke. Thus, all land under Dutch jurisdiction came into control of the duke, although the duke never received from the king a grant of land in Delaware.

In 1667 Nicolls was succeeded as governor by Colonel Francis Lovelace, who announced that he would allot land in Delaware, at an annual land rent to the duke of five bushels of wheat per hundred acres.

Captain John Carr was appointed commander at New Castle, assisted by Peter Alrich, with others as councilors. Alrich, the former governor for the City of Amsterdam colony, professed allegiance to the English, was given some authority in the colony, and was granted Burlington Island. D'Hinoyossa and van Sweringen, and many others who had their land confiscated, went to Maryland. William Tom was appointed collector of land rents for the duke.

Swedish and Finnish settlers became dissatisfied with the land regulations and other interferences by the English and started an insurrection, led by Marcus Jacobsen, "the long Finn." He was arrested and whipped, imprisoned in Manhattan for a year, and then sold into slavery in Barbados.

Various grants of land about New Castle were made by Governor Lovelace in 1671 and settlement was rapid about Appoquinimink Creek, at a reduced annual land rent of one or two bushels of wheat per hundred acres, payable to the duke.

Deeds for land that had been granted by the Swedish governors to persons not subjects of Sweden, such as the Dutch, stipulated that they should be held as long as the holders continued subject to the Swedish authority. As the country was now in possession of the English, the non-Swedish holders were obliged to declare allegiance to England, or give up their land. They availed themselves of the opportunity to obtain grants from the Duke of York. All applicants for land were summoned to appear at New York.

A large part of the land on which Wilmington is situated was granted by Lovelace to Johan Anderson, who had come from

Holland as a cook on a Dutch ship, and to Tymen Stidham, probably a Finn. [45]

The settlers in Delaware had to contend with foes, not only from across the Atlantic, but with repeated attacks by Calvert's buccaneers from Maryland, to say nothing of the usurpation at a later period of their government and land rents. by Penn.

Governor Lovelace, at New York, wrote the commander at New Castle of a threatened invasion by Calvert forces and said: "Put yourselves in the best posture of defense possible by fitting up the fort, keeping your companies in arms, both there and up the river, and that all soldiers be at an hour's warning." [139]

Captain Jones, with thirty horsemen, under authority of Calvert in Maryland, in 1672 went to Horekill (Lewes), captured and bound the magistrates, intimidated the people, disrespectfully treated them and robbed them of all their furs and other Indian goods, and threatened to proceed to take possession of all the land up to 40° (Philadelphia). That attempt was defeated.

Governor Lovelace, ever grasping for more land, to his own final undoing, possessed himself of a tract in Delaware, which he rented to a tenant. Land grants to others continued to be made, with rents payable to the duke.

New Castle was granted corporate powers by the governor, and a bailiff and six assistants were appointed. When settlers complained about the land rents and taxes, Lovelace gave orders to "lay such taxes on them as might not give them liberty to entertain any other thought but how to discharge them." [45]

England and France entered a war against Holland in which the Dutch, in July, 1673, recaptured New York and again established Dutch sovereignty over New Netherland, including Delaware.

The major part of the English magistrates, constables and inhabitants in New York, New Jersey and Delaware, swore allegiance to the Dutch States General and Prince of Orange. Anthony Colve, a captain of infantry, was appointed governor. Other Dutch officials were appointed, including Peter Alrich. Three courts were established: Upland (Chester), New Amstel (New Castle), and Horekill (Lewes).

A treaty of peace between England and Holland seven months later provided that whatever places had been taken by either during the war should be returned. This again put the English in possession of New York, New Jersey and Delaware.

The Duke of York appointed Major, afterwards Sir, Edmund Andros to govern all his territory between the Connecticut River and the east side of Delaware Bay. However, Andros assumed command in Delaware also, and made land grants there, with land rents payable to the duke.

Andros reappointed all the previous English officials on the Delaware, excepting Alrich and Captain John Carr, the previous English commander on the Delaware. Carr had gone to Maryland and his land was seized by Andros. Cantwell and William Tom were authorized to take possession of the fort and stores at New Castle, for the king's use.

Alrich had served the Dutch during the two Dutch regimes and, in the interim, the English, swearing allegiance to each in turn. He was a versatile politician, with an engaging personality, always ready to accept official appointment from the conqueror, but the English wanted no more of him.

The site of New Castle, Delaware, has been fought over and taken and retaken in armed conflict by different European powers—Swedes, Dutch and British—and its name changed oftener than any other place on the Western Hemisphere. Known successively as Grapevine Point, Sandhoec, and Delawaretown, the town became Fort Casimir when the Dutch in 1651 built their fort there. The Swedes battled for and captured it in 1655, and named it Fort Trinity. The Dutch recaptured it the following year, and named it New Amstel. The English fought for and captured it in 1664, and named it New Castle. Again recaptured by the Dutch in 1673, it was renamed New Amstel. The following year it was restored to the English by treaty and finally became New Castle. It was once more captured by the British during the American Revolution.

All grants of land theretofore made by any of the successive governments were confirmed by Governor Andros, and additional grants were made at an annual land rent to the duke and his heirs for ever of one bushel of wheat per hundred acres.

Andros gave notice that, having in 1675, for encouragement, remitted the land rents for the first three years on all lands to be taken up and occupied, he now found that many had taken up land on speculation to exact an increased price from later arrivals, without occupying it at all. Andros therefore wisely revoked the offer,.except where the land had been occupied and improved. This order was published at Upland (Chester), New Castle and Horekill (Lewes). In 1678 the land on which Middletown is situated was surveyed.

Two Labidists—Dankaerts and Schluyter—came from Europe to America in 1679, seeking land for an American branch of that truly peculiar sect. They left a diary in which they said New Castle, Upland, Burlington and Salem were the only villages on the Delaware River. They also made some observations on conditions thereabouts which are not creditable to the fifteen years of English rule.

Social and economic conditions greatly improved during the succeeding eighteen years, as evidenced by a letter from Rev. Eric Biork, the Swedish pastor, who then wrote: "This country is delightful, taxes are light, grain plentiful, fresh meat abundant, and people well clothed. There are no poor in this country, they all provide for themselves; for the land is rich and fruitful." Nevertheless, there was continued opposition to payment of land rent to the duke.

Andros was determined, as were Stuyvesant and Printz before him, to prevent development of land speculation in the colony, as "being a social canker."

The court at St. Jones (Kent) County, made grants of land aggregating 9,500 acres to sixteen persons and give liberty to thirty-three persons to take up 18,663 acres. Failure to occupy or improve the land within one year from date of survey would nullify the grants.

Stirred by the investigation by John Lewin, whom the duke had sent to America to investigate uncollected land rents due him (as related in the chapter on New York), the court at New Castle called upon all landholders to pay their land rents to the duke's collectors.

Planters declared they had no wheat with which to pay. They

found tobacco, which they grew almost to the exclusion of wheat, to be a more profitable crop than wheat. The court requested the governor to accept tobacco in lieu of wheat. However, the planters were not zealous about paying, even in tobacco. The land rents were giving considerable uneasiness; some of the settlers, referring to the Biblical text that "The Earth was created for the equal use of all the children of men," declared that no man has a right to exact a price of another for the use of land.

William Penn Claims Delaware

William Penn received from King Charles II in 1681 a grant of all the land in Pennsylvania. But not satisfied with that large domain, and a partnership in all the land in New Jersey, he also wanted all the land in Delaware.

Before he left England to go to America with his grant of Pennsylvania, Penn began negotiations with James, the Duke of York, for the Delaware territory, then in control of Governor Andros, who represented the duke; this, notwithstanding James had no grant from the king for land beyond the shore of New Jersey.

Penn wrote to Sir John Werden, secretary to the duke, proposing that the duke confer on Penn what the duke's agent, Nicolls, had captured from the Dutch in and about New Castle. He also asked that the islands in the Delaware thereabouts be included in the grant. Werden, who was ever on the alert that Penn did not gain some advantage over the duke, replied: "I never heard the islands mentioned before, and this is quite a new proposal. I have all along believed the west shore of the Delaware to be your eastern boundary. The duke is not pleased to come to any decision on it."

The duke, without having received from the king a grant of any land west of New Jersey, made to Penn two inefficacious grants of the land in Delaware. One, dated August 24, 1682, was for land within a twelve mile circle around New Castle, and the other, dated three days later, was for the land south thereof to Cape Henlopen. By these, Penn was to assume jurisdiction over Delaware, and the duke was to participate equally with Penn in the profits of land dealing in lower Delaware. But the grants were ineffective because the duke was not in possession of the land which he was presuming to grant to Penn.

Penn, en route up the Delaware to Pennsylvania, went ashore at New Castle in October, 1682, and announced that "the illustrious prince Duke of York, has granted unto me the town of New Castle and the two counties to the south thereof."

Whereupon, John Moll, in charge at New Castle, knowing of the personal intimacy between Penn and the royal family, presented to Penn the key to the fort, and transferred to him the land and jurisdiction thereof. The *modus operandi* was the delivering to Penn of a bit of turf with one twig upon it, representing the land, and a mug of water from the river. Andros, the duke's governor at New York, relying upon Penn's statement, proclaimed that due submission should be made to Penn in Delaware.

At this New Castle meeting, Penn requested those holding land to bring, at the next meeting, all their patents, grants, surveys and claims, so that he might "adjust" them; by which he meant that he would make a list of them and compile a rent roll for payment of land rents to him.

Penn commissioned the justice of the peace at New Castle to receive petitions from persons wanting land, not to exceed three hundred acres to a master of a family, nor one hundred acres to an unmarried person, at an annual land rent of one penny per acre, or value thereof in produce, payable to Penn. It will be noted that this was a marked increase in the land rent over the one bushel of wheat per hundred acres, which the duke's agents had been exacting.

Many grants of land in Delaware had been made by the Dutch, Swedish and English governors prior to the advent of Penn. He renewed them upon request, with the land rents payable to him, but with the provision that all land granted and not occupied within the time limit should be accounted vacant land and let to others. All future grants were to be occupied within one year, or the grant would be void. All grants made successively by the Swedes, Dutch and English, to avoid land monopoly and speculation, had been dependent upon occupancy within a limited time. This provision should have been continued after the formation of the American government, but the spirit of land speculation, grasping for the unearned increment, was too strong to permit it. From this failure comes much of the social distress and unrest which has prompted so many persons, seeking better conditions, to advocate fascism or communism as means of fancied relief.

At the meeting of the first Pennsylvania assembly, at Upland (Chester), in 1682, a petition from Delaware, prompted by Penn's statement that all the land in Delaware had been granted to him, was presented, requesting a union of the three Delaware counties with Pennsylvania, which was granted. Delegates from Delaware, equal in number to those from Pennsylvania, sat in the Pennsylvania assembly for about twenty-one years, after which Delaware had its separate assembly, but the governor was appointed by Penn. However, the crown kept a hold on Delaware by stipulating that the appointee for governor of Delaware by Penn must have royal approbation, and that the appointee should exercise jurisdiction only during the pleasure of the crown, and should not prejudice the right of the crown to the land in Delaware.

Penn required that all inhabitants, including officials and members of the assembly, must first declare fidelity and obedience to him, his heirs and assigns, as the rightful proprietor and governor. To hasten applications for land, Penn stipulated that no inhabitant would be entitled to vote, or be elected to the assembly, unless he had fifty acres of land, of which ten acres was occupied and cleared, or was otherwise worth £50 sterling, clear estate. Through all of these requirements Penn held a firm grip on the people, on legislation, and on the land.

To encourage the duke to urge his brother, the king, to perfect the grant of Delaware, by which Penn and the duke would reap the future unearned increment in land value, Penn wrote the duke's secretary: "I have ordered two manors for the duke of a thousand acres apiece and intend two more. The annual land rent is a penny per acre and their value, besides the land rent, will be great in a few years."

Assuming that from across the ocean all land in Delaware would look alike to the duke, Penn was clever enough, in his own behalf, to allot these promised manors down in uninhabited Kent County, around the Murderkill, where he ordered a survey of ten thousand acres, instead of in the more populous New Castle County.

Penn, in February 1683, wrote to Lord Hyde: "Sir John Werden, I hear, is too Spanish, for my agents can hardly make him understand the duke's commands without a more powerful interpreter." (Werden had been *chargé d'affaires* at the British embassy in Spain). Perhaps Sir John understood full well and was not receptive to the urging of Penn's agents for those islands and other land grants.

Seven months after the inefficacious grant by the duke to Penn, King Charles, on March 22 (o.s.) 1683, had a draft for a grant prepared by which the land about New Castle would be granted to the duke. The terms thereof being unsatisfactory, it was returned to the king for cancellation, with a request for its revision, and it was recorded on April 10, as canceled. Three days afterwards a new grant was drafted, which cited cancellation of the contemplated aforesaid grant.

Charles, having already granted all land to the water's edge in both New Jersey and Pennsylvania, but having overlooked the river itself, proposed in this patent to grant to the duke all the river, and islands therein, and all land on the west side of the river and bay between Cape Henlopen and the Schuylkill, and extending many miles inland. The grant was to be good "notwithstanding any former letters patent or grants for the premises, or any part thereof, granted by our progenitors unto any persons whatsoever." In effect, Charles would have granted to the duke part of the land which his father, Charles I, had granted to Calvert forty-nine years previously, and part of the land in Pennsylvania which Charles himself, only two years previously, had granted to Penn. But such overlapping of boundaries in grants of land in America was a common practice with the different Stuart kings.

But just then the attorney for Calvert, in London, protested that all the land in Delaware was within the grant to Calvert and petitioned that such patent not pass the great seal until the king was satisfied of the boundary between Maryland and Delaware. This prevented further proceedings towards King Charles' making a grant to the duke, to be passed on by the duke to Penn.

Collectors of land rent in Delaware were appointed by Penn at an early date, but agents of Calvert caused settlers to refuse payment, and a rent strike developed.

Governor Calvert believed that his northern boundary of 40° North, was approximately at Naamen's Creek, above Wilmington. In September 1683 he sent George Talbot, a cousin, with a number of men to Philadelphia to demand possession of the land.

Talbot, who designated himself his lordship's commissioner for disposing of land in New Ireland (being the land in Delaware) was, in the following January, sent to Delaware to persuade settlers to become tenants of Calvert, on a land rent, or to buy land at 2s (50¢) per one hundred acres. To assert his claim to the land, he built on the Christiana, six miles northwest of New Castle, a fort which was afterwards abandoned.

At a conference with Calvert, at Chester, it was found that 40° was even farther north, possibly (as it actually is) as far north as the northern edge of Philadelphia. This frightened Penn and gave him a fresh incentive to obtain from the duke, as quickly as possible, and at all hazards, a grant of the Delaware territory.

After spending a year and ten months in Pennsylvania and Delaware, while the fight between him and Calvert had been transferred to London, Penn hastily sailed for England in August, 1684, to press his claim before the Committee of Trade and Plantations, to which the matter had been referred.

The committee in the following October decided that the land granted by Charles I to Calvert was intended to be only such as at that time was "uncultivated and not inhabited except by savages," and that the west shore of the Delaware Bay had been planted and inhabited by the Dutch. But even at that, the contention between Penn and Calvert, and their respective heirs, continued until the middle of the following century.

Charles II at his death in February, 1685, was succeeded by his brother, the Duke of York, as King James II, who thereby personally inherited the claim to all the land in America which had been claimed by Charles. Penn, therefore, had high hopes that James would now make the proposed royal grant to him. But James procrastinated.

Being spiritually a Roman Catholic, though on a Protestant throne, he was in sympathy with Penn's purpose, as he had been with Calvert's in Maryland, to establish religious toleration in their respective colonies, for Quakers, Puritans and Catholics alike. But he had become disappointed at the outcome of the Calvert effort in Maryland, where the vast majority of the people were Protestants, including the Maryland provincial assembly, which enacted Protestant protective acts against Romanism. He probably feared a similar outcome in Pennsylvania and Delaware, and therefore became less concerned about Penn's efforts for religious toleration.

Then, too, the contention about the Calvert land boundaries the northern limit of which was defined to be land, "which lieth under 40° North uncultivated and not inhabited except by sav ages," may have been a restraining influence.

In addition to these reasons, James had received a favorabl report by his agent, John Lewin, whom he had sent to Ameri to ascertain who was getting the land rents. James now believe that as landlord of the vast American territory he could reap large annual income by exacting tribute in the form of la d rents from the people in Delaware. He therefore held off maki g a grant of the land in Delaware to Penn. Penn, then in Lond n, kept after James with a persistency born of despair at the thou ht that Calvert might, by reason of his grant from Charles I, obt in not only all the land in Delaware but also territory up to he fortieth parallel. This outcome would have taken from Per a a large slice of land now in Pennsylvania; a strip along the e tire southern boundary, including the settlement of Philadel hia (which at that time was the fastest growing town on the A erican continent), and the present locations of York, Chan bersburg and Uniontown.

This strip of land was within the area which had been g anted to Calvert, but Penn's position as a royal favorite enabled him to push his entire southern boundary twenty miles south of the fortieth parallel. [48]

The committee of the Privy Council in England, in November, 1685, made a recommendation, which James approved, that the Delaware peninsula be divided between Calvert and Penn by a north and south line, substantially that now existing.

Not until the autumn of 1688 did Penn succeed in circumventing Sir John Werden, who was fully aware of Penn's grasping propensities for land and ever watchful in the protection of his master from Penn's intrigues.

James was at last prevailed upon by Penn and a patent was prepared by Sir William Williams, solicitor-general of England, embodying a proposed grant of Delaware to Penn.

James became apprehensive of the injudicious provisions of the previous inefficacious grant by him to Penn which would have made James, then Duke of York, but now King, co-partner with Penn in the profits of a land deal. This proposed royal grant by King James stated that Penn was relieved from paying to James one-half the rents and profits from the land in lower Delaware, as had been stipulated in the duke's inefficacious grant of August 24, 1682.° The grant also cited that Penn was pardoned of any felony or treason which might be charged against him for having illegally assumed jurisdiction over Delaware and proposed to grant to Penn all the land in the eastern half of the Delaware peninsula (as now defined within the boundaries of Delaware), the consideration being ten shillings.

This proposed grant was ready for King James' signature, and only the great seal was essential to make it valid. At three o'clock the next morning, receiving an unsatisfactory reply to his overtures to William of Orange, who was coming into England to assume the British crown as William III, James, in a small boat, fled to Gravesend, and on his flight to France threw the great seal in the Thames River. James had abdicated.

Once again, and this time for ever, were Penn's efforts to obtain royal sanction to ownership of the land in Delaware frustrated. After that, the British crown claimed title to all land in

°Pa. Archives.

Delaware and compelled Penn to acknowledge the validity of that claim in the commission of every governor of Delaware he was allowed to appoint.

But Penn was not deterred from continuing boldly to proclaim that he owned all the land in Delaware.

After thirteen years had elapsed, on October 28, 1701, Penn presented to the assembly, composed of Pennsylvania and Delaware delegates, the proclamation: "William Penn, proprietor and governor of Pennsylvania and territories belonging [territories was the term used at that time to designate the Delaware counties], to all to whom these presents shall come, sendeth greetings:

"Whereas, King Charles II gave and granted unto me and my heirs and assigns for ever this province of Pennsylvania, etc.

"And Whereas, the king's dearest brother James, Duke of York and Albany, etc., by his deeds of feoffment under his hand and seal duly perfected, bearing date of the 24th day of August, 1682 [The aforesaid ineffective grant], did grant unto me, my heirs and assigns all that tract of land lying and being from twelve miles north of New Castle, to Cape Henlopen, together with all royalties, franchises, jurisdictions and privileges thereunto belonging. . . ."

This was received in the assembly, and due to the unbounded confidence the people had in statements made by Penn, and also due to lack of knowledge by them of the actual facts, it was approved by the assembly. One year later Governor Hamilton told members from Delaware that the right of Penn to Delaware was disputed in England.

To show how Penn had knowingly deceived the people of Delaware, as well as the Pennsylvania assembly, by falsifying facts when he presented this proclamation, it is only necessary to cite that he, a year and a half afterwards, on May 11, 1703, wrote the Board of Trade in London offering to relinquish the government of Pennsylvania for a consideration. Replying to their inquiry as to his terms, he exacted, among other things, a grant to him of all the land in Delaware. Nothing resulted from the proposal, but it showed that Penn was well aware that the land in Delaware had not been granted to him.

This offer by Penn to relinquish the government (but not the land) of Pennsylvania was, no doubt, prompted by his belief that, inasmuch as the proprietary governments of New Jersey and Carolina had been taken over by the crown, the government of Pennsylvania might be the next to be taken over, and that in the negotiation he might as well bargain for the grant to him of the land in Delaware.

James Logan, a former secretary of Penn, speaking of the Lower Counties (Delaware), said: "From their separation, in 1704, they have always accounted themselves governed only by the king's authority couched in the approbation." [130]

Settlers in Delaware continued to be harassed by buccaneers from Maryland. Calvert asked Queen Anne, in 1707, to confirm his title to Delaware, which she declined to do.

The Earl of Sunderland, who had been an intimate friend of Penn, and had assisted him in getting his grant of Pennsylvania, now that Penn was incapacitated and nearing death, applied in London for a grant of the three lower counties, asserting, in 1717, that he was ready to prove that those counties belonged to the crown. His petition was referred to the attorney-general for an opinion on the crown's title, and the attorney-general issued a summons to William Penn to appear for a hearing. Penn had suffered a stroke of apoplexy five years previously, and was incapable of transacting business and unable to appear. The attorney-general and solicitor-general reported, "No grant of land in Delaware by Charles II to the duke had ever passed the great seal." Penn's actions in regard to Delaware were an attempt by usurpation to lay the settlers in Delaware under contribution for land rents for his personal profit. William Penn died in 1718.

Seven years later the Earl of Sunderland filed a second petition for the land in Delaware, and four other persons filed petitions for grants of islands in the Delaware River.

Calvert and Penn and their heirs had made grants along the boundary lines of Delaware and Maryland, and they agreed that, pending location of definite boundaries, each should collect the land rents from their respective tenants.

The Penn heirs, John, Thomas and Richard Penn, sons of William, though having no ownership of land in Delaware, and

Charles Calvert, fifth Lord Baltimore, agreed fourteen years after the death of Penn that the boundary between Delaware and Maryland should be substantially as at present. This was confirmed twenty-eight years later.

In a suit between the Penn heirs and Calvert, in 1750, Lord Hardwick, Chief Justice of England, decreed Delaware to the Penns, based upon this agreement. Just how that could be, when no grant had ever been made to Penn, is as difficult to understand as is the decision of the United States Supreme Court fixing the boundary between Delaware and New Jersey. Perhaps it was merely an easy way for the British Chief Justice to dispose of a contention that had been plaguing the English courts and officials for more than two-thirds of a century. Since it was, and continues to be, a fixed principle of law, unacceptable to Blackstone, that all land must have an owner, the Penns seemed to be the logical claimants.

Based upon this decree, the Penn heirs in 1757 claimed that Delaware settlers owed them £31,815 land rent. The Penns continued to rent land and collect land rents in Delaware until after the American Revolution.

The Penn heir in England, in 1770, twenty years after the Hardwick decision, wrote his brother, Governor John Penn, in Pennsylvania: "The Lords of Trade made objection to our entitling ourselves 'true and absolute proprietors' of the lower counties. Avoid giving that offense."

A statute of the Delaware assembly in 1793 imposed a fine on any inhabitant accepting a grant of vacant or uncultivated land, except from an official acting under authority of the state, and the following year enacted: "Whereas, the claims of the late and former pretended proprietors of this state, to the soil and land contained within the same, are not founded either in law or equity. . . ."

The Delaware assembly thus divested the Penn heirs of all land and land rents which they claimed in Delaware and paid them nothing. Henceforth, the people of the newly formed state, instead of paying land rents to the Penns in England, began to pay the equivalent as taxes into the public treasury for roads and bridges, and for other public benefits.

Disregarding this proof of Penn never having received an effective grant of land in Delaware, bounded within a twelve mile circle of New Castle, or otherwise, the United States Supreme Court, in 1934, two and a half centuries after the incident, defined the boundary between Delaware and New Jersey as being at low water mark on the eastern side of the Delaware River, within the twelve mile circle around New Castle. This had the ridiculous effect of extending Delaware jurisdiction to include pier-heads in the town of Penns Grove, on the New Jersey side of the river.

The *Newark News* in a leading editorial, January 11, 1944, said of a recent decision: "Bewildering have been the conflicts in judicial reasoning by the present members of the Supreme Court of the United States . . . only to emphasize the unpredictability of decisional law . . . One will have to search far back in the records of the Supreme Court decisions to find a comparable parallel of confusion."

15

Maryland

ALL the land in Maryland was within the grant by James I to the Virginia Company in 1606.

The earliest recorded, but little known, settlement of Europeans in Maryland was on Palmer's Island, in the Susquehanna River, in 1625. Nearly a hundred men were sent there from Jamestown, Virginia, to establish a station for trading with the Indians for mink, otter, beaver and muskrat skins.[a] That was six years before Claiborne made a settlement on Kent Island, and nine years before the grant of the land in Maryland to Calvert.

Palmer's Island, now known as Garrett Island, supports the piers of the Baltimore & Ohio Railroad bridge crossing the Susqehanna River, just above Havre de Grace.

It was in 1625 bargained for with the Indians by Edward Palmer, a man of education, from Gloucestershire, England, who lived on the island a number of years before the advent of the Calvert colony.

The land system of Maryland was formulated by the Calverts. George Calvert was born in 1582, the son of Leonard Calvert, a Yorkshire farmer of Flemish descent. After attending and receiving a degree at Oxford University, he married Alice Wynne, a granddaughter of Sir Thomas Worth, commissioner in Ireland for Queen Elizabeth. (Calvert later succeeded to a similar office.) Calvert was an under-secretary of state to Sir Robert Cecil, for whom Calvert named his eldest son.

By advocating the marriage of the prince, afterwards Charles

[a]Historic Havre de Grace

273

I, to a Spanish princess, upon which the father, James I, had set his mind, Calvert became a favorite of that monarch.

In 1617 he was knighted and, two years later, was appointed principal secretary of state to James I. The king granted him a large area of land at Baltimore, on the southwest coast of Ireland, and shortly thereafter granted him, in fee simple, 3,900 acres at Longford, Ireland, which he began colonizing. Calvert was soon raised to the Irish peerage. His wife, the mother of eleven children, died in 1622.

In 1623 James granted to Calvert and his heirs, for ever, the southeastern part of Newfoundland, the government of which was to be a palatinate and, in effect, was to be a kingdom within the British Kingdom.

Calvert was a member of the Council of New England. Upon the revocation of the Virginia charter in 1624, he was appointed one of the provincial council for the government of that colony.

Upon the death of James I, in March, 1625, the throne fell to his son Charles I, and Calvert sold his secretaryship of state to his successor for £6,000.

After receiving the Newfoundland grant, Calvert promptly sent a group of colonists there to occupy the land, but he himself delayed going until 1627, when he went with a retinue, including a lady friend.

After nearly two years' residence there, he wrote Charles that the climate was too severe for successful colonization and that he intended going with about forty persons to Virginia, "where, if your majesty will be pleased to grant me a precinct of land, with such privileges as the king, your father, was pleased to grant me here, I shall endeavor to the utmost of my power to deserve it."

The king wrote Calvert in reply: "Weighing that men of your condition and breeding are fitter for other employment than the forming of new plantations, which commonly have rugged and laborious beginnings," he thought fit to advise him to desist from further prosecutions of his designs.

Calvert and his party from Newfoundland reached Jamestown, Virginia, in October, 1629, where, meeting with disfavor because of his Romanism, he sailed for England. Disregarding the king's advice, he petitioned the privy council for an area of land in the

Virginia region; at first specifying the territory between the James and Chowan Rivers, but afterwards selecting the Chesapeake region. Calvert also asked the council to instruct the Governor of Virginia to aid in returning to England, the lady whom he had left in Virginia.

The charter for Newfoundland was so liberal in all respects to the grantee, that Calvert, in his petition, copied its provisions for his proposed grant in Maryland.

William Claiborne, a younger son of an old Westmoreland family in England, was sent to Virginia in 1621 by the Virginia Company, as a surveyor. After the Virginia charter was abrogated in 1624, he was appointed by Charles I as secretary of state for Virginia.

A year before the grant of Maryland to Cecilius Calvert in 1633, Claiborne had located a settlement on Kent Island, in the upper Chesapeake, and had established a lucrative trade with the Indians along the Chesapeake Bay and the Potomac and Susquehanna Rivers. He exchanged beads, knives and other trifles for beaver and other valuable peltries, which he shipped to England. From this he prospered greatly and acquired land in Virginia.

In 1631 Claiborne was sent to England by the Virginia assembly to oppose the proposed grant of land to Calvert anywhere within the original Virginia territory, which extended from below the present Wilmington, North Carolina, to above Wilmington, Delaware.

When James I annulled the charter of the Virginia Company, both he and his successor, Charles I, stated that it merely abolished the government of Virginia by that company and did not diminish the land rights of the company stockholders. This was further shown by the fact that for years afterwards Virginia Company stock certificates were received in payment for land.

Clearly, then, the grant of Maryland to Calvert was a grant to him of land which belonged, by grant of James I, to the shareholders of the Virginia Company.

Upon his arrival in England, Claiborne conferred with Clobery & Co., his factors in London, to whom he had been consigning furs, and they aided him in opposing a grant to Calvert.

He had a license from the governor of Virginia to trade with the Dutch and English along the North Atlantic seaboard. While in Britain, he applied for, and was granted, a Scotch license to trade in any part of North America which the king or his predecessors had not granted to others.

In opposing a grant to Calvert, Claiborne and his factors stated that Claiborne had bought Kent Island from the Indians —the kings of that country—and had settled the island before George Calvert came to Virginia. Furthermore, Claiborne said the Calvert grant read that Calvert was granted land which was *hactenus in culta;* that is, land which is unsettled and unimproved, whereas Kent Island had been already settled by him as a part of Virginia and was represented by delegates in the Virginia House of Burgesses.

Further objection was made to the grant in that it was surreptitious, and invasive of the charter rights of Virginia; that King James had granted the same land to the adventurers and planters of Virginia; that these actually possessed Kent Island long before; that it granted too extensive trade privileges and the power of granting "any part of the land in fee to whom he please."

Claiborne then proposed that he pay to his majesty an annual rental of £50 for the island, and £50 for land twelve leagues (thirty-six miles) in width on each side of the Susquehanna River, extending from the mouth thereof to the head "of the grand lake of Canada," and down the Chesapeake Bay on each side to the sea.

George Calvert having died in April, 1632, at the age of fifty-three, before the grant of Maryland passed the great seal, the grant was in the following June issued to his eldest son Cecilius, aged twenty-six, who became second Lord Baltimore.

The commissioners of plantations in England, to whom Claiborne's petition was referred, ruled that Claiborne had only a license to trade with the Indians, which gave him no warrant to land; that under the grant just issued to Calvert the land belonged to Cecilius Calvert, his heirs and assigns; and that the only redress Virginia had was to bring suit against him.

Cecilius, when eighteen years of age, had married Lady Anne Arundel, daughter of Thomas Arundel, Lord of Wardour, who was implicated in the Gunpowder Plot to blow up the House of Parliament in 1605. Arundel was said to have converted George Calvert to Roman Catholicism, and advocated settling Catholics in Maryland. Cecilius was never in America.

Opposition to the Calvert grant continued after it had passed the great seal. The case was tried before the privy council which, as was to be expected, decided in favor of Calvert.

The charter conferred upon Calvert rights and privileges which have never been granted by a sovereign of England to any other individual—in effect, a despotism. The grant included all the land, minerals, rivers, bays and fishings within the present state of Maryland, and a considerable area now in Pennsylvania and Delaware.

It granted to Calvert the right to confer titles, incorporate cities and towns, levy import and export taxes, dispose of land, erect manors, establish courts of justice, appoint all officials, declare martial law, muster and train men to make war; to pursue men and put them to death; and included the patronage and advowsons of all churches to be built.

The king bound himself and his successors not to levy any tax or contribution whatever on the people; but this did not extend to customs duties. No appeal on any controversy between Calvert and the settlers in Maryland could be taken to any British court.

Enactments of the Maryland legislature were not required to be submitted to the king in council, as later was provided in the grant to Penn. Maryland was constituted a palatinate equal to a principality.

To induce purchase of land and migration to Maryland, Calvert advertised the desirable climate and soil and the possibility of making more than 100 per cent profit on the labor of every indented servant which land buyers would transport there.

At the initial offering in England, before sending a colony to occupy the land, Calvert announced that: "Every first adventurer during 1633, who shall transport five men [inferentially indented servants] between fifteen and fifty years of age, shall receive for himself and his heirs for ever, a grant of two thousand acres of land at a yearly rent of four hundred pounds of good wheat—twenty pounds rent per hundred acres.

"Whoever during the following two years shall transport ten men shall receive two thousand acres at an annual rent of six hundred pounds of good wheat—thirty pounds per hundred acres.

"After the third year, and until further notice, for every five men transported, a thousand acres will be granted at an annual rent of 20 shillings payable in commodities of the country"—two shillings (50¢) rent per hundred acres.

These grants of land were not to be made to the men who were transported as indented servants, share croppers or tenants, but to those who sent them and paid their transportation.

A party of colonists in the "Ark," 350 tons, and the "Dove," 50 tons, sailed from England for Maryland in November, by the course usual in the early days, via the Azores.

Cecilius was busy defending his grant against attack in England and appointed his brother, Leonard Calvert, then twenty-six years of age, to go as governor of the colony.

After departure of the colony for Maryland, Cecilius wrote the Earl of Strafford that he had sent a hopeful colony to Maryland: "There are two of my brothers gone, with very near twenty other gents of very good fashion, and three hundred laboring men well provided in all things."

There is reason to believe they were mostly adherents of the Church of England, sent as indented servants; only two of the twelve who died at sea professed adhesion to Roman Catholicism. The governor was assisted by two councillors—Thomas Cornwallis and Jerome Hawley—both of whom were Protestants. [108]

After tarrying a while in the West Indies, they reached the Chesapeake the following February and presented to the Virginia governor a written command of Charles I, that: "The king desires to encourage the noble purpose of Lord Baltimore, and requires that all lawful assistance be given in seating [locating] him and his associates in Maryland." But as the Virginia settlers considered the Maryland territory had been stolen from their province, the presence of the Maryland settlers was resented.

The colony proceeded to the Potomac River and made a landing on an island which they named St. Clement. There, a priest set up a cross and took formal possession of the country, "for our Savior, and for our Sovereign Lord the King of England." They found the woods swarming with deer, bison, bear and turkeys.

The following month they moved to a large tract of land which the Indians had cleared and cultivated. This they named St. Mary's. The Indians were friendly and were given hatchets, hoes and cloth, and the colonists were shown how to cultivate corn and make succotash, corn pone and hominy—all delicious and nutritious food, for which civilization is indebted to the American Indians.

Owing to the facility of the cleared land, the colonists were able at once to plant and, at the end of the first season, to send a shipload of corn to the Massachusetts colony, for which they received in return a supply of salted codfish.

Calvert planned the foundation of an aristocratic state, with large tracts of land possessed by individuals, who would thereby uphold his authority. An assembly, composed of landholders, to act under Calvert dictation, was established at an early date.

Leonard Calvert promptly notified Claiborne that if he wished to retain Kent Island he could do so only as a tenant of, and by paying land rent to, Cecilius Calvert as lord proprietor. Receiving no response, Governor Calvert, six months later, issued an order that if Claiborne would not submit to his government he should be seized and punished.

A pinnace, the "Long Tail," belonging to Claiborne was captured by Calvert forces for trading with the Indians in Maryland waters, without a license from Calvert. In reprisal, Claiborne armed a shallop, the "Cockatrice," and manned it with about thirty men under command of Lieutenant Ratcliffe Warren, whom he commissioned to seize any vessels belonging to the government at St. Mary's. Calvert, learning of this, sent two pinnaces, the "St. Helen" and "St. Margaret," duly armed and equipped, under command of Captain Thomas Cornwallis. The two expeditions met in Pocomoke River in April, 1635. The Warren party fired on the Calvert vessels, killing two men, whereupon the "Cockatrice" surrendered.

About two weeks later another conflict occurred on the Great

Wicomico River, a tributary of the Pocomoke, in which Thomas Smith, commanding a vessel of Claiborne, defeated the Calvert forces. Smith was afterwards captured, tried before the assembly, and hanged for piracy.

In 1636 Cecilius Calvert, in London, announced that any person transporting to Maryland from any other place (having in mind especially Virginia and New England) persons of British or Irish descent should have granted to him, or his assigns, fifty acres of good land for each person. The grant was to be holden in socage tenure, paying yearly for every fifty acres to his lordship (Calvert): for the first seven years, the rent of one shilling sterling in silver, or in commodities, as his lordship or his officers should accept; for the next fourteen years, one bushel of good wheat, or three shillings silver and, thereafter, the twentieth part of the annual yield (the last named, in effect, an annual ground rent based on the annual rental value), or twenty shillings in silver or gold yearly.

The object of this was to induce men of means to buy land and settle tenants or indented servants thereon and, as population increased, to increase the land rents. Calvert well knew that land sales at increasing prices depended upon increasing population.

The announcement continued: "Every adventurer or planter shall cause so many persons to reside upon the land granted as per conditions, and in default thereof, after due notice, shall pay to his lordship, Calvert, two bushels of good wheat yearly for each person missing, and it shall be lawful for his lordship and his heirs to seize fifty acres upon which there is no person, and let the same to any other person for any term not exceeding three lives, or twenty-one years, paying such adventurer or planter and his heirs or assigns a tenth part of any rent obtained over and above the land rent reserved by his lordship upon the original grant."

Calvert was willing to sell land to all applicants, including the Puritans in New England, as shown in an entry in the journal of Governor Winthrop of Massachusetts: "Lord Baltimore being owner of much land near Virginia . . . made tender of land to any of ours that would transport themselves thither, with free liberty of religion and all other privileges which the place affords, paying such annual land rent as should be agreed upon." Winthrop added that none of his people had "any temptation that way."

Thomas Copley, a Jesuit, in accordance with conditions of the plantation, demanded of Calvert four thousand acres for transporting into Maryland himself and twenty able-bodied men at his own charge. [108]

The Jesuit brotherhood and others were active, in the early years of the settlement, in obtaining land rights from the Indians, which prompted Calvert to issue the order that such rights were void and that land titles not obtained from him, as lord proprietor, were not valid, as he held a monopoly of all the land in the province by royal grant. He further declared there should be no land held in mortmain (by an organization). This also brought him in conflict with the Jesuits.

Calvert promoted his brother, Leonard, by appointing him lieutenant-general, admiral and commander, and also chancellor and chief justice of the province, with power to grant land. Leonard was directed to assemble the "freemen," to whom he was to announce that the lord proprietor dissented from the laws made by them at the previous assembly and that he would submit to them laws to be enacted by them.

When these proposed laws were considered at the next assembly, there were fourteen votes, including proxies, for them, and thirty-seven votes in the negative. This was the beginning of a prolonged struggle between the people and the Calverts. [169]

The settlers on Kent Island continued in rebellion and Governor Calvert, with a force, reduced it in February, 1638. Palmer's Island, occupied by people from Virginia, also was in rebellion and it too was reduced and a fort erected thereon.

After four years of contention and fighting with Claiborne, the governor for a few years established and maintained his government throughout the Chesapeake region, but the settlers on Kent Island, feeling they had been unjustly treated by the Calvert rule, resented as unjust the land rents levied upon them.

Claiborne had failed in his attempt to retain possession of the island by force and was sent by the governor of Virginia to England, to seek what remedy he might have there.

King Charles sent commissioners to Maryland to look into the situation. They naturally reported in favor of Calvert, which the king confirmed.

Virginia then ceased opposition to the Calvert charter and grant, and recompensed Claiborne by granting him a large area of land in Virginia. He also obtained land in the Bahama Islands, being part of the grant made by the King of England to the Providence Company, another English colonization project.

Cecilius, in London in 1638, ordered that any law passed by the assembly shall be in force "till I or my heirs signify dissent thereto, and no longer."

It is evident that many persons in England obtained land in Maryland which they had no intention of using. In 1639 an act for peopling the province provided that if any one who had received a grant of land on condition that he would have a specified number of able-bodied persons settled thereon, neglected such settlement for three years, "his lordship is empowered to grant or lease any part of such land to others for a life of seven years."

Refusal of the settlers on Kent Island to pay land rent persisted in 1640, and Calvert issued a commission to the sheriff to demand the unpaid rents. For every fifty acres the rent was 12*d* sterling, or of that value in commodities; that is: four pounds of tobacco, at 3*d* per pound or one peck of wheat. One capon was valued at eight pounds of tobacco, or two pecks of wheat (50¢). Failing to collect, the sheriff was ordered "to distress upon the land and chattels."

A tract of four thousand acres on the Potomac River, above Port Republic, was laid out in 1641 to Captain Thomas Cornwallis, who had come over with Leonard Calvert, and had commanded the Calvert naval fleet against the Claiborne forces. He became the most substantial resident in Maryland and built in the colony the first brick house of which there is any record. [108]

Notwithstanding the land rents which Calvert was exacting of all the settlers, the assembly in 1643 granted him 5 per cent tax on all tobacco exported to countries other than England, Ireland and Virginia. Four years later he was granted, for a period of thirteen years, 10s per hogshead on all tobacco exported.

At the time the assembly was granting him the tax on the product of the tobacco growers, he was sending an order from Bristol, England, that all his indented servants on his West St. Mary's plantation be sold forthwith, to be replaced by laborers to be paid from the products of the farm, "if sufficient."

A proclamation in 1643 required that all persons who had settled on land assigned to them must take out grants for the same and pay land rent, on pain of being refused grants thereafter.

The council of state in London issued an order to apprehend Cecilius Calvert, charged with coining and exporting money; the coins bearing his image, name, and coat-of-arms. [108]

Being under charges in England, he had given bond not to leave there, whereupon Leonard went to England in April, 1643, to confer with him; appointing Giles Brent as acting governor during his absence.

Claiborne took advantage of the governor's absence to renew active opposition, by "attacking Calvert's land rights, declaring that all persons who had transported themselves into the province were entitled to land and might take it up at their pleasure without reference to Calvert." [19]

Richard Ingle, who had lately arrived in Maryland from England and become a tobacco trader, upon departure of the governor, started an agitation to deprive Calvert of all his rights of government, if not to the proprietorship of the land, in the province. Arrest of Ingle for treason was ordered.

Cecilius was dissatisfied with Brent's acts and, in December, notified Brent that he intended going to Maryland in, or before, June next. Meantime, he suspended granting land until his arrival.

Cecilius did not go to Maryland as promised and, instead, ordered Leonard to return to Maryland forthwith. Upon his arrival there he found that Claiborne and Ingle had joined forces and with an armed vessel had seized St. Mary's, the capital, and that Claiborne had retaken Kent Island. Whereupon Leonard fled to Virginia, and a general uprising occurred in favor of Cromwell and the British Parliament. Cornwallis' brick house was seized, "with the plate, linen, hangings, brass, pewter and other household effects worth £1,000; also his cattle, a shallop and a pinnace."

The province was in control of these contestants for the six months ending in August, 1646, when Acting-Governor Brent captured the armed vessel and expelled both Claiborne and Ingle. During this rebellion, the land records at St. Mary's were lost or stolen, which caused much doubt about many land titles.

The following year, the settlers on Kent Island again rebelled and refused to take the oath of allegiance or pay land rent to Calvert as lord of the province.

Governor Leonard Calvert died that year, and Margaret Brent, sister of Giles Brent, was named his executor. She was a woman of forceful personality and was active in taking up land.

The late governor had commissioned Thomas Greene, a member of the council, as his successor. England then being under Cromwell, and Cecilius apprehending encroachment of Parliament on his Maryland domain, deemed it prudent that the governor be a Protestant. Thereupon, to save his privilege and land-rentals, he appointed William Stone, of Virginia, a Protestant, as governor and changed his council (not the assembly) from all Catholics to one-half Catholics and one-half Protestants. [60]

Notwithstanding this the attorney-general in England was directed by Parliament to take under consideration the validity of the royal grant of Maryland to Calvert. [108]

Stone, having occasion to go to Virginia, appointed Greene as deputy-governor. Greene, being a royalist, grasped the opportunity to proclaim Charles II, but Greene's commission was soon terminated by the return of Stone. Greene's action embarrassed Calvert in his relations with Cromwell.

A group of Puritans who had come from England in 1621 under the leadership of Richard Bennett, son of a wealthy London merchant, and settled along the Nansemond River in Virginia, were forced by religious intolerance to leave Virginia. They moved to the Severn River in Maryland in 1649 and later were followed by several hundred more. They founded Providence, afterwards named Annapolis, and divided a tract of land into lots of fifteen acres each.

There they found they were obliged to take an oath of loyalty to Calvert. Having objection, because of religious scruples, to taking an oath of any kind, a modified oath was compromised upon with Governor Stone. Calvert rejected this and proclaimed that all who would not take the oath within three months should be expelled from the province and their land seized to his lordship's use. [60]

To establish and perpetuate a feudal aristocratic society in Maryland, and to increase land sales, Calvert in 1648 ordered that each land grant of a large area should be constituted a manor, "to be of an indefeasible estate of inheritance in fee simple to them and their heirs for ever."

Manors were laid off in different parts of the province, and some of the choicest locations were reserved for Calvert; other locations were reserved for the benefit of his relatives and friends.

Calvert promulgated the terms and conditions upon which he would grant land for manors, as follows: "On two thousand acres each, at an annual land rent for the first seven years, £2 sterling in silver or gold, or value thereof in products, payable to Calvert or his heirs; the next fourteen years, the annual rental to be forty bushels of wheat, or £6 sterling in gold or silver at the choice of his lordship or his heirs; and after the said fourteen years, the twentieth part of the annual yield and profits of such manor, or in lieu thereof, £10 silver, at the choice of his lordship or heirs. For every two thousand acres, and every three thousand acres, and every one thousand acres of land so to be granted to any adventurer [there] shall be created . . . a manor, to be called by such name as the adventurer shall desire. Also to grant within every manor, to him and his heirs, a court-baron and court-leet."

This was stretching out aristocratic features in the province— a feudal mode of parcelling out lands by subinfeudation. [15]

To assure their continuance, and make Maryland a feudal state as far as human foresight could dictate, Calvert ordered that: "the sixth part of the land of every manor shall be set apart by meets and bounds and never be alienated, separated, or leased from the royalties and lord of the manor for a term exceeding seven years, but the lord of the manor shall have power to grant or convey any other part of said manor to any other person of British or Irish descent, either in fee simple or fee-tayle for life, lives or years, under such rents as they think fit, not prejudicial to his lordship's [Calvert's] royal jurisdiction, and liable to the payment of such land rents to his said lordship and his heirs for ever."

With the knowledge that an ever increasing population automatically increases the rental value of land, he determined to reap that unearned increment. While such rentals look small today, we may be assured they were the utmost Calvert could exact while there was a sparse population in a wilderness.

These conditions of plantation were calculated to induce men of some wealth in England, who were able to bear the expense of transporting servants and dependents, to take up land on which to place them, and often themselves to emigrate to the province. [15]

To protect such adventurers, the Calvert assembly made it a felony for any indented servant to depart secretly from his master, the penalty being death.

Fiske, [48] in *Virginia and Her Neighbors,* in giving an excellent account of these manors in Maryland, said: "The manor was the land on which the lord and his tenants lived, and bound up with the land were also the rights of government which the lord of the manor possessed over his tenants, and they over one another.

"The manor house was usually of generous dimensions, containing a large dining hall, paneled wainscoting and family portraits; there was the chapel, with the graves of the lord's family beneath its chancel, and the graves of the common folk in the churchyard.

"Surrounding or near by the manor house were various buildings for the numerous negro slaves, and for cooking and preserving; for the extensive stable of horses, and for coaches and farm implements; for cattle, and for carpentering, blacksmithing, wheel-wrighting, carding, weaving, painting and shoemaking; and a more or less primitive mill for grinding grain. In the distance were the dwellings and farm buildings of the white tenants. Here and there the dwelling of a white freehold tenant, with ample land about it, held on lease of twenty-one years.

"These manors were little self-governing communities. The

granting of a manor usually included the right to the grantee to hold court-leet and court-baron. The court-leet was like a town meeting. All freemen could take part in it. It enacted by-laws, elected constables and other local officers.

"It set up stocks and pillory, and sentenced offenders to stand there; for judicial and legislative functions were united in this court-leet. It empaneled its jury, and with the steward of the manor presiding as judge, it visited with fine or imprisonment, the thief, the vagrant, the poacher, the fraudulent debtor.

"The court-baron was an equally free institution in which all the freehold tenants sat as judges determining questions of law and of fact. Each was a little world in itself. This court decided all disputes between the lord and his tenants, or escheats. Here actions for debt were tried, and transfers of land were made with the ancient formalities."

It is probable that court-leets or court-barons were seldom held, and on some manors not at all, and that their functions were taken over by the county courts as soon as county courts were brought into existence.

Any estates and manors forfeited for treason or felony went to the lord proprietor.

A grant of three thousand acres was made to William Mitchell on the usual terms, in consideration of his sending thirty persons to Maryland. St. Thomas' manor of four thousand acres was granted in 1649.

A manor on the Patuxent River was granted in 1650 to Robert Brooke of England, to constitute "one whole county to be created thereabouts, with all such dignities, privileges and profits belonging to said place." Brooke arrived with his family and many servants, and a pack of hounds. In the same year a manorial grant on Kent Island was made to Robert Vaughan. A manor of ten thousand acres was granted to Edward Eltonhead.

Thomas Gerrard, gent, a member of the council, was granted Saint Clement manor of 11,400 acres on the north side of the Patuxent River. This was the largest individual manorial grant in Maryland, and was adjacent to Basford manor, in the same ownership, and to a manor of 61,000 acres reserved by Calvert for himself. Original manuscript records of court-baron and court-leet held in Saint Clement manor, from 1659 to 1672, are in possession of the Maryland Historical Society.

Calvert in 1665 ordered that in every county at least two manors, each not less than six thousand acres of the choicest soil, be surveyed and set apart for himself. These to be leased to tenants on payment of land rent.[b]

Johnson, in his excellent essay on *Old Maryland Manors,* cites the manors of: George Evelin, lord of the manor of Evelinton in St. Mary's County; Marmaduke Tilden, lord of Great Oak manor, and Major James Ringgold, lord of Eastern Neck manor, both in Kent County; Giles Brent, lord of Kent Fort, on Kent Island; George Talbot, lord of Susquehanna manor, in Cecil County; and notes the sale, in 1767, of twenty-seven manors embracing a hundred thousand acres. The last named were sales by Frederick Calvert when the assembly levied an increased tax on all land.

Cecilius Calvert, at Bath, England, in 1648 announced: "Every adventurer or planter, before having any land granted to him, shall take an oath of fidelity to his lordship and his heirs, as follows: '[I] do faithfully and truly acknowledge the Right Hon. Cecilius, Lord Baron of Baltimore, to be the true and absolute lord and proprietary of the Province of Maryland and the islands thereto belonging . . . and shall defend and maintain his lordship's and his heirs' right, title, interest, privilege, royal jurisdiction and domain over and in said province . . . that I will not purchase or possess any land from any Indian, etc.' "

An act of assembly, about 1649, provided that: "All persons making mutinous or seditious speeches tending to divert the people from the lord proprietary or his heirs, shall be liable to be punished with imprisonment of one year, banishment, boring of the tongue, slitting of the nose, cutting off one or both ears, whipping and branding with red hot iron on the hands or forehead." Further: "All purchases of lands made or to be made, not deriving a lawful title thereto by, or from, his lordship or his heirs under the great seal, shall be void and null. It shall be lawful for his lordship to seize, possess and dispose of any such lands purchased from Indians or others."

The Calverts did not permit any pecuniary advantage to escape

[b]Md. Archives

them. Their private ownership of all wild animals and game was declared, and it was enacted: "Inhabitants trading with the Indians for beaver or other commodities are obliged to pay one-tenth in weight and value to his lordship."

After driving the aborigines to remote parts, giving them mere trifles as assumed compensation, and often nothing at all, Calvert, under his great seal, allotted some tribes a tract of eight to ten thousand acres at the head of Wicomico River. On a thousand acres of this, as was usual in grants of manors, the Indians were obliged to pay Calvert an annual land rent of one shilling for each fifty acres, payable in furs. Bozeman, [15] a Maryland historian, said: "After appropriating their land he rented it to them! His Lordship's benevolence! He made copyhold leases to the Indians at St. Mary's, which changed the status of the Indians from free inhabitants to rent-paying tenants."

An act for relief of the poor, passed in 1650, is the first record that any poor existed. This prompted Bozeman to comment: "As long as civil society consists of an aggregation of families, and property is allowed to be descendible, such a law is essentially necessary."

Only a small portion of the large domain was granted to others during the first seventeen years, and settlements existed in only three places: St. Mary's County, Kent Island and along the Severn River.

The British Commonwealth, under Cromwell, assumed the government of Maryland in 1652, whereupon Calvert closed the land office, and, in disregard of others who needed land on which to live and work, kept it closed during the six years of the administration of the Cromwell-appointed governor.

Calvert in 1653 directed Governor Stone to cause all persons who had failed to take out patents for their land, or had not taken the prescribed oath of fidelity to the proprietary, to take out patents, and make the prescribed oath within three months, upon pain of forfeiture of their land.

The revolution in Maryland, during the Cromwell regime, prompted a complaint from Virginia to Cromwell that Calvert was holding vast areas of land unused: "We think it agreeing to reason that he should show his right to it by sending people over to use it, otherwise, how unreasonable it is that he should possess two-thirds part of the Bay of Virginia, and yet in twenty-one years has not more men there, except such as have gone there from Virginia, than can, or do, use only as much as is contained in a small corner thereof."

The assembly, being relieved of Calvert dictation, and influenced by the renewed agitation by Claiborne for freer access to land, passed a resolution that: "all those that transport themselves or others into the province have a right to land, by virtue of their transportation."

Richard Bennett and Claiborne, parliamentary-appointed commissioners, deposed Stone, an appointee of Calvert, and in August, 1654, appointed Captain William Fuller of Providence (Annapolis) governor and commander of the militia, with a Puritan council. Having mustered a force of 175 rebellious Marylanders and Virginians, they prepared to meet Stone.

Stone, at St. Mary's, mustered all males capable of bearing arms and, with 12 boats and 130 men, started to the Severn River; some going by water and others overland. Stone flew the Calvert colors and Fuller those of the Commonwealth of England. Fuller obtained possession of two merchant ships, one being the "Golden Lion." The two forces met on the Severn the following March. The Puritans were completely victorious. About twenty of Stone's men were killed and thirty wounded, and nearly all the remainder, including Stone, who was wounded, were taken prisoners. The loss by the Puritans was trifling. Ten prisoners were condemned to death, of whom, however, only Eltonhead and three others were executed. The estates of those who had opposed them were confiscated. [169]

Disputes having arisen over the boundary line between Maryland and Virginia on the Eastern Shore, Calvert, aiming to increase his adherent population thereabouts, gave instructions to cause the land bordering on the disputed division line to be granted and settled upon as soon as possible, even at half the price of land in other parts of the province.

Calvert appointed Josias Fendell governor of the province, in 1656. He was promptly arrested by the Puritans and kept in jail two months. Later that year, Philip Calvert, half-brother of Cecilius, was sent to Maryland as a member of the council and secretary of the province, and three years afterwards was appointed governor. He was a son of George Calvert, first Lord Baltimore, by the lady who had accompanied him on his voyage to Newfoundland and Virginia. He was succeeded two years afterwards by Charles, the eldest son of Cecilius.

The conflict continued between the two sets of governments until March, 1658, when an agreement was signed by which the claims of Calvert were recognized.

Calvert directed donations of land to several of those who had been conspicuously faithful to him during the late rebellion; To Josiah Fendell, governor, 2,000 acres; to Luke Barber, 1,000; to Thomas Trueman, 1,000; to George Thompson, 1,000; to John Langford, 1,500; to Henry Coursay, 1,000; and to Philip Calvert, 6,000 acres, to be erected into one or more manors. Spesutie Island, "Utie's Hope," at the head of Chesapeake Bay, was granted to Colonel Nathaniel Utie who, with a squad of soldiers, had been sent by Governor Fendell on an unsuccessful mission to the Delaware. He had been instructed to direct the Dutch either to depart from there or take the oath of allegiance to the lord proprietor of Maryland; neither of which proposals the Dutch accepted. Land was granted on rental to foreigners in the same manner as to the British or Irish.

Upon Charles II becoming King of England in 1660, Claiborne at last realized that it was futile for him to continue to war against the favorites of the monarch in England. He retired to his landed estate in Virginia, where he died at over eighty years of age, with the conviction that he had been robbed of what rightfully belonged to him.

Josiah Fendell, whom Calvert had appointed as governor, deserted Calvert. He and several others were arrested upon orders from Calvert and sentenced to forfeit their estates and to be banished. These sentences were afterwards reduced to disfranchisement. Fuller escaped arrest by flight. [112]

In the early years of the province, warrants for land were issued for a certain number of acres, wherein the boundaries were seldom specified, other than that they were abutting on a certain stream and began at some particular point. Subsequent surveys often showed overlapping of grants, which caused confusion and uncertainty as to titles.

When transfers of land were made between individual holders, they were often made by the method of "livery of seizen," this being the entry of the grantor and grantee on the land accompanied by witnesses; or by "seizen by the rod," which was by similar entry, the grantor and grantee both taking hold of a twig, breaking it apart, each keeping one part as evidence of the contract of transfer. At a later period, transfers were recorded by endorsement on the original deeds. It was not until about twenty years after the first settlement that provision was made for registration of transfers.

Calvert's name was used in all writs and processes, as the name of the king was used in England, and indictments charged the offences to be against the Calvert government. Fines imposed in courts of justice inured to Calvert, as the foundation of justice.

The grant to Calvert extended to the south and west shores of the Potomac River, which gave him ownership of the entire river. Whereupon he levied tolls on all vessels belonging to Virginians sailing on the river. The Virginians naturally were incensed at this and vigorously objected. But as Calvert owned the entire river, as well as all the land in Maryland, the Virginians had either to pay toll or keep off the river. The Calverts never would give up this monopoly, and not until after the Revolution was any part of it relinquished, and not until 1927, being 293 years after the grant, was it fully relinquished.

Metal money was very scarce in all the colonies and tobacco became the medium of exchange in Maryland and Virginia for payment of all services and obligations. Laborers who were seeking a piece of land for a habitation were often paid for their services by allotting them a small tract. A large landholder on the Patuxent River, who had clay on his land, gave a piece of land in payment for labor in making brick with which to build his mansion.

Augustus Herman of Bohemia, a surveyor who came to America with the Dutch prior to 1647, was prominent in the Dutch councils in New Netherland. He and Resolved Waldron, as stated in the chapter on the Delaware Region, were in 1659 sent by Stuyvesant as ambassadors to Calvert, in Maryland, respecting the Calvert claim to Delaware, which was then occupied by the Dutch.

After his conference with Calvert and Fendell at St. Mary's, Herman made a trip to Virginia and does not appear to have returned to the Delaware, but settled in Maryland. There were several influences which probably determined him to desert New Netherland and become a citizen of Maryland.

Several years previously he had written a letter denouncing Stuyvesant and, like many other of the leading citizens of New Amsterdam, he was often in discord with the tyrannical governor. Notwithstanding which, Stuyvesant entrusted him with the important ambassadorship to Calvert.

But affairs at New Amsterdam were not altogether to Herman's liking. He saw that Calvert controlled a great domain —an empire—free from foreign entanglements, as was the plight of the Dutch. At that time, there was no opposition within the colony, and Calvert's government, of which he had been deprived six years, had been recently resorted to him.

Then, too, Herman took a liking to the Chesapeake and its tributaries—declared it God's country, as do so many persons who have sailed, fished and gunned over it—and the thought came to him, as a surveyor, that he would propose to Calvert, if in fact Calvert himself had not hinted at it, to make a much needed map of Maryland, in consideration of the grant of a manor.

Such an arrangement was concluded, and Herman selected twenty thousand acres, to which he gave the name Bohemia Manor, along the Elk and Bohemia Rivers in Cecil County. This location was in the path of the shortest trade route between the Delaware and Chesapeake. Herman was instrumental in construction of a road between the headwaters of Bohemia River, a tributary of the Chesapeake, and Appoquinimink Creek, which flows into the Delaware, and on which Odessa is situated.

Herman acquired the confidence of the people of both Maryland and Delaware. He was influential in averting an attack by the English in Maryland on the Dutch, and instead, led to the opening of trade between them over his trade route, to their mutual advantage.

Some years later he deeded 3,750 acres to the Labidist sect, of which Peter Sluyter was the leader. Upon dissolution of the order, after fifteen years' possession, the land was partitioned and Sluyter "retained as his share enough to make him wealthy." Bohemia Manor was held by Herman and his descendants, as lords of the manor, for 128 years, and the name continues.

Several acts of benefit to the people passed by the assembly, were, after five years of operation, disallowed by Calvert. The Maryland people could never be certain that acts passed by their assembly during the Calvert reign would not be disallowed by the proprietary. [112]

Suffrage was restricted to those holding fifty or more acres, or possessed of personal property of £50. Similar suffrage restrictions prevailed in all the proprietary colonies, through acts of the proprietary-controlled assemblies, and in some of the New England colonies through restrictions by the Church.

Calvert sent strict orders in 1670 to prepare a revised rent roll, to learn whether any one was holding land on which they were evading payment to him of land rents. The number of land leases had so increased that two receivers-general were appointed to collect the rents, and they were to appoint deputies to assist.

Following previous export taxes levied by the assembly for Calvert, a law, enacted in 1671, laid an export tax of 2s per hogshead on tobacco, to continue eleven years. The proceeds, instead of being applied wholly for the advancement of the province, were to be divided equally between the public treasury and Calvert. [19]

Cecilius, after enjoying in England for forty-one years the land rents collected from the landholders of Maryland, died in 1675, aged sixty-nine. He was succeeded as lord proprietor by his son, Charles, the third Lord Baltimore, who had been living in Maryland for the previous fifteen years. He was the first Calvert proprietary ever to be in Maryland. He went to England the following year and remained there four years.

Approximately at that time, sixty manors, averaging three thousand acres each, had been created, tilled mostly in small tracts by tenants on a land rent basis. George Talbot of Rascommon, Ireland, a cousin of Calvert and surveyor-general of Maryland, was in 1680 granted thirty-two thousand acres, upon agreement to bring 580 British and Irish into the province. The grant was for ten miles along the east side of the Susquehanna River, one-half of which was later found to extend into Pennsylvania.

Penn, who had received a grant of Pennsylvania from Charles II in 1681, urged Calvert, unavailingly, to move his southern boundary line farther south on the Eastern Shore, so that Penn's southern line might be correspondingly shifted farther south to give him an opening at the head of Chesapeake Bay. He then offered to buy of Calvert land at the head of the bay, which Calvert was willing to accede to, if Penn would relinquish to Calvert his claim to Delaware. But Penn was unwilling to do that.

Upon recommendation of the privy council in 1685, a north and south line was run on the Delaware-Maryland peninsula, to divide that area between Penn and Calvert, approximately as it is today.

The method of acquiring land at the prevailing land rent, by bringing in indented servants, was discontinued in 1683, but importation of indented servants continued until the time of the American Revolution.

Transportation of young women for wives for the settlers became a lucrative business for ship captains, and many were brought over. The cost per wife, to pay for their transportation, was 100 pounds of tobacco.

Settlers continued pouring in to get land for homesteads. They found all the choice locations already appropriated, but mostly held unused or only partially used. An act was passed which provided that land long unsettled and uncultivated should revert to the proprietary, to be granted to others.

Charles Calvert, after four years in Maryland, again went to England in 1684 and remained away five years. He left his minor son, Benedict Leonard Calvert, fourth Lord Baltimore, as nominal governor. George Talbot was made chief of a commission of deputy-governors, by whom the government was administered.

[60]

The assembly in 1688 ordered sixty-two towns to be laid out, generally at the head of navigation of the numerous rivers and their tributaries. Each was to have "commons" of from fifteen to three hundred acres, mainly for pasturing domestic animals. Some of them had a whipping-post and pillory. Charlestown, on the North East River, was later laid out by promoters, on five hundred acres, with broad streets, two hundred lots and a commons. Fairs were held there annually, and other attractions offered while the boom lasted, to induce purchase of lots. Being at the very head of navigation on the bay, the boast was that it would become the metropolis of the province. The depth of water was pronounced insufficient, a fact which promoters must have known beforehand, and Charlestown lapsed into a quiet village, now a flag station on the main line railroad.

King William of England issued a *scire facias* against the Calvert charter in 1691 and appointed Sir Lionel Copley as royal governor of Maryland. Calvert had returned to Maryland two years previously, after five years in England. In resentment at the king's move, he shut up his land office, true to past Calvert practice, refused to grant any more land to the oncoming settlers, and left for England.

He continued to live in England for the remaining twenty-four years of his life. The revenue from land rents was forwarded to him by his agent, after being collected from the lords of the numerous manors and from the hard-working farmers. Meanwhile, he had none of the burdens of government of the province.

Whereupon, to meet the demands of settlers for land, the assembly, now beyond the control or influence of Calvert, in 1692 passed an act which provided that those who had obtained warrants for land were to enjoy the land, without patent from Calvert.

Episcopal parishes were established that year, and a tax of forty pounds of tobacco per poll for support of the Church of England was levied on rich and poor alike, regardless of their church affiliation. After being in effect eighty years, Charles Carroll of Carrollton, a Roman Catholic, led a legal assault against this illogical tax. To many of these churches, Queen Anne, during her reign, presented silver communion plate.

The crown governed Maryland twenty-four years, until 1715. Governor Nicholson succeeded Copley as royal governor and the provincial capital was moved from St. Mary's to Annapolis.

St. Mary's, Patuxent and Pocomoke, the three ports of entry, each had three tax officials at the close of the seventeenth century, viz.: collector of duties exacted by Calvert, collector of customs for the king, and the collector for the king of revenue from sale of prize, forfeiture, and other royal levies. An export tax on furs, an important labor product, was in 1694 levied for schools.

The land rents, created automatically, solely by the mere presence of the people, were being sent to the absentee lord-proprietor in England, instead of being used to provide badly-needed roads, bridges, and schools, and for other public purposes in the development of the province.

William Penn, whose affairs were so entwined with those of Calvert, became physically incapacitated in 1712 and died six years later.

Charles Calvert died in 1715 and was succeeded by his son, Benedict Leonard Calvert, fourth Lord Baltimore. Benedict, in a move to regain the government of Maryland, renounced the Roman Catholic faith and petitioned that the government be restored to the Calverts.

He died within six weeks after his father, whereupon his son, Charles, the fifth Lord Baltimore, aged sixteen years, a Protestant, and grandson of an illegitimate daughter of King Charles II, had the government promptly restored to him, and he became governor of Maryland at that early age.

Controversy broke out anew in 1732 between the heirs of Penn and Calvert, respecting the boundary between them. The grant to Calvert specified as his northern boundary, the parellel of 40° N. (which is at the northern edge of Philadelphia), while the grant to Penn, of later date, specified as his southern boundary the "beginning of the fortieth degree of North latitude." This caused a conflict of interpretation.

By the previous persistency of William Penn, and his personal friendship and influence with Charles II and the Duke of York, Penn, at that time, had his southern boundary line run due west from a point fifteen miles below the southernmost point of Philadelphia, to contact the twelve mile circle north and west of New Castle.

Anxious to settle the long and vexatious controversy and expensive lawsuits, which had existed between the Penns and Calverts for fifty years regarding the boundary, the respective heirs entered into an agreement. Charles Calvert, then in Maryland, consented to the more southerly boundary of Pennsylvania, by which Maryland contains about three million fewer acres than were presumed to be included in the grant by Charles I to Cecilius Calvert. That area now includes the cities of Philadelphia, York, Chambersburg and Uniontown.

A while before this agreement between the Penns and Calvert was entered into, Calvert granted to Thomas Cresap five hundred acres on the Susquehanna River, below Columbia. To prove the claim of Calvert to that region, Cresap built a house on his grant. A fight ensued, in which Cresap was driven from his home by Pennsylvania citizens and his house destroyed by fire. After being captured and taken to Philadelphia, he was released and then left for other parts.

The population of Maryland in 1748 was estimated as: free whites, 98,357; indented servants, 6,870; Negro slaves, 42,764. This does not show the number of indented servants who had lived in Maryland. By that time, thousands had served their terms of indenture and become free, and others were constantly arriving.

A tract of sixty acres near what is now The Basin in Baltimore Harbor, owned by Charles and Daniel Carroll, was sold by them in 1729 at £2 per acre. The following year it was laid out in streets, and lots were offered for sale. The water-front lots were soon sold. But the town grew slowly and after twenty years, by 1749, had only about twenty houses and a hundred inhabitants. It became a flour exporting port, and forty years later had increased in population to twenty thousand, making it the fourth most populous city in English America.

A tract of two hundred acres was granted to Jonathan Hagar in 1739, on which Hagerstown was laid out twenty-two years afterwards.

The English law of primogeniture was in effect in Maryland

from the beginning until 1786; even after that date, the eldest son generally received the larger share of the family estate. This built up vast holdings, power, and importance in favored land-holding families.

The Carroll family was probably the largest landholding and wealthiest family in the upper, if not in the entire Chesapeake region.

Charles Carroll, of Annapolis, father of the signer, was a fore-most citizen of the province. He long had been agent and re-ceiver of rents for the Calverts. In addition to the manor of Donghoregan of 10,000 acres, in Howard County, he held 60,000 acres elsewhere in Maryland; also 20 lots and houses in An-napolis, and 300 slaves and other property, comprising a fortune estimated at £90,000.

Land in Maryland tripled in price between 1730 and 1760. In 1774, when John Adams met Carroll's son, Charles Carroll of Carrollton, at the Continental Congress in Philadelphia, he noted that he was "of the first fortunes in America. His income is £10,000 sterling a year, will be £14,000 in a few years, they say; besides his father has a vast estate which will be his."

Charles Calvert died in London in 1751 and was succeeded by his son, Frederick, sixth, and last, Lord Baltimore. Frederick, like his forebears of the Baltimore barony granted by King Charles I, 119 years previously, lived in England in the lap of luxury, on the fat of the land, from unearned land rents wrung from the farmers in Maryland. He was a licentious and dissolute rake who cared nothing for Maryland or the Maryland people, except as providers of funds with which to keep up his dissipa-tions.

While the American colonists were in the agony of the French and Indian War, Frederick Calvert was writing his governor, Horatio Sharpe, in Maryland, to find good places for favorites whom he sent to Maryland to feed at the public trough; to see that his rents were collected and the revenue remitted promptly; to keep a sharp eye on the Roman Catholics; and to send him Maryland partridges and dried rattlesnakes.

When the assembly levied a tax on all land, including the proprietary's manors, Frederick sent orders to his governor to sell his manor lands, of between three and four hundred thousand acres. That vast area was too great to be readily realized upon, but a hundred thousand acres were presently sold.

This is a demonstration of the economic fact so universally ignored, that a high tax on unused land will bring land into the market and make it easier to get land upon which to labor and create wealth.

Governor Sharpe, an appointee of Calvert, in signing the new tax bill said: "It is better for the proprietary to pay a tax on his manors than to lose his rents and his manors to boot." Eleven years later, when Robert Eden, who had married Frederick's sister (forebears of Anthony Eden), was governor, the records show the sale of twenty-seven manors, comprising a hundred thousand acres.

Frederick died in London in 1771, without legitimate children, and the barony became extinct. He willed all his landholdings in Maryland to an illegitimate son, Henry Harford, for whom one of the Maryland counties is named.

The American colonies having in 1776 declared their independence, the new State of Maryland sequestered all the remaining landed domain of Henry Harford. The state afterwards paid Harford £10,000 in compromise of litigation and the British government needlessly and foolishly presented him with £90,000, by levying taxes on all the British people.

Giving Calvert, his heirs and assigns, the right for ever to collect, for their personal profit, the rental value of land created by all the people of Maryland was without logical justification. But justification for it became impregnated in the minds of the settlers, through repeated assertions by Calvert agents, and was supported by royal practices of that age. Seemingly this continues in the minds of most of the otherwise enlightened people of Maryland to this day.

All the land that had been disposed of by the Calverts was, in effect, on annual ground rent leases, to be held so long as the annual ground rent was paid to the Calverts and their heirs and assigns.

The people of Baltimore, those of the older generation at least, are familiar with ground rents, because so much land in

Baltimore was held in that way. But those annual ground rents were payable, not to the municipal or state treasuries, but to private holders—assigns, directly or indirectly to the Calverts.

The legislature of the new State of Maryland granted title in fee simple to the holders of land and then levied taxes on them for public revenue. It could have, just as well, continued these leases (and made leases on land subsequently granted by the state), with the ground rents payable to the state and municipalities; the annual ground rent to be based on the value of the land held by each lessee—increasing as population increased the annual rental value. This would require no more clerical help or bookkeeping than the present system of collecting taxes.

Had it done this, the revenue from ground rents, no doubt, would have been sufficient to have avoided the necessity of ever levying taxes, or ever creating a bonded debt.

Every municipality in Maryland, except Baltimore City, has the legal power, now, to collect its necessary public revenue by a tax on land value alone, in substitution for levying taxes on improvements and commodities; and any of them would be acting wisely if they would exercise that right.

16

New Jersey

ALL the land in New Jersey was in 1606 with certain provisos, included by King James I of England in his grant to the Virginia Company. Three years afterwards, this grant was amended to include land in New Jersey only as far north as Barnegat.

The Dutch were trading with the natives on Manhattan Island in 1614, and it is believed that some Dutch settled in Bergen County between 1617 and 1620.

Captain Cornelius Jacobson Mey, of a Dutch expedition, sailed up the Delaware in 1620, giving his name to the Cape. He built Fort Nassau at Timber Creek, five miles below Camden, the first settlement of white people ever made on the Delaware.

Michael Pauw, a burgher of Amsterdam, and a director of the Dutch West India Company, was granted by the company in 1620 some land at Pavonia, which became the patroonship of Pavonia.

In November of the same year, King James I of England granted to twelve English lords and knights, and their twenty-eight associates, all the land between 40° and 48° North latitude (Philadelphia and Gulf of St. Lawrence), which included all land in New Jersey north of Camden and Toms River. But no settlement, under any of these English grants, was made in New Jersey.

Pauw and his small colony lived at Pavonia for a while and later received a grant of land on Staten Island. Finding the New Jersey grant unprofitable, he failed to comply with its conditions and the company paid him twenty-six thousand guilders (guilders rated at 40¢) to relinquish the grant. There were two houses built there.

"We, Director and Council of New Netherland, residing on the Island of Manhattan, at Fort Amsterdam, under the jurisdiction of Their Noble Highnesses, the Lords States General of the United Netherlands and of the Incorporated West India Company, Department of Amsterdam, attest." Such was the introductory wording of a grant of sixteen miles square at Cape May, made, "subject to the usual conditions," by Peter Minuet, as director, in 1631 to Samuel Godyn, an Amsterdam merchant, and Samuel Bloemaert.

Peter Heyser, captain of the ship, "Whale," and Giles Coster, commissary, representing the grantees, negotiated with nine Indians named therein as the "lawful owners," who conveyed it for "a certain quantity of goods." The Indians agreed to have the sale confirmed by the other co-owners.

The same grantees had settled a colony on a grant across the bay in Delaware. Massacre by the Indians of all the settlers there, and a suit and counter-suit between the company and the grantees, terminated both projects.

Governor Kieft, successor to Minuet, in 1638 sold Paulus Hook for 450 guineas to Abram Isaacsen Planck (Verplank), who leased the Hook to Cornelius Arissen and agreed to build a barn for him. [168]

This grant to Planck was confirmed by Philip Carteret when he became the English governor of East Jersey in 1668. It was sold by Planck to Cornelius van Vorst in 1699, for £300 "current money in New York." For sixty-five years it was cultivated as a part of his extensive farm. [168]

Aret van Teunissen van Putten of Holland was, in 1641, granted the site of Hoboken and erected a brewery on it. [111]

All the land extending from Newark Bay along the valley of the Hackensack River towards Tappan, New York, was in 1641 granted to Myndert Myndertsen van der Horst of Utrecht, Holland, and a colony was established there. [16]

Constable Hook was in 1646 granted by the Dutch to Jacob Roy, chief gunner at Fort Amsterdam; and it is recorded that the following year Francisco, a Negro, was given a piece of land along the Hudson River.

The same year, Claas Carstensen was granted land in the Greenville section, and Maryn Andriasen, land at Weehawken.

Augustyn Heermans (Herman) was in 1651 granted a large tract along the Raritan River, for Cornelius Van Werckhoven.

All the land on Long Island apparently having been granted during the first thirty years of Dutch rule (though sparsely settled, and a large portion of it held unused on speculation), twenty Englishmen from there went in a sloop to the Raritan River, to acquire land of the Navesink and Raritan Indians. As the Dutch had already acquired Indian grants there for large areas, Stuyvesant, the new Dutch governor, sent Kregier and Loockermans, with some soldiers, through the Kill van Kol to resist the English. [16]

The town of Bergen, now Jersey City Heights, was established, and land granted there, by the Dutch in 1660.

In an endeavor to allay the restlessness of the English, who were pressing towards Manhattan from Massachusetts, Connecticut and Long Island, the Dutch in 1661, to prove to the King of England that they entertained no hostility against the English settlers and welcomed them to New Netherland, issued and distributed posters throughout the British Kingdom, inviting English settlers to locate on land along the seashore in New Jersey, "which was wholly unpopulated except by Indians." [111] Excepting immediately along the seacoast, this section is sparsely settled even today.

Regardless of grants of the same territory to others by his predecessors, Charles II in 1664 granted to his brother James, Duke of York, all the land between the Connecticut River and the east side of the Delaware.

The apparent immediate reason for the conquest of Dutch New Netherland by the English in 1664, and the consequent grant of New Jersey to Berkeley and Carteret, are given in the chapter on New York.

Following are excerpts from the grant issued while the British squadron was on the high seas, on the voyage of conquest of the territory granted:

"This Indenture made 23rd day of June, 1664, between his Royal Highness James, Duke of York and Albany, Earl of Ulster, Lord High Admiral of England and Ireland, and Constable of Dover Castle, Lord Warden of the Cinque Ports and Governor of Portsmouth of the one part; John Lord Berkeley, Baron of Stratton, and one of his majesties most honorable privy council, and Sir George Carteret of Saltrum in the county of Devon, Kent, one of his majesties most honorable privy council of the other part.

"Witnesseth that the said James, Duke of York, for and in consideration of the sum of ten shillings to him paid doth sell unto the said Berkeley and Carteret all that tract of land lying westward of Long Island and Manhattan Island, and bounded on the east part of the main sea and part of Hudson's River, and upon the west, Delaware Bay and River, extending southward to the main ocean as far as Cape May, thence crossing in a straight line to Hudson's River, which said tract is hereafter to be called New Cesarea or New Jersey, and all rivers, mines, minerals, woods, fishings, hawking, hunting and fowling, and all other Royalties, profits, commodities and hereditaments whatsoever to the said lands and premises belonging. To have and hold and paying therefore unto the said Duke of York, his heirs and assigns, the rent of a pepper-corn upon the feast of the Nativity of St. John the Baptist next ensuing the date hereof (only if the same be demanded)."

It is interesting to know something of Berkeley and Carteret, and of their association with King Charles and the Duke of York, and why they were thus favored with the grant of all the land in New Jersey.

John Berkeley, born in 1607, commanded the army against the Scots in 1638, and was knighted. He became conspicuous in the civil wars which followed in England, supporting Charles II and the royal cause, and accompanying Charles in his exile in 1652.

Six years afterwards, Charles raised him to the peerage. On the Restoration of Charles in 1660, he was placed at the head of the duke's establishment, managed the duke's receipts and expenditures and became a member of the privy council.

Nine years later he became lord lieutenant of Ireland, which appointment he held for two years, and was then appointed ambassador to Versailles.

George Carteret, born on the Island of Jersey in 1599, entered the British navy and at the age of twenty-seven was appointed by Charles I joint governor of his native island. In 1640 he was comptroller of the navy and five years later was created a baronet. On the ruin of the royal cause, he afforded an asylum on the island to Charles II and about three hundred other refugees of distinction. In 1651, after seven weeks' siege by the parliamentary (Cromwell) forces, he surrendered and fled to France to join other refugees. At the Restoration of Charles he formed one of the immediate train of the restored monarch on his triumphant entry into London. His clinging to the royal cause gave him influence at court. He and Berkeley were members of the council of plantations and were two of the six favorites to whom Charles, in 1663, granted all the land in the Carolinas and Georgia. Neither one of them ever was in America. Four years subsequent to date of the grant, Berkeley was detected in selling public offices and became discredited. The following year Carteret was accused of embezzlement and expelled from the House of Commons. Bancroft, [5] the historian, designated him as "the passionate, ignorant and not too honest Sir George Carteret."

Notwithstanding the unsavory reputation of both Berkeley and Carteret, all land titles in New Jersey rest upon their signatures and public officials continue to perpetuate their memories by giving their names to streets and school houses.

Colonel Richard Nicolls, who was in command of the expedition for the conquest by the English of the Dutch in America, as cited in the chapter on New York, carried with him his appointment by the Duke of York as governor of all the Dutch territory which was to be conquered.

Immediately after the conquest, Nicolls received an application for a grant of land in New Jersey. The applicants thus addressed the governor: "We make bold with all humility to petition your honor that you will grant us liberty to purchase and settle a parcel of land to improve our labor upon in New Jersey and, some of us being destitute of habitation where we are, we crave your early answer." Signed by John Bailey and five other persons on Long Island.

Governor Nicolls consented to this petition on condition that they first make terms with the Indians, which they did, but the only valid Indian who signed had previously parted with whatever interest he may have had to another white man, as was a common practice with Indians.

Regarding the purchase of land from Indians, the United States Supreme Court gave a decision that Indians had no ownership of land, that all deeds for land must run from the lords proprietors. A summary of this decision is given in the chapter on Indians.

This tract, which included land that had been granted by the Dutch to Herman thirteen years previously, became known as the Elizabethtown tract. It was bounded on the south by the Raritan River; on the north by the Passaic River; on the east by the Arthur Kill; and on the west by twice the length and breadth. Nicolls granted it for ever, "at a yearly land rent which would accord with the rentals to be later established by the duke."

Governor Nicolls announced in April, 1665, that with his consent and approval William Goulding and eleven associates of Long Island had acquired land of the Indians, and he granted the land to Goulding and associates, bounded as follows: "Beginning at Sandy Hook, running along the bay to the mouth of the Raritan River, thence along the river to a certain marsh which divides the river in two parts, thence in a southwest line twelve miles, thence to the ocean, together with all lands, soils, rivers, harbors, minerals (royal mines excepted), quarries, woods, lakes, fishings, huntings and fowling, and all other profits; to hold for ever, on condition that the grantees shall within three years manure and plant said land and settle thereon one hundred families at least. In consideration whereof I do grant that said grantees shall enjoy said land for seven years free from any payment of land rent, custom or tax. But after expiration of seven years, whoever possesses them shall pay the same rate which others within the duke's territories shall be obliged to pay."

These two grants occasioned extended litigation and great

disorder in the province for many years, having been granted by Nicolls after the duke had granted all New Jersey to Berkeley and Carteret—of which Nicolls had not received notice. The litigation was not ended when the American Revolution began, 110 years later, and ended all such controversies. (See Elizabethtown Bill in Chancery 1747–59.)

Nicolls also made grants of land on Staten Island and in the Hackensack region to his military and naval officers.

Upon receiving the grant, Berkeley and Carteret, designating themselves the true and absolute lords proprietors of all the Province of New Jersey, though neither of them was ever in America, issued a proclamation of "Concessions and Agreements" and to put it into effect appointed Philip Carteret (a relative of Sir George) as governor, during their will and pleasure. He was given power to sell and to rent the land of the lords proprietors at a yearly rental, and to nominate a council of from six to twelve selected men, who would become landholders.

This proclamation provided that he should "lay taxes to raise money or goods, upon all land or persons in the province, except the lands unallotted by the lords proprietors." He was to appoint members of an assembly (later to be elected from among those who became landholders) who should make provision for the support of the governor, and the necessary charges of the government. Judges and constables were likewise to be appointed by him, the constables to collect the lords proprietors' land rents free of cost to the lords and pay the same to the receiver of rents, whom the lords would send over from England. To encourage purchase of land, none but landholders were to be appointed or elected to public office. A register of land titles was to be kept in both New Jersey and England. The governor was to arrange to erect forts; provide ammunition and other habiliments of war; train soldiers to suppress mutinies and rebellion; make war upon the Indians if occasion required; grant land according to the terms of the concessions, and make rules for laying out land and casting lots for locations.

It was also provided: "Upon planting land, one-seventh of each tract shall be reserved for the lords, the remainder to be allotted on rent or sale to those willing to build thereon. Tres-

passing or grazing of cattle on unsold land of the proprietors
. . . was not permitted upon penalty of fine." This last provision
to avoid subsequent claim that the unenclosed land of the proprietors was a commons.

". . . in all assembly meetings the governor and his council
are to sit by themselves and the deputies (assemblymen) by
themselves [to lend greater dignity to the governor and his
council], and whatever the assembly do propose, to be presented to the governor and his council and, upon their confirmation, to pass for an act of law, and to remain in force only
when confirmed by us. In case of foreign invasion or intestine
mutiny or rebellion the governor and his council shall call to
their aid any person whatsoever whether landholder or not."

[To induce immigration] . . . "any one who settles themselves
in New Jersey before January, 1668, shall receive a grant of 150
acres, and an additional 150 acres for himself for every able
indented or other male servant they carry with them. Every
master and man servant must be armed with a good musket,
ten pounds of powder and ammunition of twelve bullets to the
pound, with bandolier, and have six months' supply of provisions. Females to receive seventy-five acres, and all indented
servants a like acreage at the expiration of their term of service.
Arrivals during the ensuing two years shall receive a reduced
acreage. Provided, always, that for the space of thirteen years
following, said land shall be occupied." This was to prevent
speculation in unused land.

Not any of these grants were free gifts, but entailed payment
to the lords of a perpetual annual ground rent of either one-half
or one English penny per acre, according to location value of
the land and the settlers themselves were to make what "presents" were required by the Indians. Land was granted free for
highways, streets and necessary public buildings, and each par-
ish received two hundred acres for use of the church.

In the summer of 1665 Philip Carteret arrived at the present
location of Elizabeth, where he established headquarters. Then
it was, for the first time, that Nicolls learned of the grant of all
New Jersey to Berkeley and Carteret and of its alienation from
his government at New York.

Four families had settled on the Elizabethtown tract which had been granted by Nicolls to Bailey and his associates. The tract granted to Goulding and his associates, known as the Monmouth purchase, on which Middletown and Shrewsbury developed, was in process of settlement. These settlers and their immediate successors refused to recognize any authority or ownership of land by Berkeley and Carteret.

Governor Carteret in 1665 issued town charters to several towns in northern Jersey. An extract from the usual form of granting land runs: "We, John Lord Berkeley and George Carteret the absolute lords proprietors of the Province of New Jersey have granted to ——————————— a certain tract of land. [Here more or less indefinitely described] with all the upland, meadows, woods, fields, pastures, marshes, rivers and rivoletts, together with all the gains and profits thereunto appertaining; to have and hold, his heirs and assigns for ever. Yielding and paying to the said lords proprietors their heirs and assigns, one-half penny yearly for every acre herein conveyed."

To applicants for land to make a settlement on the Delaware River and Bay, the governor replied: "I cannot grant any exemptions from the payment of the half-penny per acre annual rent, it being the advantage which the lords proprietors reserve to themselves."

Governor Nicolls, in New York, wrote Lord Arlington at London that the grant of all New Jersey to Berkeley and Carteret was of inevitable prejudice to the New York colony, and suggested that they be given a tract of a hundred thousand acres, of twenty miles on each side of the Delaware River and Bay, which was recovered from the Dutch.

Governor Carteret sent emissaries to Connecticut in 1666 to endeavor to induce settlers there to move to New Jersey. Thirty families, led by Robert Treat, located at Newark, paying the proprietors half-a-penny per acre annual land rent. They divided their tract into town lots of six acres each, and each family drew for a location. Treat was allowed two extra lots in consideration of his leadership. Governor Carteret did not live up to his purported agreement to clear the land of any Indian claims, and the settlers, rather than risk being scalped, presented the Indians with some rum, coats and trinkets.

Carteret, two years later, issued a proclamation saying: "The province is in a probable way of being populated, there now being a considerable number of families in it," and called for appointment of freeholders (landholders) by each town to form an assembly.

The first assembly ever convened in New Jersey met at Elizabethtown in May, 1668. At a session six months later there arose the question of the legality of those titles to the land which had been granted by Nicolls. Deputies from Middletown and Shrewsbury, which were located on such land, refused to take the required oath of allegiance to Berkeley and Carteret and were dismissed. Nor would the authorities of those towns publish the laws enacted by the Carteret assembly. They contended that the Indian title confirmed by Nicolls was supreme and that, if the settlers at Middletown and Shrewsbury could not get relief from payment of land rents exacted by Berkeley and Carteret, they would organize an independent government.

Richard Hartshorne, a Quaker, who arrived in New Jersey in 1669 and located at Middletown, went to Gravesend and bought of William Goulding his interest in the Monmouth tract. [139] Hartshorne wrote an enticing account of New Jersey, which was circulated in England and induced considerable immigration. He afterwards became active in public affairs. [162]

It was decreed by the governor and council that every male over sixteen years of age should pay a personal tax, and a tax on every acre of land under fence, and on all livestock. Inasmuch as the lords had not fenced any land they would be exempt from the land tax. The settlers were to pay all taxes.

Governor Carteret ordered the surveyor-general to survey the Elizabethtown and Newark meadows and lands, irrespective of the claims of the Nicolls grantees, who would not take out deeds from the lords proprietors.

The governor proclaimed to the people of Woodbridge: "There are several persons admitted to your town meetings who have no land by the lords proprietors' authority, to the prejudice and hindrance of all other honest-minded men, and also endangering your town charter by suffering such malignant spirits to live amongst you."

That is, they had land which had been granted them by Nicolls, and Indian purchase, which grants were not recognized by Carteret, who consequently designated the grantees as "malignant spirits."

When the date for beginning collection of land rents arrived in 1670, there were revolts, and in some places riots, as far away as Perth Amboy, by those who objected to the land rents. Two years later they elected as "President of the country," over the proprietory governor, James Carteret, apparently a rather wayward son of Sir George, who was then tarrying in New Jersey, en route to the Carolinas.

Settlers asked Governor Carteret: "How did the king come into possession of the land which he conveyed to the Duke of York? Did not a predecessor of Charles II long ago grant to others all the land that Charles gave to the duke?"

They further protested against any potentate beyond the Atlantic Ocean assuming ownership of all the land on this side, to be granted by him as private property to his favorites in England, and used by those favorites to exact an annual land rent of the settlers in New Jersey.

Land rents exacted by the absentee lords proprietors were continually in arrears in New Jersey, as they were in all the colonies. Payments were avoided when possible and often resisted. Collections became especially difficult by reason of contentions arising from the Nicolls grants and they were enforced by constables by distress. Payment of rents in grain was refused; gold and silver being demanded, of which there was almost none in the colonies.

The council of seven appointed by the governor addressed the proprietors in London, asking that they accept payment of the land rents in produce of the country at merchants' prices. This was acceded to by the proprietors as the only way to collect the land rents.

Governor Carteret issued a declaration against James Carteret and his followers for styling themselves deputies, or representatives, for the country, and for electing a "President of the country," and other mutinous and rebellious acts contrary to the concessions promulgated by the lords proprietors.

The council requested the governor to go to England, which he did in July, 1672, acquainting Sir George with the affairs and grievances of the province, and suing to have his son desist from such irregularities.

Limiting the franchise for the purpose of bringing pressure on the Nicolls grantees to pay land rent to them, Berkeley and Carteret issued a "Declaration of the True Intent and Meaning of Our Concession," in which they stated:

"No person shall be counted a freeholder nor have a vote, nor hold office until he actually hold his land by grant from us. Sensible of the disorders in the province, we declare that all land granted by our governor to July 27, 1672, and confirmed by patent, shall remain to the particular owners, their heirs and assigns for ever, with all the benefits, profits and privileges therein contained. That all grants not derived from us we declare null and void.

"We utterly disown any grant made by Colonel Richard Nicolls and demand that holders of land pay the land rent to us, and unless so paid we hereby order our governor and council to dispose thereof. That the constable in every respective town shall take, by way of distress from each individual inhabitant within their jurisdiction, the rent due as yearly, beginning March 25, 1670.

"That it is in the power of the governor and his council to appoint courts; that all appeals from the courts shall be made to the governor and council, and thence to the lords proprietors in England, and then to the king. That the governor and council may dispose of land according to our direction.

"Although our concession call for payment in lawful money of England, we shall accept it in merchandise and produce of the country at merchants' prices.

"We will build a prison out of proceeds of land rents, and will send guns and ammunition as a magazine, but all other charges are to be defrayed by the province [the settlers]. That all strays of beasts, and wrecks at sea, belong to us."

Berkeley and Carteret, writing from Whitehall, London, in 1672, issued directions that Governor Carteret buy land of the Indians, in the name of Berkeley and Carteret, and that every person who took up land was to reimburse the lords proprietors what they paid the Indians, in addition to the usual land rent to them.

While Governor Carteret was in England, John Berry, deputy-governor, notified settlers to take out land patents (and become rent-payers), otherwise they would lose the benefits of the lords proprietors' favor and forfeit such land as they were settled upon.

The Duke of York wrote Colonel Lovelace, who had arrived at New York to succeed Nicolls as governor of New York, as follows: "On June 24, 1664, I granted to Berkeley and Carteret all the land in New Jersey, and on November 28 following, so advised Colonel Nicolls, governor of all my territories in America, requiring him and all others concerned to yield their best assistance to the quiet possession of the premises.

"Nevertheless I am informed that contentious persons there lay claim to certain tracts of land under color of pretended grants from the said Colonel Nicolls, namely, one to John Baker and associates, and another to William Goulding and associates, both of which grants (being posterior to my grant to Berkeley and Carteret) are, as I am informed, void in law." This tended to quiet the colony for a brief time.

By order of his father, James Carteret left New Jersey in 1673 for Carolina, of which province his father and Berkeley were two of the eight proprietors, and where James had been made a landgrave, with forty-eight thousand acres of land.

The vessel on which he sailed was captured by the Dutch in the Chesapeake and, after being put ashore, he returned to New York. In the same year he married the daughter of Mayor Delavall. He returned to England subsequent to 1679.

Samuel Hopkins, who was a passenger aboard the captured vessel, and who had encouraged Admiral Evertsen of the Dutch fleet to attack New York, was an early settler at Elizabethtown. He was always identified with those hostile to the governor and the proprietors, having taken part with James Carteret in his attempt to subvert the established government. After capturing New York, the Dutch appointed Hopkins secretary of their government in New Jersey.

Weary of their distractions under the Carteret government,

many people of New Jersey welcomed the Dutch authority. [16]

Upon the conquest by the Dutch, the towns of Newark, Elizabethtown and New Piscataway petitioned the Dutch governor-general and council at New Orange (New York) that those towns be allowed the same privileges and freedoms given to natural subjects of the Dutch nation.

Most of the settlers, including the English, seemed to have taken the oath of allegiance to the Dutch government. The Dutch recognized the land grants made by Nicolls, which further encouraged the Nicolls patentees to resist the Carteret government after it was re-established.

A census made at that time, evidently of men capable of bearing arms, showed there were 409, "including eighteen Quakers," in the eastern part of New Jersey.

A quarter of a century of quiescence ensued at Salem after the Swedes and Dutch had driven out the New Haven English colony thereabouts, as related in the chapter on the Delaware Region.

But in the autumn of 1673, after the Dutch in their war with England had regained control of New York, New Jersey and the Delaware, a Dutch ship arrived in England with the British governor, Lovelace, aboard as a captive.

With the Dutch in control of the Carteret and Berkeley domain of New Jersey, and likely to grant it to some Dutch patroon, Lord Berkeley became concerned at the dubious prospect of ever making a fortune from profiteering in land in New Jersey. Just then falling into disrepute at court because of charges of corruption, Berkeley concluded that it would be best to try to find some one who would be willing to take a chance on his grant, to whom he might sell.

With that object he began negotiations with John Fenwick, a former major in the Cromwellian army, who since had become an ardent Quaker. Fenwick had no capital, but he enlisted the sympathetic interest of Edward Byllynge, a London maltster and a Quaker, in a proposal to establish a Quaker colony in New Jersey and divide the profits from the land venture.

George Fox, the founder of the Quaker faith, had been to New Jersey and other parts of America, and since his return to

England had been strongly advocating a mass migration of Quakers to America, to escape the unmerciful treatment they were receiving.

The treaty of peace between England and Holland, following the conquest of New York by the Dutch, stipulated that all places which had been taken by either of them should revert to the original holder. This reinstated English control of New Jersey and the Delaware. The duke appointed Major Andros as governor of New York and tributary territory, including New Jersey.

Without realizing that he would before long become a bankrupt, Byllynge, through Fenwick, in March, 1674 paid Berkeley £1,000 for Berkeley's undivided half interest in New Jersey, and received from him a grant thereof made to Fenwick, his heirs and assigns, in trust for Byllynge.

Less than a year thereafter, when Byllynge was on the verge of bankruptcy, Penn, as a mutual friend "in every way unconcerned," as Penn would have us understand, was brought into a transaction in the matter, which, so far as pertained to Fenwick's participation in West Jersey, later proved the fable of the camel's head in the Arab's tent.

An agreement was made between Fenwick and Byllynge of the one part, and Penn, Laurie and Lucas of the other part. Laurie, a merchant, and Lucas, a maltster of Hertford, were creditors of Byllynge. Lucas had been imprisoned eight years for his Quaker faith and was under sentence of banishment from England.

This was Penn's introduction to land dealing in America, which prompted him, six years later, to apply for and obtain from Charles II the grant of Pennsylvania which gave rise to his ineffective claim to Delaware.

The following year a quintuple agreement was entered into whereby Fenwick parted with a nine-tenths interest in his New Jersey venture for £400 to Byllynge, Penn, Laurie and Lucas, who agreed to the division of New Jersey into East and West Jersey. By this transaction Fenwick was on his way out: Penn was on his way in.

Brodhead [16] pronounced this deed "perhaps the most faulty

English secondary parchment in American annals, because of many omissions of essentials." By it Carteret was allotted all East Jersey with 2,981 square miles, while the Penn group took all West Jersey, with 4,595 square miles.

It is assumed that this division was with the assent of Carteret, though, as Penn was much given to dominating groups and transactions in which he took part, it is possible that he planned this division and then notified Carteret what they had done. Anyway, a year and five months passed before Carteret confirmed it in writing, whereupon Penn exclaimed, "Whose is the Earth and the fullness thereof." Five days after this transaction, Byllynge made a deed to Penn, Laurie and Lucas, in trust for his creditors.

Meanwhile Fenwick, on the strength of his remaining one-tenth interest, became on his own account a high-powered land salesman whom realtors of today might well envy. He prepared a glowing and enticing prospectus on the charms of New Jersey and the prospects of huge land profits, although it was country he had never seen and of which he knew but little. In a short while, without any authentic maps, surveys or blue prints, he sold to about fifty purchasers in England, as he afterwards showed, 148,000 acres of land along the Delaware Bay, mostly in tracts of 1,000 to 10,000 acres each.

Fenwick arrived in the Delaware in June, 1675, in the ship "Griffin," the first English vessel to arrive in West Jersey; none following for nearly two years. With him were about 150 colonists, including his three daughters, two sons-in-law, with five of their children, eight indented men servants and five women servants. He made a settlement at Salem—"peace." But instead of having peace, Fenwick was harassed by threats, prison and dire troubles during the entire remainder of his life.

Upon his arrival he negotiated for, and obtained from the Indians, the usual permission to occupy the land bordering on the Delaware Bay, in Salem and Cumberland counties. Whereupon, Fenwick granted to settlers he had brought with him deeds to land along the Salem, Cohansey and Alloways Creeks, including lots of sixteen acres each in Salem.

The following December Governor Andros, at New York,

learning of Fenwick's activities at Salem, and knowing nothing of any authority Fenwick had, ordered that he should not be received as owner or proprietor of any land, or to be allowed to trade. Andros assumed this authority by his interpretation of his appointment by the duke to act as governor of New York and the tributary territory.

In May, 1676, Fenwick attended a council meeting at New York, at which Andros and Philip Carteret were present, and in which they discussed the claim of Fenwick to land in New Jersey.

Fenwick returned to Salem where he assumed proprietary rights in allotting land, issuing licenses to distill liquor, and ejecting previous settlers from their habitations, all of which brought upon him the wrath of Andros, and imprisonment for forty days in New York.

Penn, Lucas and Warner appointed as commissioners in their interest Richard Hartshorne and Richard Gay, both of East Jersey; also James Wasse, whom they sent from England with a letter to Hartshorne, saying: "We desire you to have a meeting with John Fenwick and the people that went with him and show him he has no right to sell any land there. See if he be willing to peacefully let the land he purchased from the Indians be divided into a hundred parts, casting lots for the same. We are content to pay our ninetieth part of what was paid the Indians.

"Also to get land surveyed, and divide into lots for a town or settlement of four or five thousand acres, and divide into one hundred parts. Lots to be sold at £200 each." [139]

Penn, with his grant of Pennsylvania from Charles II, arrived in the Delaware in October, 1682.

James Nevill of Salem wrote Governor Penn at Philadelphia complaining of the boasting of Fenwick. He enclosed an account of land sold by Fenwick in England, after his conveyance to Eldridge and Warner. The list included: three tracts of 10,000 acres each; five of 5,000 acres each; two of 3,000 acres each; six of 2,000 acres each; twelve of 1,000 acres each and seventeen tracts each of smaller area. Nevill added, "I am informed he sold 148,000 acres in England and showed a schedule thereof to Thomas Woodroofe."

The following, signed by Penn and witnesses prior to his departure from England, was subsequently found. It lacks the signature of Fenwick and merely shows what Penn wanted of Fenwick: "March 25, 1682. Deed from John Fenwick to William Penn and assigns, for half of New Jersey, for ten shillings and other valuable considerations, including his interest in the ten equal parts mentioned in a deed to Penn and others in February, 1674, (except always 150,000 acres in that tract of land called Fenwick's colony) with power to keep court under the government of William Penn."

Fenwick having died in 1684, his executors agreed with William Penn, as follows: "Agreed that excepting 150,000 acres already allotted to the heirs of John Fenwick, the neck of land between Salem Creek and Oldmans Creek is hereby allotted to William Penn to dispose of, he making full report of same." By this time the camel had its entire body in the Arab's tent.

Following the entanglements of Fenwick has led us beyond the time of some of the principal occurrences pertaining to this chapter.

After the recapture from the Dutch, Charles II, on June 29, 1674, renewed to the duke his former grant of land in New England, New York, and in New Jersey to the east side of the Delaware, saying that the right of conquest is greater than the right of descent. Whereupon, the duke granted to George Carteret (Berkeley having sold his interest to Fenwick), his heirs and assigns for ever, all that tract of land lying westward of Long Island and Manhattan to a line run from Barnegat to Rancocas Creek. Carteret was to pay yearly to the Duke of York, his heirs and assigns, twenty nobles of money of England, if demanded. This boundary was not adhered to by Penn, as noted in the quintuple agreement.

Land in East Jersey ordinarily sold for eight or ten times as much as land in West Jersey. East Jersey had seven fair-sized towns, comprising 3,500 people, besides being near New York, a place of great trade. [162]

Andros, with a body of soldiers, returned to New York as

governor in October, 1674, and shortly thereafter assumed to act as governor of New Jersey, confirming all land grants in East Jersey previously made by Berkeley and Carteret.

Philip Carteret, who had been in England during the Dutch possession of New Jersey, arrived in the same frigate, having been reappointed governor of East Jersey by Sir George.

In his instructions to Governor Carteret, Sir George recited the instructions formerly made by him and Berkeley.

Sir John Werden, secretary to the Duke of York, who disapproved of the grant by his master to Carteret, and who later took the same attitude towards the grant of Pennsylvania by Charles II to Penn, wrote Governor Andros at New York: "We have as yet done nothing towards adjusting Sir George Carteret's pretensions in New Jersey, where I presume you will take care to keep all things in the same posture as to the duke's prerogatives and profits as they were in your predecessors' time, until you shall hear of some alterations agreed to here."

Andros went to New Castle, in 1675, to meet and enter into a treaty with the Indians of Delaware and West Jersey.

The following year a tax was levied in East Jersey on all land which the proprietors had deeded to others. The Morris family was granted a large tract of land near the Raritan River, with the right "to dig, delve and carry away all such mines for iron as they shall find." [169]

The West Jersey proprietors living in London appointed commissioners resident in West Jersey, to manage the affairs of the province: "The method for division and sale of land is by proprietaries, that is to say, each one hundred parts is designated a proprietary, judged to be twenty thousand or more acres; the bounds to be marked on trees, and divided among the proprietors. Two or more may join in purchase of a proprietary. As each proprietary is settled upon another will be opened.

"Each one hundred parts, as occasion may require, to be divided in ten equal parts or shares. Five shares are to be granted to Thomas Hutchinson, yeoman of Beverly; Thomas Pierson, yeoman of Bonwick; Joseph Hemsley, yeoman of Great Kelk; George Hutchinson, distiller. of Sheffield, and Mahlon Stacy, tanner of Hansworth, all of Yorkshire, England, for themselves and friends. The remaining tenths, each containing about two thousand or more acres, to be granted to later purchasers of shares who may go to West Jersey to inhabit.

"To promote speedy immigration, any person arriving before April 1677 shall have seventy acres, and an equal acreage for himself and every able-bodied male servant that he may transport. Indented servants, at expiration of their service, shall have fifty acres for himself and heirs; a lesser acreage for females.

"All such shall pay yearly rental to that proprietor to whom the land belongs, one pence an acre in towns, and half a pence elsewhere. Later arrivals to pay an increased land rent; provided always that the land shall be actually occupied for ten years. All other proprietors shall, for the first ten years, keep upon every lot of land at least one person, and if it exceeds a hundred acres, one person on each one hundred acres; otherwise it shall be subject to forfeiture.

"The constables shall collect the rents for the proprietors who live in England, Ireland and Scotland, and shall pay it to the receiver of rents appointed by the proprietors, unless the general assembly to be constituted shall prescribe some other way of collecting the rents free of expense and trouble to the proprietors. A register of land deeds shall be kept both in West Jersey and in London. Commissioners have power to locate towns."

A charter of Fundamental Laws of West Jersey was proclaimed in 1677, as a "Declaration of Concessions and Agreements," which provided that: "These rights and privileges of West Jersey are individually agreed upon by the proprietors and freeholders to be the foundation of the government, which is not to be altered by legislative authority, or free assembly, hereafter. Should any person of the assembly move, or excite anything that contraverts them, he shall be proceeded against as a traitor to said government.

"Religious freedom is granted. Inhabitants have the privilege of fishing in the Delaware River and on the seacoast, and of hunting and killing wild game, except on surveyed land. Taxes may be laid by the general assembly upon land or persons.

"No ship captain shall transport any person from the province except that the court give permission, after the name of the intended person to depart had been posted in three public places for three weeks.

"The assembly of West Jersey is to consist of landholders, to have power to make laws, provided they be not against any of our concessions before mentioned.

"To keep the members of the assembly, and the people, in mind of these conditions, they shall be read at the beginning and dissolution of every meeting of the assembly, and further, shall be read in a solemn manner by the chief magistrates four times a year in the presence of the people.

"Any land to be taken up from the Indians by the proprietors, the Indians shall be made acquainted of the intention of the proprietors to do so, and given what presents they shall agree upon, for their good will and consent."

The ship, "Kent," the second English vessel to sail into the Delaware, brought the commissions representing the West Jersey proprietors, and also 230 settlers, mostly Quakers, from London and Yorkshire. It arrived in August, 1677. Calling en route at New York, the settlers showed Governor Andros deeds for land in West Jersey, which Andros refused to recognize until so advised by the duke. However, he gave them permission temporarily to locate on land along the Delaware, subject to his government. [105]

There was an interregnum between Andros' appointment as governor of the duke's territory (after repossession by the English) and the date of the grant by the duke to his subsequent grantees of New Jersey. During this period, Andros forcibly asserted authority as governor, and for a time, between 1677 and 1679, his authority was widely recognized by settlers, regardless of the presence of Governor Philip Carteret. In 1678 he appointed six commissioners in West Jersey, as a minor court, subject to appeal at New Castle.

Soon after the first settlements, the West Jersey proprietors divided 500,000 acres among themselves as the first land dividend. Later there were four dividends, each of like area, each proprietor taking his portion of 2,500,000 acres, [139] which is 85 per cent of the entire land area of West Jersey.

Clarkson estimated that the number of settlers sent to West

Jersey through Penn's agency, during the first five years, was about eight hundred, mostly Quakers. [65]

The Penn group had been acting these six years on the strength of the Byllynge purchase of Berkeley's interest in West Jersey. It was not until August 6, 1680, that the Duke of York made a grant of that region to Penn and his associates: "To have and to hold for ever, and likewise have given and granted to Byllynge all power of government."

Immediately after the death of Sir George Carteret, early in 1680, Governor Andros, in New York, assumed a dictatorial attitude towards Governor Carteret in New Jersey and continued to make grants of land in New Jersey.

A grant by James, Duke of York, to Sir George Carteret, grandson of the original proprietor, dated September 10, 1680, reads: "For and in consideration of a competent sum of money for the better extinguishing of such claim His Royal Highness may have had in East Jersey, hath sold to said Sir George Carteret, his heirs and assigns, all the entire premises called East Jersey, with all islands, and hereby grants the government to Sir George Carteret, his heirs and assigns to be held, enjoyed, exercised and executed by him."

The power to institute government was considered as one of the proprietary rights, which was as transferable as property in land. [105]

Governor Carteret wrote Lady Carteret, advising her that "surrender of Staten Island (which is yours as much as any other part of the province) is refused," and asked that Governor Andros be punished, "now that you have him in England, else we shall never be at peace."

Sir John Werden, writing from Edinburgh to Sir Allen Apsley said: "You have often heard what the consequences would be of the release of New Jersey to the Quakers and Sir George Carteret, viz., certain loss of the trade and revenue of New York, because of no import tax collected in New Jersey."

At a meeting of the governor, council and assembly of East Jersey, in October, 1681, there was acrimonious contention over the requirement that the expense of collecting the proprietary land rent be borne by the settlers. Many encroachments had been made upon the "Concessions" of 1664. Deputies asked that it be declared void and debated. The governor replied: "If you had the benefit of understanding you would neither have desired nor expected them to be made void." The deputies declared the inhabitants were not obliged to conform thereto.

At this time, the cost of passage from England to New Jersey, including food, passengers supplying their bedding, was usually £5 for adults and 50s for grown children. The rate for goods was 40s per ton. [139] Sometimes ships went from Dublin and Hull, some calling at Leith, Dundee, Aberdeen and Ayr, in Scotland, and at Waterford, Ireland.

New Brunswick was founded in 1681. The first legislature in West Jersey met at Burlington that year, and a contention arose between assemblymen and Penn representatives as to ownership of islands in the Delaware River.

Penn's long coveting of the islands in the Delaware was engendered by the hope of the prospective grant to him by the Duke of York of an area within a twelve-mile circle of New Castle, which would have extended his holdings to the New Jersey shore. Although this proposed grant was never made effective, Penn repeatedly asserted his claim. This is fully treated in the chapter on the Delaware Region.

It was ordered in 1681 that, "each tenth of ten proprietaries shall have their proportion of frontage on the Delaware River or Bay, and so far back as will contain sixty-four thousand acres. All land sold by a West Jersey proprietor shall be settled upon within six months, or be void and free for other purchasers, and they shall seat it within one month. . . . no person shall have more than forty perches front on a river or navigable creek."

Surveyors were ordered to measure the entire river and bay from Assanpink Creek (below Trenton) to Cape May, and to find the division line of each tenth. [144]

A lease (sale) from Elizabeth Carteret, widow of Sir George and guardian of the younger Sir George, and the trustees, to William Penn of all the land in East Jersey was made in London, February, 1682. With Penn in the deal were: Robert West; Thomas Rudyard, gent; Samuel Groome, mariner; Thomas Hart, merchant; Richard New, merchant; Thomas Wilcox, goldsmith; Ambrose Rigg, gent; Thomas Heywood, skinner; Hugh Hartshorne, skinner; Clement Plumsteed, draper; and Thomas Cooper, tailor. All were Quakers resident in England; they were the first twelve proprietors of East Jersey.

The lease stated: "That, by and with the consent and direction of Dame Elizabeth Carteret . . . for five shillings, has granted and sold that entire tract of land in New Jersey easterly of a line drawn from Little Egg Harbor to the headwaters of the Delaware River, and all the islands, minerals and all other royalties, franchises, rents, profits and powers of government."

The sale also included assignment to the purchasers of all arrears of land rent due the Carteret estate. In addition to the five shillings named therein, £3,400 (about 85¢ per acre) was paid for all the land in East Jersey, which Carteret, the original holder, had received as a royal gift.

The proprietors, after completing the purchase in London, sent a greeting to the settlers in East Jersey, saying: "Since it has pleased Almighty God to order it so by His Providence as to give us the interest we have in this province, we desire that you may find yourselves happy in this our purchase." And they might have added: "in paying to us absentees a perpetual annual ground rent for the privilege of using land in New Jersey from which to earn your living."

Samuel Groome was appointed by the new proprietors as receiver-general and shortly after his arrival in New Jersey, wrote: "I purpose demanding all arrears of land rents. Captain John Berry [who served as deputy-governor during the absence of Governor Carteret in England] is £200 to £300 in arrears. I'll begin with him and either have the money or the land." [135] The tax levied on improved land could be paid in money, or in wheat, corn or other produce. [105]

Robert Turner, a wealthy English Quaker who had been imprisoned for his religious belief, bought a proprietary share in both East and West Jersey, and bought land in Pennsylvania. [106]

Some West Jersey proprietors sold their individual proprietaries, or fractional shares thereof. Byllynge and his trustees sold one proprietary, in 1675, to William Peachy for £350, which seems to have been the going price at that time, and it was divided with seven others, a one-eighth share going to each. Another sale, six years later, was made at the same price, and an eighth was sold at £50. Fractions grew smaller, down to one sixty-fourth, [144] and the price grew larger. In the course of time the feudal element was gone, and those holding land then became plain landholders.

Instructions from the proprietors in London to Gawen Laurie, on his departure for East Jersey to succeed Thomas Rudyard as deputy-governor, in July, 1683, were: "Consider the best means of dividing the land among the proprietors, especially the 10,000 acres to each proprietor, being 240,000 acres now to be divided, as formerly ordered. Also, where any persons are behind in payment of rents they shall consent to turn back to the proprietors what land they are not using. That in laying out Perth [Amboy, which was done in 1684] be sure that the streets be made wide and that the 1,500 acres in the town be divided into 150 lots of 10 acres each, to be divided among the 24 proprietors; 60 acres to each, leaving 6 lots for market place, prison, townhouse and wharfage. The price of each lot to the end of this year to be £15; later £20 (£2 per acre). Each purchaser to be obliged to build a dwelling house on his lot and to clear 3 acres within 3 years.

"The 6,000 acres on the south side of the Raritan River at Amboy Point [South Amboy] to be divided among the proprietors.

"In laying out counties, one-seventh of the area shall be retained by the proprietors, and the other six-sevenths to be open to settlers on rental. [139]

"Since the population has increased, land rent is advanced to 2d sterling per acre, or may be bought at 12 years' purchase price, which would be 50s for 25 acres, or 2s per acre, but [looking forward to the accruing unearned increment] no one to have more than 100 acres at those prices, and must build a dwelling house thereon within 7 years. In case of default one-half of the land to revert to the proprietors."

In 1682 there were supposed to be 700 families, or about 3,500 inhabitants in towns in East Jersey; and in adjacent plantations about half as many more.

The seat of government in East Jersey was ordered to be moved to Perth, "a sweet, wholesome and delightful place," and a ferry boat was established between it and New York.

In March, 1683, Penn and his associates sold, and the same was confirmed by the Duke of York, "as far as in him lieth," one proprietary share of the domain in East Jersey to each of the following: James, Earl of Perth; Robert Barclay; John Drummond; Robert Gordon; Arent Sonmans; David D—— Jr., all of Scotland, Gawen Laurie, merchant; Edward Byllynge, gent; James Braine, merchant; William Gibson, haberdasher; Thomas Barker, merchant, all of London, and Robert Turner, merchant, of Dublin. These twelve new shareholders were made proprietors, and made, with the twelve original proprietors already named, twenty-four proprietors in all; Wilcox having sold to Barclay and Hartshorne dropping out. These twenty-four Britishers thereby became possessed of all the land in East Jersey, nearly two million acres, on which they exacted an annual ground rent from all settlers.

These proprietors were mostly strangers to one another, linked only in the endeavor to profit from the increase in land value created by the settlement of a virgin country.

The interest awakened in the British Isles over the New Jersey project was highly stimulated by the diverse interests of the men comprising the board. [94]

Among the twenty-four proprietors there was a strange commingling of nationalities, religion, professions and occupations. The five most prominent were the Earl of Perth, a Roman Catholic, who virtually conducted the government of Scotland under King James; John Drummond, his brother, later Viscount Melford; Robert Barclay, the great Quaker philosopher; Arent Sonmans, a Hollander residing in Scotland, and Robert Gordon. The majority were Quakers. [144]

(The New Jersey bill in chancery in the case of the Nicolls grants shows descent of land titles among the proprietors until 1745.)

Charles II confirmed the deal for the purchase of East Jersey by the twenty-four proprietors, together with all powers of government. "His majesty commands the inhabitants in said province to submit and yield all due obedience to said grantees, their heirs and assigns, as absolute proprietors and governors thereof, who have the sole right derived from the Duke of York, and his majesty, to dispose of the land of said province upon such terms and conditions as to them shall seem meet, requiring due compliance from all persons, as they will answer to the contrary at their peril." [162]

Among the direful expressions sometimes used by their majesties when occasion required to intimidate settlers were, "Upon pain of incurring our high displeasure," and, "Being proceeded against with due severity."

The West Jersey assembly, to settle disputes on the subject, resolved in 1682 that the government of West Jersey had been granted with the land. This was confirmed by Charles II the following year.

The proprietors in England and Scotland made an inquiry in 1683 as to what authority Governor Nicolls had for governing and granting land in New Jersey immediately after the conquest of the Dutch. They pointed out that prior to the reconquest, the Duke of York had granted all New Jersey to Berkeley and Carteret, who had appointed their own governor to make land grants.

Thomas Rudyard, deputy-governor, in 1683 wrote: "The fresh and salt meadows in East Jersey are very valuable for livestock." Mostly unusable, and actually held unused, they have since proven much more valuable, and still are so proving, as pawns in land speculation.

In a memorial from Salem, in 1683, to Governor Samuel Jennings, inhabitants complained "of frequent changes of proprietors and ask that the assembly be called to prevent future mischief and inconveniences, that we might live with security, and hope for our children, and die with comfort." The governor was granted six hundred acres for his services.

Penn, while in Pennsylvania in June, 1683, appointed a commission to treat with the governor and council of West Jersey, and another for East Jersey. He also demanded: "satisfaction for great wrongs done me and this Pennsylvania province by some inhabitants of New Jersey for spreading false reports on 'change, and in coffee houses and booksellers' shops, in London, about wars in Pennsylvania between Penn and Lord Baltimore, and that Baltimore claimed all land up to the falls of the Delaware

River [Trenton], leaving Penn no place where ships could come; thereby discouraging hundreds ready to buy land and provoking others in England who had bought and not paid to fling up their contracts." The commission to West Jersey was, among other matters, to settle about trade, and to claim the islands in the Delaware River. [162]

To induce purchases of land, and at the same time to have assembly members and officials guard the proprietors' land privilege, the fundamental constitution of the Province of East Jersey, issued by the lords proprietors in 1683, provided: "Voters and candidates for public office must have fifty acres, of which ten acres have been cultivated, or if in boroughs, a house and three acres, or if a tenant, £50 in stock. Bribery will forfeit the right to vote or hold office for ever. Three committees of management shall be provided, of twelve members each, of which eight shall be proprietors, or their proxies, and four freemen [landholders]. All officials shall solemnly promise to be true and faithful to the King of England, and to the lords proprietors.

"Whoever holds five thousand acres shall be eligible to be chosen as a proprietor, but this is not to take place until forty years after adoption of this constitution and, if after twenty years after said forty years, twenty-four such cannot be found, then not less than three thousand acres. No proprietor shall at any time hold more than his one twenty-fourth part of the country. To avoid innumerable laws, no act except this fundamental constitution shall be in force more than fifty years." [162]

Samuel Groome wrote the proprietors in London in 1683: "There is not an industrious man that may not have a comfortable life and plentiful supply of all things necessary in East Jersey. Some people from New England and elsewhere were tampering with the Indians for land but, seeing no hopes of coming in at that door, they now apply to us to become our tenants. It may be well if the twenty-four proprietors will agree to each take one twenty-fourth part of the lands as we lay them out and cast lots for locations." [139]

The proprietors in Scotland and London joined in instructions to Deputy-Governor Laurie in East Jersey "to tighten the exactions for payment of land rents and of recapturing excess land from those who are in arrears in rent." [162]

Apparently, squabbling among the English and Scotch proprietors over the method for dividing the land in East Jersey between themselves caused delay in opening up the land to meet the requirements of incoming settlers. Also, according to one account, "the proprietors in January, 1684, were stiffening the terms on which they would let settlers have land; some saying they will not rent at 2d per acre and may not at 4d." The rent had been half-a-penny.

A month later they ordered that "ten thousand acres shall be set out in the best places for each proprietor. All who have purchased one-twentieth of a proprietary may have five hundred acres in one tract."

To all demands on settlers to pay their land rent, the reply was an exhibition of Indian titles. To this stand, Governor Barclay, in London, replied in 1684: "We have sent over Gawan Laurie, one of our fellow proprietors, and expect a compliance on your part to our proposals, made or to be made by him. We are troubled to find there are too many dissatisfied persons among you seeking to subvert our interest. But we will make it manifest that those who think to possess our land by unreasonable claims will find themselves mistaken. We hope, by the assistance of God and the king's favor towards us, to prevent such practices in the future. We find you lay stress upon your purchase of land from the Indians, but we inform you that thereby you have acquired no right unless you would renounce the protection of the King of England." [162]

Sir John Werden, writing from St. James's, London, to Governor Dongan in New York in March, 1684, said: "The commissioners are unanimous that no land beyond East and West Jersey ought to be separated from your government upon any terms and, to prevent obstructing the peltry trade of New York, you should prevent all you can the uniting of any part of either Jersey with Mr. Penn who, as you observe, is very intent on his own interest in those parts."

Deputy-Governor Laurie wrote the proprietors in London: "I oblige all who buy lots at Perth [Amboy] to build a house within a year. A lot of thirty-six acres is priced at £40, or 4d land rent per annum. If the rents come in, I will build some houses for the proprietors, which can be rented. There is not a poor person in the province. Pork and beef are 2*d* per pound; oysters enough to serve all England."

Some proprietors, who had gone from England to East Jersey, formed a board of proprietors in 1684, to grant land, settle disputes and help advance the colony. A similar board was, four years later, formed in West Jersey. [112]

Sir John Werden, in 1684, wrote Governor Dongan at New York: "You say Captain Billop will sell his plantation on Staten Island [opposite Perth Amboy]. If he do you should have some inhabitant of New York, rather than any of New Jersey, buy it. Whoever buys land on Staten Island, it being under your New York government, must be liable to the laws thereof."

Dongan wrote the Earl of Perth, in Scotland, one of the East Jersey proprietors: "Your agents in East Jersey have dispersed printed papers to the disturbance of the inhabitants of Staten Island. It is peopled with about two hundred families and has been in possession of the Duke of York about twenty years, except when the Dutch had it. I would mention how convenient it would be to regain East Jersey [for New York], and I assure you some of the proprietors are of the same opinion."

Dongan wrote Werden: "Please look into the last patent of East Jersey. In case the duke cannot retrieve East Jersey, it would do well to secure Hudson's River and take away the East Jersey claim to Staten Island. The Lord Perth has writ me a very angry letter."

The letter from Dongan to Perth is said to have caused the recall of Dongan as governor, through the influence of the East Jersey proprietors with James. [162]

Upon the death of Charles II, in February, 1685, the Duke of York succeeded to the crown, as James II.

The proprietors of East Jersey not having the cash with which to pay the deputy-governor for services during the past year, he was granted a thousand acres. They ordered that "no land be rented or sold below the price fixed in the first printed proposal, viz., 2*d* per acre rent, or £10 sterling for each hundred acres sold and, in addition, the purchaser to pay an annual land rent of 6*d* for every one hundred acres. But for more durable land the sale price or rent may be increased by the governor. Land for settlement to be plotted according to the method in Pennsylvania and Long Island; as for instance, a five or ten thousand acre township to be taken by ten or twenty families; that is five hundred acres to a family. Where there is a plot of twenty-four thousand acres, as we are informed at Barnegat, it is to be divided into twenty-four parts, being a thousand acres for each proprietary.

"Wherever there is a choice spot of land so esteemed by the surveyor-general or any two commissioners, either for soil or location, it shall be reserved for the joint interest of all the proprietors and shall not be meddled with." [162]

Governor Barclay wrote Laurie: "All indented servants imported since March, 1682, as soon as their term expires, may have twenty-five acres at 1*d* per acre annual land rent, instead of 2*d* as previously stated by mistake. We forbid the selling of any of our land rents whatsoever."

Laurie and Surveyor-General Rudyard each had five thousand acres allotted them, each selecting a thousand acres of the choicest land at Cangoraza, "on the water side." But the proprietors, learning that it was choice land, penalized Laurie by counting the thousand acres as equal to three thousand in his total allotment of five thousand acres. The thousand acres selected by Rudyard being found to be even better, his thousand acres were counted as equal to four thousand acres.

Of the twenty-four East Jersey proprietaries, all but five had, within a few years, parted with a portion of their holding, some share divisions being one-quarter, others one-eighth, one-twentieth, one-thirty-second or one-fortieth of a proprietary.

Dr. Daniel Coxe was physician to the queen of Charles II, and later, to Queen Anne. He and his son, Colonel Daniel Coxe, speculated extensively in colonial land claims. The doctor bought Sir Robert Heath's defunct claim of the Carolinas and endeavored to obtain its validation, by which to justify his effort to obtain land in Louisiana.

Dr. Coxe acted in league with William Dockwra, a London merchant, secretary for the East Jersey proprietors, and later accused of fraud in taking up land. [144] Coxe said: "The West

Jersey proprietors gave about £18,000 for the land which cost the earlier holders not much above £4,000, and then were forced to buy every acre over again from the Indians, who daily raise the price of land as they understand our want of it. But we humbly hope that should the king resume all American governments into his own administration, his justice and goodness will preserve to us our lands." [162]

East Jersey proprietors wrote King James in 1687: "The most considerable of the proprietors would not be concerned in this province except on the particular approbation of the present king and the assurance of his favor and protection; as a pledge whereof the king gave them the land and a grant of the free use of all rivers, bays and waters for navigation, free trade of fishing, and with the right of government."

The proprietors proposed and prayed that his majesty would confirm title to their lands and land rents, and the monopoly power of purchasing land from the Indians, as was enjoyed by the proprietors in other provinces. [105]

Dr. Coxe bought the entire West Jersey interest of Edward Byllynge, which included the right of government of the colony. In March, 1692, he and his wife, for £9,800, transferred to the West Jersey Society, a corporation, all rights to their American lands, which included more than one-fifth of all land in West Jersey; two hundred thousand acres in Minnisink, between the Delaware River and the Blue Ridge Mountains in Sussex, Ulster and Orange Counties; Merrimac lands in New Hampshire; and ten thousand acres in Pennsylvania. Also a pottery in Burlington, town lots in Perth Amboy, land in Gloucester and Cape May counties, and at Egg Harbor, together with the right to govern West Jersey. Notwithstanding these varied and extensive land holdings, to say nothing of the right to govern all West Jersey, Dr. Coxe was never in America.

On the same day as the purchase from Coxe, the West Jersey Society issued sixteen hundred shares of stock, subject to a payment not to exceed £10 each, to pay for, manage, and improve the land bought. [162]

The following December, the proprietors of West Jersey in England wrote Governor Basse in New Jersey: "We have bought of Coxe the remaining one-third of the land, of which he sold us two-thirds in the first purchase. Also, four thousand acres at Cohansey." From this it may be surmised that the West Jersey Society acted for the West Jersey proprietors.

To Basse they added: "The two proprietaries above the [Trenton] falls, containing fifteen thousand acres, which Dr. Coxe bought for £1,250, and which we bought of Dr. Coxe, is said to be the best land in the province. You may sell any part for £12 per hundred acres, except reserving some part of it near the Delaware River where the best oaks grow. Dr. Coxe tells us land is sold at £10 per hundred acres but, rather than fail, you may sell above the falls at £5 per hundred acres. Do not sell any land at Cape May, or along the seashore, for that we will not sell, because of the convenience for the whale fishing." [162]

Each of the twenty-four East Jersey proprietors had, by September, 1690, paid in £55, with another £10 shortly to be paid. [162]

William Dockwra, secretary, wrote Governor Hamilton in 1692: "You are to cause our receiver-general to forthwith demand all arrears of land rents due the proprietors from any town, or person, in the province and if any town or person shall refuse to pay such land rent, or to secure the same, you are to order our receiver-general to destrain upon goods and chattels of such town or persons and in default of distress to sue them in due course of law for recovery." [162]

A year later Dockwra wrote Hamilton: "The government and inhabitants of New York, according to their wonted custom, have been again soliciting at court for annexation of both Jerseys to New York, but have been frustrated."

A petition of Elizabethtown people (Nicolls' grantees) to the king, in 1693, pleads: "We have planted and improved our land, but about one hundred, or some other great number, calling themselves proprietors, pretend that they have a title thereto by several mesne conveyances from Berkeley and Carteret, to whom the duke conveyed the land before he, or any other of him, had ever been in possession of said land; and after your petitioners had enjoyed the same quietly for near thirty years, to force them to pay a large land rent for same.

"In this pretended court, and before these pretended judges of their own making, the said pretended proprietors did, in 1693, bring an action against Jeffery Jones for part of said land in Elizabethtown, and the same came to trial, and although upon full evidence the jury, chosen by the said proprietors and their creatures, gave a verdict for Jones, and yet the judges being either of, or the appointees of, said proprietors, were so partial and arbitrary, as contrary to law and justice, to give judgment against Jones, which your majesty has reversed.

"That your petitioners are now destitute of any lawful government and groaning under oppression of said usurpers, we plead to be placed under the government of New York. If Nicolls' patents are disallowed it will not be safe for any man to make improvements, nor to purchase land. The land rents ought to be paid to the crown." [162]

Had the annual land rents been paid into the public treasury all these years, for public purposes, instead of being paid to absentee landholders, New Jersey need never have had a public debt, and would be more highly developed than now.

Thomas Gordon, one of the Scotch proprietors of East Jersey, settled at Scotch Plains in 1684. Eleven years later, to represent the New Jersey proprietors resident therein, he was sent to England, in the controversy with the Elizabethtown claimants. Upon his departure, he was instructed by Governor Hamilton to say: "The land rent of the Nicolls Elizabethtown patent is indefinite and refers to 'such rent as may be established in other of the duke's colonies.' Such later patents in New York were as much as half-a-penny per acre. If the proprietors may not let out the land upon what land rents they please, where is their advantage in purchasing the province? We offer to the proprietors, as our opinion, that they sell off the land rents since it breeds so great heart-burning amongst the inhabitants. Instruct the council in East Jersey for how many years' purchase they will sell the land rents. But if the price is set too high it will discourage them." [162]

An opinion given by eight English lawyers, presumably at the request of the proprietors stated in part: "All grants made by Nicolls after date of the Berkeley and Carteret grant are void, for the delegated power of Nicolls could last no longer than his majesty's interest. . . . By the law of nations, if any people discover a country of barbarians, the prince of the people who make the discovery has the right of the land and government, and no people can settle there without the consent of the prince, or of such persons to whom the right has been conveyed, and payment to them of such rent for the land as the proprietors require."

It is unlikely there was any law on the subject at that early day, and the "right" referred to was but an usurpation by the reigning monarch for his individual profit, or to reward some favorite. As Mulford [105] said: "If there was any defect it must have been in the right of the king to make such conveyance."

The proprietors in England appointed Basse, then in England, as governor of both East and West Jersey, and he returned to New Jersey in the spring of 1698, where he remained until the next year. They instructed him that "upon non-payment of land rents you are to levy and sell, but not to sell any land rents at less than twenty years' purchase-price and, in addition, to reserve not less than half a penny per acre perpetual annual land rent upon any landholder to whom you sell. That you do not consent to any law that may lay any tax or imposition whatsoever upon any of the uncultivated land in said province." This particularly included the lands of the proprietors and, naturally, would enable them more easily to hold their land unused until buyers appeared. One harmful effect was to make land artificially scarce, which promoted land speculation by others.

Lewis Morris, at Tinton, in East Jersey, wrote Secretary Dockwra: "Any tax on land, the proprietors lands pay nothing . . . Their land rents are an unjust tax upon us and our heirs for ever. I would be glad to hear any one of their admirers instance one good thing the proprietors have done for the country, show where they have performed any of the many promises they have made in their 'concessions' and by their governors; what trust, what faith, is there in them? what truth in their letters? where is their integrity, justice, honesty and fair dealing with the country?" [162]

A memorial of the proprietors of East Jersey, in 1699, proposed, ". . . surrender of the government if his majesty will confirm to them the laws of said province [which laws the proprietor's assemblies had enacted] and the land rents reserved upon the grants of land already made and to be made. To have the sole privilege, as has been always practiced, of purchasing from the Indians what land remains unpurchased of them. That the twenty-four proprietors of East Jersey may be lords of the land and hold courts for the lands in the proprietorships, and appoint all officers that relate thereto. That all goods and chattels of traitors, felons, deodands, fugitives, estarys, treasure-trove, mines, wrecks, royal fish [whales] that shall be forfeited, found or taken within East Jersey, and within the seas adjacent, to be for the proprietors, with all other privileges and advantages as amply as in the grant and confirmation to them in 1682." [162]

William Sandford became owner of fifteen thousand acres, upland and meadow land, between the Passaic and Hackensack Rivers. He was a member of the councils of the two governors, and president of the court of Essex County at Elizabethtown. At a session of the court, in 1700, Samuel Carter, leading a group of discontents, railed at, and outrageously abused, the justice; calling the president a liar, which led to rebellious actions. Carter was held without bail.

The settlers continued dissatisfied about the land policy, and renewed disorders occurred in Middletown, incited by an English sheriff being displaced by a Scotsman. The settlers resented the Scot's arresting their neighbors and they beat him. Colonel Hamilton came from Burlington with forty or fifty armed men and was met by 170 unarmed.

The proprietors of East Jersey in London, in December, 1700, wrote the Lords Commissioners of Trade and Plantations in London: "The proprietors by themselves, or by licensing settlers to do so, purchase the land from the Indians, and afterwards confirm the same to the settlers by grant from the proprietors under land rents. This was the method of granting lands within this province from the first planting of it, and the grantees usually paid their rents till some of the settlers broached and advanced an opinion that the king's right to the American countries was only notional and arbitrary, and that the Indian natives are the absolute independent owners of the lands and have the sole disposal of them.

"In consequence, some of the planters, who after purchasing

from the Indians, and taking deeds from the proprietors now refuse to pay their land rents, and others who have since bought of the Indians, refuse to take deeds from the proprietors. If this notion should receive encouragement and prevail, the proprietors are advised that all pretenses of the crown to, and their grants of, American colonies have been wholly illusory and royal frauds, and the petitioners may, and in all probability will, deny his majesty's right to government, as well as to the land of these countries, and set up a government of their own, which the proprietors hope your lordships will think it worthy of your consideration to prevent.

"As was the usual practice, the proprietors licensed one John Royce, now a great asserter of the Indians' sole right to the land, and he did purchase twenty thousand acres of the Indians, and had about six thousand acres granted to him by the proprietors at 2d per acre yearly land rent. But now Royce, puffed up with the notion of the sole right of the Indians, and of no right in the king and his grantees, refuses to pay land rent, and claims all the land he bought of the Indians.

"The proprietors humbly submit to your lordships' judgment, that they, and the proprietors of West Jersey, had unanimously agreed, before this complaint arrived, to surrender the government of both provinces to his majesty, under terms and conditions as they are advised are proper." [162]

Through the sale of fractional shares, the number of proprietors became so great, and so divided in interests and aims, that their councils were uncertain and wavering, and their resolves but feebly pursued. [105]

The proprietors of East and West Jersey in August, 1701, submitted a statement of their views, signed by twenty-two from East, and thirty-two from West Jersey. Relative to surrender of their governments, they asked the sole power of purchasing land from the Indians; any title from Indians to other persons to be null and void; that no person be capable of election as representative who should not have a thousand acres of land, and no one was to vote who had not a hundred acres.

Queen Anne, second daughter of James II, came to the throne in March, 1702. Her husband, Prince George of Denmark, was made high-admiral of England. One of her first acts was the acceptance, in April, of the surrender by the lords proprietors of the governments of East and West Jersey. Upon which, William Penn exclaimed: "The surrender of the governments to the crown is an ugly preface." He obviously feared Pennsylvania might be the next to be taken over. After Penn arrived with his grant of Pennsylvania, he seems to have given no attention to New Jersey affairs, except to receive his allotments of large areas of land in New Jersey when declared as dividends, and in resenting statements derogatory to Pennsylvania, sent to England by some New Jersey gossips.

The New Jersey proprietors, by their surrender of the government, lost a claim to authority which they had been scarcely able to enforce, but they were now secured, under royal assurance and direction, in the private ownership of the land. [105]

England declared war against France in 1702, and the French advanced against the colonies from Canada.

The Queen appointed her cousin, Lord Cornbury, as the first royal governor of New Jersey and also governor of New York. Her instructions to him: "Liberty of conscience to every one except Papists; that Quakers be allowed to affirm; no printing press to be set up without the governor's permission."

Governor Cornbury, in a speech to the assembly said: "I am commanded to recommend to your care a bill whereby the rights and property of the proprietors may be confirmed to them, together with all land rents and all other privileges."

The leaders in the assembly were opposed to the proprietary claims and, it was suspected, and even alleged, that Governor Cornbury really was not desirous that the assembly should confirm the proprietor's title to land and land rents. [139]

The assembly, in 1703, enacted that no person except one holding a right of proprietary, and obtaining a license of such, could purchase land of the Indians, under penalty of 40s per acre. [46] This shut settlers out from getting land except upon the terms exacted by the proprietors.

Colonel Robert Quarry in 1703 wrote the Lords of Trade and Plantations: "The assembly bill asserted the right of the East Jersey proprietors to all the land on Staten Island, the government of which has been in actual possession of the crown for the past forty years.

"East Jersey had been a long time in the hands of a Scotch governor, Morris, and about twenty Scotsmen, who always carried it against more than a thousand others. The major part of the assembly are proprietors. West Jersey is chiefly in the hands of Quakers, mostly proprietors.

"But what seems the most extravagant in the proprietors is that they should cheat so many of their own brethren, and to have picked and culled all the choice land throughout the province to themselves and their heirs. Others must take up the barren land, or none, while the rest have from twenty thousand to sixty thousand acres apiece of the choicest land, worth a vast sum of money; a few of the topping proprietors in England are taken care of by those proprietors here.

"The assembly, at the request of the Queen, has levied the most unequal tax. There are a great many men in the province, besides the proprietors, that have obtained great estates by land-jobbing, whose business is to buy all good land and parcel it out to vast advantage. The support of the government lies on the poor industrious farmer of fifty to one hundred acres of improved land, who must pay a tax for his land and also his horse, cow, sheep, servants and what other stock he has. This injustice they shelter under an instruction recommended by the proprietors to her majesty." [162]

And the New Jersey legislature today, like those of other states, continues this illogical and impolitic system, supported by the selfish motives of energetic real estate boards. These present-day speculators are so without vision for the public welfare, when their unearned increment seems impaired, that but few of them realize the tax system they support is against their own business interest, as well as a social canker.

Peter Sonmans, son and heir of Arent Sonmans, stated, in 1704, that he possessed five-and-a-quarter proprietaries in East Jersey, and two in West Jersey, inherited from his father. He and William Dockwra, with other proprietors, asked for a hearing about possession of Staten Island.

Governor Cornbury wrote the Lords of Trade in London, "Her

majesty's instructions to me were not to allow any person besides the proprietors or their agents to buy land of the Indians. I consider this will hinder the country from being cleared and peopled so soon as it would be otherwise, for the proprietors will not sell or lease any land but at certain rates, which these proprietors who live in the province have agreed among themselves shall be the price, and people go to Pennsylvania. I believe certain land rents should be fixed, and that licenses issued by the governor to buy land of the Indians would settle the country much sooner." [162]

Secretary Dockwra, Sonmans and Colonel Coxe, in 1705, wrote the Lords of Trade: "The Quakers should be excluded from the council and assembly and all other places of public trust."

The same year the proprietors of West Jersey wrote that no act should be made to lay any tax upon unused land; and complained that: "Governor Cornbury has encouraged, and assented to, a bill in the assembly for taxing all land without distinction. There is no other colony in America wherein uncultivated land is taxed. So none more effectual could have been contrived to prejudice the proprietors. For if any man who has a thousand acres or more (as most of the first holders have), which he does not use, he must pay a tax for this land which may eat up the greater part of the profit of what he can, and does, cultivate; or he must desert the whole; and if we who have great tracts of land of many thousand acres to maintain our agents or servants, we must pay a tax for all the residue which yields us nothing. In consequence of this act several persons, who have agreed with our agents for land, have renounced their bargains and removed into those provinces where they can purchase great tracts of land and preserve them for their posterity, and we, unless relieved from this oppression, must deliver up our lands or our purses. If the exclusive right of the proprietors to purchase from the Indians be taken from the proprietors—the grantees of the crown—all grants of the whole main land of North America have been royal frauds under sanction of the great seal of England, and no man will ever after purchase lands under that title. 'Tis not the want of power to purchase lands from the Indians, but the taxing of unused lands, that has occasioned persons to remove to Pennsylvania and other colonies." [162]

The above is a convincing reason why unused land should be heavily taxed. It can be readily seen why persons who contemplated buying land to hold unused, to "preserve for their posterity," should have preferred to go, to speculate in land, to those parts where unused land was not taxed. Land speculation, prompting the holding of land unused, retards development of any state or community, and thus restricts the production of wealth.

Lord Lovelace arrived in New York in December, 1708, as successor to Cornbury. Queen Anne died in 1714, and was succeeded by George I.

A fourth dividend of land to the West Jersey proprietors was made that year, comprising 205,374 acres above Trenton. William Penn and Colonel Daniel Coxe received abnormally large portions. The Indian consent was acquired by giving them an insignificant amount of goods. [144]

Surveyor-General Leeds was charged with having altered the survey records. Contention about land, which had been going on for some years, made life-long enemies, with cries of "grab, grab and fraud." Two tracts, one of 2,000 acres, and one of 1,250 acres, at Morristown, were granted by the lords proprietors in 1715 to John Kay, Helly and Stevenson, all absentees. [144] In 1719 the province had a population of thirty thousand, and was heavily in debt.

The London Land Company in 1736 claimed ten thousand acres from Arent Sonman, and there arose a demand by proprietors for a distribution of land below Trenton as the fifth dividend.

Some New Jersey people made a plea to the crown for a government separate from that of New York, and this was granted in 1738.

A bill in chancery, respecting the Nicolls' Elizabethtown grant of eighty-one years previously, was filed in 1745, to which, six years afterwards, an answer was filed by 449 landholders and inhabitants.

The old dispute concerning land titles, which at earlier periods had been the cause of so much confusion and strife, was revived in 1745 and riots ensued. Large areas of land were held by Indian titles in disregard of the proprietors' orders and the proprietary-enacted laws. The proprietors had not been able either to compel payment of the land rent or to obtain the land. Colonists declared that "the Indians have a right from the Great and Absolute Proprietor of the Whole Universe, which stands registered in the best record on Earth." [57]

Instead of showing land titles from the lords proprietors, the settlers showed deeds "procured from strolling Indians for a bottle of rum." It would seem that white men were roaming about the country, over meadows and mountains, with a bottle of ink and a goose-quill pen in one hand, and a bottle of rum in the other, seeking Indians to sign deeds for land.

The defense of the settlers was that "so called" lords proprietors had, in 1744, surveyed all the unused land in Essex County, including many acres in the Horseneck Purchase and in the Van-Geisen Purchase, which the settlers had obtained from the Indians and improved, and upon which they had lived for many years. The proprietors began to sell the land to others and eject the settlers. Threats were made to dispossess all who would not yield to the proprietors, and also those who had grants from the proprietors, but would not pay their land rent, a sum amounting to £30,000. Settlers were arrested and jailed. [57]

Settlers who had been decided against in the courts, and been committed to prison, were released by force. For a time the laws became powerless. Memorials and counter memorials upon the subject were presented to the king. [105]

In 1747 there were land riots in Morris, Somerset and Hunterdon Counties, and the following year in Newark and Perth Amboy. Arrests and imprisonment were followed by attacks upon the jails and release of the prisoners. Again, in the two succeeding years, land riots occurred in Hunterdon and Bergen Counties. [46]

The proprietors claimed that any one who held land by an Indian deed alone virtually declared the "Indian grantor to be the superior lord of the land and disowned the crown of England to be so. Such one withdrew his allegiance from the crown of England, for within his domain all lands were held immediately or mediately from the king; that to attempt to establish the dominion of the Indian, and to destroy the dominion of the crown of England, was an overt act that approached high treason." [57]

By these arguments the proprietors attempted to maintain their land privilege, and justify their actions in arresting and imprisoning settlers who could not show a title from the proprietors. But with all their arguments, they could not control or influence the colonists. The governor appealed to the assembly, but public opinion was with the colonists. [57]

The colonists answered that they had the following license: "You [including many names] and company have liberty to purchase from the Indians within this government what quantity of land you shall think convenient, in this province, etc., and for so doing, this shall be your Warrant. Given under hand and seal of the governor." Signed, Philip Carteret, July, 1666.

Settlers claimed that this warrant had been given them in 1666. Abram Pierson of Newark, during his pastorate at that time, was sent, at the request of Carteret, to confer with the governor at Elizabethtown. The minister declared that, while there, this document was taken from his pocket. So, when production of the warrant was requested, as authority to purchase from the Indians, it could not be produced. In later years it was found among Carteret's papers. [57] However, the warrant did not imply revocation of the land rent provision.

Purchases under this warrant were made before the law of 1703, which declared all further purchases from Indians illegal. The lords proprietors claimed that there was no confusion in the colony which "the rioters and their accomplices had not made, with the hope of wresting from the proprietors both their rents and their lands."

The governor and his council, with an air of superiority, frequently referred to the settlers as ignorant people who did not know what was good for them and who were misled by vicious demagogues. Colonists claimed they believed their land titles good, but asserted they could not secure justice in the proprietary appointed courts. The proprietors secured all the able lawyers in New Jersey and New York, so colonists could not get competent legal advice to defend the multiplicity of suits brought to try to ruin them. [57]

But, at about this period, proprietary deeds to extensive portions of land, held by the settlers, were acquired by men of authority and influence, who were disposed to enforce their claims. These included Chief Justice Robert Hunter Morris, James Alexander, secretary of the province, and other prominent officials.

Writs to eject the settlers were issued and suits for recovery of the land rents were commenced against many holders of Indian deeds. These defendants, who formed a large portion of the population of some counties, associated together and resolved that, whatever might be the decision of the law, they would maintain their possessions. [105]

For nearly a century, land titles and land rents in New Jersey were sources of great public disturbances and often, as shown, were the cause of riots. By 1755 the French and Indian War had diverted public attention, and drawn into the army many of riotous disposition, which allayed the rebellious spirits.

Nevertheless, after ten years' persistent effort, the settlers lost their farms and homes, and the resulting poverty and suffering were acute.

After the lords proprietors had acquired the land of the Indians, the province, in 1758, following the example of Calvert in Maryland, put the Indians on a three thousand acre reservation at mosquito-infested Indian Mills in Burlington County. Two hundred of their descendants lived there during the next forty-four years.

The First Presbyterian Church in Newark, the only church until 1719, was in 1696 granted two hundred acres, in different tracts. In 1754 it rented a part of its donation at a rental of £2, 6s, and the next year increased the rental one shilling. This is the earliest record of increasing land rent in New Jersey.

From that time to the present, with successive recessions and recoveries, land rent and the selling price of land in New Jersey have increased, solely as the result of increase in population and public improvements; and because of a too low tax on all land value.

Foreseeing that landholding would soon return a steady unearned income from rent and sales of land, speculation in land began to develop.

The trustees of the First Church in 1760 induced David Young, heir of the oldest patentee, to deed to their church the two hundred acres which had been granted in fee by the lords proprietors for the use of a church. Great haste and secrecy were displayed in getting this deed, because of the developing strength of other churches. [57]

However, after half a century of conflict between the churches over the unearned revenue from land rent, the First Church, in 1787, granted to the church in Orange, and to the Episcopal Church, a portion of the annual income, since then grown to a large sum from the land rents.

Even before the time of this transaction, land had been made artificially scarce by speculators holding large areas unused, which increased the price of land and made it more difficult and costly for people to get desirable locations upon which to live and work. Then poverty began to arise. Instead of collecting this community-created annual land rent for public purposes, including relief for the poor, the poor were sold at auction to whosoever would care for them at the lowest monthly charge. This disgraceful method continued in effect for the next half-century. And even today, any beings so unfortunate as to have met with adversity, must, to get poor relief from their municipality, declare themselves to be paupers.

The most characteristic feature of the economic development of West Jersey, at an early day, was the establishment of a land-owning class, through the formation of a plantation-owning aristocracy. Wealthy members of the Society of Friends sought to marry their daughters to some worthy young man of another land-owning family and join the two estates; thus thousands of acres came into the possession of a comparatively few families. There grew up a social condition not unlike that of tidewater Virginia and Maryland. [94]

Staten Island was clearly in the grant of New Jersey, but was lost, apparently through neglect of the New Jersey proprietors, and of the New Jersey assembly (after 1702 controlled by the crown), to continue to assert ownership. After 165 years of intermittent contention it was, in 1833, recognized as a part of New York.

Thomas Budd, one of the early English settlers in West Jersey, arrived in Burlington with a group of Quakers in 1678, and in some way acquired possession of Absecon Island, on which Atlantic City is now situated.

Subsequently, Jeremiah Leeds claimed he bought all the land on the island, from the ocean to the meadows, and from the Inlet to the present city limit at Jackson Avenue, for which he paid (presumably to Budd's heirs), 40¢ per acre.

When the Camden & Atlantic Land Company was formed and Atlantic City founded, at the opening of the railroad in 1854, the Land Company paid Leeds $128,000; being $17.50 per acre for the same land, composed mostly of sand-dunes.

Due solely to increase in population, this land (not including buildings) has increased in value and is now officially assessed at $44,000,000. It produces, or is worth to the holders, a land rent of more than $3,000,000 annually, over and above taxes thereon.

The question naturally arises, "Who created that great land value and land rent since the days of Thomas Budd and Jeremiah Leeds?" Certainly not Budd or Leeds, or the individual holders of lots and unused land, but all the people, including bathing beauties and other visitors who congregated there.

Consequently it is a publicly-created value, and in all reason should be collected for the city treasury to pay public expenses. Were this annual land rent so collected, instead of inuring as increased value to holders of lots and unused land, the city would have all the revenue it needs, without a bonded debt, or being in the financial plight it long has been.

There is only one main avenue in the city sufficiently wide to accommodate the present traffic without congestion. When the future city was planned, the city engineer recommended wider streets than were proposed, but the speculative land company officials rejected this, because it would reduce the number of saleable lots. Consequently, those who use the streets, now or hereafter, must endure congested traffic as a tribute to land speculation.

While the beaches and sand-dunes along the New Jersey coast early passed into private ownership, upon the principle that no land was too poor to be without an owner, there was but slight recognition of individual bounds. Faulty surveying, changes in natural monuments, and alterations in contour caused by tides and subsidence, threw boundary lines into the greatest confusion. [94]

Practically, the beaches—a free gift of nature to all the people— were commons, open to everybody, until within recent years, when holders of title to the land fronting on the ocean have erected wire fences along the north Jersey shore. They thus exact toll of everyone bathing, or even wading, in the ocean, and of all those in the fishing industry in those waters. This, in effect, gives private ownership not only to the beaches, but also to the Atlantic Ocean immediately along the north Jersey seashore.

It is believed that most of the land in West Jersey has been located in surveys, but there are intervals, here and there, where surveys already made do not completely cover all the land.[a]

In 1864 a law was passed by the legislature relating to riparian lands, and since that time, the state has claimed and exercised the right of ownership thereof, which had been previously part of the proprietary interest. The state now leases tens of thousands of acres of it to users, especially for oyster culture, at an annual rental payable to the State School Fund, thereby reducing the state-wide school tax on all property.

With this as a precedent, and with the ever-increasing population and pressure for land use, the state may presently, in one way or another—possibly through a surtax delinquency—assume ownership of unused land. These areas may be leased at a perpetual annual land rent, if unsuitable for industry, or be dedicated to the many social uses, private and public, to which land may be put, including slum clearance, athletic fields, public golf-courses, playgrounds, parks, forestry and wild-life sanctuaries.

[a] Benj. A. Sleeper, civil engineer.

17

The Carolinas

THE section now known as the Carolinas was first named Florida by the Spaniards and the French adopted the name. The English, after colonizing Virginia, called it Southern Virginia.

In 1629 the name Carolina was indefinitely applied to that region, and not until the territory was made the subject of a grant by Charles II, in 1663, was it definitely so designated.

After the French abandoned their settlement at Port Royal in 1563, no other European settlement was attempted in the Carolinas until the ill-fated Raleigh colony settled at Roanoke, in 1585, followed by the Chowan settlement, sixty-eight years after Roanoke. Meanwhile, English colonization had been successfully established in several parts of Virginia, New England and Maryland.

All the land in tidewater Virginia having been pre-empted by settlers, and by absentee holders living in England, Robert Green, in 1653, led a company of a hundred pioneers from Virginia into the Chowan River region, bordering on Albemarle Sound, North Carolina. Governor William Berkeley of Virginia (later one of the Carolina grantees) had granted them a thousand acres; and an additional ten thousand acres were offered, if occupied by a hundred settlers. [5]

A party from Massachusetts had settled on Old Town Creek in the Cape Fear region in 1661, but at the end of two years they had become so discouraged that they had left their cattle with the Indians and returned to Massachusetts. Evidently chagrined, and thinking that others might attempt a settlement there, they affixed to a post "a writing which disparaged the land about the river, and to the discouragement of all who should thereafter come there to settle."

George Durant obtained an Indian grant on a neck of land in North Carolina in 1662, and a year later, Governor Berkeley of Virginia granted to George Cathmaid a large tract there, for having located sixty-seven settlers along Albemarle Sound.

Governor Berkeley in 1663 granted to Thomas Rolfe, son of Pocahontas, his heirs and assigns for ever, 750 acres along the Pasquotanck River in North Carolina, at an annual land rent, payable to the king, of 1s for every fifty acres; provided that, if not seated or planted within three years, it should be subject to allotment to others. Grants were made, similarly, to Robert Peel, 350 acres for transporting seven persons thereto; to John Harvey, 850 acres at Currituck; and to John Jenkins, 700 acres. [134]

Charles I of England had in 1630 conveyed the Carolina territory to Robert Heath, his attorney-general. Thirty-three years afterwards, the privy council in England declared that, as no settlement had been made in the country, and as no one had responded to its notice to present his patent, the Heath grant was declared void.

Upon the Restoration of Charles II in 1660, there were many loyal, if not servile, supporters of the old monarchy to be rewarded, and many creditors with claims upon the treasury and the bounty of the new sovereign. Some of these were recognized by Charles in his grant of the Carolinas on March 24, 1663. This grant [145] was made to Edward, Earl of Clarendon; George, Duke of Albemarle; William, Lord Craven; John, Lord Berkeley; Anthony, Lord Ashley; Sir George Carteret; Sir William Berkeley, and Sir John Colleton.

The grant comprised all the land now within the boundaries of North and South Carolina, and most of the present state of Georgia, westerly to the South Sea (Pacific Ocean). The grantees were empowered to build forts, establish markets, enact laws, appoint judges, create counties, baronies and colonies, erect manors, confer titles of nobility, and to raise a militia and declare martial law. In consideration, the grantees were to pay Charles a yearly rental of twenty marks, and one-quarter of all gold and silver found. Two years later the Bahama Islands were annexed to the grant.

Bancroft [5] said: "To satisfy the greediness of favorite court-iers, Charles II, in 1663, narrowed the limits of Virginia by giving to eight favorites the basis of an immense speculation in land, through the Carolina grant, a territory large enough to have given each one of the eight grantees a tract as extensive as the kingdom of France."

It may be of interest to know who these eight men were, to whom Charles granted this princely domain: George Monk, the turncoat general of the Parliamentary Army served with Crom-well in opposition to the monarchy, was captured and imprisoned two years in the Tower of London. At the death of Cromwell he became singularly conspicuous in the Restoration of Charles to the throne, who then rewarded him by elevation to the peer-age, as the Duke of Albemarle. He was made privy councillor, endowed with the Order of the Garter, made prime minister and loaded with pensions, inheritances and honors. [5]

Anthony Ashley Cooper, for whom the Ashley and Cooper Rivers were named, had been particularly recommended to Charles by George Monk to be one of the king's council. He was regarded as a politician; had espoused the cause of mon-archy, then of the parliament, and then again of monarchy, as it suited his ambition. Yet he long retained the favor and con-fidence of the king and became chancellor of England and Earl of Shaftsbury. He was the most influential in the early policy of the Carolinas. [126] "The most unprincipled of ministers and most unprincipled of demagogues" [97]—and the protector of vested rights. [5] He was later imprisoned in the Tower.

Edward Hyde, Earl of Clarendon, capable, covetous, but arrogant, had lived abroad fourteen years when he became the companion of Charles in his exile and, after the death of Crom-well, had materially contributed to the re-establishment of the monarchy. [126] Hated by the people, he was faithful only to the king. When the Clarendon ministry fell, eight years after the Restoration, he became an exile. [5] His daughter married the king's brother, the Duke of York, who became King James II; and their children, Mary and Anne, became queens of England.

The Earl of Craven was an old soldier of the German discipline, and distinguished for his military service. He was one of Charles' privy council, held a military command and was supposed to be husband of the Queen of Bohemia. [5]

Sir John Colleton had been an active partisan of royalty by his uncalculating zeal in its cause. After the ascendancy of Cromwell he retired to Barbados. Upon the Restoration of Charles, he returned to England and was made a baronet. [126] He was of no historical notoriety. [5]

Sketches of the other two grantees, John Berkeley and George Carteret, are given in the chapter on New Jersey.

The proprietors held their first meeting in London, appointed officers, and ordained rules for the government of the Carolina province. No fixed policy was ever established and their acts were usually vacillating and injudicious. Most selfishly, they proposed that: "the first colony of settlers may, at its own expense, fortify the seacoast, and the entrance to the river on which they locate, and that a court house and other public buildings be erected by the colonists on land to be granted by us on some small payment."

Meanwhile, the proprietors dispatched to Barbados the ship "John and Thomas" with arms and ammunition to be *sold* to those who desired to undertake, "on liberal terms," risking their lives in a settlement of Port Royal. This town was to form a barrier between the proprietors' land in Carolina, and the Spaniards at St. Augustine.

"Every person who goes, or sends an agent, well armed, to Carolina shall have one hundred acres, at an annual rental payable to the proprietors. Later arrivals to have a reduced acreage." Many pamphlets were issued to induce settlers and thereby sell land.

The proprietors promptly committed the care of their interests on the Chowan to Governor Berkeley of Virginia. He appointed William Drummond (whom he afterwards hanged) as governor of Albemarle County, bordering on Virginia. The proprietors advised Berkeley that one-half-penny per acre, per annum, land rent was "as low as it is possible for us to descend, and we hope to have settlers upon better terms for us."

Colonel John Yeamans, a Barbados planter, father of Major William Yeamans, arrived at Port Royal early in 1663 in the ship "Adventure." He had with him some commissioners to explore the Carolina coast with the view to making a settlement. They found Spaniards and hostile Indians there and decided to go to the Cape Fear River, which Yeamans ascended for a long distance.

Later in the same year, a second expedition went from Barbados to the Cape Fear River in the ship "Adventure," in command of Captain William Hilton. They found that the cattle and swine, which had been left there by the Massachusetts people, had increased in number.

Negotiations were had with the Indians for a location on the river. Upon arriving back in Barbados, the following January, they gave a favorable report and many settlers went there. A proposal was made to the lords proprietors, by "several gents and persons of good quality," for a thousand square miles (640,000 acres) of land, on which to locate two hundred settlers.

Colonel Yeamans, in 1665, brought several hundred settlers from Barbados to the Cape Fear River, in a small frigate, a vlei-boat of 150 tons, and a sloop. The vlei-boat stuck on the bar and was lost. The sloop, when sent to Virginia for provisions, was wrecked on Cape Lookout, and two men were lost. [132]

These adventurers, together with some English, and some Dutch who had come from Manhattan after the English conquest there, brought the population in the settlement to eight hundred. Yeamans received a grant of land for his colony and was knighted and appointed governor of all the territory within the grant. Dissatisfaction arose respecting the location and the land allotments, and two years later the colony disbanded; the settlers scattering to Albemarle Sound, to Nansemond, Virginia, and some to Massachusetts.

The Massachusetts people, who had, a few years previously, abandoned their Carolina settlement, became active in claiming the land, when they learned that all the Carolina region had been granted to the eight lords proprietors. However, the lords ordered Yeamans "to make everything easy for the people of New England, from which the greatest immigration is expected, as the southern colonies are already drained of people." Within a quarter of a century, all this land relapsed into its original condition, roamed over by deer and Indians.

Showing the effect of increased population and community development in creating an unearned increment in land value, which is then charged upon industry and private initiative, a tract of 111 acres of formerly valueless land with a frontage of 1,800 feet on the Cape Fear River, below Wilmington, was, in 1939, being 275 years after the Yeamans settlement, sold for $69,000, as a location of an oil terminal.

In 1665 the proprietors proclaimed to the settlers what they designated the "Concessions and Agreements of the Lord Proprietors of the Province of Carolina," in which they stated: "The assembly may levy taxes equally to raise money on all lands excepting the lands of the lords proprietors. May erect baronies and manors, with the necessary courts, jurisdictions and privileges as to them shall seem convenient. May erect forts, cities, and villages, and the same to fortify from public funds [taxes] but they may not at any time demolish such forts. Shall make provision for the maintenance of the governor appointed by the lords, and for support of the government; also the constables of the counties shall collect the land rents payable annually to the lords, and pay the same to the receiver that the lords shall appoint, whereby the lords may have their land rents duly collected without charge or trouble to them."

It was made illegal, as it was in all the proprietary colonies, for any individual, other than the lords proprietors, to purchase land from the Indians. The proprietors claimed, by the king's grant, to be the sole owners of every acre of land in the Carolinas and most of Georgia, westward to the South Sea. They expected their colonies to be established by driving the Indians away from their homes and the graves of their ancestors. [126]

The treaty of peace between England and Spain in 1667 acknowledged the claim of England to its possessions in America, whereupon the Carolina proprietors directed their earnest attention to the settlement at Port Royal, under Ashley Cooper, Earl Shaftsbury.

To induce speedy immigration, all free persons over sixteen years of age settling in the colony before March 25, 1670, were to have 150 acres, and an additional 150 acres for himself for every able indented man servant, and 100 acres for every indented woman servant, or man servant under sixteen years, that he should bring. For later arrivals, a decreasing acreage in the next two succeeding years was provided. All indented servants at expiration of their term should have a hundred acres each as their own; provided all such grantees should pay to the lords proprietors an annual land rent for every acre. The statute *quiaemptores* was set aside, thus allowing subinfeudation (subtenantry) in Carolina, although it had been forbidden in England during the preceding 379 years.

More settlers came from England, New England and the West India Islands, but, to get land, they were obliged to engage to pay the lords proprietors in London an annual ground rent of from one-half to one penny an acre.

The "Fundamental Constitutions" were solemnly adopted by the proprietors in London, in 1669. Under them, the eldest proprietor was to serve as palatine, or governor, with regal authority. An hereditary nobility was created by the eight lords proprietors, each of whom selected a large area of choice land as a barony, with the hereditary title of seigniory. They sold large areas, as baronies, to those upon whom they conferred the hereditary title of nobility of landgrave, or cacique. These titles were secured, and their dignity supported, by making their land for ever inseparable from the titles and privileges of the respective orders of Carolina nobility.

All grants of land obliged the grantees to pay an annual land rent of one-half-penny per acre; increased twenty years later to one penny.

Any lord of a seigniory or barony was to be permitted to lease a part of his land to others and, if in one piece of between three thousand and twelve thousand acres, it might be constituted a manor.

The lord of each seigniory, barony or manor could try his leetmen or vassals (tenants and indented servants) in all civil and criminal cases, without appeal, except by previous registered agreement. Nor could any leetman or leetwoman have liberty to go off from their particular lord and live elsewhere, without license of said lord under hand and seal. The tenants were American serfs in a feudal land system, as had been the settlers under the Dutch patroons in New Netherland.

Of these baronies, one can today find the Colleton barony, the Wadbro barony, the Broughton barony and others, owners of which are drawing rents from the labor of those who cultivate them. [21]

The lords proprietors and their deputies (each proprietor living in Britain had the right to appoint a deputy resident in Carolina) were in the nature of sovereigns. Landgraves and caciques had an hereditary right of succession and the pernicious and unnatural law of primogeniture was recognized. Those of Carolina title of nobility, resident in Carolina, largely composed the upper house in the provincial assembly.

Freeholders or freemen were landholders below the nobility, and had the right to vote for, and to be elected, members of the provincial assembly, but no one holding less than five hundred acres or otherwise worth £1,000 was eligible to election.

Ever changing the conditions for disposing of land, it was ordered in 1669 that for five years landholdings be restricted to 660 acres, except by proprietors, landgraves and caciques.

The area a colonist might take up on land rent was reduced to sixty acres for himself, and fifty or sixty acres for each person brought with him. Later it was fifty acres, without distinction, for each person that came in. [8]

In Albemarle, land was granted to anyone upon request, the annual rent of one-half-penny per acre to begin three years after date of the grant.

Population and development, at Chowan and Albemarle, were retarded by selection of unfavorable locations; and when the rents became due the people became dissatisfied. Instead of sudden wealth, the colonists there gained a living by raising cattle, cultivating tobacco and corn, felling forests to export lumber, and trafficking with traders from New England; the remuneration from which, however, left them nothing beyond bare subsistence and nothing with which to pay land rent.

Settlements subsequently expanded southward to the Pamlico and Neuse Rivers, by immigration of Huguenots and Swiss, and of Germans from the Palatinate. A governor was appointed for the northern region, and an assembly held, but this section was largely neglected by the proprietors and the government at Charles Town, and occasionally the Albemarle settlement was without any government. [112]

The members of the board of proprietors in London contributed £500 each towards sending an expedition to Carolina. A fleet of three vessels, in command of Joseph West, with Governor William Sayle, and equipment, ammunition and provisions for eighteen months, sailed from England in January, 1670, stopping at Kinsale, Ireland, to take on twenty or more indented servants for the proprietors. They arrived at Port Royal the following March. Their determination not to build at Port Royal, which was chosen for them by the proprietors, was, no doubt, because of its exposure to attack by sea and land by Spaniards at St. Augustine, and by warlike neighboring Indians under Spanish influence.

Governor Sayle, with about two hundred colonists, started a settlement on the west bank of the Ashley River. Here they laid off streets and town lots, and built a fortification and dwelling houses fifteen by twenty feet. They named the settlement Charles Town (not the present Charleston). More colonists from Bermuda arrived at Port Royal but later went to Charles Town.

The governor was directed to make presents to the neighboring Indian chiefs to secure their good-will and friendship, also to deliver to needy persons merchandise, guns and ammunition from the storehouse of the lords, on credit, at 10 per cent interest.

The ship "Blessing," owned by the proprietors and carrying a crew of ten, was in 1671 sent from Carolina to New York, and returned with settlers.

The proprietors in England wrote Mr. West in Carolina: "The carrying of passengers to Ashley River is the main end of our sending out this ship." Shipmasters were forbidden, as they were in Penn's domains of West Jersey and Pennsylvania, to carry away any settlers, without previous posted notice.

Cultivation was chiefly by white indented servants and Indian slaves, the latter purchased from their Indian captors, who had taken them in warfare. Sir John Yeamans in 1671 brought Negro slaves from Barbados to cultivate his plantation, the first Negro slaves ever seen in Carolina, fifty-two years after their first importation into Virginia.

Yeamans was instructed by the proprietors to lay out a "grand modell" of a town, in plots of three hundred feet square. Immediately adjacent to the town there was to be a common, one-third of a mile in width, open to the use of all inhabitants, on which to graze their cattle. With each square, as a town lot, eighty acres in the colony, and four hundred acres elsewhere in the precinct, were granted on land rent. [112] Some preferred buying land outright, rather than pay annual land rent to absentee proprietors.

Creation of baronies, as provided in the fundamental constitutions, began in 1671, and orders were given to have land surveyed for any of the provincial nobility who requested it. [112]

The royal grant had guaranteed to the settlers an assembly, but this had been largely nullified by the proprietors, who at first constituted their legislature and for some time remained chief wielders of the law-making power. [8]

Eight years after the initial settlement, the proprietors wrote the governor: "You are to summon the freeholders and require them in our name to elect twenty persons who, with our deputies as our representatives, are, for the present, to be your assembly to make such laws as you shall find necessary. You are to require the assembly to choose five freemen, to be joined with five deputies of the proprietors who, with the five eldest men of the nobility—being fifteen members—are to be your grand council. There is no thing to be debated or voted in the assembly but what is proposed to them by the council." All freemen elected to the council were obliged to swear allegiance to the king and subscribe fidelity and submission to the proprietors, and the form of government.

The landgraves and caciques being created by the lords proprietors, the proprietors would have a majority in the assembly. The proprietors themselves, in England, had the final vote on all laws passed by the provincial assembly. Whatever was proposed therein must first have been passed by the grand council.

No law passed by the assembly could come permanently into force until ratified by the palatine himself and three lords proprietors. All laws were to expire at the end of sixty years. Such was the grand model of government which the proprietors stated to be for "establishing the interest of the lords proprietors and that would avoid erecting a numerous democracy."

It was ordered by the grand council that the people should settle on the land allotted them; four poles of land within the town, for a town lot, and five acres outside the town, for a planting lot, for every person in each family. The lots were to be designated (allotted) by the freeholders by chance.

The neighboring Indians, realizing in 1671 that they were being more and more dislodged from their hunting and fishing grounds, and that they were being driven closer to enemy Indian tribes in the interior country, declared themselves in favor of the Spanish garrison. Urged by the Spaniards, they made depredations on the white settlers. The grand council ordered war on the Indians; the soldiers' remuneration for services was the ancient soldiers' pay of sale, or ransom, of their prisoners.

A specimen bill of lading of that time read: "Shipped by the Grace of God, in good order and well conditioned, for the account of the lords proprietors of Carolina, in and upon the good ship, 'William and Ralph.'"

The proprietors in London wrote the governor: "We being informed that there are many whales upon the coast of Carolina, which fish are reserved to us, we hereby grant to our colonists the privilege of catching them for their own use during the next seven years. We prohibit the coasting for ambergris, spermacetti and wreck-goods to any but such as our governor, three of our deputies, and our agent shall license. We would have none licensed to coast for ambergris, etc., but such as will give security to make good to us one-fifth part of the ambergris they discover."

Besides securing to themselves the largest share in the administration, the principle was announced by the proprietors that a balanced government chiefly depended on the proper proportion of landed estates held by the proprietors, the nobles, and the common people.

Concessions on land rents were, in 1672, offered people in Ireland to migrate to Carolina.

Rivers [126], a Carolina historian, notes that "the unalterable laws" of 1669 avowed the objects of the proprietors to be: a pure aristocracy, to avoid a "numerous democracy," and that the welfare of the settlers was not so much regarded as the pecuniary advantages and political importance of the lords proprietors.

The settlers completed a fort at (original) Charles Town in 1672. Streets and sixty-two town lots were laid out. The same year, Oyster Point Town (modern Charleston) was laid out, and some settlers at Charles Town moved thereto. Seven years later all the settlers moved there, taking with them the public offices and the name; and thirty houses were erected.

The following year the lords proprietors in London wrote the governor: "Take notice that Oyster Point is the place we appoint for the Port Towne, which you are to call Charles Town. Each of the proprietors is to have five acres reserved within the said towne. You are to grant land to others beneath the degree of proprietor, with the proviso that his house shall be erected within two years; and any one having erected one house shall have more lots, provided that within twelve months after taking the lot he erect a house of a least sixteen by thirty feet, two stories high, with garret."

While those "beneath the degree of proprietor" were erecting buildings and developing the community, the proprietors alone were allowed to hold land unused, to reap the unearned increment created by others.

Ten years after the charter was granted the same cause for dissatisfaction of the settlers—that of land rents—which had existed at Chowan and Cape Fear now existed at Charles Town and in other proprietary colonies.

The proprietors in London in 1674 wrote to Andrew Percivall, their agent in Carolina: "You are to grant land to none that comes to settle but upon conditions they settle in townships and take up land according to the draft herewith, viz., five acres for a house and garden, ten acres in the common cow pasture and thirty-five acres in a piece beyond the common, and an out-lot contai..ing three hundred acres in one piece in the same colony whenever they will take it up. The home lot shall always inseparately belong to the house in town, which, whenever it is not inhabited and kept up, the house and home-lot shall devolve into the hands of the lords proprietors."

Five of the proprietors decided to form a coterie to trade with the Indians, and forbade the governor, the council and other inhabitants of Carolina to trade with the Indians, "it being in justice and reason fit, that we should not be interrupted by them in our transactions with the Indians, with whom by our grant and charter from his majesty, we alone have authority to treat."

The governor was instructed by the proprietors that, since beads were highly prized by, and had a high monetary value with the Indians, particular care should be taken not to allow every settler to barter beads with them, lest such articles should become too common and cheap in their estimation.

At a meeting of the committee of trade and plantations in London, in 1679, it was ordered that, for the transportation of French Protestants (Huguenots) to Carolina, two ships, each drawing not above twelve feet of water, be fitted out in England.

With the increase in population, land in Charles Town increased in value; cleared and fenced land twenty miles from town rented at 10*s* per acre per annum. [132]

Some planters had as many as eight hundred head of cattle. Salted beef began to be exported to Barbados, Jamaica and New England. Lumber, pipe staves, ginger, indigo, silk, cotton, wine and wax were exported to the West Indies, and sugar, molasses and rum were received in return. Only seventeen years after the first settlement was made, as many as sixteen trading vessels to carry this commerce were at one time at anchor in Charles Town harbor.

The third "fundamental constitutions" were put in practice in 1682, by which the proprietors again changed conditions in making new deeds to land. At first land was allotted at an annual rent of a penny an acre "or value thereof." The new constitutions left out the words, "or value thereof," and added the right of re-entry by the proprietors if the land rent was not paid. Re-entry was not mentioned in the first deeds.

Many who had arrived early did not at once take out deeds, and these must now accept the new form of deed. Requests that the land rent might be paid in produce, at "the value thereof," were met by the reply of the proprietors: "We insist to sell our lands in our own way," with the result that, as one chronicler wrote: "Many hundreds of people have deserted the colony and many thousands have forebore to come hither." This led, some years later, to the overthrow of the government of Governor Colleton.

The proprietors in 1682 proclaimed: "Any of the squares [a square being 12,000 acres] of a county that are made choice of [selected] by a proprietor shall be a seignory for ever belonging to that proprietorship. Any landgrave or cacique that is not in Carolina may have his attorney take up the said land belonging to his Dignity."

Instructions of the proprietors for granting land provided: "No man that hath a right to land in Carolina by purchase, and is under the degree of a proprietor, shall have liberty to choose the land due to him until he have subscribed in the book to bear allegiance to our sovereign lord the king, his heirs and successors, and to be true and faithful to the palatine and the lords proprietors, their heirs and successors."

Minute instructions were given for laying out the land. In the deeds it was provided that, "On any default in payment of the annual land rent for ninety days, it shall be lawful for the proprietors, their heirs and assigns, to enter and distrain, and the distresses then and there found, to take, lead, carry and drive away and impound, and to detain and keep until they shall be paid all arrears of the said rent."

Land was usually allotted on an annual land rental, but some was sold at £50 per thousand acres. For making wine, Francis de Vowsery was granted eight hundred acres, and Arthur Middleton an equal number for making oil and cotton, subject to payment of land rent.

The proprietors agreed with certain Scots for a settlement in Carolina, whereupon Lord Cardosse, a Scot, arrived at Port

Royal in 1683. With him were ten families; among them, those of the name of Hamilton, Montgomerie and Dunlop. They founded Stuarts Town. The charge for passage from England at that time was £5. The following year, in July, Lord Cardosse wrote: "I was, and still continue to be, taken ill of the fever and ague." He returned to Scotland.

In 1686, though Spain was at peace with England, Spaniards from St. Augustine landed at Edisto, fifty miles south of Charles Town, with three galleys and a force of Negroes and Indians. They broke open the house of Joseph Moreton, then governor, murdered his brother-in-law, and carried away all his money and plate and thirteen slaves, to the value of £1,500. Two slaves returned. Demand was made on the Spanish governor for the remainder. He replied that he could not deliver them without an order from the King of Spain.

The Spaniards committed other depredations, and the English fitted out two vessels, with four hundred men, well armed, to attack St. Augustine. But James Colleton, who had just arrived from Barbados, with a commission as governor, threatened to hang the English if they proceeded, so they abandoned their plan. A chronicler said, "I am well informed there was a design to carry on a trade with the Spaniards."

Attempts to collect land rents on both cultivated and wild lands, in 1687, met with resistance, and the assembly defied the governor. [5]

Suit was brought in 1689 against Governor Seth Sothell for nine years' arrears of land rent of £36, on four thousand acres at 2s per hundred acres. [12]

The agent of the proprietors was directed in 1677 to "sett out" one whole colony of twelve hundred acres to John Berkeley, Simon Perkins, Anthony Laine and John Pettitt, upon their landing in Carolina.

The proprietors in 1689 wrote Governor Colleton advising him that he had been made a landgrave, with forty-eight thousand acres, and adding: "We have sent some further instructions for the method of passing acts of assembly which you are to observe."

Thomas Smith was a landgrave, with forty-eight thousand acres. The twelve thousand acres which had been held by John d'Arsens, were assigned to Smith when he married D'Arsens' widow. Thomas Amy was granted twelve thousand acres in 1694. John Price was created a landgrave, with forty-eight thousand acres, and Dr. Christopher Dominick was granted twelve thousand acres. But it seems that such large areas were seldom deeded to those to whom they were granted.

The proprietors in 1690 wrote from London to their agent, Andrew Percivall, complaining of the unsatisfactory condition of affairs in Carolina: "As to the land grants, it is the manner lands are granted here in England, wherein land rent is reserved. Though the annual rent is 1*d* per acre, we are willing to take the rents in indigo and other commodities at prices current. We are informed that some of the first settlers have discouraged any people of worth that have come amongst you; they discouraged above five hundred people who arrived in Carolina in one month, including the Scots and French.

"The Scots intended to have sent ten thousand people there. We doubt not but there would have been many thousands more men in Carolina, but wise men who have anything will never come into a country where there is no settled government . . . By our charter from the crown, power is given to us to exercise martial law."

From the letter of Lord Cardosse, just quoted, it might appear that the prevalence of fever and ague, the attack by the Spaniards on the Scots at Port Royal and disturbances about land rents, regarding all of which the settlers had naturally informed their friends in Scotland, had actually discouraged further migration from Scotland.

A colony from the French (Huguenot) settlement on the James River, in Virginia, settled along the Pamlico in 1690.

Contentions between the settlers and the proprietors continued respecting land rents and arbitrary government. The proprietors wrote from London to their governor: "We require that you ratify no law that diminishes or alters any of the powers granted to us in our charter from the crown."

The assembly presented grievances on the conveying of land, and appointed a committee to meet a committee of the upper house (representing the proprietors), to consider the form of granting land and a system of government, but no committee from the upper house appeared.

The proprietors insisted upon their own interpretation of their powers and kept the terms of disposal of land alterable at their pleasure. There was continued impotency, misrule, disaffection and opposition.

Rivers [126] wrote: "We cannot refrain from remarking that the 'true and absolute lords' of the immense region of Carolina, with all its mines, quarries and fisheries, whose objects were declared to be the diffusion of the Christian religion among those who knew not God—must now have appeared to the colonists to have abandoned their dignity and best policy, for sordid calculations. Instead of the Gospel, the Indians were offered only glass beads; and the colonists, though needy and still struggling to maintain themselves, were required, by preparing cargoes of timber 'at moderate rates,' to repay, with 10 per cent interest, what advances had been made them. Unless punctual payment was made, the settlers should expect no more ammunition or fish-hooks, blankets or provisions. At the same time, the first set of fundamental constitutions was repudiated by the lords, and repeated amendments with essential alterations substituted, to the detriment of the colonists, and despite charter requirements, numerous laws were enacted without the concurrence of the people, and to which they were expected to yield unmurmuring obedience."

John Locke, the eminent philosopher, secretary of the council, had framed this fantastic constitution, said to have been inspired by Lord Shaftsbury. Locke's ideas of landownership underwent a radical change during succeeding years, probably influenced by the atrocious terms of that constitution. Twenty-one years after the issue of the constitution, Locke published his renowned *Essay on Civil Government,* an excerpt from which is given in the Epilogue herein.

This constitution was abandoned within three years after publication of Locke's essay, but the ill effects of absentee landholding which it created continued.

Its interest today lies in the fact that it reveals the type of society which Whigs, the most liberal of the governing classes in England, would have established in America, if they had not been defeated by the irrepressible and stubborn realities of life on the frontier. [10]

And, as the Beards say, the realities of the frontier did defeat the grandiose plan of the proprietors. Judge Henry A. M. Smith, writing in the Carolina Historical Magazine, on "The Baronies of South Carolina," states that the land was not laid out nor taken up in squares, nor were seigniories or baronies of twelve thousand acres laid out for the proprietors, landgraves and caciques, but cites sixteen baronies, of which the largest, for twelve thousand acres, was for the Earl of Shaftsbury.

The value of the swamp and river lands along the coast was unknown, until, in 1693, a ship from Madagascar (undoubtedly one of the many pirate ships that rendezvoused about that island, and frequently harbored at Charles Town) put into Charles Town with a bag of rice aboard. The rice was planted in the low land and produced a bountiful crop. Rice became a staple commodity, which caused increased importation of slaves. Cotton production was unimportant until Eli Whitney invented the cotton gin in 1792, resulting in the establishment of cotton factories in England.

Popular ferment continued regarding the tenure of land, payment of land rents and naturalization of Huguenots. "We part with our lands only on our own terms" reiterated their lordships. "And," retorted the people, "we consider your deeds invalid, because only some of you have set your hands and seals thereto."

Discontent in the colony was so acute that Governor Smith advised the proprietors to send over one of their own number, whereupon they sent John Archdale, a pious and intelligent Quaker, who had obtained a proprietorship through purchase of Lady Berkeley's share. The assembly solicited him to remit the arrears of land rent, which now was a grievous burden upon all the people.

After many months, Archdale consented to remit arrears of rents, provided the remaining debts were secured, the town fortified by means of taxes and prompt payment of land rents was promised in future.

Land rents were to be held at a penny an acre, or the value

thereof in indigo, cotton, rice, silk, peas, beef or barreled pork. In case of non-payment of the rents, the receiver could distrain—the land to revert to the proprietors if payment was delayed seven years.

New settlers were to be exempt from land rent for five years. The sale price was fixed at £20 per thousand acres (about 10¢ per acre), with an annual land rent in addition of 12d per hundred acres. The land was not revertible until non-payment for twenty-one years.

After thirty-five years of contention, the fifth and last revised set of the "unalterable" constitutions was submitted to the assembly. It omitted mention of manors and leetmen. It still created landgraves and caciques, with the hereditary right of succession to the upper house of the assembly, and continued to proclaim that land was the foundation of "all power and dominion" in Carolina.

With these constitutions, six engrossed certificates with blank spaces for filling in names of new landgraves, and eight for caciques, were sent to be distributed to those who would be the most influential in behalf of the proprietors. The latter complained that settlers took up more land than they would cultivate and then complained of a want of neighbors. At the same time, members of the assembly, in an address to the proprietors, complained: "Such great tracts of land are permitted to be taken up in one entire piece to the great prejudice of the colony and the inhabitants thereof. We request that in future no more than a thousand acres may be taken up in one piece, which would much strengthen this settlement; that your lordships will condescend to grant the freedom of whale fishing for twenty-one years; and intercede for taking the British import tax off of rice, turpentine, pitch and tar imported from this colony."

Edward Randolph, who had been sent by the Lords of Trade in London to report on conditions in the colonies, reported from Charles Town, in 1699: "There are but few settlers in this province, the lords having taken up vast tracts of land for their own, which prevents peopling the place and makes them less capable to preserve themselves. The civil government differs from that in other provinces. There are not above eleven hun-

368 The Carolinas

dred families, English and French here, and five thousand slaves; with four Negroes to one white man. The inhabitants complain that during the French War the proprietors never sent them a barrel of powder or a pound of lead to help them, and his majesty did not send any soldiers."

Of the Huguenots who came to America, some preferred the warm climate of South Carolina. Grants of land on land rent were made them late in the 1600's, and within two years they acquired more than fifty thousand acres. After being admitted to full citizenship, they became influential citizens.

Towards the end of the seventeenth century, four or five grants were often made, through fraud in head-rights, against the arrival of one indented servant, and large tracts near settlements were likewise obtained by speculators. The proprietors directed that, thereafter, no more than five hundred acres should be granted to any one person, except to landgraves and caciques.

England declared war on Spain in 1701—the War of the Spanish Succession—which continued thirteen years. The Carolina assembly enacted an import and export tax for defense, but the proprietors revoked it; upon which the colonists declared they would hazard conquest by the Spaniards rather than acknowledge the right of the proprietors to repeal their laws. However, the following year, the assembly voted an expedition of ten vessels and 350 men by sea, and a land force of a hundred white men and five hundred Indian allies. "The encouragement to the soldiers being free plunder and a share of all captives to be sold into slavery."

Threats to have the proprietors' charter annulled were met by expressed doubt as to whether it might not involve "an infringement on the privileges of the proprietors," who were peers of the realm; consequently action was withheld.

A protest signed by 150 inhabitants in June, 1705, cited: "These proprietary monarchs have their eyes upon the land rents; their concern is of interest; they are step-fathers and strangers in the government, and they have shown it, for their ears are stopt and shut to the complaints of their oppressed people; they govern them by sub-tyrants and connive at their tyrannies." [134]

A settlement of French Huguenots was made between the Neuse and Trent Rivers in 1707.

For inducing Huguenots to settle in Carolina, Rene Petit and Jacob Grinard were each granted four thousand acres, [21] on a land rent basis.

Baron Christopher de Graffenried, who had been made a landgrave, and Lewis Mitchell, engaged to found a settlement of six hundred Germans and Swiss at Newbern, on the Neuse River. Each family was to have 250 acres, paying 2d per acre rent annually after five years.

The town of Beaufort, named for the Duke of Beaufort, who had become a proprietor, was ordered laid out into lots in 1710. Huguenots, Swiss and Germans were among the early settlers.

Carolina was that year divided into North and South Carolina. Taxes for extraordinary purposes were raised from land, improvements and personal property, and generally from export and import taxes.

The price of land was increased to £20 per hundred acres, with an annual land rent of 10s in addition, with all minerals found thereon reserved by the lords proprietors. Some planters had a thousand cattle (two hundred was a common herd), swine in great numbers, grains, vegetables and fruits in abundance.

Encroachment of the whites on the hunting and fishing grounds of the Tuscarora Indians, the most powerful tribe in North Carolina, on the shores of Pamlico Sound and along the Roanoke River, caused an attack upon the settlers in 1711, which continued three days. Three hundred whites were killed. A force of fifty whites and a thousand Indian allies was sent 250 miles overland from Charles Town to the Neuse River, where they attacked the Indian fort and killed, it is recorded, fourteen hundred Indians.

The North Carolina assembly voted £4,000 for defense, and to build three forts. Appeal for help was made to Virginia and South Carolina. Virginia voted £4,000 to assist, provided North Carolina would mortgage to it a strip of land along the northern boundary of the province.

The Tuscaroras and allied Indian tribes were so nearly destroyed that the remnant went to New York, where they joined the Five, which then became the Six, Nations. This was the first important Indian war in the South and the worst single Indian disaster experienced by the English east of the Alleghenies. [112]

During the forty-two years preceding 1712, the Carolina people drove from office six of their fourteen governors. During the same period, there were two rebellions, and constant unrest. Because of irregularities, the proprietors closed the land office in 1712. Many squatters settled on land, and validity of titles was disputed. [12]

A vicious war broke out in 1715 between the whites and the Yamassee Indians, in which the Indians complained of the whites seizing their land, fraud in the purchase of peltries, sale of intoxicating liquors to the Indians, and seducing their women.

The agency of the province, which had been established in London, getting no response from the proprietors for help in the war, had an address sent to the king, which was referred to the Lord Commissioners of Trade. They gave the opinion that Carolina, being a proprietary territory, its government should be surrendered to the crown, if the crown must protect it.

Sir George Carteret, in London, then palatine, wrote the board: "We, the proprietors of Carolina, find that we are utterly unable to afford our colony suitable assistance, and unless his majesty will graciously interpose we can foresee nothing but utter destruction in those parts."

The assembly proposed to raise money by selling to settlers the land near Port Royal, which the settlers, at great loss of life, had taken from the Yamassee Indians. But the lords proprietors laid claim to the conquered territory, and sent orders that fifteen baronies, each of twelve thousand acres, be laid out for their private use in the Yamassee territory, with no more land to be granted to any person whatsoever.

The assembly having offered a bounty for importation of white indented servants, the deputy-governor, in 1716, informed the assembly that he had bought thirty Highland Scots, rebels captured in the Scottish rebellion, and wished for power to purchase more. The assembly sanctioned the purchase, but wished no more "until we see how these will behave themselves."

Attacks by Indians on the whites continued in 1717. Many settlers abandoned their farms, and upon returning to them after the war, found all their lands in possession of speculators. Upon seeking redress, by law, many settlers and their attorneys were arrested, imprisoned for weeks, and then heavily fined. The wrath of the land speculators fell upon all who opposed their schemes. [140]

At the first meeting of the assembly, in 1717, Governor Johnson inveighed "against addresses being sent from the colony to England, as such were disrespectful, unjustifiable and impolitic." The governor asked the assembly to order a rent-roll made for the benefit of the proprietors, saying, "If you will not do this they will pursue other methods to recover their just land rents. If you will look over their charter you will find them to be your masters."

The proprietors had, in 1709, if not earlier, limited to 640 acres the acreage to be granted to any one man, other than grants to landgraves or caciques. They complained of the many exorbitant and illegal grants, and ordered that all who desired land must apply to the proprietary board in London. Three years later this was revoked and grants, not exceeding five hundred acres, were made as they had been ten years earlier. Abuses continued, and the proprietors in 1718 revoked this privilege, and again required that application for land must be made to the board in London. [140]

The assembly laid a tariff tax of 10 per cent on imports of British manufactures. This caused threats in England of prosecution against the charter, if the act were not repealed.

The proprietors in 1719 wrote to Governor Johnson: "The lords proprietors' right of conferring and repealing laws was so particularly a privilege, granted to us by the crown, that we can never recede from it. We name such persons as we think fit to be of the council with you. You are commanded hereby to dissolve the assembly."

The assembly appealed to the king as follows: "All the inhabitants of the province are convinced that no human power but your majesty's can protect them, and fervently desire that this once flourishing province may be added to those under your protection."

Yet the charter was not revoked. A committee of the British Parliament appointed to consider the malfeasance of all the charter governments in America, and to prepare a bill for resuming their grants, found various personal claims and conflicting influences and hesitated, even for great national advantages, to subvert by its vote the vested interests of the lords proprietors.

The people became greatly incensed at the arbitrary actions of the proprietors in monopolizing land, and complained, among other things, about their refusal to part with an acre of their immense uncultivated domains to settlers, against the expressed design of the charter. Especially so, after the colony had expended thousands of pounds sterling to bring several hundred immigrants from Ireland. These immigrants were each promised two hundred acres of land, which upon arrival was refused them, and they now must starve in Carolina, or beg the means of returning to Ireland.

The colonists asked: "Have the proprietors at any time helped the colony in its distress, beat back the Spaniards from St. Augustine, or quelled an Indian horde? And after all these provocations if we choose to rebel, and throw your vaunted absolutism to the winds, where are your forces to suppress our revolt?"

The people in general were prejudiced against the lords proprietors to such degree that it had grown almost dangerous to say anything in their favor. Governor Johnson, in addressing the assembly, tried to frighten and subdue the colonists by saying that if the charter were revoked it would also cause revocation of land titles made under it to the colonists.

The assembly formed itself into a convention, and by acclamation of the people, proclaimed James Moore as governor, in the name of his majesty, the King of England. This was subsequently approved by the crown.

Disturbances became so pronounced it was proposed that the British Parliament appropriate funds, with which the king could buy the land from the lords proprietors. Carteret, who was one of the eight proprietors, and at that time palatine, refused to sell his share. The other seven consented and, in 1729, were paid £50,000 for their shares; whereupon the proprietary government ceased, and the two Carolinas became two crown provinces, each with a governor appointed by the king.

Carteret retained a one-eighth undivided share in the land in the two Carolinas and in Georgia and the western region until 1744, when he relinquished all claims in return for the grant of a strip of land in North Carolina, forty miles wide, extending along the North Carolina northern boundary, "from the Atlantic to the Pacific."

John, Lord Carteret (Earl of Granville), son and heir of Sir George, inherited this land, which he utterly neglected. His grant being confiscated by the new state during the American Revolution, he strove until his death to re-establish his claim. [169] Holding claim to the land, but not using it, and in no probability having any intention of ever using it, he brought suit to eject settlers, who were cultivating some of it to maintain themselves and their families.

His claim was disallowed by the United States Supreme Court. Consequently, the £7,143 sterling which Sir George was offered and rejected eighty-three years previously, with interest during all that time, was lost to the Carteret estate.

To diminish as much as possible the remaining area of land which the crown had purchased of the proprietors, the governor, prior to actual transfer, secretly disposed of land on whatever land rent terms he could find takers for; even issuing deeds in blank. [5] He granted four hundred thousand acres to the commissioners who ran the boundary line between North Carolina and Virginia.

The large grants to landgraves and caciques were often not surveyed, or recorded in the land office; consequently, it was difficult to determine how much land had been granted and how much the crown was entitled to receive in the purchase. After the purchase, the attorney-general and solicitor-general in London declared, in 1730, that the grants to the landgraves and caciques were illegal, because they did not designate the exact location of the land conveyed.

A court decision in Charles Town held that a landgrave grant indefinite as to time and place, and not taken possession of during the lifetime of the original grantee, was, nevertheless, valid, and the title of the succeeding holders good in law. [140]

Following the revolution in Carolina in 1719, the proprietors closed the land office and it remained closed until two years after the crown had acquired the land. Meanwhile, as population increased, holders of old grants began to seize all the desirable land and new colonists suffered from inability to get land. It was afterwards estimated that, while the land office was closed, about eight hundred thousand acres of the most valuable land were granted by the lords proprietors to landgraves and caciques. [2]

A law afterwards passed guaranteed the validity of all grants made by the lords proprietors, notwithstanding any defects in describing the land, provided some part of it had been actually surveyed by a sworn surveyor. Practically all grants made to landgraves and caciques were thus confirmed, because a large part of the province had been surveyed between 1720 and 1730, and two years' additional time was allowed to complete the surveys, which led to great frauds. [140]

After the purchase of the land by the crown, land continued to be subject to the payment of rents, with the rents payable to the King of England. The arrest of a man in North Carolina, in 1737, for non-payment of land rent caused a mob of five hundred to join in "cursing his majesty, and uttering many rebellious speeches." After forcing release of the prisoner, threats of vengeance were made against any official who dared to demand land rents.

The limit of royal grants at that time was 640 acres. The crown recommended the passage of a law compelling all grantees at once to settle on and cultivate their lands. It was also urged that future grants be restricted to fifty acres for each member of a household, including indented servants and slaves.

This was wisely aimed to discourage speculation in unused land, and to attract settlers but, in anticipation of this, many old settlers who were already land-poor, obtained some six hundred thousand acres. By avaricious grabbing of land by those who could not use it, there was not a thousand acres within a hundred miles of Charles Town, or within twenty miles of a navigable stream, not already taken possession of.[a] New settlers were obliged to locate on undesirable and uneconomically situated land.

Henry McCullough, a London merchant, and his associates, held patents to 1,200,000 acres in the Piedmont section of North Carolina, free of rent for the first twenty-one years. In 1739 the king sent him to Carolina, to adjust the land rent problem in the two colonies. He antagonized everybody and, during the seven years he was there, he accomplished nothing. [12]

Grants were made in 1744 at 3s sterling or 4s proclamation money for a hundred acres; the rate established in North Carolina by the royal government. [12]

The assembly of South Carolina endeavored in 1745 to get a bill passed requiring holders of township lands to cultivate them, on penalty of forfeiture. But the council, protecting the speculators holding unused land, induced the assembly to desist. [140]

The following year the assembly claimed that there had been great abuse in granting land, and unwarranted fees charged. The settlers demurred at paying the land rents. [5]

The council, prior to 1760, was for the most part composed of leading merchants and importers of Charles Town. Representing, as they did, the creditor class, they allied themselves with the crown officials, in opposition to the planter element in the assembly. [140]

By 1771 the assembly superseded the council as the potent influence on legislation. Because of the unsettled conditions in the colony, the king in 1773 directed that the land office in South Carolina be again closed. During the remainder of the Colonial Period there was but little effort made to check fraudulent land grants, but all the best land already had been granted, or otherwise grabbed.

The large grants to the landgraves and caciques were mostly in South Carolina. There were very few large estates in North Carolina; the inhabitants there being mostly small landholders. Land being readily obtainable, the poor whites, including re-

[a]Pub. Rec.

leased indented servants from the southern section and from Virginia, had a chance to improve their condition by getting land.

At the outbreak of the American Revolution, the North Carolina Declaration of Rights, which asserted that the land belongs to the people, was incorporated in the state constitution, and all royal land rents were abolished.

Instead of paying land rents to the British king, the settlers now paid taxes levied by the new state on all property.

Since the constitution recognized that the land belongs to all the people, it would have been wiser to have collected from the private users the annual rental value of the land for the public treasury, instead of, as was done, and still is, levying taxes on privately owned improvements and personal property. Levies on capital and labor are suppressive taxes on industrial development, home-owning, and creation of wealth.

18

Georgia

A LARGE part of the land in Georgia was within the grant made by Charles II, in 1663, to the eight Carolina lords proprietors.

Sir Robert Montgomery in 1717 was granted by these proprietors all the land between the Savannah and Altamaha Rivers. He published a pamphlet to attract settlers, proposing districts or allotments, twenty miles square, [50] but apparently nothing came of it. Spaniards objected to the English settling in Georgia, claiming it as Spanish territory.

In 1729 the crown bought of the Carolina proprietors a seven-eighths undivided part of the Carolina-Georgia grant.

General James Oglethorpe, a member of the British Parliament, became interested in relieving the distress of the many persons of respectable families who were confined in prison in England as insolvent debtors.

Upon a petition by him and other influential persons, George II, in 1732, made a grant of land to a board of trustees for the purpose of establishing a colony where these unfortunates and others might find homes; and at the same time be a military outpost against the Spaniards.

This grant was for land lying between the rivers just named, running west in two parallel lines from the sources thereof, extending in a direct line to the South Sea (Pacific Ocean), with all islands lying within twenty leagues (60 miles) of the Atlantic coast. Annual land rent was 4s per hundred acres, payable to the king.

Contributions amounting, it has been stated, to £200,000, including £10,000 by Parliament, were made to promote the object. This was the only American colony which apparently did not emanate from a desire by the promoters for personal profit through land ownership.

Georgia was granted a charter as an independent colony. Oglethorpe was appointed governor and, in November, 1732, with 130 men, women and children, sailed from Gravesend in a chartered vessel, the "Anne," of two hundred tons. Included were necessary artisans and equipment for a pioneer settlement.

They arrived at Charles Town after a two months' voyage, where they were cordially received, and were recognized as forming a protection to the Carolina settlers against attacks by the Spaniards and Indians from the south. The Carolina assembly presented them with one hundred head of cattle, also hogs, and a barrel of rice.

Proceeding to the Savannah River, where they found the Indians friendly, they entered into a treaty with an Indian chief.

On a high bluff they cleared the land of heavy timber and erected tents. Streets, a public square and forty home lots, each sixty by ninety feet, were laid out. Erection of the first house, of clapboards, and a palisade, were begun that day, to become the future delightful city of Savannah.

Fifty acres were allotted to each family by tail male (inheritance thereof limited to male descendants), of which five acres were for a garden. Allotments of outlying land were limited to tracts of five hundred acres each. Augusta was founded five years afterwards.

More than one thousand colonists were sent to Georgia by the trustees, while hundreds of other immigrants, including thirty-eight Salzburgers, came at their own expense. There were Swiss, Germans, Moravians, Portuguese Jews, Italians, Piedmontese, Highlanders and English, and some settlers from New England. All were allotted land along the river. [119]

The qualification for a voter was fifty acres in his district; for a representative five hundred acres anywhere in the province. This latter permitted legislation by land speculators, who soon became possessed of large areas, to the detriment of future settlers. [169]

The charter had reserved a perpetual annual land rent of 4*s* per hundred acres payable to the king; and the colonial government added 20*s* per hundred acres for revenue for its support, the rent beginning ten years after date of each allotment of land. But on town lots, the rent was 2*s* per fifty acres, with a purchase-price of 5*s* proclamation money. For large tracts, rentals were reduced, which encouraged speculative holding of land unused. With land to be had in other colonies at less cost, the legislature, ten years after the initial settlement, declared that land cost should be reduced to attract settlers.

The trustees in London proposed to the king repeal of the royal land rent, so that land could be granted on more favorable terms. The Board of Trade in London, representing the king, favored a reduction from 4*s* to 2*s*, which was adopted, to begin at the end of the tenth year after allotment. [12] No rent roll was ever prepared for the crown and apparently no attempt was ever made to collect land rent for the king.

Complaint was made later that the colony was suffering through Oglethorpe's selfishness, greed, despotism and fantastic pursuits of social chimeras. [169] The probabilities are that these complaints arose from his restricting the greed of some of the colonists for more land, to be held by them on speculation, free of rent during the ten years' no-rent period—later to be sold by the speculators at increased prices, created by the demand for land by the influx of settlers.

The Cherokee and Creek Indians, who inhabited that region, were amiable until the outbreak of the French and Indian War, when the Cherokees, incensed at the appropriation of their lands by the whites, plundered and killed some of the settlers.

The charter had prohibited slavery and liquors for the first twenty years but in the nineteenth, the trustees surrendered the charter and Georgia became a crown colony, with a royal governor appointed by the king, and a council and assembly. Negro slavery and liquors were then permitted. Land tenure was "enlarged and extended to an absolute inheritance, or private ownership in fee, and alienation of land was permitted."

Thirty years after the first settlement, there had been granted 546,770 acres, in addition to 89,400 acres granted along the Carolina border by the governor of South Carolina. [12]

The population, five years after that, is placed at fifty thousand, perhaps one-half slave. [48] As this would represent an average of only twenty-five acres for each white person, no doubt large tracts held by speculators had not been registered.

By the treaty between Great Britain and France at the close of the French and Indian War in 1763, the western limit of British sovereignty was fixed at the Mississippi River, and that river, instead of the South Sea, became the western limit of all royal colonial land grants that had been made. At the same time, the king extended the Georgia grant to the Florida border, and forbade white settlers locating west of the Appalachian Mountains.

Population in Georgia increased slowly until after the American Revolution, when the new state took possession of the unallotted land. In 1786 it granted to one Webb and associates 165,000 acres.

Georgia claimed all the land between its present western boundary and the Mississippi River, details of the sale of which, through bribery of members of the legislature, and resulting frauds, are related in the chapter on the Gulf Region.

Within the present area of Georgia, the state, between 1803 and 1831, distributed by lottery 22,404,250 acres, in 130,000 lots, averaging 172.3 acres each, but only about three-fourths of them were taken up.

19

The Gulf Region

DE SOTO'S expedition of several hundred Spaniards, which explored from Florida to west of the Mississippi River, was an unsuccessful quest for gold and added nothing to geographical knowledge, or to the advancement of civilization, but left a legacy of half-breeds and disease.

After his people departed, in 1542, one and a third centuries passed before another white foot trod the regions of De Soto's explorations. The French from Canada, learning from the Indians of a large river in the west, Louis Joliet, a young American-born French fur-trader, and Jacques Marquette, a Jesuit priest, thirty-five years of age, with five French companions, and a number of Indian canoeists, were in 1673 sent from Green Bay, Wisconsin, in search of the river. Finding it, they went as far south on it as the Arkansas River. Learning there of Indian warfare farther down the river, they returned north; having travelled twenty-five hundred miles.

Seven years later, Rene Robert de la Salle, aged thirty-seven, of a wealthy French family, floated and paddled down the river from Mackinac and reported having reached the Gulf. Thereupon he proclaimed possession of the entire region for the King of France and named it Louisiana, in honor of Louis XIV.

Mark Twain, in his *Life on the Mississippi,* wrote: "Then, to the admiration of the savages, the Frenchmen set up a cross with the Arms of France upon it, and took possession of the whole country for the king, the cool fashion of the time; while the priest consecrated the robbery with a hymn, and they drew from the simple sons of the forest fealty to Louis over the sea. No one even smiled at this colossal irony."

La Salle returned to Fort St. Louis, where he had left Tonti, an Italian companion, in charge, and then left for France, by way of Quebec, to report his discovery.

In a frigate and three other ships, with 280 colonists, La Salle returned to the Gulf in 1685, but unable to find the entrance to the Mississippi, he disembarked in Matagorda Bay, Texas. He had lost three vessels and the other one returned to France.

Some of his men mutinied and killed him near Navasota, on the Brazos River. The colony perished, except seven who made their way to Canada. This exploit, which was long before the English had any knowledge of the Mississippi Valley, was the basis of the French claim to the Mississippi River and all its tributaries.

Tonti, with fifty Canadians and Indians, went down the river that year in search of La Salle, but, not finding him, returned to the mouth of the Arkansas River where he established a post.

Pierre La Moyne d'Iberville, a native of Quebec, with other Canadians, had fought the English in Newfoundland, and had part in the capture by the French of Pemaquid in Maine. He promoted a French expedition to the Gulf coast thirteen years after La Salle, and sailed from France with the "Badine," of thirty guns, the "Marir," and two harbor boats of forty tons each.

On board were his brothers, Bienville and Sauvolle, and two hundred colonists, mostly Canadians who had been fighting with the French forces in Europe; also some women and children. They were joined at Santo Domingo by a French warship of fifty-two guns. [119]

Arriving at Pensacola, he found three hundred Spaniards from Vera Cruz had established a battery there, commanded by General Roalli, who claimed the entire country bordering on the Gulf. Roalli planned to drive out the French but concluded they were too strong for him to attack.

A fortification was erected by the French at Biloxi, with a garrison of seventy-six men and boys.

There appeared an armed English ship of twelve guns, which had been sent by Dr. Daniel Coxe, of England, that inveterate monopolist of land in New Jersey. Coxe claimed the Mississippi region as part of the defunct Heath English grant of the Carolinas, extending from the Atlantic to the Pacific, an interest in which Coxe had bought as a gamble. The French dissuaded the English commander by asserting the French claim to all the land, by prior discovery and settlement.

This incident prompted the French to explore the Mississippi. Proceeding there in small boats, manned by crews under Bienville, then eighteen years of age, they advanced up the river, and at about fifty miles from its mouth established a fort. At about 175 miles from the mouth they came to an Indian village (presumably near present Baton Rouge), where they were told of the La Salle expedition of seventeen years previously. [169]

D'Iberville, with two frigates, sailed for France the same year, but soon returned from there with instructions to investigate and report on the natural and agricultural resources of the country, including the propagation of silkworms and buffalo. Explorations were made throughout what is now Louisiana, Arkansas, Mississippi, Alabama and Tennessee.

French missionaries from Canada, and other French voyagers, were traversing the country between the Great Lakes and the Gulf coast to such extent that, together with the French forts, the French controlled the Mississippi River and all its tributaries. Search was made for Spaniards, but none were found to be in that region. [169]

Not until 1700 did the French, under D'Iberville, found a permanent colony. D'Iberville made frequent trips between France and Louisiana and was appointed commander-in-chief of the "Colony of the Mississippi." But three years afterwards, while on an expedition against the British, he died of yellow fever in Havana. Bienville had been, and continued, in actual command of the colony. [169]

Twenty-three girls, of "spotless chastity, and industrious," sent from France, arrived in 1704, and within a few days were all married to the men in the colony. Bienville asked the home government to send thirty additional marriageable women, to form home ties for the Canadian men, who were roaming the country for Indian women. In due course, twelve arrived, but they were so homely only two of them promptly found husbands, the remainder, as officially reported, would likely remain unmarried for quite a time. The report begged that in future, when exporting women to Louisiana, more consideration should be given to beauty and less to chastity; otherwise the men would prefer the Indian women. [119]

The French built Fort St. Louis de la Mobile, on Mobile Bay, which was the seat of government for nine years and, in 1711, they founded Mobile.

King Louis XIV granted to Anthony Crozat, a French merchant, the exclusive right for fifteen years to mine and trade in the French territory, with the further right to appropriate land for actual use, but not to be held unused; also the right to import Negroes from Africa to be sold as slaves. [169]

By the treaty of Utrecht, in 1713, the Mississippi River watershed was recognized as a French possession. La Mothe Cadillac arrived from France that year, with a commission as governor of the colony, to succeed Bienville, and served for a brief period.

The king in 1716 ordered that trading-posts be established at Natchez and at Fort Toulouse, in Alabama. Several forts were ordered along the main river, beginning with one among the Natchez Indians, with eighty soldiers; also it was ordered that salt-makers be sent to Louisiana, who, after working there three years, were to receive land; and that one hundred hospital girls be sent annually to increase the population.

The king presented Bienville with the Island of Come, not as a fief, but in villanage tenure.

Five years after Crozat received his grant, he found the burden of it too great and relinquished it. A new grant was made, to the Company of the West and, subsequently, to the Company of the Indies. This company, with a capital of a hundred thousand livres, and John Law as director, was in 1717 given for a period of twenty-five years a monopoly of commerce in the region, and of the Indian trade in beaver skins from Canada.

It had power to make grants of land, dig mines, establish forts, levy troops, make munitions, appoint public officials, build vessels of war and churches, and pay the clergy under the ecclesiastical jurisdiction of Quebec. It was to transport to the colony six thousand whites, including convicts from French prisons, and three thousand Negroes.

It made a grant of twelve miles square on the Arkansas River to John Law, on which two hundred Germans settled. Numerous other grants of land were made, some as far up as Natchez, and colonists were sent to inhabit them.

Bienville was appointed commandant-general and, in 1718, laid the foundation of New Orleans; the same year that the Spaniards, crossing the Rio Grande, founded the Alamo Mission at San Antonio. The French company sent troops and men and women —voluntary and involuntary—emigrants. [169]

Bienville complained that these colonists were undesirable; that he needed carpenters and laborers; the same complaint that was made at the founding of Virginia by the English, more than a century before, and by the Swedish governor on the Delaware.

The peaceful acquisition of Pensacola from the Spaniards was urged by Bienville in 1719, as affording a better harbor. But the Spaniards, asserting ownership through the bull of Pope Alexander VI, two and a quarter centuries previously, refused to part with it; whereupon Bienville took it by force. It was retaken by the Spaniards and recaptured by the French, but four years afterwards was, by treaty, returned to Spain. [169]

The cultivation of rice, indigo and tobacco had begun, but the whites could not endure the work and it was given over to Negro slaves. Lumber was exported to the West Indies.

To protect its monopoly, the company issued an edict in 1720, forbidding any vessel, under penalty of confiscation, to enter any port in the colony. Inhabitants were required to buy and sell commodities at the company stores, at arbitrarily fixed prices. Economically, the whites and blacks were on the same basis.

The company developed some trade on the Guinea and Hindoostan coasts [5], but greater development was hampered by climate, malaria and monopoly. [169]

Through wild speculation in its stock in Paris, and entanglement in French finances, the company became famous as the Mississippi Bubble. The bubble collapsed in 1720, causing thousands of people of all classes, who had participated in the widespread speculation, to lose their life's savings.

The commandant at the fort near Natchez, in 1728, wanted some land on which there was an Indian settlement. The Indian chief objected and called a council of surrounding tribes, who determined to forthwith exterminate the French garrison and colony. More than two hundred French were killed. Three years later the French, with an army of 650 soldiers and 350 Choctaw Indian allies, attacked the Indians at Natchez, and returned to New Orleans with 427 captives of the Natchez tribe, who were sold as slaves in Santo Domingo.

The Indians who had escaped capture fled to the Red River, where they made attacks on the French settlements, in which ninety-two Indians were killed. This ended the existence of that tribe. Governor Perrier caused four Indian men and three women prisoners to be publicly burned to death in the street in New Orleans, in 1732. The following year Bienville again became governor.

In 1763: Spain ceded East and West Florida to England in return for Havana, which the English had captured. The same day, France ceded to England all the French territory east of Pearl River and the right of free navigation on the Mississippi River, and ceded Louisiana to Spain without defining any north or west boundaries.

To encourage settlement and improvement of the country along the river, the Spanish governor the following year offered small tracts of land to families that would settle upon them. The families were, within three years, to build and keep in order a levee and a road along the river banks, which was the beginning of the levee system.

General Thaddeus Lyman, of Connecticut, who had served in the Colonial Army during the French and Indian War, spent several years in London prior to 1772, endeavoring to obtain a grant of a large area of land in America. He reported at that early day that all the land in Connecticut had been privately appropriated, and he applied for 150,000 acres along the Mississippi River, between the Gulf and the Ohio River. He did not succeed in that, but was given twenty thousand acres in West

Florida, between Pensacola and the Louisiana border. Many others of influence each received grants of from four thousand to twenty-five thousand acres in the same region.

Land grants of five thousand to forty thousand acres each, aggregating 594,000 acres in East Florida, were, in 1773, held by thirty-five titled Englishmen[a]—held, not for use by them, but for the despicable purpose of exacting a purchase price of future settlers.

At the time of the American Revolution, the British government made efforts to attract settlers to their Florida possessions by making grants of land, at an annual land rent of a half-penny per acre, to begin two years after date of the grant. Many Tories migrated there from the American colonies and, being beneficiaries of British land grants, remained loyal to the British crown.

Carondelet, the Spanish governor of Louisiana, to encourage immigration of royalists fleeing from the French Revolution, granted to Baron de Bastrop twelve square leagues (36 square miles) on the Washita (Quachita) River; to Marquis de Maison Rouge, thirty thousand acres; to De Lassus and St. Vrain, ten thousand square arpents. These grants were not settled upon by the grantees. Most of the land in Louisiana was held in large tracts by French aristocrats who were absentee holders. [118] All land so held by individual grantees meant that the United States would receive just that much less land for the public domain when it purchased Louisiana from France. Individual Americans had to later buy the land from these French holders.

The De Bastrop land was afterwards bought by Stephen Girard of Philadelphia and Edward Livingston and Robert Goelet of New York. Because of fault in title, Congress refused for years to confirm, but, in 1854, validated the title. [21]

Great Britain recognized the independence of the United States on January 20, 1783, and the same year ceded Florida to Spain. Twelve years afterwards, Spain sold West Florida to France.

Georgia claimed, under the Oglethorpe charter from King George II, all the territory between 31° and 35°N. lat. between

[a]Dartmouth Manuscripts

the Atlantic and Pacific Oceans; subsequently limited by treaty
with France to the Mississippi River on the west. The Spaniards
had fortifications at different points, and prevented American
occupation of it. Notwithstanding, the Georgia legislature, in
1785, organized a government for the territory between the
present western boundary of Georgia and the Mississippi River,
and offered lands for sale.

Secretary Knox reported this as, "dictated by the avaricious
desire to possess the fertile lands possessed by the Indians." In
1789, members of the Georgia legislature, being bribed, authorized, and Governor Telfair approved, a conditional sale of the
larger part of this domain.

In the middle counties of Mississippi, 5,000,000 acres were sold
to the South Carolina Yazoo Company for about $60,000. In the
northern counties of Mississippi 7,000,000 acres were sold to the
Virginia Yazoo Company for about $92,000. In the northern
counties of Alabama 3,500,000 acres were sold to the Tennessee
Yazoo Company for about $46,000. All these represented grabs
at a trifle more than 1¢ per acre.

Georgia, Spain and the Indians each claimed this land. President Washington, who was then engaged in endeavoring to settle
the boundaries between them, fearing complications from these
extraordinary sales, issued a proclamation against them.

The Tennessee Company disregarded this and sent agents,
speculators and settlers down the Tennessee River to Muscle
Shoals, where they located on an island and built a fort, intending to sell land situated along the river.

A band of Cherokee Indians, organized by William Blount
(afterwards governor of Tennessee and United States Senator),
who was promoting land speculations in his state, to stifle competition destroyed the buildings by fire. Other efforts were made
to colonize, but were defeated by the Cherokees and Chickasaws
and the Federal government.

The South Carolina Yazoo Company, attempting to colonize
its lands, raised troops in Kentucky and prepared to attack the
Spaniards at Natchez. The Spanish Minister to the United States
protested, and President Washington sent a military force which
arrested the leaders. [119]

All these companies presently failed to make payments due to Georgia, and the state legislature rescinded the sales; which brought charges of swindling innocent purchasers. President Washington was abused by the speculators and denounced as a tyrant.

But more scandalous Yazoo operations occurred six years later, in 1795, when the treaty between the United States and Spain became known, by which the former acquired from the latter an area of land a hundred miles wide from the eastern boundary of Alabama to the Mississippi River, a distance of about 350 miles, between 31° and 32°28′ N. The Georgia "Yazoo" land frauds, the most notorious and widespread of the early American land gambles, were then promoted.

By bribery of members, the Georgia legislature again sold vast areas of Yazoo lands to speculators in each of the hastily-organized groups: Georgia Company, Tennessee Company, Georgia-Mississippi Company and the Upper-Mississippi Company.

These sales comprised 21,500,000 acres for $500,000, or 2⅓¢ per acre. Later surveys showed the actual acreage to be 35,000,000 acres, at less than 1½¢ per acre.

Shares or scrip in these early land companies were offered to the public. Philadelphia, New York, Hartford and Boston were the principal centers, each having its own "deal" and selling its shares throughout a wide area. The purchasers extended from Lake Erie to the Gulf of Mexico and from Maine to the Mississippi.

The Duc de la Rochefoucauld-Liancourt, the French philanthropist, visiting America at the height of this speculation, wrote while in Boston: "The Yazoo agents opened a kind of office to which purchasers of land flocked in such crowds that those gents, taking advantage of this inconceivable infatuation, raised the price each day, often twice a day, for the purpose of more strongly exciting the general eagerness and taking away all time for reflection. Every class of men, even watch-makers, hairdressers and mechanics, ran eagerly after this deception, in which Boston has sunk about $2,000,000."

President Washington reported to Congress: "These acts embrace an object of great magnitude, and their consequences may deeply affect the peace and welfare of the United States." The attorney-general was instructed to investigate "the atrocious speculation, corruption and collusion by which said usurped acts and grants were obtained."

It was asserted that "bribery and corruption distinguished the proceedings of the legislators favorable to the sale." Public meetings of denunciation were held in different places, and at the next election, members who had voted for it were defeated and opponents elected, whereupon an act was passed, in 1796, revoking the sale. [119]

In its preamble the revocating act stated: "The sale of such an enormous tract to a few speculators was contrary to the rights of all good citizens, and was an injury to the State."

The promoters of the Upper-Mississippi Company, to protect its bribed purchase through becoming an "innocent purchaser," made a sale of a million acres at 10¢ per acre to its "dummy" New England-Mississippi Land Company, which included William Wetmore and other prominent New England land speculators.

Although a committee of Congress reported that this New England Company paid little or no actual part of the purported purchase price, the company, headed by some foremost Boston capitalists, lobbied in Congress for many years for an act to give it a large indemnity "as an innocent purchaser." Finally, nineteen years after the bribery, Congress appropriated $8,000,000 for the speculative holders of these several companies, and their heirs; paid, of course, by taxes levied on the American people. The power of the lobbyist!

The United States Supreme Court, guided by its famous, and infamous, ruling, first proposed by John Marshall when pleading the Fairfax case in Virginia (he later was appointed Chief Justice), decided that irrespective of bribery or other methods used to obtain the grant, the grant, once made, was in the nature of a contract, and to revoke or impair it by subsequent legislation would "impair vested rights of innocent investors." This was the first of a long list of court decisions validating grants and franchises of all kinds, obtained by bribery and fraud, and by which the American people have been robbed of land and cash. [107]

There was widespread dissatisfaction with the Federal government among citizens along the tributaries of the Mississippi, during the last decade of the eighteenth century, at being denied unrestricted navigation to the Gulf. There was also dissatisfaction among Georgians at the continued hold by the Spaniards of the land in the southern part of Alabama and Mississippi.

Genet was the French Minister to the United States under the Robespierre regime and he abetted this discontent. He went to Charleston and enlisted some Carolinians and Georgians and appointed military officers, in the name of the French Republic, for proposed warfare against the Spaniards along the Gulf; the recruits being promised allotments of land to be captured in the Spanish possessions in southern Alabama and Mississippi. [119]

The Spanish governor made active preparations for defense at New Orleans, Mobile and along the Mississippi. The governor of Georgia and President Washington both issued proclamations against the expedition, and Washington ordered all United States troops then in Georgia to resist the contemplated invasion.

Cattle from the great ranges of Kentucky and Tennessee were driven east to market, but all wheat, corn, pork, flour and lumber produced in that region were sent to the only available market, that at New Orleans. The Spaniards held the land on both sides of the Mississippi. By treaty, in 1793, Spain recognized free navigation of the river, and granted to the United States a place to deposit the produce brought down in small craft for transfer to ocean-going vessels.

Although Spain had, in 1800, secretly sold Louisiana to France, it continued in control, and Spanish officials at New Orleans, in 1802, denied to Americans the right of such deposit. They imprisoned all American citizens captured along the river; the purpose being to create popular discontent and a desire on the part of American citizens along the river for Spanish sovereignty in the Mississippi Valley, so as to secure unrestricted navigation of the river.

The great trading concern of Panton & Leslie, which had a monopoly of all the trade on the Gulf side of Florida, and some trade on the east coast, was the chief proprietor of Spanish sovereignty in those parts. Their interests were coupled with the intrigue of the Spanish emissaries.

United States Senator Blount of Tennessee was a prominent land speculator in his State. Wishing to have unrestricted navigation on the Mississippi to the Gulf, to increase the demand for, and value of, his land, he proposed to a group of Englishmen that they buy part of his land and then have the British government forcibly take possession of Louisiana and the river.

He was charged in the United States Senate with intrigue with the British to capture New Orleans and adjacent territory from the Spaniards, and was expelled from the Senate.

Meanwhile settlers made treaties with the Indians, which some of the settlers violated, and then made war on the Indians to seize more lands. [53]

The Federal government in 1802 paid Georgia $1,250,000 for its claim to land in Alabama and Mississippi—the land which had been involved in the Yazoo briberies—and added it to the public domain; the sum to be payable from sales of the land to settlers and speculators. The government stipulated that it would recognize all valid claims to grants made by Spain and Britain, but refused to admit any of the claims of the Yazoo companies, or claimants under them. [119] Nevertheless, as noted, after lobbying in Congress eleven years, Congress paid the speculators in these Yazoo companies $8,000,000, for which it received nothing in return.

Many claimed extensive tracts of land in the Yazoo region under Spanish, British and Georgia grants. Land commissioners were appointed by the Federal government, who, after investigation, allowed 2,366 of these claims, which were approved by the President.

Land in the public domain was sold on credit by the Federal government, mostly in large tracts to speculators, payable at a future date. This enabled the speculators easily to hold the land unused and to sell at increased prices, which the demand for land by the incoming settlers themselves automatically created.

At the Huntsville, Alabama, land office, in 1818 and 1819, wild land, with soil suitable for growing cotton, sold at auction at $30 per acre, and occasionally higher prices were bid. When the price of cotton fell a few years later, land prices also fell, just as wheat land in the West fell in price with the fall in the price of wheat at the close of the First World War in 1918.

By the Treaty of Paris, in 1783, recognizing American independence, the western boundary of the United States was agreed upon as the Mississippi River, and the southern boundary as 31° N. lat., which parallel runs approximately along the present northern boundary of Florida, continuing west on that line through Alabama and Mississippi to the Mississippi River; leaving below that line a small part of each of the two last-named states, which became designated as West Florida.

By the treaty of San Ildefonso (Spain), dated October 1, 1800, and revised the following March, Louisiana and the Floridas were ceded by Spain to France, but this was kept secret for two years. Napoleon had been contemplating a French Empire in Louisiana, which was unwelcome to America, and Jefferson sent James Monroe to France with authority to negotiate for the purchase of the Island of New Orleans.

War between France and Great Britain was just then threatening. Napoleon and Tallyrand, fearing that Great Britain would capture Louisiana, urged the United States to buy the entire French possessions. A purchase, known as the Louisiana Purchase, was concluded in 1803 at a cost of $27,267,222, payable in installments, partially from proceeds of land sales. This sum included interest charges on deferred payments, and various claims of American citizens against France which the United States assumed to liquidate. The purchase recognized as valid all grants of land which France or Spain had made to individual holders—many of them fraudulent, and to the subsequent impairment of the United States public domain.

The area of land in the Louisiana Purchase extended west of the Mississippi River, but how far west and north was indefinite. The only land France specifically conveyed was that "which France had received from Spain in a treaty between them dated October 1, 1800," and that treaty omitted any statement as to bounds.

Upon the United States, by this purchase, taking possession of Louisiana, contention arose between the United States and Spain (which held Texas), as to the boundary between Louisiana and Texas. The United States claimed to the Sabine River—the present boundary. But Spain claimed to about 125 miles east of there, at the Arroyo Hondo, and sent an armed force prepared to sustain the claim, which the United States checkmated by doing likewise. The troops of both rested in close proximity at Natchitoches, on the Red River, in Louisiana, and when the United States ordered the Spaniards to retreat west of the Sabine war seemed inevitable. [161]

For a possible clue to the boundaries: The grant by Louis XIV to Antoine Crozat, ninety-three years previously (subsequently relinquished), of the territory called Louisiana, gave the bounds thereof as: ". . . bounded by New Mexico, and by those of the English in Carolina. The River St. Louis, formerly called the Mississippi, from the Staghorn to the Illinois, together with the River St. Philip, formerly called the Missouries River, and the St. Jerome, formerly called the Wabash (Ohio) with all the countries, territories and lakes in the land, and the rivers emptying directly or indirectly into that part of the River St. Louis."

This could by no possible construction include anything beyond the headwaters of the Missouri River. France never afterwards claimed beyond the Rocky Mountains. [103]

The contention with Spain respecting boundaries, and the problem of the bounds of the Louisiana Purchase, were both solved by the purchase by the United States, in 1819-21, of Florida from His Catholic Majesty of Spain.

This purchase of Florida included all the land therein, and the parts of Alabama and Mississippi south of 31°, except any land which Spain had already recorded as having been granted to others; the consideration being payment by the United States of claims of American citizens against Spain, amounting to $5,000,000 for damages, mainly to American shipping.

Not until settlement had been made of the boundaries in this Spanish purchase, could there be any reasonable assurance of just what land the United States had acquired west of the Mississippi River by the purchase of Louisiana from France.

These boundaries west of the Mississippi began at the Sabine River, ran north to the Red River, thence west to the 100° longitudinal parallel, then to the Arkansas River, and to the source thereof, then by a straight line north, to a juncture with the 42° parallel.

His Catholic Majesty ceded to the United States all his rights, claims and pretensions to any territory east and north of the said line, and for himself, his heirs, and successors, renounced all claim to the said territory for ever. Likewise, the United States renounced all its rights, claims and pretensions (of which it had not made any) to the territory lying west and south of that line.

This left the United States as the undisputed claimant to all the land west of the Mississippi River within the present states of Louisiana, Arkansas, Missouri, Iowa, Minnesota, the Dakotas and Nebraska, almost all of Kansas and Oklahoma, part of Colorado and later on, as participating claimant with Great Britain, of the territory northwest thereof, which was marked on maps of that and a later period as "the unexplored region."

Inasmuch as there were a few Canadian fur traders prowling about the Northwestern region, and Spanish and British explorers hovering along the Oregon coast, the United States made no claim to the territory between the Rocky Mountains and the Pacific Ocean until later, as shown in the chapter on the Oregon Region.

Rumors of the probable purchase of Florida from Spain by the United States started a wild speculation in land at Pensacola.

During the negotiations for the purchase, attempts were made by Spanish officials to make large grants of land to Spanish favorites and thereby reduce the area of land to be transferred to the United States.

The latter demanded that all Spanish grants made subsequent to 1802 be made void, to which Spanish officials replied, with injured pride, that such demand was "offensive to the dignity of the crown of Spain." However, the subsequent grants were voided.

Any impression that the Spanish occupancy and government of Florida were legendary, or had been desultory, is disabused by the fact that, from the days of De Leon, forty-five successive Spanish governors of Florida held office uninterruptedly for 250 years, from 1513 to 1763. During the following twenty years, under the

British occupancy, there were seven British governors. Then Spain again held Florida for thirty-eight years, under sixteen successive governors, at the end of which time Florida became a territory of the United States, followed in 1845 by Statehood.

Congress in 1824 presented to Lafayette 23,040 acres of land from the public domain in Florida, situated a few miles northwest of Tallahassee. He placed several Frenchmen on it to cultivate grapes, figs, olives and silk, but without success. He never visited it, but it continues to be known as the Lafayette place. [37]

As in other states, many of the soldiers from Florida, who had served in the Indian and other wars, were paid in land scrip exchangeable for land. The "Armed Occupation Act" of 1842 was enacted by Congress for the purpose of inducing people to take up land in Florida, to awe the Seminole Indians, for which purpose it was effective. Any able-bodied man could apply for 160 acres, south of Palatka and Gainesville, for which a deed would be issued after seven years' occupancy; and 1,321 entries were recorded. At that time a very small part of Florida had been surveyed. Many of these entries were annulled, some commuted for cash, and many were deserted.

Not less than ten million acres of high and dry land in Florida have been, by connivance between state and United States agents, fraudulently classed as swamp land. And this princely domain has been parceled out by the Florida Internal Improvement Board to railroad, canal and other promoters, under the guise of aiding transportation. [37]

Grabbers of Florida lands have been so bold that they have held up honest applicants for homestead locations by declaring the desired lands to be subject to the Swamp Land Act (noted in another chapter); these lands have then been sold to large timber and turpentine operators, at a fraction of a dollar per acre. [37]

In 1881 Hamilton Disston, the wealthy Philadelphia saw manufacturer, was induced to buy of the State of Florida four million acres of land, south of Kissimmee, for which he paid $1,000,000 at 25¢ per acre. The object was to drain the land by cutting canals.

Mr. Disston, whom I knew, established a sugar plantation, erected a cane mill, and worked so assiduously to enlist financial co-operation to carry out the contract, that he died suddenly of a heart attack. He had lost heavily in the undertaking.

A very large part of the four million acres was transferred to an English syndicate and they, too, lost heavily. Since then much of this land has been bought and sold at many thousand times the original price of 25¢ per acre. [37]

The notorious Florida land boom of the 1920's brought to the state car-loads of realtors and speculators, mostly schooled in California, and well versed in all the arts of subdivision. [37] Through these men numerous gullible people all over the United States, and in some foreign countries, lost heavily in a gamble which finally collapsed.

20

Pennsylvania

LAND GRANTS by the Dutch and Swedish governors, and
settlements by nationals of various European countries, had
been made within the present boundaries of Pennsylvania
many years before the land in Pennsylvania was granted to
William Penn.

A large tract of land "on and around the Schuylkill" was, in
1623, obtained by agreement with the Indians by Arent Corsson,
a Dutch agent for trading with the Indians on the Delaware.

Swen Schute, who was in command of, and surrendered to the
Dutch, the Swedish fort on the present site of New Castle in
1654, became possessed of practically all land in the sections of
Philadelphia afterwards known locally as Passayunk, Southward,
Moyamensing and Kingsessing.

The English drove the Dutch from the Delaware in 1664, and
Colonel Richard Nicolls, having taken possession as the English
governor, granted land and confirmed some grants which had
been made by the Dutch and Swedish governors. All such were
subject to an annual land rent, payable to the Duke of York.

Of the Swen Schute land, Nicolls granted a thousand acres to
some Englishmen named Ashman and Carman. Grants were
also made to Niel Mattsen, and six hundred acres, in what became
West Philadelphia, were deeded to Jonas Nilsson, who had been
a soldier in the Swedish Fort, Elfsborg (Salem), and who was
afterwards an active member of the Swedish settlement.

Swen Gonderson and three sons, Sven, Olav and Andrew
Swenson, were in 1664 granted by the Dutch governor, d'Hino-

yossa, eight hundred acres in what is now Philadelphia, assumedly from Vine Street to below Washington Avenue. This grant was confirmed by Governor Lovelace, who had succeeded Nicolls, at an annual land rent of eight bushels of wheat, payable to the duke. He also confirmed a grant of a thousand acres in Philadelphia previously made to Peter Larrson Cock, a Swede.

The thousand acres at Marcus Hook, which was in 1653 granted by the Swedish governor to Captain Besk, a Swede, was in 1676 appropriated by the English Governor Andros, who had succeeded Lovelace. He granted it to Jan Hendrickson and five others. Two years later, Hendrickson deeded all his right thereto to Roger Pedrick. The following year Pedrick and William Hews, with others, petitioned for a division of this land among them.

Andros in 1676 granted to John Hartsfelder 350 acres on the southwest side of Cohocksinks Creek, now in the Northern Liberties section of Philadelphia, at an annual land rent of three and a half bushels of wheat. About ten years later it was sold to Daniel Pegg.

Numerous grants of a hundred to two hundred acres each were made by Governor Andros along the Schuylkill and on the Wissahickon, Neshaminie, Poequissing, Amesland, Caleb's and Moherhuting Creeks.[a] Various grants in Bucks County were made by Andros. Names of many settlers, and of the vessels in which they came, are recorded there.

Peter Rambo, an early Swedish settler, became a large landholder and claimed a tract of land in the lower section of Philadelphia, which was protested by the three Swensons as having been granted to them, before the grant to Penn. Their protest was upheld by the court. The Swensons and other large landholders were later, for a time, in the way of the fulfillment of the plans which Penn had made for the laying out of Philadelphia.

Penn, in 1672, at the age of twenty-eight, married Guhelma Springett, daughter of Sir William. Three years later some Quakers in England acquired an undivided half interest in all the land in New Jersey, and they called upon Penn, a leading Quaker, to advise them, as related in the chapter on that prov-

[a]Upland Court Record

ince. That was the beginning of Penn's acquaintance with and desire for land grants in America.

Meanwhile, for several years, Penn devoted his time to propounding the Quaker faith in England and on the continent. In 1677 he went to Holland, where he attended religious meetings at Leyden, Haarlem, Amsterdam and Hannover. At Rotterdam he met Benjamin Furley, who afterwards became an agent of Penn in sale of land and in inducing emigration to Pennsylvania.

Penn's father, Admiral William Penn, died in 1670, leaving his son William an annual income of £1,500, or more, and a claim against the government of £16,000 for back salary. King Charles II, being unable or unwilling to part with that sum, Penn proposed to Charles that he be granted a large area of land in America in liquidation, and Penn presented a formal petition to that effect.

The grant of all the land in Pennsylvania to William Penn, [145] dated February 28/March 4, 1681, read in part:

"Charles II by Grace of God, King of England, Scotland, France and Ireland, Defender of the Faith, etc., To all to whom these presents shall come, Greeting:

"Know ye that we do grant unto said William Penn his heirs and assigns all that tract of land in America with all the islands therein, bounded on the east by the Delaware River from twelve miles northward of New Castle unto the 43° North latitude. On the south by a circle drawn at twelve miles distance from New Castle, northward and westward unto the beginning of the 40° North, then by a straight line west to five degrees in longitude from the easterly boundary.

"Also all the lands, fields, woods and isles belonging and leading thereto. And all the lands, woods, mountains, hills, lakes, rivers and bays situated or being within said bounds together with the fishing of all sorts of whale, sturgeons, also all veins, mines and quarries of gold and silver.

"We do create and constitute said William Penn the true and absolute proprietor of the country aforesaid, saving unto us our heirs and successors the sovereignty thereof, yielding and paying unto us our heirs and successors the one-fifth part of all gold and silver discovered.

"We erect the said country into a province and seigniorie and do call it Pennsylvania.

"We further grant power to divide said country into towns, hundreds, counties, boroughs and cities; and to constitute fairs and markets; power to appoint judges and officers, to muster men and to make war and to pursue the enemies and robbers as well by sea as by land, and with God's assistance to vanquish and take them, and to put to death.

"We grant to said William Penn his heirs and assigns a full and absolute power for ever to sell or rent such parts of the land in fee simple or in fee-taile, and erect manors, and to hold court-baron, and view of frank-pledge for the conservation of peace."

This gave William Penn, his heirs and assigns, the power of feudal lords, with authority of a viceroy.

Penn began at once in England to sell land in Pennsylvania. Conditions agreed upon in London, July 11, between Penn and the early purchasers of land, were similar to the concessions and agreements put into operation by Penn's guidance in New Jersey seventeen years previously; and provided that an area of land should be set out for a large town.

Every adventurer (buyer) was to have one thousand to ten thousand or more acres, but not more than a thousand acres in one tract, unless within three years he had a family on each thousand acres. The purchaser of each five hundred acres in the province was to receive ten acres in the town (Philadelphia), to be drawn by lot, so long as the area in the town would admit of it.

All mines and minerals, except gold and silver mines royal, and all rivers were to belong to the purchaser of land into whose lot they should fall. From this provision, acceded to, and maintained by succeeding state legislatures, have developed the royalties that must be paid to the absentee holders of coal lands by all users of Pennsylvania coal.

In prospecting for gold and silver, the proceeds of any discovery were to go: two-tenths to the King of England, as per the terms of the original grant, one-tenth to the landholder, two-tenths to the discoverer, one-tenth to the public treasury and four-tenths to Penn. After parting with the land on the regular terms, he was to receive four-tenths of any precious metal discovered thereon.

"Whoever may take or send indented servants shall be allowed for himself fifty acres for each servant taken or sent, and the servant shall also receive fifty acres when his term of service expires."

"Every man is bound to plant, or man, his land within three years after survey, or else other applicants may be settled thereon." The urge to dispose of land by Penn, and the pressure to buy and hold land unused on speculation, while increasing population made it more valuable, were too strong to permit continued adherence to this enlightened policy.

The oldest Pennsylvania deed known is in Bucks County, dated April 1, 1681, from Penn to Thomas Woolrich of Stafford, England, for a thousand acres, the consideration being £20, and in addition, 1s per hundred acres annual rent for ever. Another deed is there for five hundred acres to James Hill, shoemaker, of England, on the same terms.

Penn addressed a letter to the people of Pennsyslvania in which he requested them to pay to his deputy, William Markham, whom he was sending to Pennsylvania as his deputy-governor, those land rents that they formerly paid to the governor of New York for the Duke of York. Markham and Thomas Holmes, surveyor, arrived in Pennsylvania July 1, 1681.

Calvert, of Maryland, disputed the exact location of the 40° N., which was the southern boundary of the Penn grant; whereupon Markham, in August, went to Maryland to confer with Charles Calvert, third Lord Baltimore, who was then the Maryland governor, but they failed to reach an agreement.

Thirteen months later, Calvert, with a retinue of twenty-one, went to Upland (Chester) to confer with Markham and found Upland to be twelve miles south of 40°. The 40° parallel is at the northern edge of Philadelphia.

Penn's instructions to Markham and Holmes: "Should it happen that the location you select for the great town has been already taken up, and not improved, use your skill to persuade them to part with part of it, and take some back land. By the settlement of this town, the back land in a few years' time will be worth twice as much as the entire quantity was before. Offer them a new grant at their old rent; nay, half their rent abated; yea, make them free as purchasers rather than disappoint my mind in this township; urge the weakness of the title of their grant from the Duke of York [their previous landlord], he having never had a grant from the king, etc. Be just and courteous to all. Avoid offending the Indians. Be grave, they love not to be smiled on. Hearken [learn] by honest spies if you can hear of anybody who inveigles the Indians not to sell land, or to raise the price upon you."

A letter from England the same year reported: "William Penn is extraordinarily busy about his new country, and purchasers present themselves daily." Penn, in England, issued literature telling people in England and elsewhere of the advantages of Pennsylvania, adding: "England swarms with beggars; now thousands of both sexes that are sound and youthful and able to work run up and down both city and country [the cause of which is shown herein in an earlier chapter]; nor is there any care taken to employ them. Such as could not marry here in England, and hardly live and allow themselves clothes, do marry in Pennsylvania and bestow thrice more in all necessities and conveniences for themselves and their children." Of the persons most fitted to emigrate he noted: "industrious husbandmen and day laborers that are hardly able to maintain their families in England, carpenters, masons, smiths, weavers, tailors, tanners, shoemakers, shipwrights, etc. Also younger brothers of small inheritances. Labor will be worth more there, and provisions cheaper. The passage will be at most £6 per head for masters and mistresses; servants £5; children under seven years 50s."

The rent on all land allotments was at a fixed rate, except on the lots fronting on the Delaware River in Philadelphia. The perpetual ground rent on these, as increasing population and commerce increased their value, was to be increased every fifty-one years to one-third of the actual rental value.

It was planned that ten families settle together in a township, each on fifty acres, as near together as possible, and each family to have 450 acres additional, extending back therefrom. Within two years, at least fifty of these townships existed and the settlers were prospering.

Penn followed the example of neighboring provinces in distribution of land, as well as his personal experience in previously allotting land in New Jersey. He appointed a secretary, auditor-general, receiver-general, surveyor-general, deputy surveyors, and the commissioners of property, who acted in the proprietary's absence, with authority to clear lands of Indian claims, and grant them at a purchase price and an annual land rent in addition.

Penn's ingenious advertising in England and on the continent drew merchants, yeoman and peasants, English Quakers, Germans, Scotch-Irish, Welsh and Irish as seekers after homesteads.

Penn, early in 1682, promoted a company by the title of "Free Society of Traders," composed of some London merchants, a doctor, leather-seller, yeoman, wine-cooper and others, granting them twenty thousand acres in and about Philadelphia, one location being a "manor" of ten thousand acres at Frankford, to Dr. Nicholas More, president of the Society, and called the manor of Moreland. The payment or rent thereof was to consist of one-fifth part of the gold and silver reserved by the king, and another one-fifth and 1s yearly rent per hundred acres to Penn, his heirs and assigns. He stipulated that no person should inspect the company's books without its consent. Dr. More, two years later, became chief justice of the province.

Laws agreed upon in England provided that every inhabitant in the province who purchased a hundred acres or up; and every person who had paid his passage and taken up a hundred acres at 1d annual rent per acre, and had cultivated ten acres thereof; and every indented servant, who after his freedom took up fifty acres and cultivated twenty thereof; and every inhabitant over twenty-one years of age that payed scot and lot to the government and professed faith in Jesus Christ, being not convicted of ill fame or unsober and dishonest, should be accounted a freeman, and be capable of electing or being elected a representative in the assembly.

The government of the province was to consist of a governor (the proprietor or his appointee), a provisional council and an assembly elected by landholders. These were soon chosen. All enactments of the assembly were to be submitted to the king in council.

The Indians were to have liberty to do all things relating to improvement of their land and providing sustenance for their families that any of the planters enjoyed. No person was to leave the province without notice thereof, posted in the market place three weeks before.

In every hundred thousand acres surveyed, Penn reserved ten thousand acres for himself. He claimed the right of strays, escheats, deodands and the right to erect windmills, and the profit of the markets and stalls.

Penn wrote from London to Thomas Holme, his surveyor-general in Pennsylvania, that during the first fourteen months he sold 565,500 acres, in parcels of from 250 to 10,000 acres. Of the latter are two lots to the Free Society of Traders, making up their twenty thousand acres sold in England, Ireland and Scotland.

Markham acquired for Penn consent of the Indians to occupy land on the Delaware River, below the falls at Trenton.

Only the first purchasers in England, whose names appeared in the parchment list of August 22, 1682, had a right to lots in Philadelphia proper, and they drew for their lots. Heirs of holders of rights to such lots usually had difficulty in obtaining their plots, which soon became valuable, and recognition depended on payment for warrants, the survey, the return, the patent and its recording, besides many inconveniences. [136]

Penn sailed from Deal in the ship "Welcome," of three hundred tons, with about one hundred passengers, chiefly Quakers, the names of whom, with few exceptions, are now unknown. He arrived at the Delaware Capes on October 24, 1682. About thirty died of smallpox on the voyage, a frequent occurrence during the early Colonial Period.

En route up the Delaware he went ashore at New Castle, where he announced his proprietorship of Delaware, as stated in the chapter on the Delaware Region; after which he sailed up the river to Upland. This was a settlement founded and plotted four years previously by some Swedes, on twelve thousand acres, divided among six persons. It had a court with jurisdiction over the neighboring territory along the river. Penn changed its name to Chester.

In December, Penn went to Maryland to see Calvert and in the following May, Calvert met Penn at New Castle.

But aside from the stated 40° as the boundary, the grant provided that this parallel was to be intercepted on the west and northwest by a circle drawn twelve miles distant from New Castle, which provided for an impossible conjunction. The dispute was due to a lack of geographical knowledge in London at the time of drafting the Penn grant.

Calvert had correctly marked the 40° parallel by a fort on the Susquehanna River, twenty miles north of the present Maryland boundary. Penn's position as a royal favorite enabled him to predominate in his interpretation of the boundary and to push his southern boundary twenty miles south of the Susquehanna fort, thereby supposedly taking from Calvert more than three million acres, along the entire southern part of Pennsylvania.

It has been truly said that Penn's charter was the source of more boundary disputes than any other in American history. [48]

At the time of the arrival of Penn, there were five thousand Europeans living along the Delaware, including English, Swedes, Finns, Danes, Dutch, Irish, Scotch and French; the number of English being equal to all the others. An act of assembly naturalized the foreign-born settlers. To extinguish titles and claims to land derived from the previous Swedish and Dutch governors, Penn confirmed some grants already made by them and made the land rents payable to himself, instead of to the Duke of York.

Acrelius said the new deeds from Penn charged three or four times the land rent that had been charged by the Duke of York.

The first habitations of the early settlers in Philadelphia, and of new arrivals for several years, were in caves dug into the high river bank. Trading and speculation in land locations had already begun amongst the sparse population of that early day. Land between the Delaware River and the Schuylkill was chosen for the first city, which Penn had decided to name Philadelphia. There was an immediate distribution of lots on several streets. A list of the lots and names of those who drew them are in E. Hazard's *Pennsylvania Annals,* but street names have been since changed.

Penn wrote from Philadelphia to the Lords of Trade and Plantations: "I have made seven purchases of the Indians, and in pay and presents they have received of me at least £1,200. I have followed exactly the counsel of the Bishop of London, by buying, and not taking, the native's land."

Penn located a manor of 6,500 acres in Bucks County, which included Pennsbury, where he built and furnished an elaborate residence. Several tracts of ten thousand acres each were laid out as manors for certain of Penn's relatives.

Robert Turner, a wealthy English Quaker who had been imprisoned for his religious belief, had bought proprietary shares in both East and West Jersey, and afterwards bought of Penn five thousand acres in Pennsylvania. He went to Pennsylvania the year after Penn arrived, taking his family and seventeen indented servants, and built a brick house in the city. Joseph Growden of England, one of the early purchasers, bought five thousand acres on Neshaminy Creek, Bucks County. [106]

During the first year more than twenty vessels arrived, with about three thousand people. Eighty houses were built and three hundred farms laid out.

Fourteen months after arriving in Pennsylvania, Penn wrote the Marquis of Halifax: "Our capital town is advanced to about 150 farmers strong. I settle them in villages, dividing five thousand acres among ten or twenty families, as their ability is to plant it; the regulation being a family to each five hundred acres, of which fifty acres for each family are in the village."

Colonists poured into Philadelphia from various parts of Europe and struck out in all directions into the new and untried regions. Plans were soon lost sight of and surveys and sales were made promiscuously, as purchasers wished. [91]

By the end of the second year there were 357 houses in the city, many of three stories, and well built. Two years later the population of the province was eight thousand, of which twenty-five hundred were in the city. This was as much as the population of New Netherland, at the end of half-a-century of Dutch occupancy.

It, therefore, is not surprising that Penn wrote: "Within one year of my arrival, the value of the least desirable lots in Philadelphia increased to four times their value when first laid out, and the best lots were worth forty times, without any improvements thereon. And though it seems unequal that the absent should be thus benefited by the improvements made by those that are upon the place, especially when they have served no office, run no hazard, nor as yet defrayed any public charge, yet this advantage does certainly redound to them, and whoever they are, they are great debtors to the country."

Penn designated ten thousand acres in Montgomery and Berks Counties to be a location for the Swedes, to which, before his arrival, he had urged Deputy-Governor Markham to have the original Swedish settlers move, from the site of the proposed city.

He also set apart for the Welsh forty thousand acres in Montgomery County, "on the west side of the Schuylkill." This was allotted in tracts of one hundred to five thousand acres. [3x] Welsh settlers became quite numerous, but considerable land in that tract was allotted to others. [91]

Another Welsh tract of three thousand acres began seven miles west of New Castle; the idea of Penn being to extend his domain as near Chesapeake Bay as possible. The terms were £12, 10s per hundred acres (about 60¢ per acre), payable in annual instalments, and in addition 1s silver per hundred acres, annual land rent for ever.

Francis Daniel Pastorius, a young lawyer in Germany, arrived in Philadelphia representing a group which had bought fifteen thousand acres through Benjamin Furley, a shipping merchant in Rotterdam, who acted as Penn's agent in Europe for the sale of land and the promoting of emigration.

All the land along the Delaware River had been already allotted, and Penn demurred at granting fifteen thousand acres in one tract, fearing that much of it might remain unused. He also demurred at honoring Furley's promise of granting three hundred acres in the Northern Liberties division of the city; saying land in that section was granted only to the first buyers of five thousand acres before he left London, when the books were closed.

The following October, thirteen families, comprising thirty-three persons, mostly Mennonites or Quakers, weavers by occupation, arrived in Philadelphia from Crefeld, Germany, being some of those for whom Pastorius had bought land.

A fortnight later, Penn deeded land in Germantown: 200 acres to Pastorius, 2,675 acres to the Crefeld group, a like acreage to a Frankfort, Germany, group, and 150 acres to one Hartsfelder, who probably represented the last-named group. This acreage was sold on condition that within a year thirty householders should be located on it, which condition seems to have been more than fulfilled, as, by 1700, there were sixty-four houses thereon.

It would appear that, in addition to this acreage, he granted them the three hundred acres in the Northern Liberties section, and three city lots between Front and Second Streets, at South Street, each lot one hundred by four hundred feet, on each of which a house was to be built within two years. Fourteen lots were laid out in Germantown. Each family there had three acres.

Penn left Philadelphia in August, 1684, terminating his first visit. After his arrival in England he made some large sales of land. To Joseph Pike, a prominent Quaker of Cork, who was always an absentee, he sold twenty-five hundred acres. Most of this land was held by Pike and his family for nearly a century, [91], and was then sold at a large profit, created, not by the Pikes, but solely by the public through increase in population.

Several speculators each bought ten thousand acres along French Creek, in Chester County, for a settlement of French Protestants. Another sale was of five thousand acres along the Schuylkill, in Whitemarsh township, Montgomery County, to Major Jasper Farmer, of Ireland, and his sons. [91]

At this time lots were in increased demand for speculation. "There was great buying, one of another."

Penn wrote Markham: "I cannot make money without special concessions. Though I desire to extend religious freedom, yet I want some recompense for my trouble." At another time he wrote Markham that he had just "refused a tempting offer of £6,000 for six shares, for a company to which I would grant a monopoly of the Indian trade south to north, between the Delaware and Susquehanna Rivers, paying me 2½ per cent rent." He reported refusing an offer of £100 and abatement of land rent on five thousand acres. Penn appointed agents in England and Pennsylvania to sell land.

In Chester County, in 1685, a tax of 2*s* 6*d* was levied on every hundred acres taken up and surveyed, but non-residents, being absentees, were to pay one-half more, or 3s 9d; a wise provision to discourage holding land unused on speculation, and one which should be in effect everywhere.

In 1685, Penn, writing from England to Thomas Lloyd, President of the Council, in Philadelphia, said: "Prepare the people to think of some way to support me, so I may not consume all my substance to serve the province."

Eneas MacPherson, of Scotland, bought five thousand acres with all the customary privileges of a manor, including the power to erect the same into the barony of Inversie. "The said MacPherson may hold court-baron, view of frank-pledge and court-leet, at an annual land rent of 1s per hundred acres."

William Bacon, of the Middle Temple, London, bought ten thousand acres. Like numerous others, he was purely a speculator and absentee holder.

Penn went to Holland and Germany, in 1686, with a German translation of his prospectus of Pennsylvania, to interest Mennonites, Schwenkfelders and other similar sects.

Penn was absent from Pennsylvania fifteen years, between 1684 and 1699. He ordered officials of the land office to make no grants within five miles of any navigable river, or adjoining any land already inhabited, as such was to be reserved for himself until it became more valuable; also not to sell in the city vacant lots that lay between those already disposed of. He tried to evade granting lots in the city.

Penn's intimacy with the dethroned James II caused him to be suspected by the new rulers of England. He had been arrested three times, charged with correspondence with James, but each time was cleared. [169]

He prepared to go to Pennsylvania in 1690, "with a great company of adventurers" (prospective land buyers), when an order for his arrest was again issued. Whereupon, for two or three years, he lived quietly in the country, or in obscure lodgings in London. [169]

Because the Pennsylvania government objected to contributing funds towards fortifying the New York frontier against the Indians, for the protection of all the colonies, and further, because of charges against Penn in England, King William, in 1692, appointed Governor Fletcher of New York to be also governor of Pennsylvania.

A threat to annex the province to New York caused the assembly, after ten months of the Fletcher government, to pass an act levying a tax on all land to provide the fortification funds.

At a hearing in 1694 Penn was cleared of all charges, but it was not until five years afterwards that he was able to go to Pennsylvania.

Surveys were not made at the time of a grant. As purchases were often made for speculative purposes by persons who never visited the province, titles were frequently defective from the outset. Penn and others bought many such from heirs of the original buyers. [136]

It was difficult for settlers to get their land surveyed until the speculators had been satisfied. Surveys of large areas were made by speculators in localities most suitable for immediate settlement. They were accustomed to hold large tracts of outlying land until fabulous prices could be obtained. [136]

No system whatever for division of land can be traced in the records of the Pennsylvania land office.[b]

The early buyers of Penn paid him 12d a year rent per hundred acres. As population and the demand for land increased, 50d or 100d per hundred acres per annum became more customary rates. At first, from every hundred thousand acres surveyed, one-tenth was to be reserved for Penn in one tract; later, his share was increased. Towns were often laid out on his portions and lots offered for sale.

The development of York was retarded by quarreling over the ownership of lots, because of failure of the land office to record deeds. [71]

In Chester County in 1695 land under cultivation was assessed at £1 per acre, and all uncultivated land at 2s per acre, which made it easy to hold unused land on speculation. Woodland was assessed at £5 per hundred acres, with a tax of 1d in the pound. A tax was also levied on mills, live-stock and on Negroes. [136]

[b]Gordon's History

Penn's first wife, the mother of three children—Springett, Laetitia and William—died in 1694. Two years later, after some weeks of traveling and preaching in England and Ireland, Penn, then fifty-one years of age, married Hannah Callowhill, for whom a street in Philadelphia is named.

Gabriel Thomas of Wales, near Bristol, arrived in Philadelphia in the first company and, seventeen years afterwards, wrote: "In twelve years from laying out of Philadelphia, lots which had sold at 15*s* and 18*s,* are now £80 silver. And others which two years ago were £3 have sold for £100. Also, land near the city, which sixteen years ago was £6 or £8 per hundred acres, cannot now be bought under £150 to £200 per hundred acres."

Nine lots in Philadelphia, and sixty thousand acres elsewhere in the province, were sold by Penn in 1699 to four Londoners: Collett, a haberdasher, Russel, a weaver, Quarre, a watchmaker and Gouldney, a linen draper, who, with associates, were known as the London Company. They were absentee holders on specu-lation, and held the land until late in the Colonial Period. [91]

This sale enabled Penn to bring to Pennsylvania his wife and daughter, Laetitia, and as secretary, James Logan, aged twenty-five, a Quaker of Bristol and a former schoolteacher. Seven weeks after their arrival, Penn's son, John, "The American," was born, for whom ten thousand acres, on part of which Norristown is located, were surveyed.

Penn also gave his son, William, a manor, which he soon sold to William Trent and Isaac Norris for £850; and 1,250 acres went as a gift from Penn to George Fox, the Quaker leader.

The frame of government, as amended in 1701, provided that no inhabitant should be entitled to vote, or be elected, unless he had been a resident for two years, was over twenty-one years of age, and had fifty acres of land, of which ten acres were occupied and cleared, or he was otherwise worth £50, clear estate. This prompted the settlers to acquire land.

Penn asserted that he would never permit an assembly to intermeddle with his land. He denied the right of the assembly to interfere in the agreement between him and the first pur-chasers in England; and complained because of its attempt to prevent him from increasing the rent and prices of land, [136] which the increased demand for land, resulting from the increase in population, made possible.

Rumors of attempts of the British government to convert the proprietary governments in America to royal ones caused Penn to return to England in 1701. On leaving the province at the end of his second, and last, visit, Penn commissioned Edward Shippen, formerly of Boston, who had settled in Philadelphia, Thomas Strong, James Logan and Griffith Owen, or any three of them, to sell land. Many well-to-do persons from Boston, New York and the West Indies located in Philadelphia.

King William III died in 1702. Queen Mary having previously died, her sister Anne succeeded to the throne. She was a friend of Penn, because of his friendship with her father, James II. That year England declared war against France and Spain.

John Evans, a young man in his late twenties, was appointed by Penn as governor and, having received, as required, the royal approbation in 1704, arrived in Philadelphia with William Penn, Jr., of about the same age. Evans became conspicuous by his conduct with Indian women, and they both gave the guardians of the peace much trouble by their roistering in the inns and other resorts of the town.

Penn stated that during the first twenty-six years of his proprietorship he had lost over £64,000. Later in life he placed the amount at £30,000, "while the speculators who have bought land of me are growing rich."

These amounts do not mean losses, but the sum invested in the promotion up to the time named. By the settlement of the province, which was going on rapidly, Penn, with millions of acres, was growing far richer than all the buyers of small tracts. The final outcome, when the state took over the unsold land, showed a very large profit to the Penns, as will presently appear.

Mr. Penn was first followed by his flock to Pennsylvania as a kind of patriarch. His failures in his conduct towards them were complained of by the assembly. It complained to Penn of the exorbitance of the land office: "Thou kept the land office shut up whilst thou sold lands in England to the value of about £2,000, and also got great tracts of land secured to thyself and relatives." [52]

Swedish resident landholders, to the number of twenty-four, in 1709, addressed the assembly: "We with great difficulty and loss of several lives, after obtaining peace with the Indians, and upon the surrender of this province to the English forty-five years ago, it was agreed on both sides that the inhabitants were not to be disturbed in their lives, liberties or estates. After that, being summoned before the government [under the Duke of York] at New York, we were obliged to take patents or grants for what land we held or desired. But since this province has been granted to William Penn he and his officers have called for our deeds under pretense of renewing them, which having obtained, would not return them again, but instead thereof, re-surveyed great parts of our lands and took it from some of us: others were required to pay greater land rents than before; and because some of us refused to pay the increased rent—on some tracts being three or four times more than we ought, or used, to pay when under the Duke of York government—we being, as we supposed, the Queen's tenants, and not liable to pay at all to the proprietor Penn, the Penn collector, James Logan, threatened to distress our goods for said rents. We solicit your help that we have our patents restored, together with the overplus of the land rents which have been extracted from us these twenty years."

Previous to 1712, there were sold in Pennsylvania and Delaware ninety-one thousand acres for £10,640, at the rate of £5 to £130 per hundred acres.° The general price of land had been £5 per hundred acres, together with a perpetual annual land rent of 1s per hundred acres in addition. This was soon changed to £10 per hundred acres, with 1s per hundred acres annual rent. After 1719 the price was £10 per hundred acres and 2s annual rent. At that time wheat was 2s to 2s 3d per bushel, corn 22d, rye 20d, and cider 6s per barrel.

By acts of the assembly, between 1696 and 1717, land which was held by Penn and the lieutenant-governor was apparently exempt from taxation. [136]

The assembly enacted in 1724 that land held for speculation was exempt from taxes. Later it was assessed for taxation at £5

°Pa. Land Grants

to £15 per hundred acres and subject to sale for non-payment. Penn contended that because unused land was not taxed in England, it should not be taxed in Pennsylvania. A tax policy that encourages holding land out of use for an increasing population which must have land, to run up the price, militates against the material development and social welfare of any state.

Shepard [136] said: "The proprietors were great landholders—feudal lords—who had been hitherto expressly exempted from assessment for taxes. The progress of the democratic spirit demanded that feudal rights of tax exemption should be abolished, and as owners of land they should be considered as private individuals. Any plea for exemption lacked the powerful support of precedent in other provinces, both royal and proprietary. The proprietors said the Board of Trade in London had told them they were no more liable to taxation than were the royal governors. But as time passed, they must submit, in part at least."

Penn suffered a stroke in 1712, and was out of his mind for a year and a half, and died in 1718, aged seventy-four. His will provided that after payment of his debts all his land and land rents should go to his widow and other trustees—Logan, Gouldney and Gee. They were to convey ten thousand acres to his daughter Laetitia and ten thousand acres to each of the three children—Guhelma, Springett and William 3rd—of William, Jr., his son by his first wife.

All the remaining land and land rents were to be conveyed to Thomas, Richard and John, children by his second wife.

Inasmuch as Penn's sons, being Quakers, declined assuming the governorship because of the oath required, Penn left to three trustees—the Earl of Oxford, Earl Mortimer and Earl Powlet—his right to govern Pennsylvania, with instructions to them to sell that right to the crown or to any private person.

After the death of the second wife of Penn, in 1726, the surviving trustees conveyed the Penn land in the province to her sons; one-half to John, and one-quarter each to Thomas and Richard. John and Thomas were, in 1732, employed in a London dry-goods store, while Richard was for a time without employment.

By other deeds executed between 1731 and 1742, the land rights of the young proprietors were established. By terms of the founder's will, his grandsons could obtain the powers of government only by purchase, and they were unable to do that.

The land of the Society of Traders, which had bought twenty thousand acres, was sold by trustees in 1723. The tract of 7,700 acres in Chester County was bought by Nathaniel Newlin. He did nothing towards developing it, and six years later sold a large part of it at a profit. The remainder he left to his children.

Settlers continued to arrive and during one week, in 1727, six ships docked in Philadelphia. The eager demand for land for homes and cultivation was so persistent that many released indented servants and newly arrived immigrants located without permission on unoccupied land. This became especially marked after 1730. By that year about a hundred thousand acres had been located on and improved without permission, including fifteen thousand acres in Conestoga Manor, Lancaster County, which were settled upon by some Scotch-Irish immigrants. They were afterwards ejected by the sheriff and his posse, who burnt their cabins.

Secretary James Logan, writing in 1727 to John Penn in London, said: "Both these sorts sitt frequently down on any spott of vacant land they can find, without asking questions. They say the proprietor invited people to come and settle his country, that they are come for that end and must live; they pretend they would buy but not one in twenty has anything to pay with. In doing this by force they allege that it is against the laws of God and nature that so much land should be idle, while so many Christians want it to labor on."

Two years afterwards Logan again wrote Penn: "The settlement of vast numbers of poor but presumptuous people, without license, have entered on your land and neither have, nor are like to have, anything to purchase with."[d] From Logan's reporting the assertion of the poor settlers that it is against the laws of God and nature to hold land out of use, when others need to use it, one may have the feeling that he recognized the justice of their assertion.

The assembly, in 1730, requested the Penns in London to

[d]Pa. Archives

solicit the crown's approval of its acts, but they refused to do so unless paid for their services, whereupon, for that and other reasons, Benjamin Franklin was sent to England as an agent of the assembly. The Penns, knowing Franklin as an opponent of their land-tax policy, then offered their services, but Franklin was on his way.

The Penns held more than twenty-seven million acres. Penn's sons, John and Richard, in 1731, estimated the value, exclusive of the Delaware River front lots in Philadelphia, to be £50,000. —a small fraction of what the Penns were paid by the new state and the British government when divested of the land.

William Penn, grandson of the founder, in consideration of £5,500 and certain specified reservations, sold his asserted claim to land and government to his uncles, John, Thomas and Richard. They mortgaged the land to the vendee as security for payment, but reserved the right of government.

The surviving trustee, failing to sell the right of government, conveyed it to these three sons of Penn. Thomas seemed best fitted for the management. In 1732, when he visited Pennsylvania, the two brothers who remained in England, urged him to sell their lands at almost any price, so they could pay their debts and avoid continual dunning; they had been paying their father's debts and cost of litigation with Calvert. After the return of Thomas to England, nine years later, none of the Penns was in America during the next thirty years. [136]

For a number of years after 1732 the regular price of land per hundred acres was £15, 10s currency, together with a perpetual annual land rent of a half-penny sterling per acre. Meantime, the proprietors offered land at auction at a bid price, with an additional 1s sterling per hundred acres perpetual annual ground rent.

An Indian deed to Penn heirs, in 1736, evidently written by Thomas Penn, then in Pennsylvania, which seems ridiculous, recited: "We do hereby promise and engage for our children and their children, that neither we nor they . . . will sell or grant to any person, other than to said proprietor, the children of William Penn . . . any land within the limits of the government of Pennsylvania." [74]

A "walking purchase" of land from the Indians, (by which the bounds that can be walked in a specified time fixes the area) in 1737, extended from Wrightsville (near York) to Mauch Chunk, thence to the Delaware River at the mouth of the Lackawaxen (Port Jervis), instead of at the Water Gap. [74]

Gettysburg was settled about 1740 and Moravians from Georgia founded Bethlehem in 1741.

Benjamin Franklin, [52] in 1754, wrote: "No one was allowed to buy land of the Indians except the proprietary. Rendered thus the sole purchaser, he reckoned he might always accommodate himself at the Indian market on the same terms with what quantity of land he pleased; and till the stock in hand, or such parts of it as he thought fit to dispose of were in a fair way of being sold off, he did not think it for his interest to incumber himself with more.

"In process of time as the value of land increased these land rents would of themselves become an immense estate. For want of a specific clause to declare their property taxable the heirs of the proprietaries insist on having it exempted from every public obligation, and upon charging the difference on the public.

"The Penn family has been doubly paid in the value of the lands, and in the increase of land rents with increase in population."

John Penn, the American born, never married. At his death in 1746, he bequeathed his one-half of all the land in Pennsylvania to his brother, Thomas, for life, then in succession to the sons of Thomas, or in default of these, to descendants of Richard, who held one-quarter. Thomas Penn, son of the founder, thus became the owner of three-quarters of all the unsold Penn land in the province.

Governor Dunmore of Virginia, in 1754, claiming the land for Virginia jurisdiction by the Lancaster agreement, erected a fort at the present site of Pittsburgh. To encourage settlements, he offered three hundred thousand acres, mostly in Pennsylvania, free of land rent for fifteen years, whereupon the Penns offered land in the same region on the same terms. Settlers and speculators increased and, in competing for Indian grants for lands west of the Alleghenies, it became a struggle between the Phila-

delphia and Lancaster merchant-speculators and Virginia speculators. This competition brought on the atrocious seven years'
French and Indian War (1754–61). The war spread over most
of the colonies, including New England, in which the lives and
homes of thousands of innocent settlers were lost. [1] Spreading
to Europe, it involved England and Prussia on one hand and
France, Austria, Spain and minor powers on the other; it flamed
up in India, deciding the fate of teeming millions on the other
side of the world. [10]

To raise the necessary funds for the war, a tax on all land
value was the foremost suggestion, to which the Penns offered
vigorous objection, claiming exemption from any tax.

The revenue of the Penns from rents of manors and other
allotted lands, was at that time nearly £30,000 per annum. [5]

The governor, Robert Morris, wrote the assembly: "It is contrary to the constant practice and usage in this, and all proprietary governments upon this continent, so far as I have been
informed, to lay any tax upon the lands of the proprietaries."

The assembly, in addressing the governor said: "Of the proprietary right to a monopoly of land, whether from the crown
or assembly, the assembly answers that those in whose favor
such monopoly was created ought to bear at least a part of the
expense necessary to secure them the full benefit of it."

In the dispute, the Penns, in lieu of a tax on their lands, offered
as their contribution, lands west of the Allegheny Mountains
free of land rent for fifteen years, as follows: "To every colonel
who shall serve in an expedition against the French on the Ohio,
a thousand acres; and [graded down through the ranks] to every
common soldier, two hundred acres. The assembly to afford
some assistance to such as should accept the same."

The assembly replied: "This offer is in effect an amusing one,
as land can be had in Virginia at a perpetual land rent of 2s per
hundred acres, without purchase price being exacted, whereas
the common perpetual annual land rent in Pennsylvania is 4s,
or 2s sterling, in addition to a purchase price, and with the same
exemption of rent in both provinces for the first fifteen years.
So that the offer to the soldiers to recover the Penns' lands out
of the hands of the enemy is no better than a proposal to reward

them with a part of the lands they were to recover, and at more than double the price demanded in the neighboring province, without the risk they were in the present case exposed to."

The assembly, in an address to the governor, seems to have had at that early day, a logical grasp of what is often designated as the tax burden. "All taxes," it said, "ought, upon the whole, to produce more good to those who pay them, than the same sum left at their individual disposal would produce, in which case taxes are no burden."

The assembly finally resolved to grant £50,000 to the king's use for the war, by a tax on all land and personal property within the province. To avoid the tax being levied on their land, the Penns sent an order on their receiver-general for £5,000, and the proposed tax on the proprietary lands for the defense fund was abandoned. [52]

Thomas Penn persisted in his effort to avoid having taxes laid on the Penn lands by having them laid on those who improved land and developed the country. That is the practice throughout the world, fostered by the powerful interests who are holding land out of use, for increasing population to make more valuable.

Thomas Penn writing from London to Richard Peters in Philadelphia said: "Taxation of land must be on true rental value only, as in England, and not upon the real value of the fee simple. All unoccupied and unimproved lands, and all ground-rents, should be exempted, and no land should be sold for non-payment of taxes. The proprietors are not on the same footing as the purchasers, for we believe our grant is paramount to the laws and constitution of the province. The assembly should not meddle with our lands without our consent," and again wrote: "No bill can pass the assembly without our consent."

Deputy collectors of land rents for the Penns were appointed, in 1756, personally to collect from farm to farm. Unless the amount of arrears was kept down, many people might object to paying anything at all. [136]

In 1757, the Penns claimed that £197,193 were due them for rent and purchase money in Pennsylvania, and £31,813 in Delaware. The total value of the Penn estate was now estimated at

£3,806,112, exclusive of the valuable lots on the Delaware River front in Philadelphia;° all this had grown automatically in seventy-five years from an $80,000 claim, inherited by Penn.

On appeal of the Penns, the Board of Trade in England, in 1758 recommended that all land within boroughs and towns, not already granted by the proprietaries, be deemed located uncultivated lands, and not as lots. In the town of Carlyle, sixty-four lots belonging to the Penns were then rated at from £8 to £15 each. Near that town, 136,372 acres of unsold land were valued at £15, 10s per hundred acres, of which three thousand acres were rated at £10 per hundred acres, and two thousand acres at £25 per hundred acres. The Penns acknowledged, in 1759, that they must submit to the land-tax, or have their lands sold. [136]

Because the high prices of land exacted by the Penns were causing migration to the southern colonies, land prices in Pennsylvania were reduced somewhat in 1751. Fourteen years later they were reduced to £5 sterling per hundred acres, with a perpetual land rent in addition of 1d sterling per acre per annum.

By the middle of the 1700's the revenues of the proprietors from land sales and rents made their position more independent. People of the province looked upon the proprietors as aristocrats, having association with aristocracy and others of social station in England. The authority of the proprietors survived royal jealousy, family dissensions and popular attacks. [136]

John Penn, eldest son of Richard, became governor in 1763, succeeding Governor Hamilton, and eight years afterwards succeeded to the proprietorship, at which time his brother, Richard, became governor and served until the outbreak of the American Revolution.

The pressure of settlers for land continued so great that the Penns began, in 1769, the sale of land west of the Alleghenies, and in four months a million acres were sold, mostly in tracts of three hundred acres each. [155]

George Croghan, a prominent and influential Indian trader in western Pennsylvania, in 1770 wrote: "Mr. Penn has sold, since the Fort Stanwix treaty with the Iroquois, all the good land within his grant west of the Alleghenies. I am sure that between

°Pa. Land Grants

four thousand and five thousand families have settled west of the mountains in that time. All this Spring and Summer the roads have been lined with wagons moving into Ohio; all wanting land to settle on."

Encouraged by the western migration, which was increasing the demand for and price of land, Croghan became an indefatigable land speculator, and an influential leader of the Pennsylvania coterie of speculators. He had Indian title to thousands of acres of choice lands in Pennsylvania, and two hundred thousand acres in the Lake Otsego section of New York.

Unable to meet the cost of surveys and recording, he failed to patent an Indian grant of two hundred thousand acres on the Ohio, near Pittsburgh. When the sheriff was foreclosing on some of his best land, he was borrowing money to make another Indian purchase of six million acres, just across the Ohio River from Pittsburgh, for the equivalent of $12,000 in merchandise; being at the rate of five acres for 1¢. Of this he subsequently sold 125,000 acres, at 4¢ per acre, to the aforementioned Dr. Walker and associates of Virginia. To validate the Indian purchase, it was necessary that the Continental Congress, in session at Philadelphia, should sanction it. This sanction was obtained by bribery, through allotting part of the land to some of the members of the Congress and other officials. [1]

Acting for eastern land speculators in 1775, Croghan paid the Six Nations merchandise worth $6,000, for Indian rights to 1,500,000 acres.

After many years of land grabbing and land speculation, and association with others similarly engaged, Croghan died impoverished in Philadelphia. Land speculation is not always profitable, but in those periods of high speculative land prices which it engenders, it restricts labor and the production of wealth.

To understand the basis of the claim of Connecticut for land in Pennsylvania centering about the Wyoming Valley, which continued for a third of a century following 1753, cognizance must be taken of: The grant of all the land between 40° and 48° from Sea to Sea by King James I, November 3, 1620, to the Council of New England, confirmed by his successor, Charles I, nine years later; also of the questionable grant by Earl Warwick, president of the council, two years afterwards to Viscount Say and Sele. This was for "all that part of New England from the Narragansett River, for forty leagues (120 miles) along the seacoast towards the west and southwest, to the South Sea (Pacific Ocean)"; confirmation thereof by King Charles II occurred in 1662.

The grant of Connecticut land by the Council of New England was sixty-one years, the Warwick grant fifty years, and confirmation by Charles only nineteen years, prior to the grant to Penn.

The boundary between Connecticut and New York, substantially as at present, had been agreed upon by a joint committee of those two colonies and confirmed. This boundary, which intervened between Connecticut and Pennsylvania, was declared by the crown lawyers in England as not affecting the claim of Connecticut to territory west of New York.

Not until all the land in Connecticut had been privately appropriated, with no land left for the increasing population, except by purchase of others, for which very few had the money, was attention directed to the virgin territory along the Susquehanna River, within the Penn grant.

Some people in Windham County, Connecticut, formed the Susquehanna Company, comprising about five hundred persons, each of whom subscribed about nine dollars to settle the Wyoming Valley. [74] They petitioned the court in Connecticut to grant them a quit claim for land sixteen miles square on both sides of the Susquehanna. They promised to pay the Indians and have the land settled within three years, subject to the jurisdiction of Connecticut, whereupon the court made the grant.

Advance agents sent to the location, in 1754, negotiated with eighteen Indian chieftains of the Six Nations for an area of land seventy miles north and south, and ten miles east along the river, and extending westward two degrees of longitude, for which they were to pay the equivalent of $2,000. Two sachems refused to sign unless they were paid $1,000 more than the other sachems agreed to take. [74]

Having paid the Indians, the purchasers considered the land, which was uninhabited by white people, as undoubtedly a part of Connecticut, and they petitioned the Connecticut assembly that they might be formed into a distinct commonwealth, if the king would grant it. The assembly granted the petition and recommended the petitioners to the royal favor. There were then about 850 shareholders. [148]

Surveyors were sent to the location and laid off tracts of four hundred acres each, designated as "rights." The company sent an agent to London to lay the matter before King Charles II, who had made the grant of all Pennsylvania to Penn, which included the Wyoming Valley. The question of the right of Connecticut to the land in Penn's domain being submitted to counsel, it was declared that Connecticut had that right.

Furthermore, since this grant to Connecticut antedated the grant to Penn, there was no reason to presume that the crown could make a valid grant to Penn of land previously granted to people in Connecticut.

It appears that fifteen years elapsed before any considerable settlement was made there by the Connecticut people. In 1769 a group of forty settlers arrived. The Pennsylvania authorities, which by that time had become aware of the incursion, arrested them, taking all of them to the jail at Easton. Upon giving bail they returned to Wyoming, and declared their intention of holding the land.

Soon the population increased to three hundred; a Connecticut government was formed, forts erected, laws enacted, a militia established and taxes levied and collected. Wilkes-Barre was laid out within the area, and named for two British statesmen.

The Pennsylvania assembly passed the riot act. Forts and blockhouses were built, besieged, and captured, by both contenders. Connecticut partisans were imprisoned in Philadelphia as hostages for the removal of others, but the Pennsylvania assembly refused further action, claiming it to be a land matter which did not affect the general government. [136]

The contention was inflamed by frauds, intoxicating liquors, fist fights, military battles, surveys, arrests, imprisonment, prosecutions, appeals, politics and by the repeated sales by the Indians of the same land to different persons.

To the steady influx of Connecticut settlers, Penn offered land as tenants, which was refused, and many Pennsylvania settlers took title from the Connecticut Company.

The Connecticut assembly annexed the territory to Litchfield County in Connecticut, practically giving it autonomy, and, in 1773, resolved: "That this assembly, at this time, will assert their claim, and in some proper way support such claim, to those lands contained within the limits and boundaries of the charter of this colony, which are westward of the Province of New York."

The Connecticut claimants sent agents to confer with Governor Penn in Philadelphia, but Penn refused to treat on the matter. Whereupon Connecticut, determined to extend its jurisdiction to the Connecticut settlers on the Susquehanna, incorporated the territory as the town of Westmoreland, and its representatives sat in the Connecticut assembly.

Meantime, however, the company had strong opponents in Connecticut, who recognized it as a land speculation project, and in March, 1774, representatives from twenty-three towns, in opposition, met at Middletown and passed lengthy resolutions against the Connecticut assembly extending jurisdiction west of New York. [148]

A military force of five hundred men, sent by Governor Penn in 1775 to drive out the Connecticut claimants, was repulsed with considerable loss of life on both sides. During the Revolutionary War, British troops and Indians massacred three hundred of the settlers on July 3, 1778. During the next seven years, the Susquehanna Company stockholders and settlers contended for the land, and the Continental Congress called upon both Connecticut and Pennsylvania claimants to desist until Congress could determine the matter.

This was presently done and, in 1786 Connecticut relinquished its claim to land in Pennsylvania but, as compensation, the Connecticut grantees retained their charter grant to western land to the extent of 3,366,921 acres, which they reserved in northeastern Ohio. Except for the bungling by Charles II and his advisors in granting to Penn land which he had only nineteen years previously granted to the Connecticut grantees, this vast Ohio area likely would have been included in the national public domain.

The contention, which had continued for a third of a century, had been for possession of more than five million acres of land, and involved the lives of hundreds, and the ruin of thousands, at the cost of millions of dollars. [74]

Land in Luzerne, Wayne, Lycoming and Northampton Counties had been bought of the Penns. The Holland Land Company held 20,000 acres; Edward Tilghmam, 75,000; Thomas W. Francis, 100,000; Henry Drinker for self and others, 150,000; William Bingham, 300,000. In addition, some other prominent Pennsylvanians held 665,000 acres. [74] This land was, of course, like all such large holdings, obtained for the purpose of exacting increased prices from the younger generation of settlers, who presently must have land on which to work and earn their living.

Disputes regarding the boundary between Pennsylvania and Virginia increased and, in 1773, the Penns appealed to the king to fix the western limits, but the contention over land continued until after the American Revolution, when the Mason and Dixon line was run and ratified by the abutting states in 1784.

During the two years prior to the Revolution, thirty thousand immigrants arrived in Philadelphia. Finding that all the land east of the Alleghenies had been taken, most of which was held unused on speculation, they could locate only on land along, and west of, the mountains.

Complaining that inhabitants of New York had endeavored to obtain land grants in Pennsylvania from the governor of New York, the Penns had repeatedly petitioned the king to fix the boundary between the two provinces. But this was not done until 1789.

With the establishment of the new state, during the Revolutionary War, confiscation of the Penns' lands loomed threateningly. Edmund Physic, who had been for thirty-three years in close association with the land office and was then receiver-general, was requested by the proprietors to prepare a financial statement, from which the following notes are taken: The Penns estimated there were in the Pennsylvania grant 27,955,200 acres. Up to 1776, there had been disposed of 6,363,072 acres, including roads, or approximately one-quarter of the area. Disregarding the receipts for the first nineteen years, the gross sum received for land, between 1701 and 1778, was £688,486, not including that which since 1757 was received for manor land. The land rents during this period amounted to £182,248, of which something more than one-third was received.

A committee was appointed by the assembly in 1779, as stated by Shepard, [136] to "examine the claims of the Penns, to report wherein they were incompatible with the happiness, liberty and safety of the state, and to prepare suitable resolutions to remedy the evils arising from such claims." The Penns retained two noted lawyers. The committee summoned the receiver-general and examined his accounts, after which it reported that the charter of Charles II having been made as well for the enlargement of the English empire, the promotion of trade, the advancement of civil society and the propagation of the Gospel, as for the particular benefit of William Penn and his heirs, it was to be considered as a public trust for the advantage of those who settled in Pennsylvania. The report conceded a particular interest accruing to William Penn and his heirs, but held that interest in nature and essence subordinate to the great and general purposes of society. Again, by the "Conditions and Concessions" announced by the founder, such portion of the land as was not reserved in the form of manors was held in trust by the proprietor for the people; and the proprietors, by imposing land rents and terms for payment of money (except on manors), had violated the concessions on which the people of Pennsylvania were induced to become settlers, usurped a power inconsistent with their own original conditions and defrauded the settlers of large sums of money.

It was deemed advisable to obtain the opinion of Chief Justice McKean on these points, who gave an opinion in favor of the Penns. However, the committee reported in favor of confiscation, with certain reservations, and drew up the Divestment Act, which was enacted November 27, 1779. This act vested in the Commonwealth of Pennsylvania all lands not recorded to purchasers prior to the date of the Declaration of Independence, July 4, 1776. It confirmed to the Penns the rents reserved for their tenths and manors. All arrears of purchase-money were to be payable to the Commonwealth.

It was enacted that £130,000 should be given to the claimants and legatees of Thomas and Richard Penn, "in remembrance of the enterprising spirit of the founder and of the expectations and dependence of his descendants."

In addition thereto, the British government granted an annuity of £4,000, which it paid annually for more than a hundred years, to the eldest male heir of Penn's second wife. At the end of that time, a member of Parliament, no doubt designated a radical, objected to the British people being taxed to make such payments, and it was compounded to a principal sum at about twenty-five years' value, equivalent in all to nearly $2,000,000, paid from taxes levied on the people of Britain.

Shepard, [136] as late as 1896 (116 years after the Divestment Act), wrote: "The larger part of what remains of the old Penn manors is in and around Wilkes-Barre, and some reserved mineral rights in different parts of the state. In Philadelphia about three dozen ground rents exist in what was the manor of Springettsbury, and one irredeemable ground rent on improved land in Race Street near 21st Street. These ground rents continued until cancelled by private purchasers making cash payment."

The Penn rule lasted eighty-five or more years. William's first visit to Pennsylvania was for twenty-one and a half months; his second and last, fifteen years later, for twenty-three months.

George Bancroft, the historian, [5] said of Penn: "The pernicious land tenure gave the colonists a century full of strife which led them to complain, to impeach, to institute committees of inquiry, to send persons and papers, to quarrel with the executive. They sought for nearly a century to compel an appropriation of the income from land rents to the public service."

When the assembly abolished the power and land titles of the Penns and gave them £130,000, it was but an illustration of what is being done everywhere today. The community alone gives value to land; in some cities, lots are valued at millions of dollars, and where funds are appropriated to buy locations for public improvements, the land speculators demand large sums be paid them from taxes levied on the industry of all the people.

We tax ourselves to pay to land speculators the values which we ourselves create.

The land office became inactive at the beginning of the war, and remained so until the new commonwealth took over the granting of land. Grants were thereafter made at £10 per hundred acres; being £5 as purchase price, and £5 in lieu of the usual 1d per acre annual land rent that had been exacted by the Penns.[*]

The legislature in 1784 offered land at varying prices, by selling warrants of survey to be located wherever the purchasers desired, but the returns were unsatisfactory. Many tracts were allotted to soldiers.

Pennsylvania paid to New York State 75¢ per acre for the two hundred thousand acres needed to extend its domain to a harbor on Lake Erie.

William Buttler wrote from Pittsburgh in 1785: "The people are flocking into this country from all quarters, settling on land not belonging to them. Many hundreds have crossed the river and are daily going with their families. I hope the council will provide against so gross and growing an evil."

Pittsburgh was surveyed at about that time, and several towns, including Erie, were laid out by direction of the state legislature. When the anthracite coal mines were opened and internal improvements were projected, intense excitement prevailed in some counties and the wildest speculation in town lots set in. It is said that in Schuylkill County nearly all the towns, including Pottsville, were laid out by speculators. [71]

John Nicholson, who had been one of the trustees for the laying-out of the national capital, left at his death between three and four million acres of idle land. Included in his estate were extensive tracts of the very richest coal deposits in Pennsylvania, held for the rising generation to make more valuable. These finally came into possession of the coal combine, through royalties paid the landholders: the royalties, with something added, being paid by the consumers of the coal.

Robert C. Macauley, writing in the *Pennsylvania Commonweal,* in 1932, said:

"Penn could not today buy, at certain points of the city he

[*]Pa. Land Grants

founded, enough land to stand his coach and team of horses on for the $80,000 for which all the land in Pennsylvania was granted him, in liquidation of unpaid salary for that amount due his father, the value of which land alone has since increased to more than *thirteen billion dollars.*

"This means that since the coming of Penn this thirteen billion dollars has been privately confiscated by title holders, out of the production of Pennsylvanians who, in addition, pay a present land rental in excess of $1,200,000,000 annually, together with taxes.

"But how did Penn get his proprietary right to the land? Charles II, King of England, who granted the land, never saw Pennsylvania, much less being responsible for its existence. After which Penn negotiated with the Indians, giving them some trinkets for possession of land already presumably his.

"The land belonged neither to King Charles nor to the Indians. Nature gave the use, not ownership, of it alike to all continuing generations of mankind. Neither Penn nor the Indians produced the land and, therefore, never could have a moral right to its ownership. Property right in anything can morally inhere only as a result of production, or purchase from the producer.

"When Stephen Girard, the wealthy ship owner of Philadelphia, died a hundred years ago, he left an estate, estimated at approximately $5,000,000, with which to found a college in that city, and on which the trustees have since then expended $43,935,468 for building and maintenance.

"The present value of the Girard Estate, according to a report of The Board of City Trusts, is placed at $89,000,000.

"It seems almost marvelous that an estate of $5,000,000 can expend more than $43,935,000 and still have a surplus of $89,000,000.

"But it will be said, money is entitled to interest. Interest on $5,000,000 at 6 per cent amounts to $300,000 per annum, and for the entire one hundred years since the death of Stephen Girard the trustees of his estate have expended an average of $439,354 annually, nearly half as much more than the annual interest.

"The Girard Estate consists chiefly of land, including one

solid block in the heart of Philadelphia bounded by Market and Chestnut Streets and Eleventh and Twelfth Streets. It is estimated that in 1834, the rental for the entire block was $46,750, according to a statement in the *Franklin Whig and Chambersburg Messenger* of December 24th of that year.

"The present rental of this block is in excess of $1,500,000 annually. This is merely for the use of the land, the improvements thereon having been either paid out of income or supplied by the tenants.

"The Girard Estate, in 1924, according to a report of The Board of City Trusts for that year, received in royalties $3,995,-338.67 for permitting twelve mining corporations to dig 2,807,-750 tons of anthracite coal from its coal land holdings, an average of $1.42 per ton, although at the time of Girard's death the royalty rate was around 7¢ a ton.

"This part of the Girard Estate, assessed at $12,340,741 shows a gross return of 32.3 per cent on that valuation. The Girard Estate, neither during the lifetime of its founder nor since his death more than one hundred years ago, ever mined a single ton of coal. It merely permits others to do so and charges them $1.42 per ton for such permission, which is paid by all who use the coal.

"The real secret of how to spend $43,935,468 out of a $5,000,000 estate and still retain a surplus in excess of $89,000,000 is the power to appropriate wealth produced by others by means of our unjust laws, which treat natural resources as private property.

"Anthracite deposits having been placed where they are by the Creator for the use of succeeding generations, any law which nullifies this, by permitting but a few to monopolize the benefit, is obviously unjust.

"A larger population, with its greater demands for fuel, is alone responsible for the use or rental-value of the coal fields. The same law applies to the increased rental-value of the central city block. Landlords and royalty collectors having rendered no service are therefore entitled to no compensation.

"Neither Penn nor the succeeding title holders of the land of Pennsylvania did anything to produce it. There was the same amount of land before their coming as after their arrival.

"The value of land is now greater, as the result of the presence, ingenuity and industry of all the people, and this increased land-value rightfully belongs to those who created that value.

"All mankind has an equal right to the use of land. When government guarantees to an individual the exclusive use of a piece of land, he owes to government (all the people) the full rental-value of the privilege it has conferred.

"Since every one agrees the Earth is the birthright of all mankind, and that the increased value of its use is due to the mere presence of population, it follows: That the rent of land belongs to the people and that the first duty of government is to collect it."

21

The Trans-Appalachian Region

EVERYWHERE in the Middle West the French preceded the boldest English adventurers and claimed the land west of the Alleghenies by priority of discovery and construction of forts.

The Iroquois also claimed all the Ohio Valley region by conquest of the several Indian tribes that inhabited it. By the treaty at Lancaster, in 1744, they ceded their rights in it to the British, who contended that cession was sufficient warrant for claiming it.

The population of the thirteen colonies, which increased from an estimated 250,000 in 1700 to 1,370,000 fifty years later, was forcing settlement in the Ohio Valley.

In 1748 John Hanbury, a merchant, on behalf of himself and associates in the Ohio Company of Virginia, applied to the British Board of Trade in London, which represented the king in making land grants in America, for a grant of five hundred thousand acres along the Ohio River, between the Monongahela and Kanawha Rivers in the present West Virginia.

Of this, two hundred thousand acres were to be granted immediately, in consideration of settling two hundred families thereon in seven years; the grant to be free of land rent for ten years from the date of the grant, and rent to be paid only on cultivated land—the land, so long as held unused by the company, to be free of rent.

The grantees were to erect a fort and maintain a garrison; then as soon as this was done, the remaining three hundred thousand acres were to be granted, with like obligation, and exemption of land rent. The royal governor, Gooch of Virginia, was ordered to make the grant, which he did in 1749.

The names of the grantees of this and other princely grants of land at that period were from the Social Register of those days, and included three members of the Washington family and four of the Lee. Other Virginia grantees included the names of Fairfax, Carter, Nelson, Thornton, Tayloe, Walker, Lewis, Preston and Henry, and others in England. They organized as the Ohio Company, with £4,000, divided into twenty shares of £200 each, which, alone, would indicate it was a promotion by people of wealth.

A year later they had located a trading-post on Will's Creek, the present site of Cumberland, Maryland. From there they cut a wagon road of approximately eighty miles in length through the wilderness, to about West Newton, the head of bateau navigation on the Yougheogheny River. This was within thirty miles of the site of Pittsburgh and access by water to the Ohio and Mississippi Rivers. It was over this road that Braddock marched to defeat and his death, in 1755.

Until organization of the Ohio Company, the British had made no attempt to possess the Ohio Valley. But without this land the English would be confined east of the Alleghenies, and without it the French would be cut off from any direct connection between the French settlements in Canada and Louisiana. [4] Importance of the control of the Ohio Valley can consequently be appreciated.

At a conference between the Indians and the French and English, at Logstown, on the Ohio River, in 1752, the chief declared to the French: "You are disturbers in this land by taking it away from us by force. This is our land and not yours. The land belongs to neither you nor the English; the Great Being above allowed it to be a dwelling place for us."

To this the Marquis Duquesne replied: "Are you ignorant of the difference between the King of England and the King of France? Go see the forts the French have established and you will see that you can hunt under their very walls. The English, on the contrary, are no sooner in possession of a place than the forests are felled, the land laid bare and the game driven away."

The French had thirteen thousand potential soldiers and maintained military posts at Ogdensburg, Kingston, Fort Duquesne (Pittsburgh), Detroit, Miami River in Ohio, St. Joseph and Fort Chartres. The French governor in Canada sent a force of 250 men down the Allegheny River to take the country between the Niagara and Ohio Rivers.

On reaching the Ohio, they nailed to trees at various locations a tin plate bearing the royal arms of France and buried at the foot of the trees lead plates bearing an inscription claiming ownership and sovereignty of the country. The Indians claimed the land and objected to these plates, some of which are now in museums.

Governor Dinwiddie arrived in Virginia in November, 1751. He was, two years later, ordered by the London government to erect a fort, and drive the French from the Ohio region, by force if necessary.

Upon the outbreak of the French and Indian War, Governor Dinwiddie called for volunteers, promising them two hundred thousand acres along the Ohio River in West Virginia, in addition to their pay. Allotments were to be five thousand acres to each of the higher officers, grading down to fifty acres for each private. At about the same time, he and the Council of Virginia granted to applicants 1,350,000 acres in the Ohio region.

At the outbreak of the war, the French and Indians captured the fort which the Ohio Company was constructing at the site of Pittsburgh, and operations of the company were otherwise disrupted, which, the company claimed, prevented fulfillment of its obligation to locate settlers on its grant within the stipulated seven years.

The large land grants were not popular with the people of Virginia. The House of Burgesses expressed disapproval of Dinwiddie's western land and military policies and requested that, in the future, the governor make small grants, to prevent further extension of land monopoly by large companies. They could see no reason for sending armed men and money to advance the personal business of land speculators. [4]

Governor Francis Farquier, successor to Dinwiddie, in 1757 disfavored large grants, such as those of the Ohio and Loyal

Companies, to be held unused on speculation, as being destructive to the proper settling of a colony.

Further land grants were deferred until after the British captured Fort Duquesne in 1758, when settlers and speculators advanced west of the Alleghenies; the speculators being backed by English capital and political influence. [3]

The British victory encouraged in the Ohio Company promoters the hope of gaining advantages from the awakened interest in the western lands, and of obtaining renewal of the lapsed land grant. [4]

The London government, to pacify the Indians, and probably at the behest of eastern landholders had, in 1763, forbidden settlement west of the Allegheny Mountains. But the demand for land was so insistent that despite the prohibition, afterwards repealed, some thirty thousand persons located there as squatters during the next five years.

After the defeat of the French, and soon after the treaties between the British and the Iroquois at Fort Stanwix, and between the British and the Cherokees at Hard Labor, in South Carolina, numerous land speculations were set afoot in the Ohio Valley, promoted by prominent eastern speculators in western lands. [30]

The treaty between the British and the Indians at Fort Stanwix in 1768 was one of the most important Indian conferences in American history. It was attended by more than eleven hundred Indians of the Six Nations, and others. It was stated that merchandise valued at £10,000 was given as presents to the Indians. For this, they relinquished claims to the lands west of the Appalachians, extending from the Mohawk River in New York to the Tennessee River in Kentucky. [155]

In the 1760's, about fifty members of prominent Virginia and Maryland families, including those of Washington, Lee and Fitzhugh, who already had vastly more land than they could put to use, organized the Mississippi Company. With the intercession of some prominent Englishmen, in London, they applied for 2,500,000 acres on the east side of the Mississippi, along the Wabash and Tennessee Rivers, to be free of rent for twelve years. They were to undertake to settle a meager two hundred families on part of that vast area—equivalent to 12,500 acres per family. Each member of the promoting company was to receive 500,000 acres, as the first land dividend.

Groups of other prominent citizens in New York and Philadelphia, relying on British political and financial co-operation, became stricken with the prevailing craze for land speculation in the trans-Appalachian region. [3]

The popular craze was to get wealth at the expense of others by land speculation, which continues unabated to the present day. It is not so much the land speculators who are blameworthy, but legislators who do nothing to prevent private appropriation of the publicly-created rent of land, thus making the Earth an object of gambling, and robbing the public treasuries of the land rents which the public has created. This necessitates higher taxes on everybody; and furthermore, holding land unused, at a price that restricts development and the production of wealth, is the underlying cause of vast unemployment, and resulting poverty and crime.

Colonel George Washington was a typical representative of these Virginia land speculators. He had a claim to land under Governor Dinwiddie's proclamation offering two hundred thousand acres to volunteers in the French and Indian War. After the war, he bought the land rights of other officers, by which he accumulated title to 32,373 acres along the Ohio and Great Kanawha Rivers in West Virginia. [3]

He then sent an agent to Great Britain and Ireland who advertised in newspapers there, persuading families to migrate to America and locate on his land.

Simons [137] wrote: "Washington used his position as royal surveyor to locate lands within the limits which he was supposed to preserve from settlement. He had helped to maintain in London what would now be called a 'land lobby' to advance his objects. When Parliament, by the Quebec Act in 1774, extended the jurisdiction of the Province of Quebec over the country west of the Alleghenies, his interests were directly threatened, and had the Revolution not occurred and been won, he would have lost his land."

Washington, at his death in 1799, had one of the largest fortunes in the country, consisting mainly of land. He owned seventy thousand acres in Virginia and more than forty-nine thousand acres on the Great Kanawha River in West Virginia, and other near-west places. In addition he owned land in Kentucky, Maryland, Pennsylvania, New York, in the National capital, and other places.

Benjamin Franklin's fortune, two years before his death, in 1788, was estimated at $150,000, mostly in land. [107]

Holders of large tracts of land in the seaboard sections, realizing that the opening of western land would reduce the expected increased demand for land in the East, and thereby retard an increase in the value of their land, endeavored to thwart the granting of land in the West.

General Gage, in their behalf, in 1770 advised London of the many forts and garrisons which would be required, at great cost, to protect settlers attracted there, and that there were millions of acres of good land lying unused in the Atlantic seaboard country. But he did not say that this idle eastern land was held at prices which pioneers were unable to pay.

John Murray, Earl Dunmore, became governor of Virginia in 1771, and was promptly taken in hand by the land speculating element of that colony, led by Dr. Thomas Walker and Colonel Andrew Lewis. Under their guidance he soon became avaricious to obtain some land grants for himself, and presently petitioned the king for a hundred thousand acres of the recently acquired Cherokee lands. [3] His petition was rejected, and three years later, he was selling for the king land along the Ohio River at 10s, or even less, per hundred acres.

In response to an inquiry, Lord Camden, lord chancellor, and Charles Yorke, shortly to hold the same eminent position, replied: "In respect to such places as have been or shall be acquired by citizens by treaty or grant, from any of the Indian princes or governments, your majesty's letters patent are not necessary, the property of the land vesting in the grantee by the Indian grant, subject only to your majesty's right of sovereignty." This was directly contrary to the attitude of the British government in the early Virginia days, when it at that time denied that the natives had any right of propietorship in the land which they had occupied, presumably for many centuries.

The first to act upon this opinion was David Franks & Co., of Philadelphia, organizers of the Illinois Land Company. In 1773 they acquired of the Indians two large tracts of land, one along the Ohio and Mississippi Rivers, and the other on the Illinois River. Two years later they obtained of the Indians two tracts on the Wabash River, and formed the Wabash Land Company, in which Lord Dunmore and several opulent men of Philadelphia, Maryland and London, were shareholders. [3]

It afterwards developed that this opinion by Camden and Yorke did not apply to land in America, but to land in India; that American promoters in London, of western American land grants had obtained a copy which they dishonestly used to their advantage, by omitting words showing that it applied to acquiring land titles from the Moguls in India. [95]

Thomas Walpole, London banker and member of Parliament, son of Horatio, Lord Walpole, and cousin to Horace, was keenly interested in obtaining American land. He had funds at his disposal, as well as certain political influence. [1]

Colonel George Mercer of Virginia was in London, soliciting renewal of the expired land grant of the Ohio Company. Samuel Wharton, a Philadelphia merchant, was also in London seeking a grant of land. They both had the co-operation of Walpole and certain members of the British nobility.

The application of Wharton, representing the promoters of the Vandalia and Indiana Companies, often mentioned in London as the Walpole Companies, afterwards consolidated as the Grand Ohio Company, was for a large part of the land in West Virginia, and part of Kentucky, comprising about thirty million acres.

This land was planned to be sold to settlers and speculators at £10 per hundred acres, about 50¢ per acre, with a perpetual annual land rent of a half-penny per acre in addition.

Terms of the grants to Walpole and associates were agreed upon in 1775, but just then occurred the battle of Lexington and the outbreak of the American Revolution, at the conclusion of which Great Britain had no further control of land in America.

Mercer and Wharton returned to America after the close of the war, when future grants, or rather, the sale, of land devolved upon the Federal government or the States. Wharton applied to Congress for recognition of the proposed grant, but it failed of approval. The original Ohio Company made repeated efforts for reinstatement of its grant, but without success.

Colonel Mercer, and his predecessor lobbyists of the Ohio Company had, in the aggregate, spent thirty years, and Samuel Wharton, ten years, in London, prior to and even all during the American Revolution, in persistent yet fruitless efforts to promote gigantic land grabs in the Ohio Valley. The distinct object was to compel American pioneers, invariably but one jump ahead of poverty, to pay to them a fictitious price for a bit of land in a wilderness, on which to labor and rear a family. Such is the object of all land speculation, but otherwise upright citizens do not hesitate to indulge in it. Their minds are so centered on the prospective profits they do not realize the harm they do.

Virginia speculators were indignant at George III for forbidding, in 1763, settlement of the lands they had acquired of the Indians west of the Alleghenies. Ten years later, the government in London proposed sale of these lands at auction; then came the Quebec Act. The royal land policy was one cause of the revolt against England. No doubt the disallowance of their claims to Indian land grants helped the group of Virginia aristocrats and adventurers to decide, two years later, for revolution. [171]

22

Kentucky

LAND companies were organized in Virginia to obtain land west of the Alleghenies.

One of these was the Loyal Company, to which Virginia officials granted eight hundred thousand acres in Kentucky, with no obligation imposed to make a settlement. It was purely for speculation. Dr. Thomas Walker, of Albemarle County, Virginia, a noted land speculator, was selected to lead an expedition in 1750 to explore and locate the land.

Crossing through Cumberland Gap, the expedition came into southeastern Kentucky, which had not been previously visited by white men. At a point near the present town of Barbourville they constructed a log cabin. Being terrified by Indians, they returned to Virginia, but continued for many years to assert their claim.

George Croghan's traders are recorded, three years later, as trading with the Cherokee Indians along the Kentucky River.

Nineteen years after Walker, in May, 1769, Daniel Boone, who was born near Reading, Pennsylvania, left his home on the Yadkin River in North Carolina with five companions. He went on a hunting expedition and in quest of the country of Kentucky, where he remained two years. [98]

Since it was the spring of the year, the corn-planting season, it has been thought this was an odd time for a purely hunting expedition. Other groups of prospectors penetrated into Kentucky, but no attempt at permanent settlement was made until four years later, when Boone, with his own and several other

North Carolina families, went there, along what became known as the Wilderness Road. The Boone group, too, later returned home. [98]

Disregarding the king's proclamation of 1763 against white people settling west of the Alleghenies, land speculators, and settlers having a desire to get possession of fertile lands in Kentucky before others could get them, located on choice tracts of land in that region.

Harrodsburg, the first settlement in Kentucky, was laid out in June, 1774, by Captain James Harrod and about thirty companions. Each man was assigned a town lot of one-half acre and an "out lot" of ten acres.

Many other adventurers, including surveyors, arrived, intending to obtain land by erecting "improvers' cabins"—merely of four sides without roof—which would create a claim for a location without actual settlement. The Indians, to protect their hunting grounds, opposed them.

By that time, 230 men had established such claims, which, for the most part, were about Harrodsburg, Boiling Springs and St. Asaph.

At the end of 1774 not a single white man had yet made his home permanently in Kentucky. [1]

Colonel Richard Henderson, a former judge in North Carolina, and eight others, who financed Boone's trips to Kentucky, acquired of the Cherokee Indians, in March, 1775, so far as Indians could grant it, about one-half of the land in Kentucky, within the Ohio, Kentucky and Cumberland Rivers. They also acquired land in Tennessee, within the great bend of the Tennessee River, for all of which they engaged to pay the Indians rifles, ammunition, blankets, beads and other articles of a stated value equivalent to $10,000. Part of this land was within the grant by King James I to the Virginia grantees and, further, its assumed sale by the Indians was in violation of the treaty made seven years previously with the Iroquois Indians at Fort Stanwix, New York, and the treaty with the Cherokees at Hard Labor, South Carolina.

Governors Dunmore of Virginia, and Martin of North Carolina, learning of Henderson's activities, each issued proclamations denouncing him and his associates and enjoined all sheriffs and other civil and military officers to prevent execution of Henderson's designs.

Nevertheless, Henderson organized the Transylvania Company, to finance the project, and offered land for sale to speculators and settlers, though the company had not received a grant of land other than an agreement with the Cherokee Indians.

To obtain a royal grant, he declared they were prepared to pay a land rent to the king if he would confirm the title; otherwise they would organize a separate government and declare their independence.

Henderson engaged Boone to go, with thirty others, to Otter Creek and erect a fort, where he was to open a land office. Upon reaching the location, Boone plotted most of the good land about the proposed fort into two-acre lots and distributed them to his companions. When Henderson arrived, seeing this, he selected another location and laid out fifty-four lots. [98]

Henderson offered no objection to the claimants at Harrodsburg. To attract settlers, he made extensive grants of land, including two thousand acres to Boone, at an annual land rent of one-half-penny per acre.

Phelan [117] said: "The immortal lines which Byron gives to Daniel Boone are poetical but they are not true. Daniel Boone was a land speculator and the agent of land speculators and, in the expressive phraseology of the day, would be called a 'land shark.' He entered enough land claims in Kentucky to have made him wealthy had he but known how to perfect his titles. He obtained numerous grants from Spain which he lost by negligence."

In the first fifteen months, nine hundred claims, for 560,000 acres, limited to 640 acres to each buyer, had been registered with the Transylvania Company. Grants were first made at 20s per hundred acres, less than 5¢ per acre; increased later to 50s per hundred acres, approximately 12¢ per acre. Buyers were offered a salesman's commission, in the form of option on 340 acres additional, for each taxable settler they brought into the country. [30]

Hasty and undependable surveying caused such overlapping of boundaries that numerous purchasers soon realized that their claims were involved in hopeless confusion. Complaints were presently made to the Virginia commission by eighty-four settlers that they had been lured into buying land from the Transylvania Company upon the faith that they were receiving "an indefeasible title"; that "the fees for entry and surveying had been increased to an exorbitant rate"; and that "the company promoters proposed increasing the price of land as their insatiable avarice shall dictate." [98]

Henderson based the validity of his purchase of the Cherokees upon the treaty at Lochber, in October, 1770, in which the Mohawk tribe reconveyed land in Kentucky and Tennessee to the Cherokees.

Both the Virginia and North Carolina governments declared the Cherokee grant void. To settle the contention, they assented to a reduced area of two hundred thousand acres on the Green River, and two hundred thousand acres in Powell's Valley.

The Virginia assembly enacted, in 1776, that the land in Kentucky was a part of Virginia and designated it as Kentucky County, after which the Transylvania Company passed out of existence. [98]

The land on which Louisville is situated was granted by Governor Dunmore to Dr. John Connolly, a former surgeon's mate in the French and Indian War.

A general land law enacted by the Virginia assembly, in 1779, permitted to each applicant four hundred acres in Kentucky at 40¢ per acre, provided they had, prior to the previous year, built a cabin and grown a crop of corn. [30]

The vast areas of good land east of the Alleghenies, held unused on speculation at high prices, drove large numbers of the increasing population to seek homes in the Indian-infested wilderness west of the mountains.

Upon the opening of the surveyor's office near Harrodsburg, in 1780, the place swarmed with applicants, many being from states other than Virginia. [1] Four years later it was estimated that thirty thousand settlers had located in Kentucky.

During this great immigration period, so many families from North Carolina, Virginia, Maryland, and Pennsylvania were moving westward that the roads were lined with them, and many became stranded by the roadside and were in want of food.

The first Kentucky convention, in 1784 resolved: ". . . that to grant any person a larger quantity of land than he designs *bona fide* to seat himself and his family on, is a grievance, because it is subversive of the fundamental principles of a free republican government . . . and because it opens the door to speculation by which innumerable evils may ensue to the less opulent part of the inhabitants . . ."

Notwithstanding these words of great wisdom, the Virginia assembly the following year granted in Kentucky: one tract of 55,390 acres, and another of 44,470 acres, to Martin Picket; 32,000 acres to Charles Willing, a merchant, of a wealthy Philadelphia family, and 50,000 acres to Philip Barbour. [21] It is quite unlikely that any of these grants were located upon by the grantees, having been obtained purely for speculation.

Kentucky continued as part of Virginia, which granted land there in fee simple to settlers and to veterans of the French and Indian War, until Kentucky became a Territory, in 1790. Two years afterwards it was admitted as a State of the Union.

A traveler through Kentucky, in 1802, noted that the "uncertainties of land titles are an inexhaustible source of tedious and expensive law suits."

23

Tennessee

THE land in Tennessee was included in the grant by Charles II to the eight Carolina grantees. The portion unsold by them was subsequently bought by the British crown. By treaty with France in 1763, the western limit of Tennessee was restricted to the Mississippi River, instead of the South Sea.

Despite inter-Indian wars, and those against and by the whites, there began, about 1769, a steadily increasing migration of Carolina people across the mountains into Tennessee. Each month, each week, brought men, women and children as new settlers. They spread down the Watauga River from valley to valley, from creek to creek. They were after free land, by which to improve their condition, and they were willing to risk what might happen to them if they could get land on which to build their homes. [117]

By treaty, about 1772, the Indians granted the use of land to Charles Robertson, who then made land allotments to the settlers, who afterwards perfected their titles at the Watauga land office.

James Robertson led a group of settlers from North Carolina to Tennessee in 1779, and founded Nashville. The rapidity with which the settlement increased and spread was phenomenal.

Throughout the Revolutionary War era, North Carolina claimed as part of its domain all the land in Tennessee, and the politics of that state were tainted with speculation in Tennessee land. Politicians, in league with surveyors and Indian fighters, controlled the government and divided the spoils.

Land had been promised the soldiers of the Revolutionary War but, in 1782, when the lands were to be allotted, it was found that "sundry families had already settled on the proposed grants and it became necessary to allow them to retain their entries to the usual limit of 640 acres."

The early history of Tennessee is filled with accounts of the troubles and conflicts which arose from different claims. Sometimes five or six claimants would appear for the same land—one claiming under a grant by the Carolina lords proprietors; one under an unrecorded grant by Lord Granville (see Carolinas); one under the laws of North Carolina; one by executors' sale, and one in possession. The various treaties with Indians, and the little regard for them by the settlers, added to the causes of confusion. [117]

In the 1780's some roads were cut through, which facilitated immigration. A land office was opened by North Carolina in 1783 for the sale of lands in Tennessee, though the Indian claim to a large part of it had not been extinguished.

Tracts of 640 acres were offered to any settler, and a hundred acres additional to his wife and each of his children, at £2 per hundred acres, being less than 10¢ per acre; preference being given to those who had already located on the land. [50] But purchases at that time were made mostly in large tracts by speculators, to be held for higher prices as population increased.

By rushing to the land entry office, even before North Carolina had ceded the land to Tennessee, the land jobbers looted the Tennessee domain of the best land. [165]

Speculators and settlers overran the Cherokee Indians, driving them into the woods, murdering their women and children, as if to extirpate these poor wretches. The Cherokees then attacked the troops sent in pursuit and only three Americans escaped. [119]

In the great bend of the Tennessee River there was a fine body of land, for which Georgia and South Carolina were rival claimants. William Blount and John Sevier were in the forefront in exploiting that region. [165]

Blount, in 1783, wrote: "This dispute between the two states will, in my opinion, be very favorable to our designs in obtaining title. . . . It now seems that every person I have seen envies us the purchase and wishes to own a part of the bend of the Tennessee."

The lands in the great bend continued to attract and engage attention for two decades. Phases of this history of Tennessee and the State of Franklin can be understood only in the light of this fact. [165]

Three years after 1783 land along the Tennessee River was selling at 1s 6d (37¢) per acre, but as demand by settlers and speculators increased, the price of desirable locations rapidly rose.

To sever connection with North Carolina, the settlers in the Tennessee region organized the State of Franklin in 1785, and elected John Sevier as governor. It continued as such until March, 1788, after which, for six years, the region was governed by North Carolina.

In ceding to Tennessee the land in that territory, the North Carolina politician-speculators stipulated that absentee-held land in Tennessee, of which they held large areas unused, should not be taxed more than other land. [69]

There was opposition by holders of land in west Tennessee to North Carolina's ceding to the national government land west of the Allegheny Mountains; and North Carolina was the last of the seaboard states to do so. But that cession proved to be the shell without the kernel, because, before being transferred to the national government, nearly all of it had been allotted to private holders. What little was possessed by the State was sold for internal improvements.

In 1792 Governor Sevier and Landon Carter, an official of the land office, held in partnership land warrants for 128,000 acres. Charges were made that Sevier (whom the State of Tennessee has honored by a statue in the capitol at Washington) was deeply implicated in fraudulent land warrants, and the charges were pressed against him. [117]

Tennessee was admitted as a State of the Union in 1796, and William Blount was elected to the United States Senate. Because his avaricious land speculations involved him in intrigue with the British (as cited in the chapter on the Gulf Region), he was expelled from the Senate.

John Rice, an Indian trader, entered a claim in the North Carolina land office, in 1783, for five thousand acres, which included a bluff along the Mississippi River, now within Memphis.

That same year, a claim for an adjoining five thousand acres was entered by John Ramsay and John Overton. The state of North Carolina was paid £10 per hundred acres, or 49¢ per acre, for these lands which, in substance and in fact, were made saleable by the national government. [165]

North Carolina had no right to sell the west Tennessee land, for until 1818 the Chickasaws were recognized by the United States government as the owners of the land, and any court would have declared the Rice and Ramsay grants illegal. [25]

Overton bought the Rice tract for $500 in 1795, and two years afterwards sold one-half of it to General Andrew Jackson, later President of the United States, for $100. Jackson, after holding it twenty-one years, sold one-eighth for $5,000. [25]

Memphis was laid out on the Rice tract, in 1819, and that year conveyance of the first lot was made. [117]

Many of the settlers on the Memphis tract had previously acquired locations from the Indians and consequently had a better claim to the land than had the more recent purchasers. To avoid litigation, the Rice holders gave lots to the old settlers. [25]

Overton, a retired Chief Justice of the Supreme Court of Tennessee, and General Jackson were partners, for thirty years, in land deals that were sometimes questionable. Overton became the wealthiest man in Tennessee. [25]

One of the surveyors of the time located and claimed 365,000 acres of land. The total of choice lands put under entry in west Tennessee must have been a staggering one. [165]

To extinguish the Chickasaws' claim to all the land in Kentucky and Tennessee, the United States government in 1818 agreed to pay them $20,000 annually for 15 successive years.

Promptly thereafter, North Carolina speculators sent agents into Tennessee to locate lands. It was stated: "By this Indian cession many speculators are at once made rich. One person obtained 123,000 acres worth, at a moderate calculation, more than a million dollars." [165]

The demand, mainly by speculators, was so great that land

along the Mississippi River in Tennessee was soon selling at an average price of $10 per acre—land which only five years previously had sold at 12½¢ to 25¢ per acre.

One of the first Carolina settlers in the Chickasaw area stated that: "of the six million acres obtained from the Chickasaws, less than two million acres fit for cultivation would remain after all the Carolina entries and warrants were satisfied. The truth is the rich soil has been divided among a few, very few. It is all a mystery, even to the people in Nashville." [165]

So many North Carolina warrants for land in Tennessee had been issued, many of them illegally, that every new area of land opened for disposal was immediately absorbed in satisfying them.

Claimants entitled to land by pre-emption in Tennessee were, in 1841, confirmed in that privilege for not exceeding two hundred acres each. The lots were on the frontier, claimants paying to the state 12½¢ per acre. After 1841 the state publicly offered land at that price. [146]

24

Texas

ALONSO ALVAREZ DE PINEDA, sent by the governor of Jamaica in 1518 to explore the north coast of the Gulf of Mexico, was probably the first white man ever to see the land which is now a part of Texas.

Spaniards from Mexico encountered Frenchmen along the Rio Grande in 1716, which prompted the Spaniards, two years later, to found the Alamo and other mission settlements in Texas. [165]

Philip Nolan, an Irish-American, was in Texas in 1801 buying horses of the Indians. He and several companions were killed by Spaniards and others were captured and confined in Mexican prisons. But American settlers west of the Sabine River still entertained, in 1819, ideas of invading Texas more deeply. [84]

Stephen F. Austin received confirmation in 1823 of a Mexican land grant in Texas. The grant was for a square league, or 4,428 acres of land, for each man to be located; it had been solicited by his since deceased father. He led to Texas the first colony of three hundred families. Hundreds of others soon followed. They located along the Colorado and Brazos Rivers, where they were squatters on the land until permanent locations were allotted them. [161]

During the next year, 247 Mexican grants for land in Texas, not exceeding forty-nine thousand acres each, were made by the governor, but all future grants were to be made by the legislature of the consolidated Mexican state of Coahula-Texas. Some of these were afterwards forfeited. Many of them were made the basis of wild land speculation in the United States. [161]

James Bowie seems to have discovered the method, under the state colonization law, of having native Mexicans apply for tracts of land of the legal limit of eleven leagues (48,708 acres), and then buying this land from them. Bowie obtained, by 1830, something more than seven hundred thousand acres.

From this precedent, with the help of profit-seeking lawyers, a considerable traffic developed. Native Mexicans in various parts of the republic came to realize that they were entitled to the privilege of being granted eleven leagues of Texas land from their government, and of then selling them to American speculators; [174]—the sale price, over any bribe they may have had to pay the Mexican officials, and lawyer's fees, being all profit.

Coahula-Texas needing funds, the state legislature in 1834 decreed that land could be sold at auction to foreigners as well as to natives, in lots of 177 acres, at a minimum of $10 per lot, but limited to 48,708 acres to any one purchaser.

The following year the legislature, wanting quicker action, authorized the sale of 1,771,200 acres at private sale, at not less than 6¢ per acre, without restrictions. The wholesale manner in which the Mexican state authorities bartered away the public lands in Texas to speculators created a scandal, and caused great indignation among the colonists. [174]

New York and Boston land speculators were obtaining Mexican grants of large areas of land in the Texas region for purported colonization. Each colonist was to have a square league, of 4,428 acres. By 1832, thirty-three colonization contracts had been made, some of which were transferred to the Galveston Bay & Texas Land Company, and others to the Colorado & Red River Land Company. From the company office at 8 Wall Street, New York, a pamphlet was issued, which computed the area of its grant at twenty million acres and stated that it was authorized to select twenty-three thousand acres additional for each hundred families it colonized.

When the Mexican national government charged corruption in obtaining these state grants, as flagrantly in violation of Mexican laws, and subject to forfeiture, these American speculators proposed forming an independent Republic of Texas. Towards this end they supplied funds for the purchase of arms and ammunition. One Samuel Williams, a banker, and others advanced funds, for which they received scrip which entitled them to 1,329,000 acres. [21]

In March, 1836, four days before the fall of the Alamo, Texas declared its separation from Coahula and its independence of Mexico, and claimed the Rio Grande as its southern boundary, with an area of 175,587,840 acres.

The Texas Congress ordered the surveying of land on the American plan, into sections of 640 acres each; issued land scrip at 50¢ per acre and provided for agents to dispose of it.

Land was granted on which some settlers built cabins in the Cherokee country. This, together with repudiation by the whites of the treaty with the Cherokees, led to strife between them.

Forging of land deeds was another grievance. Land Commissioners in one county did a profitable business in issuing forged "head right" certificates. [84]

Writing from Texas in 1838, Rev. Littleton Fowler, who was sent there as a missionary, said: "The existing and absorbing subject of locating and proving up lands has prevented many from giving attention to the Gospel. The scramble for land, not the beguilement of the Devil, is the greatest drawback to missionary effort in Texas."

Spanish and Mexican land grants, land frauds and issuance of large quantities of land scrip, gave trouble. Confusion was partially prevented in the future by establishment of a general land office by the new republic. [84]

O. Henry, the noted author, a Texan, writing in 1894 of the Texas Land Office said: "Volumes could be filled with accounts of the knavery, the double-dealing, the cross purposes, the perjury, the lies, the bribery, the alterations and erasing, the suppressing and destroying of papers, the various schemes and plots that for the sake of the almighty dollar have left their stain upon the records of the General Land Office.

"A class of land speculators commonly called land-sharks, unscrupulous and greedy, have left their trail in every department of this office, in the shape of titles destroyed, patents cancelled, homes demolished and torn away, forged transfers and lying affidavits."

After prolonged agitation for and against, the Republic of Texas became one of the states of the American Union, in 1846. In this, Texas stipulated that it retain ownership and jurisdiction of its public land, and Texas lands have never been part of the United States public domain.

Millions of acres were claimed by individuals through fraudulent or illegal titles, and the state was forced to bring suits to recover them. Other vast tracts, which had been cleared or settled upon, added to the confusion. The land question always has been a vexatious problem in Texas. In the "land grabbing" enterprises were the names of some of the most sterling Texas patriots. [161]

The Texas legislature in 1850 allotted for the endowment of public schools, four square leagues (17,712 acres) of land in each county which had been created during the previous 11 years. Large grants of land were made to the University of Texas.

In the 1870's, agents and literature were sent through the northern states, to induce purchase of Texas land and migration of settlers thereto.

Until the Texas public domain was exhausted, railroad promoters were granted twenty, in some instances thirty-two, alternate sections of 640 acres each, for each mile of railroad built and put into operation. These grants, which amounted to millions of acres, were often illegally and fraudulently acquired, and the promoters obtained more land than they were entitled to receive. [84]

The State granted three million acres, valued at $1.50 per acre, to a building contractor, for the building of a State Capitol building at Austin. During the four years following 1883, Texas sold land at $2 per acre, with thirty years to pay for it, which enabled speculators to buy and easily hold land unused, while the incoming settlers, requiring land for use, ran up the price on themselves.

25

California

MAGELLAN in 1520 showed the way to the Pacific Ocean, through the Strait now bearing his name.

The following year, Cortez completed his conquest of Mexico and, thirteen years later, commanded an expedition through the Strait and discovered Lower California, at La Paz. Three years afterwards he sent to Lower California an expedition to explore the Gulf, after which he returned to Spain.

Alarcon, with two ships, sailed up the Gulf of California in 1540, entered the Colorado River, and was the first white man to set foot in present California, though Cabrillo, a Portuguese navigator, is credited with having discovered California. [61]

Two years afterwards the Spanish governor sent out Cabrillo and Ferrelo to explore the coast northwards. They discovered the harbor which they named San Miguel, afterwards named San Diego.

They touched at Santa Barbara and, after reaching 41° N., returned south. After Cabrillo's death, Ferrelo, who succeeded to the command, sailed the following year to the vicinity of Rogue River, Oregon, and then returned.

In 1578 Drake, with three ships, sailed through the Strait, after which he lost sight of two of his ships. In the "Golden Hind," he sailed north along the Oregon coast, where he put ashore his Spanish pilot, who walked the 3,500 miles to Mexico. [150]

Drake returned to the present Drake's Bay, outside the Golden Gate, and harbored there thirty-six days; thence he sailed to the Philippines, and home around the Cape of Good Hope. He reported that while on the California coast he nailed to a post a brass plate inscribed as follows: "Bee it known vnto all men by these presents, Ivne 17, 1579. By the grace of God and in the name of Herr Maiesty Queen Elizabeth of England and herr svccessors forever I take possession of this Kingdom whose King and people freely resigne their right and title in the whole land vnto Herr Maiesties keepeing now named be me and to bee knowne vnto all men as Nova Albion. Francis Drake."

This plate was not discovered until 354 years afterwards, a short distance inland from Drake's Bay. The California Historical Society, after scientific tests, has declared its authenticity.

Vizcaino, a Spaniard, anchored with three ships in San Diego Bay in 1602, and then went to and named Monterey Bay. This bay was not visited again until 166 years afterwards, and meanwhile it was forgotten by successive generations.

The Jesuits, who had been active in establishing missions in California, were in 1768 expelled from the realm by King Charles III of Spain. Thereupon the Franciscans began locating such missions.

By order of the king, Portola, governor of California, organized an expedition, of which two divisions went by land and two by sea, to make a permanent settlement in the present California. They congregated at San Diego and were the first white men to settle in that territory.

Portola with sixty-five men, including soldiers, priests, muleteers and Indians, proceeded to, and named Los Angeles, where he discovered oil; thence to Monterey, and to the present site of San Francisco.

From this expedition there were established, during the next fifty-four years, twenty-one missions and settlements, between San Diego and the north side of San Francisco Bay. Each mission was located on the best land thereabouts. Generally, a tract of some twelve miles square constituted a farm, where presently, thousands of sheep and cattle grazed. From the seacoast to the mountains, from San Diego to San Francisco, all the land with a few exceptions, was claimed by the priests as mission property, without reference to the number of establishments. [150]

These few exceptions related to presidios (army posts), the

commander of which had authority to grant building lots to soldiers and other residents within four square leagues of headquarters, though it is uncertain that this was ever done. Another exception was that each settler in a pueblo (village) was entitled to an inalienable homestead of two hundred varas (550 feet) square, exempt from taxation for five years, after which period there was an annual land rent for the tract of one and a quarter bushels of corn. [150]

The Spanish and Mexican systems of settling California contemplated a three-fold occupation of the land: by the religious pioneers through the missions; by the military through the presidio; and by civilians congregated in pueblos. The first grant of land made within California was to a Spanish soldier who had married a native convert. [150]

The presidio at San Francisco was founded in the year of American Independence, and five years later a code of laws for California was approved by the King of Spain.

Captain George Vancouver, the English explorer, after exploring the northwestern coast, put in at San Francisco, Monterey, Santa Barbara and San Diego, in 1792. The first American vessel to call at a California port was a northwest trader, en route to China with furs, which anchored in Monterey Bay four years after Vancouver.

The Russian ship "Juno," with a cargo of Russian goods, seeking food for the Russian settlers at Sitka, arrived in San Francisco Bay in 1806. Six years afterwards the Russian-American Company built Fort Rossia, at Bodego Bay, thirty miles north of San Francisco, which Russia hoped would prove the beginning of their domination over the northwestern coast of America. [61]

Ten years later the Russian ship "Rurik," on an exploring voyage, anchored in San Francisco Bay, where the ship's company entertained the Spanish-Californians, and in turn were entertained with fiestas. Three members of the expedition afterwards wrote books respecting the country. Eight years later another Russian ship, en route to protect the Russian settlements on the northwestern coast, anchored in San Francisco Bay. [61]

Staggering under a large debt in protecting the throne against usurpation by Napoleon, the Spanish cortes, in 1813, ordered the sale of crown lands. [150]

Thomas Doake, a sailor from the United States ship "Albatross," landed near Santa Barbara in 1816, and became the first American settler in California.

Mexico having declared its independence of Spain, the governor and his military force stationed at the Monterey presidio in 1822 replaced the Spanish flag which had flown over California fifty-five years, by the flag of the new Mexican government. Similar action followed at other presidios, whereupon California ceased for ever to be a province of Spain.

The Mexican Congress in 1824 adopted a decree which promised colonization of lands and security of foreigners: land grants to be restricted to one square league (4,428 acres) of irrigable land; four square leagues where dependent on rain, or six leagues of grazing lands; and that all landholders must engage to inhabit and cultivate their lands a certain portion of time. The mission lands were forbidden to be granted until it should be determined who owned them.

Some American fur trappers from the Missouri country, who came to the San Gabriel mission in 1826, were the first white men to come overland to California from the East.

Governor Figueroa issued a decree in 1834, providing for conversion of missions into pueblos; friars to be relieved of temporal duties; each head of a family to be given a lot one hundred by four hundred varas (275 by 1,100 feet). The following year he founded a garrison, town and colony at Sonoma, on the northern frontier, as a protection against Russian or other foreign invasion. [61]

It was at this period that the missions reached their highest prosperity. According to DeMofras, the French historian of California, the twenty-one missions then held 30,650 Indians living in the communities. The horned cattle numbered 424,000; horses, mules and asses numbered 62,500, besides the wild ones running over the plains in troops; sheep, goats and swine 321,500; and 122,500 bushels of various grains.

The Russian government in 1841 sanctioned the withdrawal of the Russian-American Company from California, and sale of its fort.

The explorations by Vitus Bering, a Dane, for the Russian

government, 193 years previously, and subsequent settlements by the Russians along the coast, were the origin of the sovereignty by Russia of Alaska, covering 586,400 square miles; for the land and sovereignty of which the United States in 1867 paid to Russia $7,000,000 and $200,000 additional for the improvements.

John Sutter, a naturalized American, formerly of the Swiss army, became one of the most prominent men of his time in California. In 1841 he obtained a Mexican land grant of thirty-three square miles. He bought of the Russian-American Company, Fort Rossia, which he dismantled, and then erected Fort Sutter, on the Sacramento River, and a mill at Coloma, on the American River.

The first exploring expedition from the United States to California, comprising six vessels, in command of Lieut. Charles Wilkes, with six hundred men, including many scientists, arrived in San Francisco Bay in 1841.

That year, the first overland emigrant train, consisting of thirty-four persons seeking land, arrived in California from Mid-Western United States; there also arrived an emigrant party from New Mexico.

The first discovery of placer gold in paying quantities in California was made eight miles west of Newhall in 1842, and twenty ounces were sent to the Philadelphia mint.

Captain John Charles Fremont, leading his first overland exploring expedition, arrived at Fort Sutter in 1844. The same year, a party of some fifty men, women and children, with twelve wagons, from the Missouri River, reached Fort Sutter.

War between Mexico and the United States began May 13, 1846.

In July that year, Great Britain had nine warships in the Pacific—the largest squadron they had ever had in those waters. Commodore Sloat, in the United States frigate "Savannah," was at that time at Monterey.

There was evidence of an intrigue whereby Britain was to take over California in payment of a debt owed by Mexico to British subjects. The possible cause of this presumed action by Britain is treated in the chapter on the Oregon Region.

Without knowledge that two months previously war between

the United States and Mexico had been declared, Commodore Sloat issued a proclamation declaring California henceforth a part of the United States, and sent an officer with 250 marines and seamen ashore to hoist the American Flag over Monterey.

Gold discovered at Sutter's Coloma mill, January 19, 1848, inaugurated a nation-wide gold rush and influx of people into California.

Before this discovery became widely known, an armistice in the war was agreed upon, followed by the treaty of Guadalupe-Hidalgo (Mexico), February 2, 1848; signed by the United States the following March, and by Mexico in May.

The population of California, the year before discovery of gold in 1848, could not have exceeded ten thousand, but three years after the discovery, the population was two hundred thousand. The name of Yerba Buena was changed to San Francisco in January, 1847, at which time it was surveyed and plotted. Within three years, the population increased from three hundred to twenty-seven thousand and the price of building lots increased from $15 to $15,000 each. [33]

Judging from court records, the first alcalde, or mayor, must have been constantly occupied in making land grants. Land acquired such high value that trouble arose between claimants under Spanish and Mexican grants and those who claimed by pre-emption or actual possession. There were armed conflicts, with loss of life. The choicest part of the town was found to be covered by no less than five different Spanish and Mexican grants for the same land, every one of them having been forged after the war. Sacramento, Stockton and other sites were claimed on similar titles. [150]

American squatters on the Sutter grant challenged the validity of the Mexican grant to Sutter and defied court orders for ejectment. This resulted in armed resistance in 1850, in which four men were killed and five wounded.

That year California was admitted as a state of the Union, and a land commission was appointed by act of Congress to examine, and approve or reject, land claims, subject to appeal to the United States Supreme Court. It examined 813 claims, of which 203 were rejected and 591 confirmed, 99 of the latter by the

Supreme Court. The litigation dragged along for more than thirty years.

The large immigration of settlers, which promised a continued increased demand for land, created a desire upon the part of holders to wait for the unearned increment. This led and continues to lead to the withholding of so much desirable land, at speculative prices, that the full development of the state has been restricted. In a speech in the legislature, a member said: "It is such a holder who puts a blight on everything. He holds large areas which he refuses to sell except at prices which few, if any, can afford to pay."

Henry Miller, who came to the United States as an immigrant in 1850, acquired an immense area of the richest land in California and Oregon, suitable for cotton, grain and dairying. A report of the agents of the estate, issued in 1935, revealed that in the previous nine years, when the sale of their land in California began, 558,302 acres had been sold at $20,841,986, and that an area of just about the same value remained. All land value is publicly, and not privately, created, and should be collected for the public treasury to reduce the general tax levy.

The California Commission of Immigration and Housing made a careful investigation, some years ago, as to where some of the public domain has gone.

In Siskiyou County alone, the Central Pacific Rail Road Company held 664,830 acres. In San Bernardino County, the Southern Pacific Company held 642,246 acres, and 4,200,000 acres in other counties. The Miller & Lux estate held approximately 700,000 acres. As a comparison, the entire state of Rhode Island contains only 798,720 acres.) In the eight southern counties, there were two hundred and fifty-five holdings aggregating 4,893,915 acres. There were thirty-two holdings each of 15,000 acres, seven of 50,000 acres each, one of 183,399 acres, the last named being one-fourth the area of Rhode Island.

"By such holdings," says the Commission, "we foster unemployment, yet it is considered legitimate business to purchase land for the avowed purpose of preventing capital and labor from being employed upon it until enormous sums can be extracted for this privilege."

No problem appears to be more persistent or more universal than that of adjusting man to land. When the Commonwealth Club investigated farm tenancy in California, it recognized the conditions that led to the farm bloc in Congress. The committee concluded that tenancy does not tend to land ownership under existing high priced lands. Inquiry as to time needed for a tenant to acquire ownership brought such answers as, "three to thirty years," "maybe a lifetime."

Norma Cooley, writing in *Tax Facts,* said: "In spite of its natural advantages—really because of them—California got off to a bad start. In the first place, it was afflicted with Spanish and Mexican land grants, a policy that laid the foundation for more rascality, fraud, foul-play, sharp practice and downright robbery than, probably, has ever been practiced anywhere else within the same time and space.

"When California was transferred to the United States, this government agreed to recognize these grants as a matter of honor. It turned out to be honor among thieves. The land speculator, who is the earliest and most persistent of all pests in any Garden of Eden, was early on the scene, and has not yet departed.

"The early settlers in California were a land-hungry people— that is why they came. They had little equipment and less money, but they had their labor, and labor applied to land produces wealth, and out of the produce of their labor they were forced to meet the terms of the land grantees, whether they bought or rented land.

"The large landholdings that grew out of the Mexican grants, and the huge grants of more than sixteen million acres given to the railroad promoters, laid as fine a corner-stone for land monopoly as any one could want. With land as the source of all employment, doesn't it seem absurd that any individual, or group of individuals, should 'own' millions of acres of idle land when jobs are so scarce that here, in this fertile land, we must feed and clothe hundreds of thousands through charity? Isn't it a little odd that we boast of the natural resources of our state, yet find it a calamity when men come without bringing wealth from the outside in order to buy of private, and often absentee holders, the privilege of using these resources?

"Population and the need for land gives land its value. The land of California belongs to the people of California, but by extravagant squandering of land by legislatures during the first twenty years, at $1.25 per acre, it has passed into the hands of a comparatively few, leaving no land for the next generation except by purchase from those who happened to be born earlier and got hold of it.

"Every flivver tourist, every mendicant, that comes to California brings a mouth to feed and the labor to feed it. All he needs is access to the natural resources of the land that lie within our boundaries.

"When Felipe De Neve founded the pueblo at Los Angeles, in 1781, and imported families to constitute its citizens, the land was not given to the settlers, but allotted to their use, and could not be mortgaged or sold. Each family was entitled to a fifty-five foot lot fronting on the plaza, for business and residence purposes, and one or two seven-acre parcels directly adjacent. The balance of the thirty-six square miles was free range. But everything, including the plaza itself, remained city owned.

"With such a start as this, what happened to deprive Los Angeles of the wealth that should be filling its coffers, paying for all its departments of government and relieving tax burdened industry?

"When the city needed cash it sold some of this land at auction. The southwest corner of Second and Spring Streets (now in the center of the city), was sold for $100, and the adjacent lot for the same price; the entire Second Street frontage between Spring and Broadway, 120 feet deep, for $200.

"And thus did the city of Los Angeles sell its very heart in a three days' auction for a grand total of $7,848. As late as 1850, Los Angeles owned nearly 99 per cent of its land, about thirty-six square miles, of which the plaza was the center. Within the lifetime of one man, Los Angeles frittered away its heritage and today all it owns of its original holdings are bits of land in Elysian Park, some fragments of the Los Angeles River bed, and Pershing Square.

"What if Los Angeles had retained possession of this land? The city would have enjoyed a natural, healthy growth. As each new family moved in, it could have taken up the next available plot of ground adjacent to those that surrounded the plaza. There would have been no need to move to the outskirts to get cheap land.

"When the time came for street paving and lighting, and for police and fire departments, there would have been no such thing as running these improvements and services past many vacant lots to reach outlying homes. Streets could have been laid out, sites allotted for a civic center, parks, playgrounds, public buildings, etc. But through the years, we have paid out millions of dollars to buy back land that the city gave away with lavish hand for meager service, or sold for a song.

"Many of the downtown buildings stand on leased land now, but the land rent is paid to an individual landholder. Would the building owner be any less secure in the possession of his property if this land rental were paid into the public treasury? Certainly not. He would have this added advantage—the money that he paid for the use of the land would be all that he would be required to pay as his share of government expenses. He would not have to pay this, as he does now, and pay in addition a tax on his improvements and personal property, and on purchases of commodities. Think of that, heavily burdened taxpayers—all the ground rent of this value turned into the public treasury and not a cent of taxes to pay! Think what that would mean to Los Angeles today, or similarly, to any other city anywhere, every plot of ground used to the best advantage instead of modern fireproof buildings standing among unsightly structures and vacant lots. No taxes to pay, merely the annual rent for the use of the land.

"Imagine the financial position of Los Angeles today if it were receiving ground-lease revenues from the 36 square miles of land surrounding the plaza! The public owned the land, the founder had pointed the way we should go and had established it as a definite policy.

"Buying and selling land, the glorious game of real estate, does enrich the few—at the expense of the many. Similar practices in other states make conditions in those states likewise so intolerable that men load their suffering families into rickety cars and head for California which has been long advertised as a place of un-usual opportunities.

"If we could once get it through our heads that it is ridiculous for one individual to pay another for the right to use the earth, land would be available to all; jobs would be plentiful in town and country. We would not have this strange paradox of land barons and beggars, idle men and idle acres, homeless folk and stranded building trades.

"We must learn to recognize every able-bodied man who enters California, with or without a family, in overalls or tuxedo, as a self-sustaining individual—then see that natural opportunities are not so monopolized that we have to pass the hat for him.

"The citizens of Los Angeles are today barred from much-needed recreation beaches because they are privately owned through a grant from the King of Spain. Mr. and Mrs. John Doe and all the little Does look over the fence, longingly, at the stretch of smooth sand and sounding surf, but they may not play there, because long ago, the king of a far-away, and now somewhat decrepit, country said that the curving shore with its tawny strand was to belong to Señor So-and-So, and to his heirs and assigns forevermore. How silly!

"We might go on indefinitely, reviewing the facts and groups of facts which, when properly assembled, give us a startling picture of the economic situation in California. It is not enough to see California with its climate and its water-power, its tourist trade, its influx of 'transients,' its great land holdings, its real estate business, and its relief rolls. We must understand the con-nection between these seemingly unrelated parts."

The California State Constitution, Art. 17, Sec. 2, reads: "The holding of large tracts of land, uncultivated and unimproved, by individuals and corporations, is against the public interest."

While in its fundamental law the state acknowledges the harm-fulness, the legislature, fearing the wrath of the real estate boards, makes no move to eradicate the evil.

26

The Oregon Country

THE Oregon Country comprised the area west of the Rocky Mountains, north of California, Nevada and Utah. The word Oregon has been traced to the Orjan River in Chinese Tartary, at the mouth of which people called Kalmuchs lived. [122]

How the United States came to possess the valuable northwestern country is an interesting story.

It is the only land in continental United States, west of the Mississippi River, which the United States obtained without paying some foreign nation or potentate.

Eight recorded Spanish expeditions, during the 247 years between 1542 and 1789, made discoveries along the Pacific coast, some as far north as the delightful Kodiak Island in Alaska. Most of these discoveries were unknown to other nations until after the voyages of the British explorer, Captain James Cook. [122]

The Spanish navigator, De Fuca, is credited with having, in 1592, discovered and entered the present Columbia River, which he named St. Roc. Another Spanish navigator, Haceta, is recorded 183 years later, in 1775, as having sailed about seventy-five miles up that river.

The Spanish admiral, De Fonta, in 1640, discovered the present Vancouver Island, then voyaged to the expansive harbor of Seward, in Alaska, and proclaimed Spanish sovereignty of all the North Pacific Region.

The only recorded British explorations during those years were the buccaneering expedition of Drake, in 1578, to 44° N. and of

Captain Cook, who, just two hundred years afterwards, was the first British subject to sail to the Pacific Northwest. He made a landing at Nootka Sound, on the west side of Vancouver Island, but did not touch on the Oregon coast.

Spanish vessels often, until 1782, entered the St. Roc River but the increasing size of ocean-going vessels, with frequent disasters on the extensive bar at the entrance, caused the Spaniards to discontinue entering the river.

The report by Captain Cook of the possibilities of the fur trade along the northwestern coast awakened great interest among adventurers. The Northwest Company of Merchants, of Montreal, a rival of the Hudson's Bay Company, as early as 1784-5 projected an overland exploring expedition to the Oregon region, to develop a fur trade. [135]

Charles Bulfinch of Boston, and associates sent the ship "Columbia," of 250 tons, and the "Washington," of 100 tons, with Captains Gray and Kendrick, around Cape Horn to the Pacific Northwest, where they arrived in 1789. Thence they went with a cargo of furs to China; returning via the Cape of Good Hope.

Captain Kendrick, at Clayoquot, near Nootka, on his second voyage to that region, two years later, obtained an Indian grant of a large area of land to the southward, paying for it with muskets, iron, copper and clothing. This was the beginning of American exploration in the Northwest.

Captain Vancouver, the British navigator, was at Nootka and learned from Captain Gray about Puget Sound, which Vancouver intended exploring.

During the previous half century or more, the Russians had been establishing settlements along the Alaska coast between Bering Strait and Sitka, and even erected a fort in California, thirty miles north of San Francisco. Not until the appearance of the British and American navigators did the Spaniards awaken to the activities of the Russians.

Shortly thereafter a Spanish expedition was sent north with men, cattle and agricultural equipment to extend Spanish settlement, and to protest against the Russians occupying land which the Spaniards claimed to have occupied for many years. Three years later, under pressure of the British, the Spaniards abandoned the settlement at Nootka and withdrew to the California coast.

Captain Gray, in the ship "Columbia," in May, 1792, discovered anew, and sailed into, the Columbia River, the second largest river in the United States, which Cook had passed unnoticed. Gray gave to the river the name of his ship, replacing the Spanish name of St. Roc.

Gray's entrance into the Columbia gave the United States the first logical right to become a claimant to any part of the Oregon Country. Gray's venture was a daring one. The bar at the entrance outside Cape Disappointment was then seven miles long and three miles wide, with a narrow, winding and changeable channel.

Over this bar the breakers, extending for miles, dashed and pounded and thundered with a roar which could be heard for miles. The first ship sent to the Columbia River by Astor lay outside the bar three days awaiting an opportunity to enter. In two different attempts to enter she lost seven men. Crossing this bar, more than fifty years ago, continuously casting with two leadlines, was an experience I have vividly remembered all these years. Since that time the bar has been jettied, and a thirty-five foot channel dredged all the way to Portland.

The region west of the Missouri River was virtually unknown to the people of America when President Jefferson declared that the safety of the nation depended upon having it populated. In January, 1803, before the United States had bought Louisiana from France, he recommended to Congress, and it authorized, an exploring expedition to the Pacific.

This expedition, led by Meriwether Lewis, of Virginia, and William Clark, a younger brother of General George Rogers Clark, was composed of thirty-two persons, including four army sergeants, twenty-two privates (of whom nine were Kentucky hunters), one Negro, two French interpreters and the young Indian wife of one of the last named.

Lewis and Clark left St. Louis in May, 1804, followed the Missouri River for 2,575 miles, crossed the Rockies, and then followed the Snake and Columbia Rivers to the Pacific Ocean, which they reached at the end of eighteen months of arduous travel.

Lewis and Clark for the United States, and Thompson, a Britisher, each posted notices claiming the Oregon Country for their respective nations. [135]

After wintering in Oregon, preparing maps of their route, the explorers, excepting one man who died, arrived at St. Louis in September, 1806.

Every one in the expedition received double pay. In addition, Lewis and Clark were each granted sixteen hundred acres of land, and each of their men received three hundred acres.

John Jacob Astor organized the Pacific Fur Company, and sent a ship around Cape Horn to the Columbia River in 1811. Aboard was one of Astor's Canadian partners. Arriving there, he located a fur trading station on a site within the mouth of the river, to which he gave the name Astoria.

The war between the United States and Great Britain began the following year. A British armed ship appeared at the mouth of the river and threatened capture of the Astor post, whereupon the Canadian partner, without sanction of Astor, sold the post to the Northwest Company, a British corporation. This, in effect, placed the entire country in possession of the British.

United States and Great Britain disputed ownership of the country and in 1818 a treaty provided for occupancy of the territory between 42° N. and 54°40′ N. by subjects of both, for a stated period.

Russia's claim to Oregon, and to the North Pacific Ocean as a closed sea, was compromised through treaties between Great Britain and Russia, in 1824, and between the United States and Russia, the following year. Russia accepted 54°40′ N. as its southern boundary; now the southern boundary of Alaska.

Discussion of this treaty in Congress first voiced the thought of the United States occupying Oregon, and brought notice by the British government to the Hudson's Bay Company that Great Britain would make no claim to land south of the Columbia River.

The Northwest and Hudson's Bay Companies consolidated, and the trading post at Astoria was, in 1824, moved up the river to the present Fort Vancouver. Dr. John McLoughlin, the superintendent, was an amiable and accommodating Scotsman, who extended many civilities to the American settlers, although the policy of the company was consistently opposed to settlement of the country, as being a menace to the fur trade.

This post became, and continued for many years, the focal point of all trade in Oregon. McLoughlin, anticipating an influx of settlers, sent five Canadians, in 1829, to locate on choice farming land and mill-sites near the falls of the Willamette River. This was the first real settlement of white people in Oregon. The next settlers, three years afterwards, were two Americans from Wyeth's party of trappers. [122]

Two Americans, Hall J. Kelley, of Massachusetts, and Dr. Marcus Whitman, a Presbyterian missionary from New York State, unassociated in their endeavors, printed and distributed articles and pamphlets, and through interviews with editors and others in the East, including public officials at Washington, urged American sovereignty of the Oregon Country and its settlement by Americans. Enduring tremendous physical hardships and expense in their respective pursuits for the cause, they both reached Oregon in 1834.

A Methodist mission for the Indians was that year established on the Willamette River, sixty miles south of Vancouver. Some farmers were already located there, and half-breed children formed a nucleus for a school. Four years later a Roman Catholic mission was located thereabouts.

American trappers drifted into the Willamette Valley and, by 1840, there began a stream of genuine settlers, lured by the fact that they could there get for the taking a mile square of fertile farming land for husband, wife and each child. [90]

In 1842, although the boundary between the United States and Canada had not been agreed upon, active agitation was begun in Congress for claiming and forming a territorial government for the Oregon region, and for granting land to settlers. This stimulated migration there from the Middle West.

As a great immigration of one thousand persons, assuring a predominately American population in Oregon south of the Columbia River, the settlers inaugurated a provincial government of the territory, and adopted a land law.

The different religious missions were each allowed to pre-empt an entire township of 23,040 acres, in addition to the land held by their individual members.

Endeavoring to prevent absentee landholding and speculation,

a local legislative committee wisely provided that only actual settlers could become landholders, and shortly thereafter a provisional constitution was adopted.

Farms, ranches, flour-mills and sawmills were established, and
their products sold to the Russians in Alaska, and to the people
in the Sandwich (Hawaiian) Islands.

Great Britain was intent upon having the Canadian-United
States boundary fixed south of the Columbia River, at the forty-
fifth parallel, extending from the Falls of St. Anthony (Minneap-
olis) to the Pacific Ocean.

In the discussion on the subject with Ashburton, the British
minister at Washington in 1842, Daniel Webster, believing that
Great Britain could influence Mexico, suggested that the proposed boundary might be allowed if the United States could
obtain northern California and San Francisco harbor, then possessed by Mexico.

It is possible that it was this which prompted Great Britain,
four years later, to send a large squadron to the Pacific, centered
at Monterey, with the apparent object of obtaining California
from Mexico in liquidation of indebtedness of Mexico to British
citizens. Great Britain could then deliver California to the United
States, in exchange for the more southerly boundary for Canada.
[135]

The purchase of Louisiana from France by the United States
in 1803, and of Florida from Spain in 1819, extinguished any claim
France or Spain might have had to land west of the Mississippi
River north of 42°, and left the Pacific Northwest open to appro-
priation by the United States, barring any counter claim by Great
Britain.

The United States took no official action for absorbing the region until after the boundary between the United States and
Canada had been officially agreed upon in 1846.

The claim by the United States to the Oregon Country was
based upon: discovery by Americans (although previously known
by the Spaniards) of the Columbia River by Captain Gray in
1792; exploration by Lewis and Clark across the Rocky Mountains to the Pacific Ocean in 1805; locating of the Astor fur trading post at Astoria in 1811; settlement of the country by

Americans and contiguity of the land purchased from France and Spain.

From the agreement between the United States and Russia in 1825, fixing 54° 40′ (at the southern tip of Alaska on the Pacific) as the southern boundary of the Russian possessions along the Pacific coast, there arose in the Presidential campaign of 1844, the slogan, "Fifty-four-forty or fight," as indicating the proposed boundary between the United States and Canada. This was advocated by the supporters of James K. Polk, candidate for President. The cry went through the country with enthusiasm, and Polk was elected. The year after being inaugurated, he signed the treaty fixing the boundary at 49° N., as it now exists.

This ended the joint occupancy treaty of 1818, whereby citizens of both countries had been privileged during the preceding twenty-eight years to occupy the region between 42° N. and 54° 40′ N.

Judson [90] states, having seen letters from British vice-consuls in southern California and in the Sandwich Islands, repeating what Americans and Britishers both said of Oregon, "that it was over-rated and not worth a war."

There were, at the close of 1845, about six thousand people in Oregon, including a few hundred in the Puget Sound region, and Americans soon exceeded the British in numbers. Five years later the population of the present state of Washington was 1,111.

Meanwhile the Hudson's Bay Company sank to a subordinate position. Schaifer [135] said: "The Oregon question, so far as control of the country itself was concerned, had been settled by the pioneers . . ." He adds: ". . . the British fort, Vancouver, was indispensable to the American settlers, was in fact the condition of Oregon's early colonization; without it, the country must have remained a wilderness until others had been founded."

Upon the fixing of the boundary, Congress provided for a territorial government for Oregon, which included the present state of Washington and the country east thereof, to the crest of the Rocky Mountains.

With the expansion of lumbering in the territory occasioned by the discovery of gold in California, the population increased rapidly, the settlers taking up land.

Overcoming great difficulties, a caravan of pioneer families, on their westward trek, opened a wagon road over the mountains to Puget Sound in 1853, which facilitated migration to that section.

Immigration into the region became so great by 1851 that the Indians realized that their lands would soon be taken by the whites. This brought on a war which continued in some sections for seven years, at the termination of which, as usual in all wars that have ever occurred between the Indians and the white race, the Indians lost their lands and were forced into the back country—in this instance, onto reservations.

Schaifer [135] in *A History of the Pacific Northwest,* writing in 1917, said: "Much of the territory now held by the cattle companies was originally filched from the national government by the well-known device of the 'dummy' entrymen . . . some of it was land, falsely, or at least doubtfully, described as swamp land and as such sold at one dollar per acre . . .

"The relatively high price of farm lands delays the progress of subdividing the large farms of pioneer times, into holdings suited to a more intensive system of farming. . . . According to the census report, farm lands alone, as distinct from buildings, increased in value during the decade 217.7 per cent in Oregon, 278.3 in Washington and 276.1 in Idaho.

"The primary cause of the rise in the social value of lands here, as elsewhere in the United States, is the disappearance of the free lands. Hitherto these regulated the value of the farm lands, permitting only such advance as was justified. . . .

"A secondary cause of social values in the Northwest has been an excess of speculation in farm lands . . . A general inflation of land values influences the rate of immigration of desirable citizens from other states into this region, and defers still further the full development of the Northwestern resources. . . .

"This is disquieting to all thoughtful men and it contributes to the unrest of the industrial class who see in it the prospect of their permanent exclusion from the ranks of landholders."

The Public Domain

BY THE early British royal land grants the western limit of Massachusetts, Connecticut, Virginia, Georgia and the Carolinas was designated as the South Sea (Pacific Ocean), while Pennsylvania, New Jersey, Delaware, and Maryland were confined within their present boundaries.

By the treaty between Great Britain and France, at the close of the French and Indian War in 1763, the Mississippi River was fixed upon as the western limit of the British possessions, and of the proprietary colonial land grants.

During the Revolutionary War, all lands held by the British king or by the royal grantees were sequestered by the states in which they were situated. Pennsylvania and Maryland afterwards, as already stated, made some payment to their respective lords proprietors.

Those states having no western lands contended that the war had been waged for the benefit of all the colonies and that the western lands should be ceded to the national government, to be sold to pay the cost of the war. Maryland, especially, took a firm stand on this and refused to join the Confederated States unless this were done.

In 1780 the Continental Congress adopted resolutions asking those seaboard states claiming lands west of their present western boundaries to cede them to the national government.

Maryland, however, qualified its demand, by permitting all Indian grants made to individuals prior to the beginning of the war to be recognized. The fact that a number of important

Marylanders, including Governor Johnson, ex-Governor William Paca, Samuel Chase and Charles Carroll of Carrollton were shareholders in the Illinois-Wabash Land Company, which had acquired large areas from the Indians in the present Indiana and Illinois, gives point to this qualification. The Robert Morris group and some French agents also were shareholders in that company. [1]

Virginia ceded to the national government all its lands northwest of the Ohio River, except 150,000 acres (in Indiana) reserved for General George Rogers Clark, his officers and men, who had conquered that country for Virginia, and a contingent reservation for the Virginia troops of the Continental Army, between the Scioto and Little Miami Rivers in Ohio, supposed to contain 4,204,800 acres.

Soon after Virginia had, with these reservations, ceded its western lands, Maryland agreed to join the Union. Connecticut relinquished part of its western claim, reserving 3,366,921 acres in the northeastern corner of Ohio. South Carolina had a relatively small area along the entire southern boundary of Tennessee, which it relinquished. Georgia reserved five hundred thousand acres and exacted payment for the remaining western lands. North Carolina land-grabbing officials made strong objection to relinquishing North Carolina lands in the Tennessee area until threatened with a federal tax on such lands; demonstrating the power of a land-tax to open up idle land to settlement. But, by that time, they had issued land warrants to themselves and favored speculators for most of the Tennessee lands. The other states had little or nothing to relinquish.

To prevent grabbing of the land by speculators, it was imperative that Congress, representing all the people, should assume monopoly of the western and southern land. This it did and enacted that the government alone would make terms with the Indians, and land so acquired was to become part of the public domain.

Immediately upon the federal government becoming possessed of a public domain, Congress was flooded with petitions by settlers and speculators for grants of land.

Pelatiah Webster in 1781 proposed a wise system for distributing the public lands which, had it been adopted fully instead of in part, would have brought about more orderly development of the country: "The land to be surveyed into townships of six, eight or ten miles square, to be sold at auction, with a minimum price of one dollar per acre; purchasers should be obliged to settle and improve the land within two or three years or forfeit it; townships to be laid out in tiers and sold. Only after one tier was settled should the next tier be placed on sale."

Washington made a trip to western Pennsylvania in 1784, where by court action he evicted some squatters from land he had acquired of the Indians. He wrote to Jacob Read, a member of the Continental Congress from Pennsylvania: "Such is the rage for speculating in, and forestalling of, lands northwest of the Ohio, that scarce a valuable spot within a tolerable distance of it is left without a claimant. Men now talk with as much facility of five hundred thousand acres as a gentleman would formerly do of a thousand."

The paramount thought of the federal government, as a landholder, was to sell land in large tracts for revenue to pay the public debt, rather than for settlement; and the only buyers for large tracts were speculators.

A system for the sale of the public land was determined upon by the Continental Congress in 1785. The domain to be divided into townships of six miles square; each township comprising thirty-six sections of 640 acres each, a section being one mile square. Alternate townships were to be offered in tracts of not less than a section, at $1.00 per acre, later increased to $2.00. The first application of the six miles square township plan was at Chelmsford, Massachusetts, in 1652.

The government reserved one-third part of all gold, silver, copper and lead in each township. This wise provision could, and should have been maintained, but was later rescinded because it was inimical to the interests of those who were obtaining the land.

While Congress was offering for sale land from the public domain, Connecticut, Virginia and Georgia were likewise offering for sale land from their western reservations.

The Indians in Ohio complained at Fort McIntosh in 1785

that the white pioneers were settling and building on their lands. Soldiers were sent to eject the settlers and burn their houses and crops, but many hundreds of others came pouring in all along the Ohio River, seeking places for homes for their families. [50] These ejections were regardless of the needs of the landless people for land for homes and on which to earn their living; but as time went on Congress, though tardily, reversed this policy.

The public domain at that time comprised the land west of the Pennsylvania boundary, north of the Ohio River and east of the Mississippi, exclusive of the reservations noted. This area was organized as the Northwest Territory, which included the present states of Ohio, Indiana, Illinois, Michigan, Wisconsin and that part of Minnesota east of the Mississippi River.

Congress framed the famous Ordinance of 1787 for the government of this Territory, which became the richest field for exploitation by land grabbers, as will appear. Officials, including judges and legislators of the Territory, were each required to hold from two hundred to one thousand acres in the district. Franklin opposed limiting voters to landholders, because it would "depress the virtue and public spirit of our common people." [21]

The Ohio Company (the third company of that name) was formed in Boston by General Rufus Putman, Winthrop Sargent and the Rev. Dr. Manasseh Cutler, former chaplain of a Massachusetts regiment in the Revolutionary War. The company was subsequently joined by some members of Congress. They lobbied through Congress in 1787, a bill authorizing the sale to them of approximately 1,700,000 acres of the public domain, along the Ohio River on both sides of the Muskingum River. The following year two groups of people, one from Danvers, Massachusetts, and the other from Hartford, Connecticut, founded Marietta, named for Marie Antoinette, at the junction of those rivers.

Each of the first settlers at Marietta received an in-lot, 90 by 180 feet, and an out-lot of eight acres; the remaining land to be held for sale at a profit to the company.

At the same time, Congress granted to the Scioto Company,

the promoters of which were largely the same as those of the Ohio Company, an option to purchase five million acres along the Ohio and Scioto Rivers.

The Scioto promoters sent Joel Barlow, a poet, to Europe, to dispose of land. He sold the rights to three million acres to a company organized in Paris. The French Revolution coming on prompted a royalist emigration, and several hundred royalists, in 1790, bought and paid for tracts of this land.

No payment was as yet due or made to the government by the promoters, and the financial failure of a leading promoter prevented payment by the American buyers. Consequently the French immigrants, having paid for their land, had neither land nor money, but Congress donated to them 25,200 acres on condition of five years' residence thereon, and a settlement was made at Gallipolis. [146]

John Cleve Symmes, a member of Congress from New Jersey, and his associates, in the same year bought from the government a million acres along the Ohio River, between the Great Miami and the Little Miami Rivers, known as the Miami purchase. On this tract Cincinnati and North Bend were afterwards laid out. Symmes declared to his associates that he saw a fortune in store for "the lucky speculators who would buy land from Congress for 5s per acre and sell it to settlers at 20s."

In Cincinnati, founded in 1788, every pioneer was assigned an in-lot 86½ by 193 feet for a house and a four acre out-lot. In Dayton, each pioneer settler was allotted an in-lot, 99 by 198 feet, and an out-lot of ten acres. Speculator-promoters of other towns offered larger lots.

Payment for lands by these several promoters was to be made in Continental Certificates of Indebtedness and Revolutionary War Military Land Warrants. Purchase of these securities by the company to make payments caused an advance in the market price, which made payment more difficult and costly, and the buyers applied in 1792, for easier terms. Whereupon Congress, ever lenient in the early days with land speculators, authorized that the Ohio Company receive 214,285 acres to be paid for with military warrants, another tract of 100,000 acres, and 750,000 acres additional upon payment of $500,000 in Continental issues then selling at 12½¢ on the dollar—or actually about 6¢ per acre. [146]

For Symmes likewise having the same difficulty, Congress reduced the area sold to him to 148,540 acres, for which he paid $70,455 in Continental issues at face value, but then selling at such reduced prices that the actual purchase price was but 6¢ per acre. Symmes, who was afterwards appointed a judge in the Northwest Territory, was arrested in 1802 for selling land outside of his concession, belonging to the government.

With the rapid settlement of the country, the average price of unimproved land in the Symmes Miami area had, within twenty-eight years after the purchase, become stabilized at $8.00 per acre [13]—an increase of 356 per cent per annum.

Nicholas Longworth, a young lawyer, in the early days of Cincinnati accepted two copper stills as a fee. These he traded for a thirty acre tract, now in the center of that city, which fifty years later was appraised as worth $2,000,000. [38] Unearned increment created by the concentration of population is powerful "in founding a family."

There are significant implications in the fact that none of the great land speculator-promoters of the Eastern coteries settled in the West. They wanted the land merely for promotional and speculative purposes, and had no intention of personally undergoing the hardships of the frontier. [1]

In 1788 more than eighteen thousand pioneers, men, women, and children, from New England and other Atlantic seaboard states, went into the Ohio country seeking homesteads, where they built cabins and cleared land for cultivation. From the wooded banks of the Ohio, the Indians watched with growing resentment the steadily increasing number of flatboats bringing new settlers to take from them the land of their birth and of their ancestors.[a] Other settlers, bound for Kentucky and Tennessee, were pouring through the gaps in the mountains in the South.

The newly formed United States government was inaugurated April 30, 1789, with George Washington as President. Washington served until 1797. In the debate in the first session of Con-

[a] J. Carroll Mansfield

gress, Representative Scott made an effort "to induce the government to sell land directly to settlers," but the influence of land speculators in and out of Congress prevented action.

Instead of Congress opening this region to the thousands of landless people in the eastern seaboard states, that they might get land on which to live and work and raise their families, various acts were passed authorizing the President to issue deeds for large tracts of land to combinations of speculators, amongst whom were members of this Congress. The settlers were left to bargain with the speculators. [21] And, worst of all, President Washington sent General Harmar "to drive these squatters [so termed] from the public domain." As stated in the Annals of Congress, "the troops broke down the fences, tore up the potato patches and burnt the cabins, but three hours after they left the settlers returned."

Wayne's campaign in 1790, and the treaty with the Indians at Greenville in 1795, made the country reasonably safe from Indian attacks.

So harmful had land speculation become at that early period, Congressman Rutherford said Congress should destroy the hydra of land speculation, which had done the country great harm. "Let Congress," he said, "dispose of this land to settlers; . . . the 'monsters' in Europe acting with the 'monsters' here [are] ready to swallow up this country."

With the population of the country increasing, and all desirable land in the East privately appropriated but largely unused, there were fewer opportunities to establish homes and work there, and people sought land in the Ohio and Kentucky regions.

Pioneers going beyond the Alleghenies were homeseekers, speculators, and agents of speculators. The professional surveyor was among the early comers, seeking with practiced eye for the most desirable spots. He was frequently commissioned by others and was very often a speculator himself, ready to sell what he had laid out in his own name. [3]

The public debt inherited by the new United States government from the old Confederation was about $42,000,000. In addition, the States owed over $30,000,000, including nearly $12,000,-000 to foreign creditors. Hamilton wanted the federal government to assume all these. As a result of a trade of votes in Congress, arranged by Hamilton and Jefferson, the Southern members voted for assumption of these debts, in consideration of the new national capital being located along the Potomac.

Daniel Carroll, brother of Charles, a Senator from Maryland, owned most of the land in the District of Columbia. The price paid by the government for this land was said to be "more than three-fold the market price."

This land was conveyed to three commissioners appointed by the President, to be held in trust while laying out the city. In September, 1792, Washington directed that city lots be sold at public or private sale. Robert Morris, an irrepressible land speculator, then a United States Senator, John Nicholson and James Greenleaf formed the North American Land Company, which bought nine thousand lots at an average price of $86.34 each, payable in seven annual instalments without interest.

These speculators, in selling the lots at ever-increasing prices, were able, from proceeds of the lots sold, and with a minimum cash investment on their part, to pay the government as the instalments came due. The speculative fever then started in the capital city has not during these long years been abated.

From that time to the present the value of the land (not including buildings) on which the White House is situated has increased to $19,685,975. To build the new Department of Commerce building the government was charged $2,459,831 of the people's money for the land on which to build it—values created, not by the landholders but automatically by all the people.

Our American statesmen-promoters of a national capital were not as wise as were those of Australia when they established their capital. There, in the 1920's, a new federal capital city was laid out on virgin land, just as was Washington, and named Canberra. It occupies sixteen square miles in a federal district of nine hundred square miles. The land was acquired by the government, which retains ownership of it in perpetuity. Building lots are not sold, but leased to private builders at an annual ground-rent, adjusted every twenty years. To avoid having privately owned architectural eyesores, contiguous unused lots and slum areas, held on speculation, such as exist in Washington and in all other American cities, all lots leased in Canberra must be fully improved, within two years, from approved architectural plans. It is estimated that within twenty-five years all government buildings will have been paid for from land rents. The rental value of the lots will continue to grow as population increases— just as it has in Washington, where the increasing land values inure to private holders instead of, as in Australia, to the government.

After the organization of the federal government, the Illinois, and the Wabash Land Companies, legatees of Indian land concessions in colonial days, fused into one corporation and claimed Indian rights to two hundred miles square of land. The president was James Wilson of Pennsylvania, a justice of the United States Supreme Court, and an ardent speculator in land in different parts of the country; an injudicious combination.

With powerful political and landholding influences, the company proposed to Congress that it would surrender to the government "all the lands it claimed, on condition that Congress would reconvey to the company one quarter of the lands."[b] The Senate committee on public lands reported that the petitioners held no legal title to the lands and it declined the proposition. But in the House was the notorious land speculator, Jonathan Dayton of New Jersey, Speaker of the House of Representatives, himself putting big land jobbery through Congress. The House committee on public lands reported that the company's Indian deeds were valid and that the United States should agree to the proposal. [21]

One of the great scandals of that time was the bribery of members of Congress, by Robert Randall, to obtain a grant of eighteen to twenty million acres bordering on Lakes Erie, Huron and Michigan. In the testimony brought out in an investigation in 1795, three members said they were approached by Randall, who said he already had thirty members pledged to support his grant; that to get a majority, shares in the land grant were to be divided among congressmen, and that those who did not want shares could get the cash.[c]

[b]Journal Ho. Reps. 1795
[c]*Ibid.*

A vigorous discussion arose in Congress the following year respecting a method for disposing of public lands. Some favored selling to settlers in "small tracts of 640 acres"; some favored selling in small tracts to settlers and in large tracts to speculators; others favored selling at auction, at a minimum price of $2 per acre.

A proposal that actual settlement be required on all land sold was rejected and, apparently, that was the only time any effort was made in Congress to insist that prompt settlement must be made on land sold by the government. Had this condition of settlement been adopted, the welfare of the settlers would have triumphed over the immediate needs of the public treasury. [146]

Settlement of the Ohio lands during the early nineteenth century was retarded by the government holding land for sale only in very large tracts, which few settlers and only speculators were able to buy, and by the high prices then demanded by speculators for smaller farm-size tracts.

Holding large areas of land unused on speculation gave the incoming settlers the choice of living either on the outer frontier in deadly peril of irate Indians, or of paying a part of their future earnings to speculators for locations closer to the zone of safety. [21]

In 1800 Congress reduced to 320 acres the minimum acreage to a buyer, at $2.00 per acre, with four years to make payment. This increased sales, but it engendered rampant speculation in land by a large number of people, who bought on those terms with the idea of exacting higher prices of incoming settlers, before the four years of credit expired.

Colonel Ebenezer Zane had made at Wheeling, in 1770, the first permanent settlement on the Ohio River. He laid out Zanesville in 1799, and three years previously had been granted three sections (1,920 acres), as a bonus for establishing ferries. A similar grant was made to Isaac Zane in 1802.

Land warrants had been issued entitling the soldiers of the Revolutionary War to land. Representative Bacon, in Congress, in 1802, said that speculators sent agents among the veterans and depreciated the value of the warrants, then purchasing them at one-tenth their value. These warrants were then presented to the government at face value in payment for land.

An Ohio editor, in 1803, declared: "To such an extent has the hateful spirit of inordinate speculation in public lands proceeded, that it has corrupted the fountains of legislation and the courts of justice, as well as the body politic."

Ohio was admitted as a state in 1803. Congress relinquished to it one-thirty-sixth of the total area, as school lands, and 3 per cent of the proceeds from land sales in the state, for road construction. [9]

The United States land commissioners at Detroit reported in 1805 that lands in their district were claimed under various grants; grants in fee simple by Cadillac; by the French commandant at Detroit in the early eighteenth century, and by subsequent commandants; by the French governors of New France and Louisiana, which had been confirmed by the King of France; similar grants, but unconfirmed by the king; claims derived from the British governors; Indian grants and others by actual settlers and occupants. In all there were more than five hundred of these claims, of which only six were recommended for confirmation. [146]

The judges of the Virginia court at Vincennes, Indiana, in the Virginia Reserve north of the Ohio, which was held for General Clark and his men, fraudulently granted to themselves great tracts of the reserve. This area is situated in Clark, Floyd and Scott Counties, Indiana, but mainly in the first-named county.

A letter from General Harrison, governor of the Northwest Territory, to President Jefferson, confirmed these charges of judicial land frauds: "The whole country to which the Indian claims were supposed to be extinguished was divided among members of the court and entered upon their journals; each member absenting himself from the court on the day that the order was to be made in his favor, so that it might appear to be the act of his fellows only."

The land commissioners at Kaskaskia, in Illinois, reported in 1807 that no less than nine hundred claims were on perjured affidavits. They had confirmed to one man nearly forty such claims, for four hundred acres each, later rejecting them. [146] Tracts thus fraudulently grabbed were sold to speculators, who exacted high prices of arriving settlers.

Land in the public domain had been quite generally sold on deferred payments, which favored purchases by speculators, who depended upon selling at increased prices before the (usually five years) instalment payments fell due. Gallatin, the able Secretary of the Treasury in three administrations, feared this would increase the debtor class and, as defaults were occurring, would create in that section of the Union a powerful interest hostile to the federal government. He said: "If the cause of the happiness of this country was examined into it would be found to arise as much from the great plenty of land in proportion to the inhabitants as from the wisdom of their political institutions."

Nevertheless Congress refused to revoke the credit system. Every person who hoped to buy western lands, whether as a settler or as a speculator, insisted upon its retention. [146]

The settlers, as have so many since then, found that buying land on mortgage or other deferred or instalment terms is often hazardous. Many purchasers, when the five-year payment period approached, petitioned Congress for relief. In 1810 the Indiana legislature presented a memorial to Congress citing the situation of many persons, actual settlers rather than speculators, who had bought public land, yet for a number of reasons were without the means to pay.

The committee of Congress was not sympathetic, declaring that an extension of time would encourage settlers to make speculative purchases of larger tracts than they could pay for, and place the people in debt to the government, which would be dangerous. During the next several years many hundred farms and tracts were forfeited.

In Michigan there was virtually a repetition of the confusion in land titles that existed in Indiana. Not until 1812, by act of Congress, were land titles in Michigan placed on a definite basis. Just as later in Illinois, the long delay in doing this retarded settlement. [13]

An Ohio editor, that year, wrote against: "Those mushroom

speculators who have infested this western country by buying on credit and holding land to the prejudice of the community. . . ." Another editor wrote that: "sales for cash would nearly annihilate those speculative high prices which are to the great injury of the community."

When sales of public lands in Illinois began in 1814, most of the American settlers in the territory were squatters—on land they did not own or rent—partly because of lack of funds, and partly because of disputed titles arising from the old French claims. Many of these old claims were revived, speculation became rife and frauds were innumerable.

A petition from Illinois that year said that 284 landless settlers had located wherever it was possible, but having little cash they could not purchase land, and prayed for enactment of a law that would favor the "industrious poor." [13]

Many state banks were organized in Ohio to facilitate creating credit for speculative purchases of land. During the five years just preceding the financial crash of 1819, about 5,500,000 acres were bought, and the indebtedness of the speculators to the government for land purchased increased from $3,000,000 to $17,000,000.

The greatest land boom that ever had been known in American history was then on, but speculators, instead of realizing expected sales and profits, soon realized they had overbought. Then came broken banks, that had backed the speculators, and the widespread panic of that period.

A Kentucky newspaper declared that land speculation, "the most portentous evil that ever existed in America," was the cause of the panic and depression.

Thomas H. Benton, United States Senator from Missouri, in his *Thirty Years' View,* said: "Distress was the universal cry of the people, relief, the universal demand, thundered at the doors of all legislatures, state and federal."

The land credit system, which had been in effect twenty-four years, and had helped bring on the panic, was repealed in 1820. The minimum size of tracts to be sold was reduced to eighty acres and the price reduced from $2.00 per acre to $1.25, payable in cash. Timber lands, $2.50; mineral land $5; coal land $10, as a minimum.

A writer, in 1820, said: "It became common to see men after getting land, to maintain themselves the first year without further resources than a gun, a net and a few tools, living from these like Indians and afterwards from their land. In a few years they were able to maintain themselves and their families comfortably." That was the spirit of the American pioneers.

Congress had, in 1803, granted to Lafayette 11,500 acres from the public domain, and upon his visit to the United States, in 1824, granted him a township of 23,040 acres from the public domain in Florida; in addition to $200,000 in cash.

The Erie Canal, opened in 1825, carried to the West human cargoes, many of them immigrants direct from Europe, and brought to the East the produce of western farms. At the same time settlers were, and had been, pouring west from Baltimore by the National turnpike, and from Philadelphia, by canal and inclined planes, over the Alleghenies. Railroad construction was not begun until 1830.

The popular feeling was so widespread, in the early nineteenth century, that the public domain was inexhaustible that the Secretary of the Treasury, Richard Rush, reported, in 1827, that "it will take no less than five hundred years to dispose of and settle the land in the public domain." Actually all of it that was profitable to use in farming, and much that was not, was disposed of during the next fifty-five years.

Congressman Hayne of South Carolina said in 1828, that more than half the time of Congress had been taken up with discussing proposals respecting public lands. [149]

In the Senate, Clay, of Kentucky, urged distribution of the proceeds of sales of public lands among the states; Calhoun, of South Carolina, urged cession of the lands to the states in which they lay; John Quincy Adams, of Massachusetts, favored devoting the proceeds of land sales to Federal internal improvements; Benton, of Missouri, advocated reducing the price of land to settlers. Some other senators demanded that the land be donated as homesteads to actual settlers. [149]

A large proportion of the settlers in the Middle West in the

1830's were squatters. Four entire counties in the northwestern part of Indiana were occupied by squatters. It was said that two-thirds of the entire population in Illinois were squatters, and that there were more than thirty thousand squatters on public lands as far west as Iowa at that early day.[d] This condition was a forceful reason for granting free homesteads, and yet Congress delayed for thirty years more.

Congress in 1832 compromised, and reduced to forty acres, at $1.25 per acre, the minimum size of tracts saleable, thus making it possible to buy a farm outright for a cash payment of $50. This should have been done at the outset, but it was opposed by land speculators and by influential eastern and southern landholders, and by members of Congress, because it would draw their people to the West and depreciate land-values in their sections. Fur companies were opposed, to prevent settlement of the western sources of their fur supplies.

Western settlement not only tended to retard a natural rise in the price of eastern lands, but it reduced the supply of workers in industry, which caused Senator Foot, of Connecticut, to offer a resolution in the Senate to stop the survey of public lands and abolish the office of surveyor-general. [137]

After Congress authorized the sale of land in small tracts, a new crop of active speculators hired others to serve as dummies in making entries for them. By this method large areas of the best contiguous land and mill-sites were obtained and held until increasing population created a demand at increased prices.

Connivance of land officials, through bribery by speculators, often caused large tracts of choice land to be withheld from sale pending the demand by settlers. To intercept the oncoming pioneers, these dealers would open offices, with sales agents, along the favored routes of migration.

Settlers themselves, when able, would often speculate by buying more land than they could farm, hoping that new settlers would pay them an increased price. [149]

For decades the principal medium of tricky financial schemes throughout the West and South was land. During the whole development of the country the land shark has been a pest and

[d]Cong. Globe

an object of hatred to the homeseekers. His wiles were the terror and mystery of the honest settlers. In the early decades land-robbery was a fruitful source of violence, and at the bottom of most litigation. [18]

Many of those who had experienced the distress of the collapsed land boom and panic of 1819 having passed away, and affairs being guided by a newer generation, all classes in all sections of the country were, in the 1830's, infected with another land gambling mania. Manufacturers, merchants and farmers, instead of paying their debts, bought land on speculation.

Sales of lands from the public domain in 1834, were 4,500,000 acres, the largest of any year since the panic of fifteen years previously. The following year 12,500,000 acres, and the next year, 20,000,000 acres—mostly to speculators, who aimed to inter-cept, and supply land at increased prices to the great surge of western-bound pioneers. [99]

Highly interesting accounts of western migration of settlers are given in the novels *Vandermark's Folly* by Herbert Quick; in *Son of the Middle Border,* by Hamlin Garland, and in the moving picture *The Covered Wagon.*

Senator Walker, of Mississippi, who was charged with organ-izing speculative combinations to cheat the government in land sales, reported, in 1836, that of the thirteen million acres sold, during the past year, he believed eight million acres were bought for speculation.

The land where Chicago is situated was no more valuable, when Chicago had its beginning in 1830, with a dozen log cabins, than any other government land, then being sold through-out the West at $1.25 per acre.

When all the land about the Chicago location had been bought of the government at $1.25 per acre, a wild land speculation developed. Town-site projects mapped out on paper sprang up overnight in all directions, just as in every land boom since then.

With highly colored maps, and pictures prepared in eastern cities, the promoters at once, before the colored ink was dry, proceeded to solicit in the East, purchases of town lots in the West. Pictures showed elegant brick and stone buildings, steam-boats at crowded wharves, drays loading and unloading merchandise of all sorts, and crowds of people and vehicles, all clearly depicted as part of a future metropolis, to entice speculative purchases of lots.

Chicago lots were sold at public auction for private account to and by speculators as far away as New York, Philadelphia and Boston. In the first six years, the sale value of lots, plotted thereabouts from the recent $1.25 per acre land, had increased to $10,000,000. [75]

The receipts by the government from land sales were, as President Jackson said, but little more than credits in the banks, circulating in a constant routine from banks to speculators, to the government, to the banks, and again to the speculators for more land. Unquestionably land speculation and bank juggling often went hand in hand. [99]

Saying that the time had come to put an end to wildcat bank inflation on which speculation was feeding, and to save the new states from absentee landlordism, "one of the greatest obstacles to the advancement of a new country and the prosperity of an old one," Jackson, in 1836, wisely (but for which he was viciously attacked), issued his famous Specie Circular. This required buyers of land, except actual settlers, to pay for it in specie, which was so great a shock that the panic of 1837 suddenly broke.

Stimulated by rising land prices, caused by the rapidly increasing population, many of the states had created bond issues for unwarranted development. When the panic broke, land values evaporated, bringing broken banks, and defalcations by bank officials who had indulged in the speculation, and defaults by state governments.

In New York, six thousand men in the building trades, and in Philadelphia, one-half to two-thirds of the clerks and salesmen became unemployed. In the South, plantation owners, with reduced demand for their products, having less work for their slaves, sold for $200 slaves for which they had but recently paid $1,200. [ix]

In Chicago: "prospective building lots that had sold at $1,000 or more, but now unsalable, were plowed up for potato patches to feed the destitute. The country resounded with groans of ruined men and human misery and the sobs of defrauded women who had participated in the speculation."

President Jackson had proposed to limit the sale of land to actual settlers. Had this advice been followed the whole speculative orgy which culminated in the panic might have been averted, or its severity lessened. [99]

Jackson's successor, Van Buren, in a message to Congress, referring to the cause of the panic, said: "There was invested $39,500,000 in unproductive public lands in 1835-6, while in the preceding years the sales amounted to only $4,500,000; the creation of debt to an almost countless amount for land in existing and anticipated cities and villages, equally unproductive, and at prices now seen to have been greatly disproportionate to their real value."

Ten years after this disastrous panic, Horace Greeley wrote from Chicago: "The town is filled with land sharks, downright thieves and blackguards."

Regardless of the human distress from the previous orgy of land speculation, the craze again broke out, which shortly ended in the land speculative crash of 1857, just previous to which Horace Greeley, again visiting Chicago, wrote: "The more I see of land speculation the less I like it. Here men are grasping all the land they can get, paying exorbitant usury and everybody in debt that they may clutch more land, all of which tends to unsettle the public mind, inflame the spirit of speculation and discourage patient industry.

"The right of the human race to live," said Greeley, "is older, stronger, more sacred, than the right of any individual to retain land unused to exact of others a price for the liberty to use God's Earth."

Not until 1853 was Chicago connected by rail with the Atlantic seaboard. Still, decade after decade, owing to its unsurpassed geographical location for intercepting trans-continental traffic, Chicago grew.

With each recurring land boom there has been a new crop of speculators, with similar endings in each succeeding panic— occurring about every twenty years. But land values on the crest of every land boom are always higher than they were on the crest of the preceding boom—and that is the backlog which keeps the fires of land speculation for ever going.

Paul Blanchard, in *The Great Land Racket* wrote: "The ill-effects of land speculation did not become apparent until after the growth of cities. Then gradually we became a nation of realtors. The whole conception of land changed from something to be used, to something to be held until the community should increase its value. Landholding then became a national racket, in which the shrewd, the cunning, and the lucky grandsons of grandfathers, stood at the key cross-roads of our bustling new city life, extracting toll from every tenant, and from every purchaser of merchandise."

By 1894, a panic year, $1,250,000 was the price of a favored one-quarter acre plot of bare land in Chicago, for which 31¢ (at the rate of $1.25 per acre) had been paid the government; being an average increase of 20,000 per cent per annum on the original purchase price.

The southwest corner of State and Washington Streets, Chicago, 48 by 120 feet (about one-eighth of an acre), for which 15¢ (at $1.25 per acre) was paid the government in 1830, was valued ninety years later at $2,448,000—an average increase of 133,000 per cent per annum on the original purchase price; created wholly by the increase in population and public improvements.

The holders of these sites, in the meantime, received large and ever-increasing annual rentals for the use of them as building sites.

Quoting Myers: [107] "The land value which the mere concentration of population had created at that spot in Chicago belonged to the title holder for him to enjoy and dispose of as he pleased, and charge the public a high rental for the right to use it. This was, and still is, the system. Thoroughly riveted in law, it is regarded as a rational, beneficent and everlasting fixture of civilized life. The whole concurrent institutions of society pronounced the system wise and just, and still so proclaim it." Hence, Wealth Without Work.

A noted land speculator declared: "I have made a fortune without having ever worked a day in my life. I mean I have never engaged in actual effort to earn a dollar by the sweat of my brow. Never mind that old Biblical quotation of 'by the sweat of thy brow.' All my wealth I obtained legally, strictly according to the law; strictly in accordance with the means practiced and upheld by the church, by the press, by business-men. That is why I say never mind that old Biblical quotation."

The man who speculates in wheat on the Board of Trade is denounced by the press and public as an enemy to society; and a man who gambles in any way excepting in land, often breaks a law and becomes subject to arrest, but he who gambles in land, thus running up the price, making it more difficult for others to get land on which to produce wealth and earn a living, is protected by law as an upright citizen.

Increase in land values does not represent increase in the common wealth, for what land speculators gain by higher prices, the purchasers or tenants, who must pay them, will lose. [56]

Sales of the public lands in the Gulf region in 1834–7 were attended by professional speculators from all parts of the United States, who, by collusion, controlled the auctions in such ways that settlers, bidding for modest tracts for farms, had no chance of getting land, except by subsequently buying from the speculators at high prices. This was a common practice at all public land auctions.

West of the Mississippi, lands had attained speculative values before the purchase of the region from France in 1803; after the purchase large tracts were granted, and larger ones were claimed. Even before surveyors could begin their tasks, lands were in possession of squatters, who would swear against old residents, or more often, swear to their own long residence. [146]

Senator Linn, of Missouri, said: "The whole of Missouri had been settled by hardy and enterprising people long before the public lands were thought of being surveyed."

By act of Congress, in 1841, there were given five hundred thousand acres to each of nine states in the Mississippi Valley, from which some tracts were granted for internal improvements. Much of this land was sold to settlers and speculators; paid for in Soldiers' Bonus Scrip which had been obtained at a heavy discount.

The mania for land gambling was widespread. When lands

in one of the counties of southern Michigan were offered at
auction in Boston, that year, they sold at from 37½¢, to 60¢
per acre. [149]

The government opened land in Iowa to buyers, in 1843, and
on the date of the opening thousands rushed by torchlight into
these new opportunities.

A similar rush for land occurred at the opening of Oklahoma
Territory to settlement, during the Harrison administration, in
1889. This was an outrageously disgraceful and unfair scramble,
without justification, and unworthy of a civilized nation, in
which the fleet of foot left the less physically-able to take the
leavings. An orderly public sale restricted to actual settlers
would have been far more equitable and respectable. Subsequent allotments from Indian acquired lands were made by
lottery or auction.

Mexican Land Purchases

By the treaty of peace of Guadalupe-Hidalgo, in February,
1848, at the termination of the American-Mexican War, Mexico
sold to the United States the land now in the states of California, Nevada and Utah, and parts of Arizona, New Mexico,
Wyoming and Colorado.

For this land the United States paid Mexico $15,000,000, and
assumed claims of American citizens against Mexico amounting
to $3,250,000. The war (a fight for land) cost the lives of twenty-
five thousand Americans and $150,000,000. [11]

By this treaty, the American government agreed to respect all
land grants that had been made by the Spanish and Mexican
governments—the remaining ungranted lands within the area
named to become a part of the United States public domain.

Some of these grants were made by Spanish governors before
Mexico became independent of Spain, and others by governors
of Mexico during the thirty-three years between the date of its
independence and that of the sale to the United States.

When it became evident that some of the Mexican land was
about to pass to the United States, Pio Pico, the Mexican acting-
governor of California, at once began to issue grants of land to

favored Mexican citizens, who could then sell the land, at their personal profit, to American speculators—court records showed these grants were given for bribes.

Millions of acres of the very best agricultural, grazing, mineral and timber lands in the territory bought from Mexico by the United States were later found to be included in previous grants to Mexicans. More than eight million acres in California were claimed by some eight hundred Mexican grantees.

With the great influx of American population, following the acquisition, land came into demand and there sprang up a populous tribe of claimants. A very considerable portion of the land, including the region about the bays—natural sites for many future cities—had been granted to individuals by the Spanish or Mexican authorities. There seemed to be not an island or site for a fort, a custom house, hospital or post office but must be bought from some private claimant on his own terms. [150]

A Mexican grant of land now in New Mexico, said to have been made to Salvador Gonzales, in 1742, for "a spot of land to enable him to plant a cornfield for the support of his family," was fraudulently surveyed and enlarged to 103,959 acres—later, by an amended survey, reduced to 23,661 acres.

The B. M. Montaya Mexican grant in New Mexico, of 48,708 acres (which was the limit of area in grants under the law of Mexico), was fraudulently surveyed for 151,056 acres.

The Estancia Mexican grant in New Mexico, likewise restricted by Mexico law to 48,708 acres, was enlarged by fraudulent survey to 415,036 acres.

In 1768 Ignacio Chaves and others had petitioned for a tract of approximately ten thousand acres in present New Mexico. A fraudulent survey increased this claim to 243,036 acres.

The Pablo Montaya Mexican grant comprised in all 655,468 acres; the Mora grant 827,621 acres; the Tierra Amarilla grant 594,515 acres; and the Sangre de Cristo grant 998,780 acres.

One of the most notorious grants was the Beaubin and Miranda grant, for lands in New Mexico, afterwards acquired by an American, Stephan B. Elkins, by reason of which he obtained his original million dollars and became a multi-millionaire and a United States Senator from West Virginia. This grant was, by fraudulent surveys and other methods, increased from the Mexican legal limit of 48,708 acres to 1,714,764 acres.

The heirs of one Gervacio Nolan, twenty-two years after the war, claimed, by a Mexican grant, 1,500,000 acres in New Mexico, on which Congress allowed 48,708 acres, but a new survey was ordered and the area was increased to 575,000 acres, and the settlers thereon were evicted by the claimants.

A Mexican grant of 48,708 acres in New Mexico, to Francis Martinez, was by a fraudulent survey increased to 594,515 acres and allowed, thirty-three years after the war.

These are a few of the forged or otherwise fraudulent claims cited by Gustavus Myers, [107] who further stated that the stupendous land frauds in all the western and Pacific states, by which speculators obtained "an empire of timber and mineral lands," are amply described in numerous official documents of the period. Scores of other claims were confirmed for lesser areas, all of which grants were corruptly obtained.

Numerous other land grants, claimed to have been made by Pio Pico, bore his forged signature. The examination of the records in the City of Mexico "led to the conclusion that even the archives of that government had, in some way, become an instrument of sanctioning fraud against the United States." Irresistible proof was obtained "that there had been an organized system of fabricating land titles in California and the southwest, carried on by Mexican officials for a long time; that forgery and perjury had been reduced to a regular occupation; that the making of false grants, with false witnesses to prove them, had been a trade and a business." [150]

The many official reports describe with what cleverness claimants forged their papers, and the facility with which they bought up witnesses to perjure for them. By such evidence courts were frequently obliged to decide in favor of the claimants. [107]

The United States Attorney-General declared that it was incredible that so many grants from the Spanish and Mexican governors could have been made in good faith by any government. [150]

The frauds in the settlement of private claims for land in the United States, on alleged prior grants by Spanish and Mexican officials, were colossal. Vast areas were obtained by perjury, fraudulent surveys and entries, and by collusion with United States government administrative officials and Congress.

Prompted by the increasing demand that the proposed railroad to the Pacific should be constructed from some southern point on the Mississippi River, the United States, in 1853, bought 45,535 additional square miles for which it paid Mexico $10,000,-000. This was known as the Gadsden Purchase and included territory south of the Gila River, the southwest corner of the present New Mexico and the southern part of Arizona. The area was added to the public domain.

The terms of sale provided that the United States should recognize all valid Mexican land grants previously made in the acquired territory. The outrageously fraudulent claims in both Mexican purchases greatly reduced the land area for which the people of the United States had paid Mexico, and which should have become part of the United States public domain.

Three years after the first Mexican purchase, Congress created a board of land commissioners, to sit at San Francisco for the settlement of land claims. All claimants were required to present evidence of title within two years, and claims for 19,148 square miles were presented. Appeals were often taken to the United States Supreme Court, which became burdened with them for many years.

Henry Miller, who came to the United States as an immigrant in 1850, acquired an immense area of the richest land in California and Oregon, suitable for cotton, grain and dairying. A report of the agents of the estate, in 1935, revealed that in the previous nine years, when sale of the land in California began, 558,302 acres had been sold for $20,841,986 and that an area of just about the same value remained.

In 1850 Congress passed the Swamp Land Act, which gave to every state in the Union all swamp and overflowed land within its boundaries.

No one Congressional act ever resulted in so much fraud, or did more to rob the people and their descendants of their God-given heritage in land, than did the Swamp Land Act, nor have its evil effects subsided to this day. [37]

This act specifically provided that, to be classed as swamp land, each forty acre tract must be overflowed, either at planting or harvest season, and that the proceeds from sales of the land should be applied, exclusively, so far as necessary, to reclaiming said lands, by levees and drains.

This made possible one of the greatest land grabs in the history of the public domain; and only a small part of the proceeds ever went to the purposes intended.

Swamp land grants totaled sixty-four million acres, of which Florida received one-third. Numerous instances of fraud occurred. For example, in Illinois, the state agent listed twenty-two thousand acres as swamp, while a representative of the land office, upon investigation, found more than one-half of it to be dry land. In California, irrigation works were actually found on areas claimed as swamp. In Missouri, the agent for Monroe County selected thirty-one thousand acres, where there were fewer than three hundred acres of swamp land, and then went to Washington where, through a member of Congress and the late commissioner of the general land office, the entire thirty-one thousand acres were promptly and officially approved as swamp land. [69]

George W. Julian, of Indiana, chairman of the House Committee on public lands, said that under the Swamp Land Act some thirty million acres of the best lands in America were granted to four Gulf states and Arkansas, which were sold by them to speculators and politicians, at 10¢ to 80¢ per acre. [127]

The Land Commissioner reported, in 1866, that more than fifty-two million acres of agricultural lands in those states were being held unused by speculators—corporations and individuals—not engaged in agriculture; and that more than two-thirds of the population in that region were landless.

Notwithstanding New Mexico was a state of Mexico prior to the independence of Texas, the first Congress of the Texas Republic claimed New Mexico to be a part of Texas. Four years after being admitted as a state of the American Union, Texas exacted, and was paid, $10,000,000 for transferring to the United States government its claim to ninety-eight thousand square miles of land in New Mexico. This area was added to the public domain. How much less than the full price was turned into the Texas treasury is not recorded.

At the same time, Texas claimed a hundred and twenty-three thousand square miles (more than seventy-eight million acres) lying outside its present bounds, being the southwest corner of Kansas, the central part of Colorado, a small portion of Wyoming and the present Oklahoma "panhandle."

Texas officials visioning a large block of ready cash, proposed that the United States buy this area, to be added to the public domain, and the purchase was made at a cost of $16,000,000, including deferred interest.

A half-section of land, 320 acres, was granted from the public domain to each adult, including women in their own name, who had settled in Oregon or New Mexico prior to 1850, and one-half that acreage went to those who settled there during the next three years. This absorbed 2,563,757 acres in Oregon, and 20,105 acres in New Mexico. At that time soldiers' land warrants were being offered by brokers in eastern cities at 60¢ per acre, or less than half the government price. [69]

Land speculators were a pest in the rich soil of Iowa, where an editor wrote: "The rage for land speculation is a great impediment to agriculture. It is a species of gambling and puts a stop to the pursuit of higher objects. It is a moral upas." The actual settlers were continually complaining of the land held unused by speculators, which increased in value only as they themselves toiled and improved the surrounding lands.

Huge sales of land from the public domain to speculators, on credit, just previous to 1857, brought on another financial crisis, as similar speculation had brought on previous panics and years of depression, beginning in 1795 with the failure of Robert Morris' colossal land projects. There followed in the same pattern the panics of 1819 and 1837, and this one of 1857, which began with the failure of the Ohio Life & Trust Company. Millions of dollars of its depositors' and policy-holders' money had been loaned by it to holders of idle land, and to promoters, to build railroads through unproductive regions to attract buyers of land.

The southerners were not at that period involved in inordinate land speculation. The expanding market for their agricultural products during the Crimean War, and the threatening War between the States had absorbed their attention.

"While the panic of 1857 shook the North," wrote Percival Reniers, in *The Springs of Virginia,* "bringing northern bankers and mercantile houses tumbling, the people of the South felt the tremor, but hardly more. Their total income instead of dropping, went up. There had never been so many dollars' worth of cotton exported; the same was true of tobacco. The sugar plantations of Louisiana boiled twice as much cane as the year before and sold it at a good price. While the North was bogged, the South actually prospered." [123x]

A federal tax on real estate in 1861 produced a desired $20,000,-000. A similar tax was levied in 1798.

These taxes on land and buildings were apportioned among the states according to population as provided in the federal Constitution.

Instead of levying the tax on land and buildings as provided in the acts, many states paid their small pro-rata from their general tax revenue.

State and municipal officials, to keep down their local tax rates formed the pernicious habit during the depression of the 1930's, and continue the practice, of going with their hands out to the national government for petty local expenditures.

In this way many states have sold their sovereignty to the national government, until now there is widespread complaint of centralized government at Washington, without reference to these hand-outs as important factors in causing centralized government.

Of all the heavily increased taxes levied for the war, land value is the only thing on which there has been no increased tax.

Not only could a surprisingly large part of the national revenue be raised by a federal tax on publicly-created land, or site-value, but it should be raised in this way. What is more, it would open unused land to employment and greater production and reduce taxes on all consumption. It is a common-sense method and should be adopted by the Ways and Means Committee as part of every revenue bill it presents in Congress.

The Free Soil Party, in 1848, strongly advocated granting free land for homesteads; as did the Free Soil Democrats four years later. Horace Greeley, both as a member of Congress and as editor of the *New York Tribune,* urged the granting of free homesteads to settlers. In 1849 he introduced a bill "to discourage speculation in public lands and to secure homes thereon to actual settlers." He declared that "every person needing land should have what land he can use," and that "no one should be allowed to acquire land to be held unused; and in that way banish the land speculator, or break up his pestilent occupation."

Opposition to free homesteads, or of legislation in any way to open the West to settlement, was maintained by many southern and eastern members of Congress; the southerners because by enticing poor whites to the West it would be injurious to the plantation system and the formation of free states in the West would impair maintenance of slavery; the easterners because it would draw population from the East, and population is what created and maintained eastern land values. Fur companies added objections because it would drive the fur-bearing animals farther away.

In 1860 the Republican Party declared in favor of free homesteads. Congressman Owen Lovejoy, of Illinois, an associate of Lincoln, stated that without the pledge of the Republican Party to support the Homestead bill the first election of Mr. Lincoln would have been impossible. [69] That generation was more land conscious than is the present.

For three-quarters of a century, Congress pursued a vacillating "penny wise and pound foolish" policy respecting the public domain; playing to the advantage of land speculators, many of whom sat in Congress, and holding land at prices—and until 1820 in tracts so large—that most pioneers who needed land for homes could not get it. Homestead bills had been before Congress almost continuously for sixteen years but not until after withdrawal of the southern members at the outbreak of the war was one enacted, in 1862.

This act offered a quarter-section (160 acres) free of cost to any adult citizen, or any who would declare intention of becoming citizens, and would locate and remain on it five years.

Settlers also could have an additional acreage, possibly adjoining, under the Timber Culture Act. Within three years, more than a hundred thousand settlers, including children, went to the Middle West and located on land under the Homestead Act.

Congressman Julian said: "The war between the states has been termed a 'slaveholders' rebellion,' but it was likewise a 'landholders' rebellion.' The chief owners of slaves had been the principal owners of the land; in fact, about five-sixths of the southern lands were owned by slaveholders who constituted only one fifth of the population." Further, "that if the Homestead Act for free land had been adopted in 1832, as suggested by President Jackson, instead of thirty years later, after the war began, slavery would have died a natural death, as the Homestead Act would break up land monopoly in the South." [127]

Granting land for encouragement of various quasi-public services was practiced early in the Colonial Period, when land was granted for establishing mills, ferries, water-power, ironworks, glassworks, tanneries and other desirable works; and some phases of that policy endured during the first century of the American government.

Between 1828 and 1862 there were three grants from the public domain aggregating 2,245,334 acres for river improvements in Alabama, Wisconsin and Iowa.

Between 1827 and 1866, Congress made ten grants aggregating 4,597,678 acres, for canals in Ohio, Indiana, Illinois, Michigan and Wisconsin.

Between 1823 and 1869, Congress made twelve grants aggregating 3,276,964 acres for wagon roads in Ohio, Indiana, Michigan, Wisconsin and Oregon.

In addition, up to 1939, grants aggregating 230,386,000 acres have been made to all the states.

Of the last named, thirteen million acres were granted to the states by the Morrill Act, in 1864, in the proportion of thirty thousand acres for each senator and representative, for establishment of Agricultural and Mechanical Colleges in each state. This was an illogical basis of distribution (as has occurred in other instances of Federal distributions) which, by including senators, gives an unequal national per capita distribution.

Of the area received, the states granted 36,224,991 acres for railroad promotion, and the remainder for schools, various institutions, prisons, salt-springs, parks, game-preserves, fish-hatcheries and internal improvements.

The earliest federal grants to promote railroads were in 1850, when 2,595,053 acres were granted for the Illinois Central Railroad, 670 miles in length, and 1,156,658 acres for the 493 miles of Mobile & Ohio Railroad. The grant for the latter was the inducement for the southern members to vote the two grants. These grants brought numerous petitions for other railroad grants.

The Illinois Central railroad project, especially, was generally considered at the time as a land-jobbing project (as in fact were all the western land-grant railroad promotions). The Illinois promoters sold the land to speculators and settlers at a final average of $11.70 per acre, which produced $30,000,000, or six-sevenths of the cost of the road, [69] and the promoters held the stock and most of the proceeds from the sale of the bonds issued by the railroad company.

Thomas Benton, member of Congress from Missouri, urged Congress to build the proposed railroad to the Pacific Coast as a national work. By 1853, Stephen A. Douglas, an Illinois Senator of great power and persuasiveness, "had convinced every one" that the Pacific railroad should be built by private enterprise through grants of land from the public domain. [89]

Acts of Congress obtained by methods of bribery, granted, in 1857 alone, six million acres in Minnesota to various railroad promoters. Within twenty years, land in Minnesota was selling at $2.50 to $5.00 per acre.

The Western Union Telegraph Company built a telegraph line from Omaha to California in 1861, for which it received a grant of 160 acres for every fifteen miles constructed; in addition to a twenty years' government cash subsidy.

Land grants to promoters of railroads in Iowa exceeded four million acres, in the projection of which John I. Blair, of Blairstown, New Jersey, was the predominating figure. One-eighth of the public domain in Iowa was granted to promote railroads, most of which were owned by Blair. [107]

From 1850 up to 1871, when the last railroad grant was made, Congress granted to promoters of seventy-two railroads, 94,239,000 acres, in addition to the 36,224,991 acres granted by the states, which latter had been part of the public domain.

In grants of land to western railroads, it was provided that the land should be agricultural, coal or iron land. But by fraudulent surveys, assented to by dishonest public officials, other valuable mineral lands were often obtained by the grantees, with all the gold, silver, copper, and oil under them, and all the timber and stone above them, with all harbor rights and franchises. In addition, there were donated to the promoters of some of the roads many millions of dollars in state and municipal bonds and cash.

While all lands, bonds and cash were granted ostensibly to the railroad companies, they were in reality given or transferred to the promoters, who organized either as construction or as land companies—or both.

The method by which a railroad to the Pacific Coast should be financed was discussed in and out of Congress for many years. Only after withdrawal of the southern members, who were in opposition, were bills for construction of the road passed by Congress, in 1862 and 1864.

These bills granted to the promoters free right-of-way and 19,-457,000 acres of land, for main line construction of the Union Pacific and Central Pacific railroads, together with a loan to the Union Pacific promoters of $27,266,000 United States Government 6 per cent bonds, on which the accrued interest for the thirty years period of the loan (paid semi-annually by the government) amounted to $49,025,721; and a loan of approximately the same amount of bonds and accrued interest to the Central Pacific promoters.

The first issue of these government bonds was not made until the year after the close of the war. Apparently trustworthy statements were made that practically all the funds used in construction of the roads, and a large profit to the promoters, came from the proceeds of these government bonds and from the bonds of the railroad companies, issued as construction progressed, and from municipal donations, and from sale of land and company stock.

Notwithstanding that the public debt of the government was large, as a result of the war, these bonds were bought by investors. Had the railroad company bonds been secured by a first lien on the railroads, instead of by a second lien, and offered for sale for construction of the roads by the government, unquestionably an amount sufficient to have paid fully for the roads, and at a lower rate of interest, would have found buyers both at home and abroad. Thus could have been avoided the wasteful grant to the promoters of more than nineteen million acres of land from the public domain, and most of the $98,000,000 of interest paid on the bonds loaned the promoters.

Engineers, just then released from the army, were available for railroad construction. There could have been no valid reason why the government, from the sale of these bonds, could not have built the road as a public work, as Senator Benton had advocated fifteen years previously, and just as the Panama Canal was afterwards constructed by army engineers. In construction of the canal there was never a charge of fraud or incompetency.

To avoid graft and political job-holding, construction of the road could have been done by sectional contracts, with reliable contractors. All the frauds, waste, public scandals and ruined reputations which accompanied construction of, especially, the Union Pacific railroad, could in that way have been avoided.

The central trans-continental railroad was completed when a golden spike was driven near Ogden, May 10, 1869. Oakes Ames, of Massachusetts, a wealthy and forceful member of Congress, was the wheel-horse in the building of the Union Pacific railroad. In his enthusiasm for the project he unwisely solicited some members of Congress to buy stock in the Credit Mobilier Company of America, owned by the promoters, which had the contract for building the road—not from need of any small capital thus obtained, but to secure their support in Congress of any future desired legislation concerning the undertaking.

For this he was expelled from Congress. Many members apologized to him for thus voting to satisfy a public clamor. Without the energy and enthusiasm of Oakes Ames completion of the railroad as a corporate undertaking, no doubt, would have been delayed many years.

Two years after making the grant for the first Pacific railroad, Congress granted to Josiah Perham, a Boston wool-merchant, and associates, a charter for the Northern Pacific Railroad to connect Duluth, on Lake Superior, and Puget Sound; with a grant of, ultimately, 43,150,330 acres of the public domain.

Jay Cooke, of Philadelphia, held forty thousand acres of land near Duluth, which was the lodestone which induced him, in 1870, when others had failed, to take up the financing of the Northern Pacific road. This led, three years later, to the collapse of his financial house, and of the railroad company, which in-augurated the memorable panic of 1873.

At that period, coal, iron, copper and zinc lands, and western land grants, were largely held by incorporated stock companies, the shares in which were dealt in on the stock exchanges, and became objects of widespread speculation.

On the day of the Jay Cooke failure, these shares dropped in price so suddenly and sharply that banks and prominent brokerage houses collapsed like pins in a game of ten-pins.

On the street, within the shadow of the stock exchange, some men wept and some attempted suicide at the realization of their financial ruin.

I saw all this, as I was in the midst of it and it made a lasting impression.

Eminent citizens who had survived the catastrophe endeavored, in newspaper interviews, as is usual at such times, to assure the public that the natural resources of the country were so vast that there would be a speedy recovery.

These natural resources came into possession of private holders through colonial proprietary land grants, descending from one generation to another. Succeeding generations have leased or sold them to corporations and they to larger corporations, on royalties per ton of minerals extracted, or at increasing ground-rents.

These increasing royalties and land rents, with added charges at monopoly prices, are exacted of all industries using coal or processing the minerals. Since the charges are passed on to the consumer, chambers of commerce and industrialists have not yet awakened to these inflated underlying charges as a decided curb on purchasing-power, and consequently on all business.

Following the panic, eighty-nine railroad companies fell into receiverships, and building of new railroad mileage was largely suspended, throwing half a million men out of work. Nearly three hundred of our approximately seven hundred iron and steel plants closed. In the year of the panic, five thousand commercial houses failed; 5,830 failed the following year; 7,740 in 1875; 9,092 in 1876; almost 9,000 in 1877, and 10,478 in 1878. [ix]

Not until six years after the panic, in 1879, was there a glimmer of resuscitation. Meanwhile, there was a most distressing period of business depression, unemployment and abject poverty.

Had the Securities and Exchange Act been enacted years prior to the panic, instead of nearly two-thirds of a century afterwards, there would not have been the inducements and opportunities for the fraudulent practices in the creation of fictitious stocks and bonds, weak credits, and heartless stock-market manipulations, which accentuated this and all subsequent panics, previous to its enactment in 1934.

Meritorious as this act is, it has many opponents who, aiming to get wealth without work at the expense of others, are sitting on the side-lines, sharpening their knives to emasculate it at the earliest opportunity.

Completed in 1883, the cost of building the Northern Pacific Railroad was stated as $70,000,000, most of the funds having been supplied by the investing bondholders in the United States and Europe.

The land grant was transferred to a land company, organized and owned by the promoters and the railroad company shareholders. Subsequently, over the years, there has been realized from the sale of this land $136,000,000—or about twice the cost of the railroad—and in 1939 there were 15,838,105 acres of land remaining unsold.

As late as 1940, more than half a century after completion of the road, the Northern Pacific Railway Company, acting for the land company, in a suit in the United States Supreme Court, was claiming an additional 3,900,000 acres, against which the government charged that the company had fraudulently obtained from the public domain several million acres of valuable mineral and timber lands, to which it was not entitled by the terms of the grant.

The Northern Pacific Railroad could have been built by the government in the same manner as that suggested for building the first Pacific railroad, thus saving forty-three million additional acres of the public domain.

The land-grant railroads were required to transport government freight and passengers on government business at specified reduced rates—a minor credit.

The builders of many of the western land-grant railroads did not adhere to good construction, or to straight lines, when laying the tracks over level prairie and desert lands, but often laid them meandrically, as I observed in traveling over them at that period. The promoters thereby obtained increased mileage, on which to collect a greater acreage in land grants, and an increased amount of railroad company bonds—which were issued to the promoter's construction companies at from $15,000 to $25,000 for each mile of road constructed. The railroad company bonds were sold by the construction companies to eastern and foreign investors.

The proceeds of the sale of company bonds and stock that remained, after building the roads as inexpensively as possible, became the promoters' profit, which generally was very large.

Within less than fifteen years after they were built, most of these roads, overburdened with interest charges on bonded debts and high operating costs because of poor construction, became bankrupt, and thousands of miles of road had to be straightened, shortened and rebuilt. The operations were carried out through receiverships and financial reorganizations, at great loss to the bondholders. But the land companies continued solvent and profitable.

Gustavus Myers, in his *History of the Great Fortunes,* wrote: "Whatever superficial or partial writers may say of the benevolent origin of railroads, the fact is that railroad construction was ushered in by a widespread corruption of legislators. That Congress, not less than the state legislatures, was honeycombed with corruption is all too evident from the disclosures of many investigations, and not only did promoters of railroads loot the public domain in a gigantic way, under forms of law, but they so craftily drafted the laws on the subject of both the nation and the states that fraud at all times was easy." [107x]

Up to 1879, nearly three thousand acts of Congress relating to the public lands had been codified. Of the more important acts were the Military Bounty Land Acts of 1812–55; Pre-emption Land Acts of 1830–41; Townsite Land Act, 1844; Mineral Lands Acts, 1846–7; Swamp Land Act, 1850; Railroad Land Grants, 1850–71; Graduation Land Act, 1854; Homestead Act, 1862; Morrill Land Act, 1864; Timber Culture Act, 1873; Desert Land Act, 1877; Timber Cutting Act, 1878; Timber and Stone Land Act, 1878; following which were the Coal Lands Acts, of 1909–10.

Valuable copper and iron-ore lands in the public domain in the Great Lakes regions, some of which years later were appraised as worth $50,000 per acre, were in the early 1880's obtained by land company promoters at $1.25 per acre through the fraudulent method of dummy entries.

A tract of six hundred acres of mineral land in Idaho was granted at $5 per acre ($3,000), from which, in twenty years, $900,000,000 worth of copper is stated to have been produced. It is now owned by the Anaconda Copper Mining Company.

An agent of the Land Commissioner's Office, in Dakota Territory, in the 1880's, reported that fully 75 per cent of the land entries under the prescription (pre-emption) laws were for speculative purposes, instead of for homes or cultivation as the law required; the claimants then selling their allotments to speculators. The land commissioner reported that in California 95 per cent of the entries under the Desert Land Act were tainted with fraud.

Before and during the 1880's large areas of land in the West were bought on speculation, by wealthy Americans and foreigners. Among the latter were Lord Dunmore, who bought a hundred thousand acres, and the Duke of Sutherland, five hundred thousand acres. One German company possessed a million acres, and two English syndicates acquired seven million acres in Texas. In all, twenty million acres were obtained by foreigners. [77]

The great tracts were obtained for the purpose of having a first lien, in the form of land rents, on the earnings of hard-working American farmers, and of reaping the unearned increment in land values, to be created by the inevitable increase in population in the western country.

The unearned increment was more attractive than the earned increment, but there was always present the feeling against the unearned increment accruing to the absentee landholder. [69] Even William Penn, the most noted land monopolist in America and a beneficiary of the unearned increment, recognized and wrote of the injustice of it, as quoted in the chapter on Pennsylvania.

Spoliation of the public domain was one of the chief grievances of the Greenback-Labor Party in 1880.

A special committee of Congress, in 1883, reported: "The present land laws seem to invite fraud. You cannot turn to a single state paper or public document where the subject is mentioned, from a message of the President, to a report of the Commissioner of the Land Office, but what statements of 'fraud' in lands are found."

A little later, Commissioner Sparks—one of the very few incorruptible commissioners of the United States Public Land Office [107], stated: "The near approach of the time when the United States will have no land to dispose of has stimulated the exertions of speculators and promoters to acquire outlying regions of public lands in mass, by whatever means, legal or illegal."

He further stated: "An English firm had fraudulently obtained ten thousand acres of the choicest redwood lands in California, estimated to be worth $100 an acre, an aggregate value of $10,000,000.

"In the same manner extensive coal deposits in the West have been acquired in mass through expedited surveys followed by fraudulent pre-emption. Nearly the whole of Wyoming, and large portions of Montana, nearly all of Colorado, and the very best cattle portions of New Mexico, the rich timber lands of California, the splendid forest lands of Washington and the principal part of the extensive pine lands of Minnesota have been fraudulently seized in the same way.

"To enable the pressing tide of western immigration to obtain homes upon the public lands now appropriated these should be wrested from illegal control."

The natural result of these official statements was that the land-grabbing interests made great exertions to get Sparks removed from office. After his removal, they resumed complete domination of the Land Commissioner's Bureau. [107]

President Cleveland, at the close of his administration in 1897, stated that eighty million acres had been rescued from illegal usurpation, improvident grants and fraudulent entries and claims.

But not much of this was agricultural land. The usurpers had sought only the more valuable mineral, forest and range lands, and water-power sites.

The United States Land Office, established in 1812, has six thousand volumes of field notes, and records of more than six million patents, filed on shelves two and a half miles long.

The public domain was increased during the 1800's to nearly 2,000,000,000 acres. By 1940, it was reduced through sales and grants, to 402,104,000 acres in continental United States, and 348,-000,000 acres in Alaska. All that remains in the former has been withdrawn from settlement.

To meet the demands of the increasing population for farms, most of the remaining desirable agricultural land, and much that was decidedly undesirable, was disposed of by the government during the 1880's, and at the same time a large farm tenant class was developing.

During the early 1900's many thousands of American farmers migrated to western Canada—a portentous movement significant of the straits to which the American farmer had been driven. [107]

Free homestead allotments of 160 acres offered in the dust bowl region of western Nebraska not finding acceptance, the sites were, in 1904, increased to 640 acres. Within ten years, only about 250,000 acres remained untaken of the original seven million offered on those terms. Pressure of increasing population against a fast-diminishing proportionate area of usable land was the impelling motive.

On much of the land in the Dakotas, Nebraska and Kansas, which had been granted as free homesteads, numerous pioneer families lived in sod huts, there being no trees for log cabins as there had been for the earlier generations of pioneers, who settled between the Atlantic seaboard and the Mississippi.

The growing seasons alternated between the wretched conditions of the "dust-bowl" cyclones and the crop-destroying grasshoppers, which prevented the homesteaders earning their living.

With the hope of carrying over to better times, country bankers anxious to collect indebtedness due them from farmers, and pseudo-financiers, easily induced widespread creation of farm mortgages, at bankruptcy rates of interest, discounts and commissions. Sale of these mortgages to confiding eastern investors, during the latter part of the 1880's, became big business, followed by defaults and foreclosures of mortgages, which brought distress to thousands of investors, and agonizing hardships to the pioneer families.

One-fourth of all farms in the United States in 1890 were cultivated by men who did not own the land, and, even more impressive, there were 3,323,876 farm laborers who did not even rent land. It is probable that 40 per cent of those who did own farms held them on mortgage, the interest on which was equivalent to rent. [107]

As a consequence of absentee and speculative landholding in the more productive areas, tenant farming has steadily increased. The 1940 census showed that 2,361,271, or 38 per cent, of all farms in the United States were operated by tenants, as compared with 25 per cent sixty years previously. During the ten years between 1930 and 1940, in North Dakota, tenant farms increased from 35 per cent to 45 per cent of all farms, and in South Dakota, from 45 per cent to 53 per cent. In Kansas and Nebraska, 45 per cent of all farms are tenant farms. In Iowa, 47 per cent, while in some of the southern states, 60 per cent of all farms are tenant operated.

High prices for farm products, with wheat at $2.51 per bushel, during the First World War brought further inflation in all land prices, and farm mortgages doubled in amount. Farm lands in Iowa which the government had granted at $1.25 per acre, or as free homesteads, were, with improvements, being bought on mortgage at $400 or more per acre. The formula of the day was: "Buy more land, to raise more corn, to fatten more hogs, to get more money in Chicago to buy more land."

Insurance companies, with all the assumed financial wisdom of their officials, bought tens of millions of dollars worth of western farm mortgages, based on inflated land values, practically all of which defaulted when the boom collapsed, and were foreclosed.

There being no buyers, the insurance companies took the land and have become motorized farmers on large consolidated areas.

The great American frontier, with easy access to land, being at last gone, the foreclosed native farmers, with their families, have been driven to become "Okies"—migrants over the face of the earth.

Mark Sullivan, writing in *Our Times* in 1926, of the social and political discontent arising from disappearance of free land, said: "The free land had been for a hundred years the outlet for restlessness, the field of ambition. When that came to an end, restlessness turned in upon itself and fermented into something a little bitter . . . So long as there was free land, every man had the opportunity to create new wealth for himself by the simplest and oldest means known to mankind. With the end of free land, American men for the first time had occasion to look with envy upon the wealth of others, or with jealous scrutiny upon how they acquired it. The end of free land was the beginning of those political issues which had to do, in one form or another with 'dividing up,' or with curbing those who had much. . . . the rise of labor-unions and the treatment of them by corporation employers. The average American dwelt more upon causes that proceeded from persons or corporations. There were such causes. But they were minor compared to the ending of the supply of free land." [143x]

Epilogue

AS HUMAN beings slowly emerged from an animal existence, tribes developed who fought one another for possession of choice areas of land as hunting preserves.

The privilege of private ownership of land had its origin when the prehistoric barbaric chieftain with a club announced to his tribesmen that all the land along this river and to yonder mountain was his. Chieftains elsewhere did likewise.

As men progressed from primitive conditions to fixed settlements in different parts of the world, groups of strong-arm men assumed ownership of the land by force, and *all land titles of today run back to and are maintained by force.*

In course of time, under selfish guidance, private ownership of land became a fixed principle of subsequently established monarchial governments, with baronies and feudal landholding, after which was patterned the land system in the American colonies.

Many advanced thinkers in America, and elsewhere, have recognized private ownership of land as an injustice to the overwhelming mass of people throughout the world, and as constituting a heavy drag on the advancement of human welfare.

To cite expressions of many such writers is more than the limits of this volume will admit, but a few here given are illustrative of the development of public thought upon the subject.

Herbert E. Holmes [72], the Maine historian, wrote: "We American people cannot submit to scrutiny the title by which we hold land . . . We do not dare to examine our national conscience, else, if we did, were we not thick-skinned and materialistic, we would be overwhelmed by the consciousness of the debt of restitution which we can never liquidate. We may pass with barely a thought the fact that European sovereigns had no rights, founded on the principles of justice, to assume to grant to favorite subjects vast tracts of land in the Western Hemisphere, from which all existing land titles have emanated. For the sovereigns did not receive title to the land by gift of God."

Leo Tolstoy, in *Resurrection:* "The Earth cannot be any one's property."

Thomas Carlyle, in *Past and Present:* "Properly speaking, the land belongs to these two—the Almighty God, and to all his children of men."

Leviticus, 25:23: The Lord said to Moses: "The land shall not be sold in perpetuity; for the land is mine; for ye are strangers and sojourners with me."

Abraham Lincoln: "An individual, or company, should never hold more land than they have in actual use."—from *Lincoln and Men of His Time.*

John Stuart Mill, in *Political Economy:* "When 'the sacredness of property' is talked of, it should be remembered that any such sacredness does not belong to land. No man made the land. It is the original heritage of the whole people."

John Ruskin: "God has lent us the Earth for our life. It is a great entail. It belongs as much to those who are to come after us, as to us; and we have no right, by anything we do or neglect, to involve them in any unnecessary penalties."

Louisiana Supreme Court decision: "Land was given by the Creator for improvement and cultivation, not for speculation; and speculation in land should receive no encouragement from legislation or courts of justice."—(In Burows *vs* Pierce, 1851).

William Temple, Archbishop of Canterbury, in *The Hope of a New World:* "The treatment of the earth by man the exploiter is not only improvident but sacrilegious."

Dr. Sun Yat-sen: "For promotion of the welfare of the Chinese people, collection of the economic rent of land for the public treasury will be the basis of our program of reform."

Thomas Jefferson: "Whenever there is in any country uncultivated [unused] lands and unemployed poor, it is clear that the laws of property have been so far extended as to violate natural right."—From Ford's *Writings of Jefferson*.

"The land in any country belongs in usufruct [the right to use without title of ownership] to the living."—From *Thomas Jefferson's Works*. Washington Edition.

Herbert Spencer, in *Social Statics*, first edition, chapter IX: "We find yet further reasons to deny the rectitude of property in land. It can never be pretended that the existing titles to such property are legitimate. Should any one think so let him look at the chronicles. Violence, fraud, the prerogative of force, the claims of superior cunning—those are the sources to which titles may be traced. The original deeds were written with the sword, rather than with the pen; not lawyers, but soldiers, were the conveyancers: blows were the current coin given in payment; and for seals, blood was used in preference to wax. Could valid claims be thus constituted? Hardly. And if not, what becomes of the pretensions of all subsequent holders of estates so obtained? Does sale or bequest generate a right where it did not previously exist? Would the original claimants be nonsuited at the bar of reason, because the thing stolen from them had changed hands? Certainly not. And if one act of transfer can give no title, can many? No: though *nothing* be multiplied for ever, it will not produce *one*. Even the law recognizes this principle. An existing holder must, if called upon, substantiate the claims of those from whom he purchased or inherited his property; and any flaw in the original parchment, even though the property should have had a score of intermediate owners, quashes his right.

" 'But Time,' say some, 'is a great legalizer. Immemorial possession must be taken to constitute a legitimate claim. That which has been held from age to age as private property, and has been bought and sold as such, must now be considered as irrevocably belonging to individuals.' To which proposition a willing assent shall be given when its propounders can assign it a definite meaning. To do this, however, they must find satisfactory answers to such questions as, How long does it take for what was originally a *wrong* to grow into a *right*? At what rate per annum do invalid claims become valid? If a title gets perfect in a thousand years, how much more perfect will it be in two thousand years?"

Blackstone, in the *Commentaries,* book II, chapter 1: "There is nothing which so generally engages the affections of mankind as the right of landed property. And yet there are few that will give themselves the trouble to consider the origin and foundation of this right. Pleased as we are with the possession, we seem afraid to look back to the means by which it was acquired, as if fearful of some defect in our title; or at best we rest satisfied with the decision of the laws in our favor, without examining the reason or authority upon which those laws have been built. We think it enough that our title is derived by the grant of the former proprietor; not caring to reflect that (accurately and strictly speaking) *there is no foundation in nature or in natural law why a set of words upon parchment should convey the dominion of land."*

Bertrand Russell wrote: "Private property in land has no justification except historically through power of the sword . . . The land became the property of those who had conquered it, and the serfs were allowed to give land rent instead of service . . . It is a singular example of human inertia that men should have continued until now to endure the extortion which a small minority are able to inflict by their possession of the land. No good to the community, of any sort or kind, results from private ownership of land. If men were reasonable they would decree that it should cease tomorrow."

John Locke, the eminent philosopher, in his renowned *Essay on Civil Government:* "It is very clear that God, as King David said, 'has given the Earth to the children of men'; given it to mankind in common. This I do boldly affirm, that every man should have as much land as he could make use of, since there is land enough in the world . . . had not the tacit agreement of men to put a value on it introduced (by consent) larger possessions, and a right to them."

Roger W. Babson, in *Fighting Business Depressions,* predicts: "Some day the public will, in some way, take the benefits of the land values which the public itself creates socially and which values are largely being unearned by the great landholders . . .

Of course, it seems too bad that these social policies were not determined upon in the early stages of our country's history, but the sooner we get back to the right principle, the better off our descendants will be."

While recognizing the injustice of, and evils resulting from private collection of land rent, Henry George, [56] in *Progress and Poverty,* declared there is no need to disturb the title or possession of those who now hold land when he wrote:

"I do not propose either to purchase or to confiscate land. Let the individuals who now hold it still retain possession of their land. Let them buy and sell and bequeath and devise it. It is not necessary to confiscate land; it is only necessary to collect the annual rental-value of land for public purposes—the resulting revenue to replace taxes now levied on production and consumption.

"The complete recognition of the common rights to land rent need in no way interfere with the complete recognition of individual right to improvements or produce. Everything could go on as now, and yet the common right to land be fully recognized by appropriating land rent to the common benefit."

Private land titles sanction the private appropriation of land rent and increased increment in land value. But public ownership—nationalization—of land is not necessarily the solution.

Nationalization would create vast bureaucracies to administer the management and the leasing of land to individual users. Furthermore, public advocacy of nationalization would presently attract holders of unused sites and of mineral and forest lands throughout the country, to join in the advocacy of public ownership for the purpose of having the government buy their lands.

All the social advantages of land nationalization can be attained by the public collection of land rent. This, without bureaucracy and its attendant evils and expense, and without disturbing any private land titles whatsoever.

Land value and land rent, as shown, are created by the pressure of population. This being a value created solely by the public, it should be, in all justice, collected, just as taxes are now collected, for the public treasuries for the public benefit. This would also open for employment and development desirable lands now held unused at high speculative prices. The vast revenue from this public collection of land rent would immediately reduce, and, in time abolish, taxes on production and consumption.

That this must presently be brought about, not only in the United States but in other parts, to relieve the chaotic and complex fiscal and economic world conditions, is the belief of an ever-increasing number of profound thinkers.

W. E. Woodward, [173] in *A New American History* warns that: "It is a tendency of mankind to resist social innovations and to cherish and protect ideas that have outlived their usefulness.

"If the existing order is sufficiently flexible in mind and temper it may save itself by concessions and compromises which absorb and dilute the new social conceptions, or, on the other hand, the political structure may be so rigid that it is incapable of change. In that case, the issue between the old order and the new society evolves, by degrees, into a controversy which can be settled only by force."

In Russia nationalization of the land, and in Mexico distribution of land among the peons, were underlying objectives of the revolutions in those countries in the present century.

"It does little good to study history unless we apply its lessons to the present and future."—Editorial, *New York Times,* September 19, 1944.

Bibliography

1. Abernethy, Thomas P. *Western Lands and American Revolution.* New York: D. Appleton-Century Co. Inc., 1937
1x. Adams, James Truslow. *The Epic of America.* Boston: Atlantic Monthly Press, Little, Brown & Co., 1931
2. Akagi, Roy Hidemiche. *Town Proprietors of New England Colonies.* Philadelphia: University of Pennsylvania Press, 1924
3. Alvord, Clarence W. *The Mississippi Valley in British Politics.* Cleveland: Arthur H. Clark Co., 1917
3w. Arnold, Samuel G. *History of Rhode Island.* New York: D. Appleton-Century Co., 1874
3x. Ashmead, Henry G. *History of Delaware County, Pennsylvania.* Everts & Co., 1884
4. Bailey, Kenneth P. *The Ohio Company of Virginia.* Glendale: Arthur H. Clark Co., 1939
5. Bancroft, George. *History of the United States.* Boston: Little, Brown & Co., 1855
6. Barnes, Viola Florence. *Land Tenure in English Colonial Charters of the Seventeenth Century.* Essays in Colonial History, 1931
7. Barstow, George. *History of New Hampshire.* Concord: Boyd, 1842
8. Bassett, John S. *Constitutional Beginnings of North Carolina.* Baltimore: Johns Hopkins Press, 1894
9. Bassett, John Spencer. *A Short History of the United States.* New York: The Macmillan Co., 1924
10. Beard, Charles A. and Mary R. *The Rise of American Civilization.* New York: The Macmillan Co., 1930
11. Bicknell, Edward. *Territorial Acquisitions of the United States.* New York: Small, Bayard & Co., 1913
12. Bond, Beverly W., Jr. *Quit Rent System in American Colonies.* New Haven: Yale University Press, 1919
13. ——, *Civilization of the Old Northwest.* New York: The Macmillan Co., 1934

14. Bourne, Edward G. (Editor). *Narratives of Hernando de Soto.* New York: The Macmillan Co., 1934

15. Bozeman, John Leeds. *History of Maryland.* Baltimore: Lucas & Deaver, 1837

16. Brodhead, John Romeyn. *History of New York State.* New York: Harper & Bros., 1859

17. Brown, Alexander. *Genesis of the United States.* Cambridge: Houghton Mifflin Co., 1891

18. Brown, William Horace. *The Glory Seekers.* Chicago: A. G. Mc-Clurg & Co., 1906

19. Browne, William Hand. *Maryland—The History of a Palatinate.* Cambridge: Houghton Mifflin Co., 1888

20. Bruce, Philip Alexander. *Institutional History of Virginia in the Seventeenth Century.* New York: The Macmillan Co., 1896

21. Brunk, Thomas L. *American Lordships.* Sioux City: Union Advocate Press, 1927

22. Burrage, Henry S. *Beginnings of Colonial Maine.* Portland: Marks Printing House, 1914

23. Cadbury, George, Jr. *The Land and The Landless.* London: Headley Bros., 1908

24. Calder, Isabel M. *The Earl Stirling and Colonization of Long Island.* London: Essays in Colonial History, 1931

25. Capers, Gerald M., Jr. *The Biography of a River Town: Memphis.* Chapel Hill: University of North Carolina Press, 1939

26. Carlyle, Richard. *The Earth Belongs to the Living.* Los Angeles: Suttonhouse Publishers, 1936

27. Carpenter, William H. *History of Vermont.* Philadelphia: J. B. Lippincott Co., 1854

28. Channing, Edward. *The Narragansett Planters.* Baltimore: Johns Hopkins University Press, 1886

29. Clark, George Larkin. *History of Connecticut.* New York: G. P. Putnam's Sons, 1914

30. Clark, Thomas D. *A History of Kentucky.* New York: Prentice Hall, Inc., 1937

31. Clay, Jehu Curtis. *Annals of the Swedes on the Delaware.* Philadelphia: Hooker, 1858

32. Cobden Club (Editors). *Systems of Land Tenure in Various Countries.* London: Cassell, Petter & Galpin, 1876

33. Colton, Walter. *Deck and Port.* New York: A. S. Barnes & Co., 1850

34. Coulanges, Fustel de. *Origin of Property in Land.* Bloomsbury: Swan Sonnenschein, 1892

35. Craven, Wesley Frank. *Dissolution of the Virginia Company.* New York: Oxford University Press, 1932

36. Crockett, Walter Hill. *Vermont: The Green Mountain State.* New York: Century History Co. Inc., 1921

37. Dau, Frederick W. *Florida Old and New*. New York: G. P. Putnam's Sons, 1934

38. de Chambrun, Clara Longworth. *The Making of Nicholas Longworth*. New York: Ray Long & Richard R. Smith, 1933

38x. Delaware. *Original Land Titles in Delaware, 1646-1679*. Wilmington: State of Delaware, 1899

39. DePuy, Henry Walter. *Ethan Allen and the Green Mountain Heroes*. Buffalo: Phinney & Co., 1853

40. Douglas, Edward M. *Geological Survey Bulletin, 817*. Washington: U.S. Government Printing Office, 1832

40x. Doyle, J. A. *English Colonies in America*. Vol. III. New York: Henry Holt & Co., 1889

41. Edwards, Joseph. *Landholding in England*. London: Land Value Publication Dept., 1908

42. Egleston, Melville. *Land System of New England Colonies*. Baltimore: Johns Hopkins University Press, 1886

43. Eliot, John. *Description of New England in 1650*. New York: D. Appleton & Co.

44. Elting, Irving. *Dutch Village Communities on the Hudson River*. Baltimore: Johns Hopkins University Press, 1886

45. Ferris, Benjamin. *Original Settlements in Delaware*. Wilmington: Wilson & Heald, 1846

46. Fisher, E. J. *New Jersey as a Royal Province*. New York: Columbia University Press, 1911

47. Fiske, John. *The Beginnings of New England*. Cambridge: Houghton Mifflin Co., 1889

48. ——, *Old Virginia and Her Neighbors*. Cambridge: Houghton Mifflin Co., 1889

49. ——, *New France and New England*. Cambridge: Houghton Mifflin Co., 1889

50. Ford, Amelia Clewley. *Colonial Precedents to our Land System*. Madison: University of Wisconsin Press, 1908

51. Foster, William Eaton. *Town Government in Rhode Island*. Baltimore: Johns Hopkins University Press, 1886

52. Franklin, Benjamin. *Historical Review of Pennsylvania*. Philadelphia: O & W, 1812

53. Fuller, Hubert Bruce. *The Purchase of Florida*. Cleveland: Burrows Bros. Co., 1906

54. Futhey, John S. and Cope, G. *History of Chester County, Pennsylvania*. Philadelphia: L. H. Everts, 1881

55. Geiger, George Raymond. *Theory of the Land Question*. New York: The Macmillan Co., 1936

56. George, Henry. *Progress and Poverty*. New York: Robert Schalkenbach Foundation, Inc., 1940

57. Gilman, Frank Baylord. *New Jersey Land*. Newark: Newark Evening News, 1903–4
58. Guizot, M. and DeWitt G. *History of France*
59. Hafen, LeRoy R. and Rister, Carl C. *Western America*. New York: Prentice Hall, Inc., 1941
60. Hall, Clayton Coleman (Editor). *Narratives of Early Maryland*. New York: Barnes & Noble, Inc., 1910
61. Hanna, Philip Townsend. *California Through Four Centuries*. New York: Farrar & Rinehart, 1935
62. Hart, Albert Bushnell. *Source Book of American History*. New York: The Macmillan Co., 1890
63. ——, *Commonwealth History of Massachusetts*. New York: States History Co., 1927
64. Hartford Connecticut Proprietors. *Land Distribution, 1639*. Hartford: Connecticut Historical Society, 1912
65. Hazard, Samuel. *Annals of Pennsylvania, 1609–1682*. Philadelphia: Hazard & Mitchell, 1850
66. Hening, William Waller. *Statutes at Large of Virginia*. Philadelphia: Thomas DeSilver, 1823
67. Henry, O. *Rolling Stones*. New York: Doubleday Doran & Co., 1912
68. Heston, Alfred Miller. *Absegami* (Atlantic City). Camden: Heston, 1904
69. Hibbard, Benjamin Horace. *History of the Public Land Policies*. New York: The Macmillan Co., 1934
70. Holcomb, Robert M. *Story of Connecticut*. Hartford: Hartford Times, 1935
71. Holcomb, William P. *Pennsylvania Boroughs*. Baltimore: Johns Hopkins University Press, 1886
72. Holmes, Herbert Edgar. *The Makers of Maine*. Lewiston: Haswell Press, 1912
73. Hough, Emerson. *The Mississippi Bubble*. New York: Grosset & Dunlap, 1902
73x. Howison, Robert G. *A History of Virginia*. 2 Vols. Carey & Hart, 1846–1848
74. Hoyt, Henry Martin. *Brief of Titles, Luzerne County*. Harrisburg: L. S. Hart, 1879
75. Hoyt, Homer. *One Hundred Years of Land Gambling in Chicago*. Chicago: University of Chicago Press, 1934
76. Hull, William I. *William Penn: A Biography*. New York: Oxford University Press, 1937
77. Humphrey, Edward Frank. *An Economic History of the United States*. New York: Century Co., 1931
78. Janes, Lewis George. *Samuel Gorton*. Providence: Preston & Rounds, 1896

79. Jenness, John Scribner. *The Isles of Shoals.* New York: Hurd & Houghton, 1873

80. ——, *First Planting of New Hampshire.* Printed Privately, 1878

81. Johnson, Fred W. (Commissioner). *School Lands.* Washington: General Land Office, 1939

82. ——, *Transportation.* Washington: General Land Office, 1940

83. ——, *Land of the Free.* Washington: General Land Office, 1940

84. John, George O'Brien. *Texas History.* New York: Henry Holt & Co., 1935

85. Johnson, Charles S. *The Collapse of Cotton Tenancy.* Chapel Hill: University of North Carolina Press, 1935

86. Johnson, John Hemsley. *Old Maryland Manors.* Baltimore: Johns Hopkins University Press, 1883

87. Johnston, Alexander. *The Genesis of a New England State.* Baltimore: Johns Hopkins University Press, 1883

88. Johnston, George. *History of Cecil County, Maryland.* Elkton: George Johnston, 1881

89. Josephson, Matthew. *The Robber Barons. 1861–1901.* New York: Harcourt Brace & Co. Inc., 1934

89x. Judd, Sylvester. *History of Hadley.* New York: H. R. Huntting & Co., 1905

90. Judson, Katharine Berry. *Early Days in Old Oregon.* Chicago: A. C. McClurg & Co., 1916

91. Keith, Charles Penrose. *Chronicles of Pennsylvania, 1688–1748.* Philadelphia: Patterson & White, 1917

92. Konkle, Burton Alva. *Delaware: A Grant and Not a Grant.* Philadelphia: Pennsylvania Magazine, Vol. 54, 1930

93. Larned, Ellen Douglas. *History of Windham County, Connecticut.* Worcester: C. Hamilton, 1874–1880

94. Lee, Francis Bazley. *New Jersey as a Colony and State.* Publishing Society of New Jersey, 1902–3

95. Livermore, Shaw. *Early American Land Companies.* New York: The Commonwealth Fund, 1939

96. Louhi, E. A. *Delaware Finns.* New York: Humanity Press, 1925

97. Macaulay, Thomas Babington. *History of England.* New York: E. P. Dutton & Co., 1913

98. MacElroy, Robert McNutt. *Kentucky.* New York: Moffat, Yard & Co., 1909

99. McGrane, Reginald Charles. *The Panic of 1837.* Chicago: University of Chicago Press, 1924

100. Mershon, Stephen L. *Power of the Crown in Valley of the Hudson.* Montclair: Stephen L. Mershon, 1925

101. ——, *Shore Front Rights in New York.* Montclair: Stephen L. Mershon, 1929

102. Miller, Hugh. *Cruise of The Betsy.* New York: Carter, 1882

103. Mowry, William A. *Marcus Whitman: Early Days in Oregon*. New York: Silver, Burdett & Co., 1901

104. Muirhead, James Fullerton. *Land and Unemployment*. London: Oxford University Press, 1935

105. Mulford, Isaac S. *Civil and Political History of New Jersey*. Camden: Kean & Chandler, 1851

106. Myers, Albert Cook. *Early Pennsylvania, West Jersey and Delaware*. New York: Barnes & Noble, Inc., 1912

107. Myers, Gustavus. *History of Great American Fortunes*. New York: The Modern Library, 1907-8-9

107x. Myers, Gustavus. *History of the United States Supreme Court*. Chicago: Charles H. Kerr & Co., 1912

108. Neill, Edward D. *Early Colonization of America*. London: Strahan & Co., 1871

109. Nevins, Allan. *Gateway to History*. New York: D. Appleton-Century Co. Inc., 1938

110. Nourse, Henry S. (Editor). *Early Records of Lancaster, Massachusetts*. Lancaster: Public Library, 1884

111. O'Callaghan, Edmund Bailey. *History of New Netherland*. New York: D. Appleton & Co., 1855

112. Osgood, Herbert L. *The American Colonies, Seventeenth Century, Vols. I & II*. New York: Columbia Univ. Press, 1904

113. Page, Thomas Nelson. *The Old Dominion*. New York: Charles Scribner's Sons, 1909

114. Parkman, Francis. *Pioneers of France in the New World*. Boston: Little, Brown & Co., 1925

115. Paxson, Henry D. *Where Pennsylvania History Began*. Philadelphia: George H. Buchanan Co., 1926

116. Pepys, Samuel. *Samuel Pepys' Diary*. New York: Harcourt Brace & Co. Inc., 1926

117. Phelan, James. *History of Tennessee*. Cambridge: Houghton Mifflin Co., 1888

118. Phelps, Albert. *Louisiana*. Houghton Mifflin Co., 1905

119. Pickett, Albert James. *History of Alabama (to 1851)*. Sheffield: Robert C. Randolph, 1896

120. Pierce, Carl Horton. *New Harlem—Past and Present*. New York: New Harlem Publishing Co., 1903

121. Pound, Arthur. *The Golden Earth*. New York: The Macmillan Co., 1935

122. Powell, Fred Wilbur (Editor). *Hall J. Kelley of Oregon*. Princeton: University of Princeton Press, 1932

123. Quick, Herbert. *The Real Trouble With The Farmers*. Indianapolis: The Bobbs-Merrill Publishing Co., 1924

123x. Reniers, Percival. *The Springs of Virginia*. Chapel Hill: Univ. of North Carolina Press, 1941

124. Richman, Irving Berdine. *Rhode Island*. New York: G. P. Putnam's Sons, 1902

125. Rife, Clarence White. *"Land Tenure in New Netherland," Essays in Colonial History*. London: 1931

126. Rivers, William James. *History of South Carolina to 1719*. Charleston: McCarter & Co., 1856

127. Robbins, Roy M. *Our Landed Heritage*. Princeton: University of Princeton Press, 1942

128. Roberts, Ellis H. *Planting and Growth of the Empire State*. Cambridge: Houghton Mifflin Co., 1887

129. Robinson, Howard. *Development of The British Empire*. Cambridge: Houghton Mifflin Co., 1922

130. Rodney, Richard S. *Early Relations Delaware and Pennsylvania*. Wilmington: Historical Society of Delaware, 1930

131. Rogers, James E. Thorold. *Six Centuries of Work and Wages*. London: Swan Sonnenschein & Co., 1906

132. Sally, Alexander S., Jr. *Narratives of Early Carolina*. New York: Barnes & Noble, Inc., 1911

133. Sato, Shosuke. *History of Land Question in the United States*. Baltimore: Johns Hopkins University Press, 1886

134. Saunders, William Laurence. *State Records of North Carolina*. Goldsboro: Nash Bros., 1886

135. Schaifer, Joseph. *A History of the Pacific Northwest*. New York: The Macmillan Co., 1918

136. Shepherd, William Roberts. *Proprietary Government in Pennsylvania*. New York: Columbia University Press, 1896

137. Simons, A. M. *Social Forces in American History*. New York: The Macmillan Co., 1912

138. Smith, John. *History of Virginia and New England*. London: 1626

139. Smith, Samuel. *History of Colonial New Jersey*. Burlington: Parker, 1877

140. Smith, W. Roy. *South Carolina as a Royal Province*. New York: The Macmillan Co., 1903

141. Stanard, Mary Newton. *Story of Virginia First Century*. Philadelphia: J. B. Lippincott Co., 1928

141x. Staples, William R. *Rhode Island in Continental Congress*. Providence: Providence Press, 1870

142. Stiles, Henry R. *History of Ancient Windsor, Connecticut*. New York: C. B. Norton, 1859

143. Stomberg, Andrew Adin. *A History of Sweden*. New York: The Macmillan Co., 1931

143x. Sullivan, Mark. *Our Times*. New York: Charles Scribner's Sons, 1926

144. Tanner, Edwin P. *Province of New Jersey to 1738*. New York: Columbia University Press, 1908

145. Thorpe, Francis Newton. *Colonial Charters*. Washington: Government Printing Office, 1909

146. Treat, Payson Jackson. *The National Land System, 1785–1820*. New York: E. B. Treat & Co., 1910

147. Trottman, Nelson. *History of the Union Pacific*. New York: Ronald Press Co., 1923

148. Trumbull, Benjamin. *Complete History of Connecticut*. New London: H. D. Utley, 1898

149. Turner, Frederick Jackson. *The United States 1830–1850*. New York: Henry Holt & Co., 1935

150. Tuthill, Franklin. *History of California*. San Francisco: H. H. Bancroft & Co., 1866

151. Tyler, Lyon Gardiner. *Narratives of Early Virginia*. New York: Barnes & Noble, Inc., 1907

152. Vallandigham, Edward Noble. *Delaware and the Eastern Shore*. Philadelphia: J. B. Lippincott Co., 1922

153. Verrill, A. Hyatt. *Romantic and Historic Virginia*. New York: Dodd Mead & Co., 1935

154. Vincent, Francis. *History of The State of Delaware*. Philadelphia: Campbell, 1870

155. Volwiler, Albert T. *George Croghan and the Western Movement*. Cleveland: Arthur H. Clark Co., 1926.

156. Wallace, Alfred Russel. *Land Nationalization*. London: Swan Sonnenschein & Co., 1892

157. Ward, Christopher Longstreth. *Dutch and Swedes on the Delaware*. Philadelphia: University of Pennsylvania Press, 1930

158. Weeden, William B. *Economic and Social History of New England*. Cambridge: Houghton Mifflin Co., 1891

159. ——, *Early Rhode Island*. New York: Grafton Press, 1910

160. Wertenbaker, Thomas J. *Virginia Under the Stuarts*. Princeton: University of Princeton Press, 1914

161. Wharton, Clarence R. *History of Texas*. Dallas: Turner Co., 1935

162. Whitehead, William W. (Editor). *New Jersey Archives*. Newark: Daily Advertiser, 1881

163. Wilkins, W. G., Jr. *History of England*. London: Land Value Publication Dept., 1902

164. Williams, Samuel. *Natural and Civil History of Vermont*. Burlington: Mills, 1809

165. Williams, Samuel Cole. *History of the Lost State of Franklin*. New York. Press of the Pioneers, 1933

167. Wilstach, Paul. *Tidewater Maryland*. Indianapolis: The Bobbs-Merrill Publishing Co., 1931

168. Winfield, Charles Hardenburg. *Land Titles in Hudson County*. New York: Wynkoop & Hallenbeck, 1872

169. Winsor, Justin (Editor). *Narrative and Critical History of America.* Cambridge: Houghton Mifflin Co., 1887-9
170. Wise, Jennings Cropper. *Ye Kingdome of Accawmacke* (Accomac). Richmond: Bell Book Co., 1911
171. Woestemeyer, Ina Faye and Gambrill, J. Montgomery. *The Westward Movement.* New York: D. Appleton-Century Co., 1939
172. Woodard, Florence May. *The Town Proprietors of Vermont.* New York: Columbia University Press, 1936
173. Woodward, W. E. *A New American History.* New York: Farrar & Rinehart, 1936
174. Wortham, Louis J. *A History of Texas.* Fort Worth: Wortham-Molyneaux Co., 1934

Index

Acadia, 10

Adams, John Quincy, 487

agents sent to Connecticut induce settlers, 310

Alabama land grant, 502

Alaska, Russian sovereignty of, 459; settlements, 567; 511

Albany, French fort near, 5; 165

Alexander VI, pope, 1, 3

Alexander, William, Earl Stirling, granted land, 85; claims Long Island, 177

Alleghenies, west of: homeseekers, speculators, speculators agents, surveyors, 480

allegiance to lords proprietors required, 362

Allen, Ethan, large Vermont speculator in land, advertised land; land litigation, 160

America: French claims in, 3–4; first vessel built in, 10; European explorers; fights between; claimed by Philip II, Spain, 6; who owned; search for owner, 12; Dutch claim rights in; support of, 13; British migrations to widely advocated; first British colony to, 16; Puritan migration to, 17; French Acadians transported to, 19; migration to by European nationals, 19; only agencies for peopling; for profit, 22; material betterment incentive, 47; claimed by James I, England; granted land in, 48; land tenancy, share-cropping, began, 52; colonization in, 77; first bill of exchange

drawn, 87; British and French respective areas in, 107; British reinstated in, 202; land in, usurped by reigning British monarchs, 336; British made land grants in until the Revolution, 439

American: royal grants, percentage metal found, to king, 49; land speculation inducements, 113; trade, Dutch interest awakened in, 165; serfs in feudal land system, 182; 356; Tories land confiscated, 214; land solicitors in London; 439; Revolution, British-held lands sequestered, 474; frontier disappears; many farmers migrants, 513

Ames, Oakes, Congressman, 505–6

Amsterdam, Holland, burgomasters possess lower Delaware; become settlers' financial father; land-rent one-tenth of produce, 246; more settlers arrive, 247; revoke sponsoring, 248

Andros, Edmund, duke's grasping governor; claims land in Connecticut; attempts seize charter; demands revised deeds, increased rents or seize land, 110–1, 137, 206; assumes command in Delaware; grants land, rentals to duke, 260; assumes government New Jersey, 316, 320; refuses recognize West Jersey title, 322; attempts, disguised, to escape, arrested, 112

Anthracite coal development, wild land speculation town lots, 429

Anticosti Island, French at, 4